WOLFE ISLAND

WOLFE ISLAND

A LEGACY IN STONE

BARBARA WALL LA ROCQUE
FOREWORD BY KENNETH KEYES

NATURAL HERITAGE BOOKS
A MEMBER OF THE DUNDURN GROUP
TORONTO

Copyright © 2009 Barbara Wall La Rocque

All rights reserved. No part of this publication may be reproduced, stored in a retrieval system, or transmitted in any form or by any means, electronic, mechanic, photocopying, or otherwise (except for brief passages for purposes of review) without the prior permission of Dundurn Press. Permission to photocopy should be requested from Access Copyright.

Published by Natural Heritage Books, A Member of The Dundurn Group

Library and Archives Canada Cataloguing in Publication

La Rocque, Barbara Wall
    Wolfe Island : a legacy in stone / Barbara Wall La Rocque.

Includes bibliographical references and index.
ISBN 978-1-55488-398-1

    1. Wolfe Island (Frontenac, Ont.)--History. 2. Indians of North America--Ontario--Wolfe Island (Frontenac)--History. 3. Fur trade--Ontario--Wolfe Island (Frontenac)--History. 4. Wolfe Island (Frontenac, Ont.)--Biography. I. Title.

FC3095.W65L37 2009   971.3'71   C2009-900101-2

1   2   3   4   5   13   12   11   10   09

Front cover: Ardath Castle as it appeared during its latter years after being abandoned. *Courtesy of Queen's University Archives, V. 23.*
Back cover: (Top): Limestone house. *Courtesy of Mable McRae.* (Bottom): The first lighthouse at Port Metcalfe. *Courtesy of Della Bullis, C.H. Wall Collection.*
Design by Erin Mallory
Edited by Jane Gibson
Copy edited by Barry Jowett
Printed and bound in Canada by Marquis

Care has been taken to trace the ownership of copyright material used in this book. The author and the publisher welcome any information enabling them to rectify any references or credits in subsequent editions.
J. Kirk Howard, President

 Conseil des Arts du Canada / Canada Council for the Arts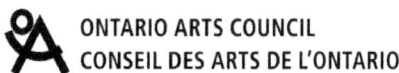

We acknowledge the support of the Canada Council for the Arts and the Ontario Arts Council for our publishing program. We also acknowledge the financial support of the Government of Canada through the Book Publishing Industry Development Program and The Association for the Export of Canadian Books and the Government of Canada through the Ontario Book Publishers Tax Credit Program and the Ontario Media Development Corporation.

    Dundurn Press   Gazelle Book Services Limited   Dundurn Press
3 Church Street, Suite 500   White Cross Mills   2250 Military Road
    Toronto, Ontario, Canada   High Town, Lancaster, England   Tonawanda, NY
        M5E 1M2   LA1 4XS   U.S.A. 14150

CONTENTS

7	*Acknowledgements*
10	*List of Maps*
11	*Foreword: A Tribute to Wolfe Island by Kenneth Keyes*
13	*Preface*
19	*Introduction: The People of Wolfe Island by Charles H. Wall, 1978*
23	Chapter 1 ~ In the Beginning
29	Chapter 2 ~ Long Island Standing Up
37	Chapter 3 ~ Enter the French
47	Chapter 4 ~ Lineage of the Barony of Longueuil
63	Chapter 5 ~ What's in a Title?
71	Chapter 6 ~ Whence Did They Come
95	Chapter 7 ~ A Teapot in a Tempest
113	Chapter 8 ~ Establishing Roots
123	Chapter 9 ~ Early Industries and Livelihoods
137	Chapter 10 ~ Down to the Sea
149	Chapter 11 ~ Garden Island: One Man's Empire
159	Chapter 12 ~ The Lifeline: Wolfe Island Ferries
177	Chapter 13 ~ Coping With the Hazards of Isolation
189	Chapter 14 ~ Establishing Transportation Links
205	Chapter 15 ~ Marysville Comes Alive
223	Chapter 16 ~ Achieving Literacy: Libraries and Schools
237	Chapter 17 ~ Essential Services for an Isolated Community
245	Chapter 18 ~ History of Wolfe Island Churches and Secular Societies
265	*Appendix I ~ Gravesites: Early Settlers from England*
267	*Appendix II ~ Gravesites: Early Settlers from Ireland*

269	*Appendix III ~ Gravesites: Early Settlers from Scotland*
271	*Appendix IV ~ The Cone Surname*
273	*Appendix V ~ Wolfe Islanders and Simcoe Islanders Who Fought for Their Country*
275	*Notes*
289	*Selected Bibliography*
291	*Index*
309	*About the Author*

ACKNOWLEDGEMENTS

I am much appreciative of the support and encouragement given by the following:

Dr. Ross Kilpatrick of the Queen's University faculty and his wife Susan, a long-time friend, both of whom have assisted me with encouragement, research material, and a course of action; Dr. Roger Martin, editor McGill-Queen's University Press, for pointing me in the right direction; Rob Leverty, executive director Ontario Historical Society, who was a catalyst in assuring me that the book would be published; Barry Penhale, publisher emeritus, Natural Heritage Books of the Dundurn Group, who never lost faith in this project from the moment my daughter Lesley, a librarian, encouraged me to give Barry a chapter to read; Alan Cumyn, Ottawa, author and faculty member of the Humber School of Writing, Creative Non-Fiction; Mark Badham, curator of the Miller Museum of Geology, Queen's University, for invaluable assistance; Noel P. James, Department of Geological Sciences, Queen's University, for a map of limestone formations on Wolfe Island; Maurice Smith, curator emeritus, Susan St Cyr, Lena Roosenmaalen, Ben Holthof, curator/registrar of the Marine Museum of the Great Lakes, at Kingston, Ontario; Mr. and Mrs. John D'Esterre for their proofing of our information on Garden Island and Hank Connell of Wolfe Island for his facilitating; Jeremy Heil, archivist, Queen's University Archives; Alexandra Cooper, library technician, Queen's Stauffer Library, map department; Wolfe Island Historical Society, Captain Brian Johnson, Victoria Stewart, and executive. Wolfe Island Business and Tourism Association (WIBTA) for facilitating webpage hook-up to their website. Lisa H. Russell, archival technician, Anglican Diocese of Ontario; James Sweeney, archivist, Anglican Diocese of Quebec; Reverend J. Appelman, archivist, Catholic Archdiocese of Kingston; Adam Burill, archivist, Ontario Archives; Librarians Barbara Love, manager, and Patricia Enwright, manager Rural

Sevices, Kingston Public Library; Sharon Hogan, assistant librarian, Wolfe Island Public Library;

Lesley La Rocque, assistant librarian, Toronto Public Library System, Toronto; David Anderson of Williamstown, for genealogical background on the McDonells of Wolfe Island.

I also wish to thank those many people who so very willingly provided me with a rich array of background information on Wolfe Island: Chris and Connie Carr, endorsement and photos; Reverend Rudy Meier, endorsement; Captain Brian Johnson, endorsement; Captain Richard F. Fawcett and Marette Fawcett, island historians; John and Joan O'Shea, island historians; Theresa Broeders, Mark Benson, Brian MacDonald, Susan MacDonald/Dill and all of the McDonell-MacDonald clan for sharing family histories, photos and information involving Scottish Settlement; the Pyke family, Grant and Margaret, George and Robert, for family history and photos of vessels of the Pyke's Salvage and Towing Co. in action; Bruce Horne and Rachel Horne, geology reference, Horne lineage and photo; Captain Leath Davis, Davis history and photos; Anne and Edmund Taggart, photos newspaper articles and books; Nicholas Taggart, paper "Nursing Alone," Louise Kenney; Theresa Fargo, History of the Catholic Church, tour through old church properties; Gepke Sjonger, photos; Ruth Ann Pearce, Tilbury, Ontario, Ellerbeck family history; Eileen Williamson, Walker family history, photos; Keith Keill, Joyceville, Ontario, Keill family history; Margaret (Johnson) Commercial, Rochester, New York; and brother James Johnson, Kingston, photos and family history; Darrell and Fern Small, Ottawa, story of Christmas Day sleigh mishap; Rod McKenna, Kingston, family photos; Mable McRae for her wisdom, knowledge and photos; Gord McRae, McRae history and visuals of artefacts; Donalda Parkes, Stevenson family history; Elaine Berry, Berry history and photo, cruse lamp; Catherine (Eves) Lyall, Newtonville, Eves family history and photos; Thelma (Eves) Butler, Newburgh, Simcoe Island photos; Harry Friend, Kingston, Friend family history and photos; Don Lane, Kingston, Kemp family history; Connie and Elwood Woodman; Norma and Isabel O'Shea; Kenneth Keyes and mother Elsie Keyes; friends Linda Bissinger, freelance editor, and Mary Byers, Toronto author, for their support and encouragement; David and Maureen Fortier for the book *Built on a Rock* by Colonel Louis J, Flynn (David's uncle); Edward and Gail Kenney, Linda J. Van Hal, Professor Duncan M. McDougall, (Queen's University), childhood resident with family on Garden Island; Eugene and Reta (Eves) Hulton; Glenn O'Shea; Arthur and Geneva Keyes; Vern Yott; Anita (O'Connell) Janzer; Doreen Joslin; Carmel Cosgrove; Margaret Fawcett; Flora Devlin; Peg White; Billy Bolton; Douglas and Michael Corrigan; Horseshoe Island, Robbie Gropp.

In particular, I would like to acknowledge those people (many deceased) who made valuable contributions during Charles's research through interviews, correspondence, and photographs: Leonard Mosier, 1930; Theresa (La Fleur) McGarvey, 1930; Mabel (Woodman) Eves, 1931; Ethel (Sudds) Eves, 1931, early Eves history; Beulah (Watts) Flynn, 1956; Mary (Brophy) Darling; Mildred Hawkins-Walton, 1970s; Captain Lewis Orr, 1970; Flora King, notes on Hitchcock lamp, 1970; Bessie (Holliday) Kenney, 1971; Weir McRae, 1978; Hugh Horne; Lillian Niles; Della Bullis; Buck

Mullin; Helen Holliday, 1970s; Norma Horne; Kathleen (Kenney) Wall.

I also wish to thank my nephew Greg Dubchak, who created and maintained my web page and prepared photo CD for designer. His wife Diane, who both assisted with marketing ideas and photography; Lloyd, my husband, for all his computer assistance, editing skills, and patience; my daughters, Karen and Lesley, champion researchers; Kenneth Keyes, a long-time Wolfe Islander who wrote the foreword to this book and who shared valuable wisdom and insight throughout this journey.

And a special thank-you to my editor, Jane Gibson, for her considerable skill and patience in supporting me through a challenging editorial process, and to my copy editor, Barry Jowett, who so commendably helped to make this book a reality. Also, my gratitude to Shannon Whibbs, senior editor, for her assistance and support during the last phase of this journey.

LIST OF MAPS

16	Map 1:	Wolfe Island, 1878.
45	Map 2:	Wolfe Island and Surrounding Islands from Survey of Lake Ontario, 1783.
51	Map 3:	A Section of Burleigh Fortification Map of 1869, showing the northwest shore of Wolfe Island including Mill and Cone Points.
65	Map 3A:	The head of Wolfe Island from J.G. Chewett's Map of 1822 indicating Crown and Clergy Reserves.
73	Map 4:	1784 Township of Cataraqui surveyed by Messrs. Kotté and Peachey.
84	Map 5:	Early Ferry Routes, Overland Passages, and Native Burial Grounds, *circa* 1800.
104	Map 6:	Detail from Walling Map of 1860, featuring: Point Alexandria, Ontario; Cape Vincent, New York; Carleton Island, New York; and the International Boundary.
144	Map 7:	"Marysburgh Vortex," Eastern Lake Ontario.
194	Map 8:	Depicting Landowners' Requested Roadway to the Foot, July 1841.
198	Map 9:	Adaptation of Railway and Canal Proposals, circa 1836.
206	Map 10:	Marysville, Wolfe Island, from the 1878 Meacham Atlas of Frontenac County.
226	Map 11:	Wolfe Island, Showing Schools, Churches, Cheese Factories and Early Quarries.

FOREWORD
A Tribute to Wolfe Island

How does an author condense and convey the history of settlement, economy, and civility of a community into a stimulating, readable text that will capture the imagination of the reader? Such has been the task undertaken by Barbara La Rocque, and admirably achieved in this major publication.

Special recognition must be given to the dedication of the author in fulfilling a personal commitment to ensure that her father's research efforts over an extended period of time would not be lost. When his manuscript of several hundred pages came into her possession, Barbara was determined to see that his work would be "preserved and shared with any and all who have a personal or passing interest in the history of Wolfe Island."

Who will read this publication? It will have a widespread appeal to the broad spectrum of the Canadian, American, and European population. For many it will be a "must read" for students at all levels of the educational system, from the senior students and the staff of elementary panel through to the doctoral students of our leading universities. It will be sought after by current and former residents of the island — from newcomers who want to know more about their adopted community to those who left the island generations ago and now have a keen interest in the genealogy of their ancestors and others who have lived on the island in the past. The list of those who will seek to peruse the in-depth study displayed herein is boundless.

This publication comes at an opportune time in our island's history. As we embark on the most expensive undertaking ever to have been initiated in this area — a $480,000,000 renewable energy wind-farm project — it is appropriate to look back and see where we have been and how we have developed to better prepare ourselves for the challenges of the future. It is also befitting to the island's namesake, as the publication of this thirty-year research project comes on the eve of the 250th anniversary of General James Wolfe's victory on the Plains of

Abraham. May his spirit of adventure and dedication energize you as you enjoy this comprehensive study of the gem and largest of the St. Lawrence River's Thousand Islands, Ganounkouesnot, Grande Île, Wolfe Island.

**Kenneth Keyes,
Fourth-Generation Wolfe Islander**

PREFACE

The following pages contain a story of passion for a place with a healthy measure of history. My parents, Charles and Kathleen Wall, should have been the protagonists, but that was not to be. Happily married for sixty-one years, my father had, all the while, been courting Wolfe Island, Ontario. His research, encompassing several centuries, included stories, pictures, and documents provided by a variety of archives, libraries, and many Wolfe Island residents.

In 1930 my father was posted to Wolfe Island when he was a captain in the Church Army, a branch of the Church of England. As diocesan funds were insufficient to support a resident priest, he was employed as the lay-incumbent for the Trinity Anglican Parish with occasional assistance of a priest from Kingston. During his tenure, he met, fell in love with, and in 1932 married Kathleen Kenney, one of the island's daughters. They subsequently moved to Toronto where, out of necessity, he shared a business partnership with his father during the prolonged Depression.

Wolfe Island, situated about three miles south of Kingston, separates the north and south channels of the St. Lawrence River. My father travelled over the island's approximately fifty-square-mile stretch of limestone, visiting and ministering to his parishioners. History of the island began to take shape as he visited cemeteries, families, friends, and historic sites, all of which whetted his appetite to such a degree that, upon retirement in 1964, he and my mother bought a house in the village of Marysville. At last, he was able to live amidst the history about which he was writing. While raising their family during the previous years, they made countless trips to the island's beloved shores for vacations, weddings, and funerals as my mother had left numerous family members behind when she moved to Toronto.

During retirement his love affair with Wolfe Island blossomed to the extent that he kept notes on its history, anecdotes, and folklore, eventually researching as much as possible about his paradise. Unfortunately, after collecting sufficient material to write this book by the mid-1980s, he was only able to complete about two thirds of the manuscript before succumbing to cancer. After his death, through the encouragement of my family, I decided that I needed to see his project become reality. My father felt very strongly about dispelling the myths, untruths, and inaccuracies that had been published over time. He was striving to create not just a factual record, but a comprehensive history of Wolfe Island and its people. Some readers may feel that facts pertinent to their families or other aspects of the island's history have been overlooked. The yield from our combined research far exceeded that which could be incorporated into this volume, and so, inclusive emphasis has been given to the island's early history. Although limited space has precluded our moving into the twenty-first century with our findings, we hope that what has been documented will be enlightening.

My quest for information to expand upon recent church history led me to Reverend Canon Christopher Carr, the priest in charge of Trinity Anglican Parish. He willingly complied with my request for an endorsement of my venture:

> One of the wardens of this parish refers to the persons "living behind the church." "The cemetery?" I asked for clarification. For him and others here, the cemetery is much more than the place where we lay our departed to rest. Our Wolfe Island cemeteries represent the living presence of unforgotten history continuing to impact on daily life.

Ms. La Rocque is completing research begun by her father many years ago when he served as lay pastor of this community. This work of completion is in the spirit of her father's efforts: extremely detailed and conscientious, always to the fact that every story can be further spun. Her work reaches far out into the history of the island, and out beyond the present shores to get stories from descendants who remember but who have moved away. Her work promises to tell parts of the Wolfe Island story not so far written. Having read several of the histories of the island and had some special conversations with the author, I can attest to that. She has made a serious effort to get the stories of those many souls, not least, that of her own father who "lives behind the church."

There are frequent references made to my father throughout this history as he tells of his personal experiences and as I relate others concerning him. With support from my family, I have done much further research and hope that our efforts will open the readers' hearts and minds to the story of Wolfe Island, and its importance in the history of Canada and in the hearts of the generations who have lived there.

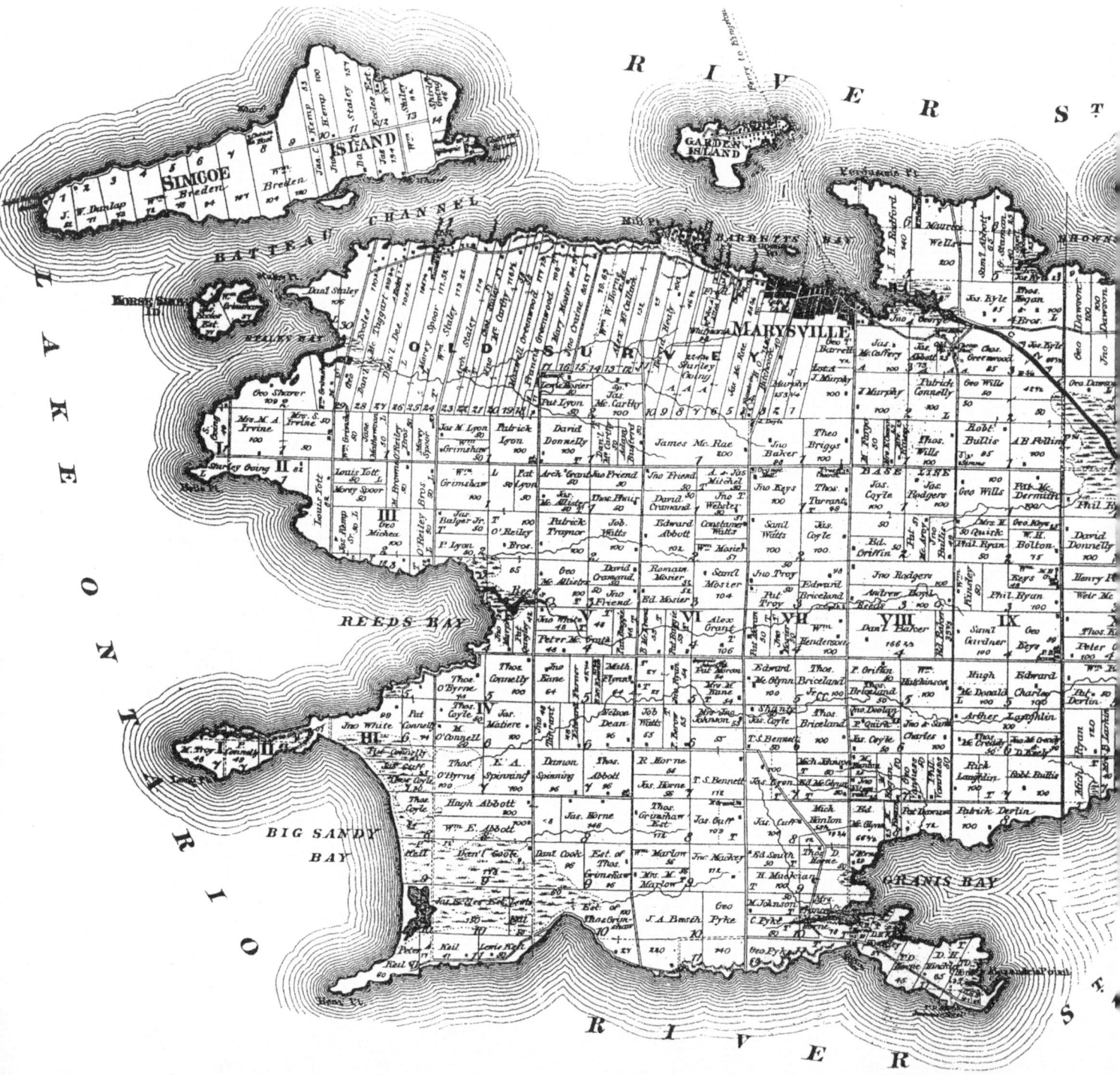

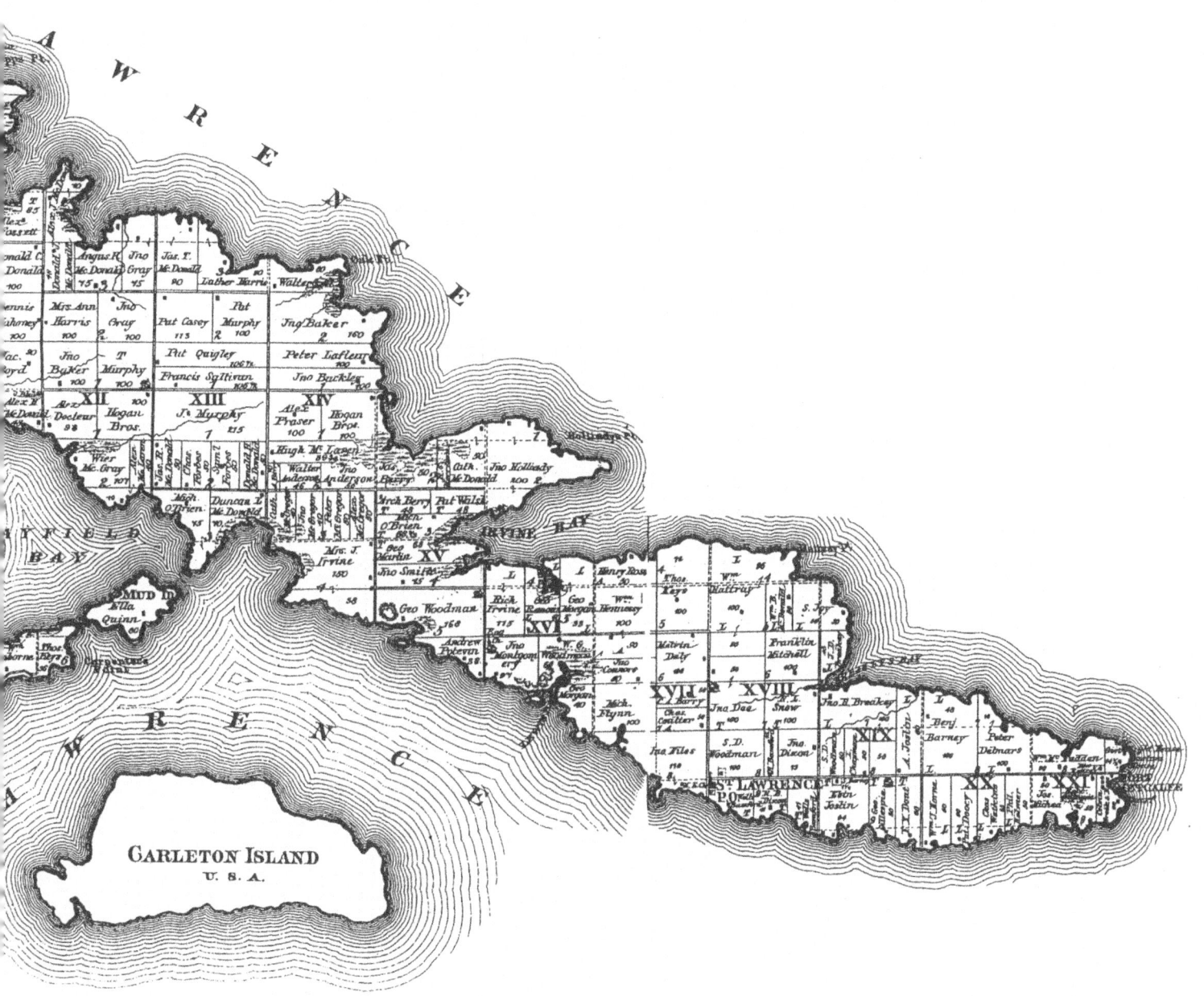

Map 1: Map of Wolfe Island, 1878, reflects the island's population explosion of the 1860s. From the *Illustrated Historical Atlas of Frontenac, Lennox and Addington, Ontario*, 1878.

INTRODUCTION
The People of Wolfe Island

On this pleasant July day we are standing on the upper deck of the *Wolfe Islander III*, which left Kingston, Ontario, about fifteen minutes ago, headed in a southerly direction across the north channel of the St. Lawrence River. We have just passed Garden Island to our right, and in the distance further to the west we can see Simcoe Island. Ahead lies our destination, Wolfe Island. These three islands, together with the smaller Horseshoe and Bayfield islands, comprise the Township of Wolfe Island.[1]

From our vantage point on the ferry, we can see an outline of low-lying trees bordering each of these islands. Two hundred years ago, our eyes would have seen huge timbers and dense forests, and probably we would have speculated as to why Europeans would ever have chosen to set down roots in such a forbidding place. That such early ventures did take place is evidenced by descendants of pioneer families flourishing into their sixth and seventh generations, while the giant trees of the forests have perished.

Much has been spoken and written concerning these islands and their people, but the story of the way of life of these particular Canadian pioneers remains largely untold to this day. What motive drew people from such diverse origins as France, the British Isles, Lower Canada, and the United States to these prohibitive, windswept, isolated islands when mainland life would have been so much more inviting? This location offered little more than timber, soil, and fish coupled with the opportunity for relentless toil. Elements such as these were part of the pioneer scene everywhere in Upper Canada, but the added dimension of living so isolated from the mainland for long periods of time deserves recognition.

In pioneer times there were physical, mental, and spiritual components to the segregation experienced by Wolfe Islanders. These factors are no less apparent today when the ferry is in dry dock for repairs, or needed for an emergency trip to Kingston during the night. What inner urge prompted the first settlers to forsake the mainstream of life and lay down roots in island isolation with only a rowboat to connect them to the mainland? Early Wolfe Islanders and newcomers alike mysteriously persisted in clinging to this mode of living, albeit somewhat more technically advanced today. The ferry is the lifeline to these islands. There have been many times when that lifeline has been broken, necessitating an airlift of food, supplies, and passengers. Is the ferry the best means of contact with the mainland in this day and age? Why not a bridge? Would it mean the end to a special way of life?

This island is actually closer to the United States than to mainland Canada, yet its history reveals that, subsequent to the lengthy aboriginal tenure, it has always been part of Canada and the people have remained true to Canadian tradition. During the early 1800s, ever-vigilant islanders sought out and captured or routed British militia deserters and armed American invaders. Whether motivated by self-preservation, loyalty to their country, or both, successive generations of islanders experienced, on occasion, the need to repel those who posed a threat to their safety.

The islanders have always been a closely knit society, irrespective of political or religious background. Surnames that once were representative of solely Protestant families are now Catholic, or both, and vice-versa. Political meetings can still muster enthusiasm and bring out hecklers. Nevertheless, islanders have generally been able to transcend social differences. In the not-too-distant past when temperance groups were fighting the taverns, and the "wets" were fighting the "drys," enmity was temporarily put aside for the sake of community, church picnics, dances, and socials, because all were united in a common endeavour.

Regardless of periodic tragic setbacks such as the great depressions of the late nineteenth century and the 1930s, or the loss of lives through the ice or the perilous, immobilizing ice storms, the islanders' *modus operandi* has not been altered greatly by the passage of time. New methods of communication, granted, have enhanced the islanders' way of life, but sadly, Wolfe Island still lacks some basic mainland infrastructure. Survival of pioneers in this, their chosen piece of the New World, required many skills to initiate industry. These early settlers provided much-needed timber for Europe, island-quarried limestone for construction, commercial fishing, cheese production, and shipbuilding — the list ever expanding as the need arose. Necessity became the "mother of invention" on Wolfe Island. One of the early settlers created and patented the Hitchcock Lamp, which travelled all the way to the Arctic in 1881 on the noted Greely Expedition. Another early settler, Mr. Shirley Going, a dedicated farmer, devised and patented a mowing machine before 1857.

Cheesemaking was in full swing throughout southern Ontario in the 1800s, but Wolfe Island is credited with producing the first cheddar cheese in the province. The spirit of competition, an outstanding trait of islanders, has been evidenced not only in social and sporting events, but also in business and agriculture. Wolfe Island competitors consistently went beyond the local level to achieve victories at the county, provincial, and national levels. Whether the event was rowing, hockey, baseball, ploughing, cheesemaking, or honey culture, Wolfe Islanders have earned their laurels. This know-how and ability to perform at a high level of competence is the product of ingenuity born of isolation.

In spite of deficiencies in formal education on these islands, and still the lack of a public library or reading room,[2] younger generations by and large aspired to higher education obtainable on the mainland. Over the years, secondary school and university education prepared many young islanders to return and practise their professions within their community. Others, influenced by the economy of their time, of necessity went further afield to gain employment. Whether inspired by the resident schoolteachers, clergy, physicians, or parental encouragement, islanders have demonstrated independence, resilience, and the ability to change with the times.

Though this township has been poor in cultural amenities, it has been rich in the quality of mercy. Whether in sickness or need, the islanders' will and ability to cope were evidenced with actions rather than words. In spite of this spirit, one might wonder why it took 150 years for medical facilities to evolve from the care provided by one lone midwife to those offered by a modern medical clinic. Could it have been the dedication and skill of the resident midwives and doctors throughout the years, coupled with the unusual good health and longevity of these hard-working pioneers, that made such a venture seem unnecessary? Change and improvement of facilities, medical or otherwise, on Wolfe Island have always required financial assistance from at least one level of government, often resulting in an impasse. One needs to live the life of isolation in order to become acutely aware of these needs. Decision-making government officials have rarely "walked in the shoes" of Wolfe Islanders, and, consequently, timely and adequate funding for necessities has been difficult to obtain. The residents of these islands, though hampered at times by social and economic inadequacies, have accepted these challenges and made them work to their advantage. They are an unassuming, quiet people with a heritage of which to be genuinely proud.

We began this introduction to the Wolfe Island Township aboard the ferry crossing from Kingston to the village of Marysville on Wolfe Island. Our trip, which two centuries ago would have occupied the better part of a morning, has taken only twenty minutes. Now, as we walk toward the main street, I invite you to step back in time while I introduce to you some of the island's illustrious visitors: Champlain, Frontenac, Montcalm, and Sir John A. Macdonald. As we proceed, I should like you to meet some of the township's more prominent residents: Baron de Longueuil, a member of the legislative council and owner of Longueuil (Ardath) Castle on Wolfe Island; Dileno D. Calvin, owner of Garden Island's timber and ship-building enterprise; Coleman Hinckley, one of the earliest Loyalist immigrants, builder of the first steamer, *Pierrepont*, which linked Kingston to Cape Vincent, New York; and Samuel Hitchcock, owner-proprietor of the first passenger ferry, launched in 1802, which travelled between his home wharf on the island and Kingston. But more especially, I would like to acquaint you with the rank and file whom we would probably meet at church or in a pub. Saints or sinners? Hardly. They are merely individuals, busily involved in living, who, along with their fellow neighbours, helped to create a historical heritage worthy of preservation.

Charles H. Wall, 1978

CHAPTER 1
In the Beginning

For countless decades, Kingston, Ontario, has been referred to as "Limestone City." Much of the limestone for its buildings was quarried from nearby Wolfe Island and the Kingston area and used to create an array of architecturally diverse buildings. A stroll through the downtown streets, surrounded by the bluish-grey countenance of churches, the city hall, and old hotels, is a reminder of the city's history.

During early surveys, geologists found Wolfe Island's limestone to be of very fine quality, much revered for its high tensile strength. This stone was hauled on barges during the 1800s and early 1900s and used in the construction of the Rideau Canal and the repair of the Welland Canal. Portions of the Kingston Penitentiary, the tower of St. Mary's Cathedral in Kingston, and countless other substantial structures were also fashioned from the bowels of the island.

The story of Wolfe Island begins with the origin of this fifty-square-mile mass of rock lying in the mouth of the St. Lawrence River, three miles south of Kingston. Around one billion years ago this area consisted of a huge mountain range stretching from Labrador in the northeast to Mexico in the southwest. Approximately five hundred million years ago these mountains had been substantially eroded, leaving behind the "basement," or oldest rocks in the area.[1] Some 470 million years ago, Wolfe Island, Kingston, and indeed most of the North American continent were submerged under the Ordovician Sea. Over a period of ten million years, layer upon layer of lime mud was deposited on this ancient ocean floor, ultimately forming the sedimentary limestone rock that makes up the present-day surface of the island.[2]

The most recent major geological event to shape Wolfe Island occurred during the last Ice Age when the remainder of the glacial ice sheets advanced across the region. At their greatest extent, around fourteen thousand years ago, the ice sheets flowed in a southwesterly direction across present-day Kingston as far south as the Finger Lakes region south of Lake Ontario.[3] The incredible weight of the mile-thick sheets of ice formed great cavities in the earth's crust, and, as the ice melted, the resultant water filled these depressions, ultimately creating the Great Lakes.[4] Huge glacial lakes formed around the present-day site occupied by Lake Ontario. Periodically, new drainage routes would open up as the ice melted and these lakes would empty. When the ice sheet blocking the St. Lawrence River drainage route finally retreated from the area, the water levels in Lake Ontario and the St. Lawrence Valley were drastically lowered, allowing approximately seventeen hundred islands to lift their heads above the waters, thus forming the world-famous Thousand Islands, the largest of which is Wolfe Island.

Originally, the configuration of Wolfe Island was two islands with a narrow strip of slightly submerged land between them. In the mid-1800s a channel was cut through, creating the Wolfe Island Canal. The island's irregularly contoured shoreline boasts many points and bays, but the waters obscure the dangerous presence of rocky or sandy shoals. The points reach out, appearing to beckon vessels to safe harbour, but the irregular depth of the water has damaged many sailing vessels and caused the loss of many lives.

GEOLOGY

The billion-year-old rocks of Ontario's Precambrian Shield underlie the entire Kingston region, and likely form the nucleus of Wolfe Island itself, under its limestone cover. The city of Kingston and the islands in the mouth of the St. Lawrence River are all situated directly on top of this rock formation, known as the Frontenac Axis.[5] Geologists examining the strata from bottom to top have found the layers in the Kingston area to be from the Ordovician Period. Each strata or layer, mostly limestone, is identified by the fossilized fauna known to have existed during the same time frame. As the Frontenac Axis was submerged during this era, the variety of sedimentation, deposited layer by layer over millions of years, caused the diversity in limestone discovered in surveys of Wolfe Island.[6]

The date of the first geological survey of Wolfe Island is not known, but evidence indicates that the south shore from Carpenter Point to Bear Point was surveyed in 1874. The first survey report, completed in 1903, confirmed the presence of an abundance of the Cambro-Silurian limestone that was highly valued in the construction of public buildings.[7] Several other surveys of Wolfe Island and the surrounding territory culminated in the reports compiled between 1959 and 1969 by geologist B.A. Liberty and his team. Liberty's studies set the benchmarks for subsequent investigations. They state that Wolfe Island's limestone, known as Trenton, dates back over 450 million years into the Paleozoic Era.[8]

Charles Wall, my late father, had been puzzled about the age of a piece of fossilized rock he turned up on his property on Wolfe Island in 1976. He sent the rock to the Royal Ontario Museum for identification and was told that the rock was limestone of the "Trenton" variety and 460 million years old. In cross-section, about fifty percent of the rock was actually fossilized coral and a prominent fossil exhibited on the limestone surface was of the genus *Actinoceras*, a squid-like animal known from the Ordovician-aged rocks of the Kingston area.[9]

LIMESTONE FORMATIONS

Liberty describes the bedrock structure as being of three limestone formations known as Gull River, Bobcaygeon, and Verulam. While each formation outcrops in different parts of the township, they actually recline one on top of the other. Gull River, the oldest, is situated at the bottom and Verulam, the youngest, at the top. The appearance of older formations at the earth's surface indicates that the younger formation was probably scraped away by glacial action and other agents of erosion.[10] The Gull River formation, which includes Garden and Horseshoe islands, covers all of the foot of Wolfe Island east of the canal as well as a one-half-mile-wide strip along the north shore from the canal to the Head. This formation, varying in thickness from twenty-five to fifty feet, is fossiliferous and well-exposed on the northwest shore. Because of this limestone's high quality, compact structure, and tensile strength, eight of the ten Wolfe Island quarries of this Gull River formation were located toward the north shore.

In 1900, a geologist observed that this formation contained boulder-like masses near the water level in the western part of Marysville. These masses may be quartzite cobbles that were sitting on the eroded Canadian Shield surface when seas flooded the continent. The boulders were surrounded by lime mud and eventually cemented into the lowermost limestone beds in the area.[11]

The Bobcaygeon formation takes in Simcoe and Horseshoe islands and about one half of the head of Wolfe Island. It stretches from the canal to the west shore and lies between the Gull River formation on the north shore and an irregular line running in the same direction as, but south of, Reeds Bay Road. Being younger than the Gull River formation, the Bobcaygeon contains more identifiable fossils. Liberty stated: "the fauna is reasonably abundant and varied"[12] and named twelve different kinds known to this area. He observed: "This formation varies from twenty to thirty feet in thickness" and can readily "be seen two miles southeast of the village … and on the south shore of

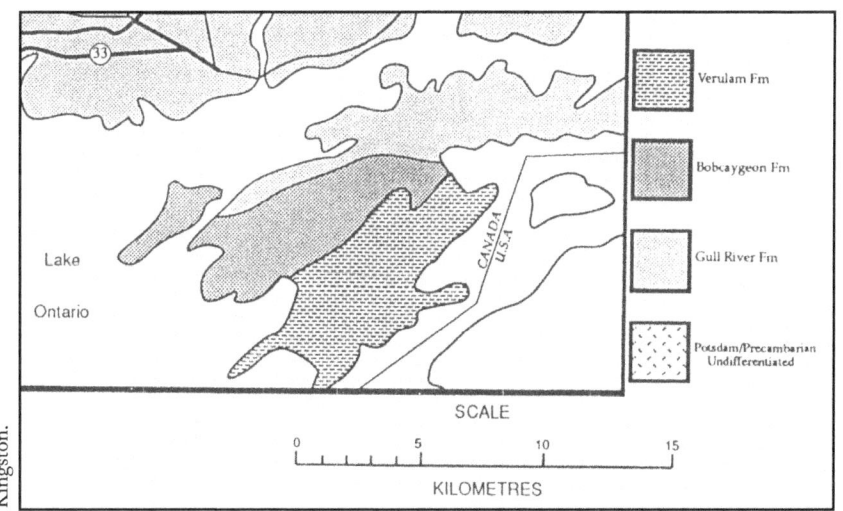

The various limestone formations found on Wolfe Island. The types of limestone and the accessibility of the finest (Gull River) along the northern shoreline are shown in the legend. The diagram is from Black Riverian and Trenton Fossils of the Kingston Area, *published by Queen's University.*

Simcoe Island."[13] The Wolfe Island location would be near the old quarry at Seventh Line and Base Line Road. The third formation, the Verulam, includes all the area south of Reeds Bay Road, and, although millions of years old, is the youngest bedrock formation in the Kingston district.

THE RIDGE

A scarp, which islanders refer to as "the Ridge," is evident on Wolfe Island in the general vicinity of the Ridge Road or the Eighth Line. However, surveys indicate that it rises near the north shore a few hundred yards south of the spring (Cold Springs), located a mile and a half east of Marysville, and is traceable in a southwesterly direction to the western end of the island. Its average height is eight to ten feet throughout its length, with an approximate depth of seventy feet. During times past, the Ridge has been mostly drifted over with soil, however, it marks nature's boundary between the Black River Group of limestone to the north of the island and the Trenton Group to the south.

GLACIAL SCRATCHES

Wolfe Island has remained relatively unscathed by erosion except for glacial striations left behind on smoothly polished rock surfaces as the glaciers retreated. Despite their rigidity, the limestone beds have recorded the paths of these moving glaciers. Wolfe Island's prime exhibit can be found at Bass Rock (the flat rocks) on the north shore just west of the village, where grooves measure twelve or more inches in width. Water levels, which have risen over the past forty years, now obscure visibility of this wide expanse of rock at the shoreline.

Courtesy of the C.H. Wall Collection, Photo 1972.

Bass Rock, pictured here, depicts glacial striations etched in the flat rocks found along the shoreline of the Front Road on Wolfe Island.

Throughout my childhood, the area was accessible to all for many purposes: picnics, sunbathing, car-washing, wiener roasts, and the like. Liberty has also indicated that many glacial markings similar to Bass Rock are evident on the shoreline outcroppings near Murray Bay, Holliday Bay, Chub Point, and McDonell Bay, between the Seventh and Eighth lines at Reeds Bay Road, as well as at the mouth of Reeds Creek. Numerous additional locations were noted just off shore.[14] During the process, a mixture of pebbles, clay, and boulders called "till" were deposited in the Kingston area by these melting glaciers,[15] along with boulders or "glacial erratics" transported from elsewhere and deposited over a stretch of the foot of the island. These pinkish granite-like boulders may have travelled from the Lyndhurst area, approximately thirty miles north of Kingston.[16]

WATER QUALITY

A seemingly limitless supply of fresh water was available to people who lived on or near the shoreline. As forests were cleared and people began to move inland, wells were created to hold the spring water in the bedrock. During the 1970s, my father consulted a knowledgeable Wolfe Islander about the supply of fresh water. Leonard "Tupper" Mosier, a descendant of one the first Loyalist families to settle on Wolfe Island, had worked as a maintenance patrolman for the Ontario Department of Transportation and Communication for over thirty-one years and had learned much about the natural resources of the island. During their discussions, Tupper recounted instances where individuals had struck oil while drilling for water. During the early 1900s, the first oil was discovered on the present De Reuter land (Sixth Line), which, when ignited, burned for several hours. Some years later, in 1935, on the same concession, oil was found on Glenn Mosier's property while he was drilling for water. This time it was capped. Several days later the cap was removed and a lit match briefly ignited the small amount of accumulated gas. No appreciably economic amount of oil or gas has ever been tapped in this area.[17]

When Europeans arrived in this thickly wooded limestone-rich island, it was surrounded by clear fresh water, abounding in varieties of fish and shellfish. In a conversation with Mrs. Theresa (La Fleur) McGarvey, who lived on the west side of Holliday Bay during the late 1800s, my father recorded her childhood recollections:

> There was a good beach in front of our home and we, as children, enjoyed playing on it and in the water.... The water was so clear we could see shells on the riverbed even when we were far out in deep water. In winter, there was clear blue ice on the river and even when we looked through the ice we could see the shells on the river bottom far below.[18]

The water's present murky colour, the lack of fish, the barren land, and the abandoned quarries are not necessarily the fault of the pioneer Wolfe Islander, but they are a commentary on our collective ability to pollute and destroy our environment.

CHAPTER 2
Long Island Standing Up

Ganounkouesnot ("long island standing up") was the aboriginal name for Wolfe Island. Although Count Frontenac (Louis Henri Buade) named it "Île Buade," the French usually referred to the island as "Grande Île." The English, using the aboriginal description, later called it "Long Island"— a name that continued into the late 1800s. In 1792 it was officially named "Wolfe Island" by Lieutenant-Governor Simcoe to honour General Wolfe, who had died on the Plains of Abraham in 1759. But it is the Native people who were the first known inhabitants of Wolfe Island. To record the history of the North American aboriginal peoples in a logical way, archaeologists created four main time periods from 9000 B.C. through to A.D. 1000, comprising several cultures — namely, the Paleo-Indian, the Archaic, the Initial, and the Terminal Woodland periods.

PALEO-INDIAN PERIOD

For a number of years, anthropologists and archaeologists generally believed that these early people likely originated in Siberia, having crossed the Bering Land Bridge.[1] However, new controversies are emerging to challenge this theory and "new technologies, especially DNA analysis, should help to unravel the mystery of who arrived here first and their place of origin."[2] The early residents are referred to as the Clovis Culture, their name coming from the town of Clovis, New Mexico, where artifacts were discovered in 1938. They had the technology to hunt big game, and it is known that their members (11,000 to 700 B.C.) roamed or occupied the southern Ontario region, as some of their distinctive fluted projectile points have been discovered east of Trenton and west of Kemptville. As the Clovis, and ensuing cultures who lived in southeastern Ontario, also occupied the northern part of adjacent New York

State, it is reasonable to assume that some would have ventured to Wolfe Island.

WOODLAND PERIOD

The successors to the Clovis Culture in this area were known as the Laurentian Eastern Group, who in turn were followed by the Point Peninsula Culture. These people inhabited or visited Wolfe Island for many centuries between 700 B.C. and A.D. 1000. Semi-nomadic, they hunted, fished, and gathered roots or seeds for food while moving about over a vast region. At some point between 500 and 900 they adopted agriculture, tobacco smoking, pottery making, and the practice of burial mounds. Although basic in style, their pottery appears to have originated at three different sources in the St. Lawrence Valley, each group depicting a decorating technique essentially its own.

BROPHY POINT

Brophy Point, on Abraham's Head, is a place where Wolfe Island's history can be traced back more than two millennia. Abraham's Head, so named because of its shape, juts out from the north shore into the north channel, a few miles east of Marysville. Easily accessible by canoe, it became a focal point of habitation for the Point Peninsula people. By this time, land was well-forested, and Wolfe Island was teeming with wildlife such as moose, deer, wildcat, and beaver. By trapping game and catching fish so plentiful in the surrounding waters, the people were able to survive. Over the years, farmers turning the soil around Abraham's Head found numerous artifacts from this civilization and others have washed up along the shoreline, but never in such abundance as during archaeological digs. Initially discovered in 1952, Brophy Point became the third chronologically and possibly the most significant archaeological location on Wolfe Island.[3] Guy Bromley, of Kingston, a collector of aboriginal relics, reported the find to the National Museum of Man in Ottawa.

Major James F. Pendergast,[4] the assistant director of the museum, visited the area in 1959 and returned to spearhead a research dig in 1964, which was sponsored by the museum. This site, covering 160 acres on Abraham's Head, has been known since the mid-1800s as Brophy Point, named after the owners at that time. Pendergast believed the area was one of the most important archaeological locations in eastern Ontario. During the dig, reporters kept pace with the team's discoveries. Brian Small of the *Kingston Whig-Standard* wrote in July 1964 that "centuries of history are carefully being uncovered at an ancient Indian fishing village on Wolfe Island." Similar reports were found in the *Ottawa Citizen*. This four-week, painstaking exercise uncovered artifacts of successive Native cultures, and each were catalogued for time, depth, and location. The bottom-most layer of the site yielded objects belonging to the Point Peninsula Culture and each subsequent layer gave credence to Major Pendergast's "superimposed layer" theory. He was confident that evaluation of their findings would confirm that "nearly all the peoples who occupied eastern Ontario stopped here." The pottery and tools are sufficiently different at each level of the excavation to be recognizable as belonging to separate and distinct eras, with the top layers identified as belonging to more current Native cultures. Items of French and British trading groups such as coins, cannonballs, lead shot, beads, and copper arrowheads were also found in the upper layers.

The Brophy site excavation, which was about eighteen inches deep and covered sixteen hundred square feet, produced hundreds of objects, including arrowheads, spear points, harpoons, net sinkers, hammer heads, tools, scrapers, pottery shards, and pipe fragments. One of the most important finds was an unbroken soapstone pipe dating back to A.D. 800. An abundance of fish bones and fragments of moose, deer, wildcat, and beaver bones were found, thus indicating an ample supply of food. There were no human bones.

My father had followed information on the dig at Brophy Point with great interest, and, while involved in his own research on Wolfe Island, contacted the major in 1975. Although the major's report had not been completed, he telephoned to confirm that a photocopy of a paper by Michael W. Spence of the National Museum of Canada was en route to Charles. This work, entitled *Anthropology Papers #14,* enabled my father to elaborate on the foregoing archaeological findings. Spence had documented several burial mounds along the St. Lawrence Valley in his paper, which preceded the major's work on Wolfe Island. With this fact in mind, Major Pendergast indicated that burial grounds must be somewhere near the village.

The finds on Wolfe Island are not stated here in a chronological fashion, but rather in order of significance, with the information gleaned from Major Pendergast shedding new light on previous discoveries.

The burial practices of the Point Peninsula people were much the same as their ancestors until two thousand years ago when a new ritual was introduced — that of burying their deceased in large earth mounds. Archaeological research indicates that bodies were laid on the ground in a circle with the feet to the centre and the heads directed outward. After a burial ceremony, earth was piled on the body to a depth of four or five feet. Sometimes a mound was built close to a regular burying ground where the bodies were laid in a row. Most of the mounds, burial sites, and camping grounds were in the St. Lawrence Valley, with at least two on Wolfe Island. They are known to archaeologists as the Pyke Farm Site and the Button Bay Site.

PYKE FARM SITE

A burial site was discovered in 1880 on the farm owned by Dexter H. Pyke. Archaeologist W.J. Wintemberg, in describing the find, said, "twenty-five skeletons, pottery fragments, and stone and copper artifacts were found in graves … near Point Alexandria, Wolfe Island, Frontenac County in 1880."[5] He also noted that, although some of the objects were of unknown use, the items found were made of a variety of materials, including stone, copper, shell, bone, antler, and earthenware. Many of the artifacts were identified as follows: a small double-pointed copper awl-like tool; a stone adze; a slate pendant; a slate gorget (a piece of armour to protect the throat); polished Ohio fireclay block-end tubes; and a knife with a Robbins-stemmed blade of flint from a quarry near Warsaw, Ohio. It appears that these Early

A sampling of Native artifacts that were found on Gordon McRae's Wolfe Island property. These were identified by the Kingston Archaeological Association as worked stone tools: adze/celts, pendant/gorget with drilled hole, fragments of spear points, and a scraping tool.

Woodland people were in contact with, or at least influenced by, their neighbours to the south.

In addition to the usual grave furniture, Spence found a large collection of other items that he said "proved to cover a broad range of time."[6] Thus, the oldest relics could have come to the Point Peninsula people by way of trade routes, or they may represent the burial objects of earlier cultures that occupied this area. He also noted that among other things found at the Pyke Farm Site were sixty-one spearheads and similar projectile points belonging to at least five other cultures. This collection was given to the Royal Ontario Museum in 1887 by a Dr. Dickson of Kingston.

BUTTON BAY SITE

The Button Bay Site, situated close to the water's edge, contained a burial mound as well as the usual cemetery. It may never have come to light had it not been for one of those fierce windstorms, well-known to generations of Wolfe Islanders. William L. Stone wrote about the 1879 Button Bay discovery made by his daughter and H.M. Livingstone of Saratoga Springs:

> [S]everal feet of the Button Bay shoreline was washed away by a strong east wind disclosing some large Indian spears, innumerable arrowheads and some skulls…. The skulls, which were encased in mica … by the native people before burial, were well preserved even to the teeth.[7]

Nearby was a mound containing more skeletons. Because the bodies had been laid in perfect order, Stone deduced that the burials had been made during a time of peace. After examining the island's artifacts, Spence concluded that the Pyke Farm Site and the Button Bay Site were part of a Middle Woodland burial complex in the St. Lawrence Valley, extending from Wolfe Island to the Long Sault Mounds near Cornwall. The local Native people referred to this area as *Manitonna*, meaning "garden of the Great Spirit."

TERMINAL WOODLAND PERIOD

The Terminal Woodland Period in Ontario's prehistory began in 900 and continued until the arrival of the Europeans in the sixteenth century. On Wolfe Island the early Natives were succeeded by the Owasco of northern New York and southern Ontario, who in turn were driven out by the Pickering of the Rouge region east of Toronto. The latter group successfully established a fishing village that existed on Brophy Point for about two hundred years. The Pickering people were the first in the area to rely on agriculture for sustenance, supplemented by hunting and fishing. Among other things, they are credited with developing the custom of pipe smoking. By 1400 they had evolved into a new culture known as the Huron-Petun, noted for their agricultural pursuits, particularly the cultivation of corn, beans, squash, sunflower seeds for oil, and tobacco.

Once contact with Europeans occurred the Native way of life was irrevocably altered. Their resentment of the intruders led to ongoing unrest among themselves and with the Europeans. After firearms were introduced, problems were exacerbated, and in time human greed eroded the centuries of peace and tranquility on Wolfe Island.

In 1615, Samuel de Champlain led the first Europeans known to have set foot on the island's shores. In 1615, he and his party, en route from Sackets Harbor, New York, to the Cataraqui River, walked across Wolfe Island. Their footsteps would signal the onset of a tumultuous period to come.

HURON, ALGONQUIN, AND MISSISSAUGA

As time passed, the Algonquin, who lived to the east and north of the Iroquois in Ontario, began to expand their territory by occupying land vacated by the Huron. Wolfe, Grindstone, and Wellesley islands were the first to be overtaken and when they eventually defined their territory, the Algonquin controlled the shoreline from Belleville to Gananoque and the islands lying off this southern shore of the mainland. The Mississauga, a sub-tribe of the Chippewa Algonquin, made their home in the Kingston-Wolfe Island area. Mississauga Point at the foot of Gore Street, Kingston, was named for those early residents.

While the French were busy exploring and creating settlements in Canada, the Huron, Iroquois, and Algonquin, each in turn, were living in the Kingston area. In addition to the Wolfe Island sites, it is possible that there was a Native village at the east end of Garden Island. In the 1850s human remains were uncovered when the Calvin Company — a Garden Island shipbuilding company — was excavating a foundation for a new workshop. The relics dug up were intact, suggesting that this had been a peaceful burial. However, as neither the remains nor the site were subjected to a thorough scientific examination, it was impossible to date the approximate time of death and thus establish whether these were the remains of aboriginal people or Europeans.[8]

This early Native culture thrived for many years, the fishing village at Brophy Point being one of their centres. By the year 1000, five distinct nations had emerged: the Oneida, Onandaga, Mohawk, Seneca, and Cayuga. The Tuscarora, driven from the United States into Canada by the British and Cherokee in the late 1700s, were admitted as the sixth nation in the Iroquois Confederacy in 1720.[9] After thousands of years of living off the land and criss-crossing Wolfe Island, they left the island as they found it, unspoiled and unpolluted. Over time, the Europeans, having been the beneficiaries of Native customs, gradually began to adopt strawberry season, maple sugar feasts, and, after the corn ripened, thanksgiving to the Great Spirit for the gift of life. The Native people had willingly shared their knowledge with the Europeans.[10]

Father Picquet, a Sulpician, the King of France's missionary and prefect apostolic to Canada in 1751, sought out bands of Native people to convert to Christianity. He crossed from Cataraqui to Wolfe Island, and, after providing the local Native groups with a feast, invited them to move to his new mission at Ogdensburg, New York, which he had founded in 1748. From that time on, the permanent aboriginal population dwindled in this portion of the Garden of the Great Spirit. As the Europeans increasingly began to settle on Wolfe Island, the Natives gradually moved off, but returned each fall with crafts to sell or to trade with these pioneers. The last group of Native people known to have come to Wolfe Island for subsistence reasons camped on Henry Hinckley's property toward the south shore in the early 1900s. They are said to have landed quickly and quietly like ghosts in the night and left in the same manner. They arrived in canoes in the spring, set up camp, raised a garden, and fished, then just "disappeared" in the fall.

Frequent discoveries of Native artifacts over the years indicate the extent of their activities throughout the island. Small fishing villages are believed to have existed on Holliday Point as well as the foot of the island, where many items were found in earlier days. According to some older Wolfe Island residents who shared information with my father during the 1930s, the Natives lived in the rectangular barrel-shaped huts, two of which were located circa 1800 in the present area of Marysville along with additional artifacts.

Although the utensils, implements, and pottery used by local Native people appear to have originated elsewhere, oral history passed down through generations of Wolfe Islanders suggests the Natives' creative talents were mainly in the weaving of baskets and the plaiting and weaving of mats and rugs. The raw materials used, such as wood splints, marsh and coarse grasses, and corn husks were all gathered close at hand, but, due to their perishable nature, many of these handicrafts have long since disappeared. Mrs. Mary (Brophy) Darling told my father in the 1970s that some early islanders had reported seeing Native women camping on several consecutive summers at one particular spot on Brophy Point. It seems that they were weaving the local grasses and brush into baskets for sale at the Kingston market.

CHAPTER 3
Enter the French

Early French explorers, pressing up the St. Lawrence River towards Cataraqui and the Wolfe Island area, helped set the scene for France's eventual ownership of Wolfe Island. The king of France had commissioned Jacques Cartier to search for gold and spices and a northwest route to Asia through the New World. Though unsuccessful in 1534 and again in 1535, Cartier's latter expedition did take him much further west along the St. Lawrence River. On August 10, 1535, he entered the mighty river and, as this was the feast day of St. Lawrence, some historians presume that he named it in honour of the Catholic deacon martyred in Rome centuries previously.[1] Others, however, believe the river's name is the result of a cartographer's error.

NEW FRANCE

On January 15, 1541, the king invested Jean-François de La Rocque de Roberval, a Huguenot nobleman, with the title "His Majesty's Lieutenant General, head leader and captain" of a new venture to the New World. Roberval, who later became governor of New France, accompanied Cartier, armed with the mandate to establish a French colony to counter Spanish-American claims to this new territory. Under Cartier's command, five ships set sail on May 23, 1541, loaded with prisoners, as immigrant volunteer sailors were not forthcoming.[2] After three months at sea, they reached Stadacona (Quebec City), and as they sailed up the St. Lawrence and approached Hochelaga (Montreal), they could see Native villages and fishing camps. The first French attempt at settlement, however, ended in failure as they were unprepared for the severity of winter. Nonetheless, Cartier, largely because of his later explorations, has been credited for much of France's influence and claims within New France. Motivated by what the indigenous people called this land, Cartier adopted the name *Canada*.

Europe's growing penchant for fur, especially beaver, spurred Louis XIV's determination to dominate the fur trade in the New World. In 1603 he dispatched Samuel de Champlain to carry out this mission. Successful in establishing trading relations with the Natives, Champlain formed an alliance with the Algonquin that would last for decades. He was also responsible for the construction of forts at Quebec and establishing a settlement at the site of present-day Montreal. The widely travelled Champlain and his young scout, Étienne Brulé, were undoubtedly the first Europeans to sight Lake Ontario.[3] According to his diaries, Champlain and his Huron allies waged an attack on the Iroquois in 1615, near present-day Sackets Harbor on the southeastern shore of Lake Ontario. During the attack, two Iroquoian arrows lodged in Champlain's leg and he had to be carried, like the other wounded, in a basket on the back of a survivor — a humbling experience for this man of great endurance. On their route back, via Wolfe Island, part of their mission was to collect fish and game as winter was approaching. They sojourned for a short while on Bear Point, the island's southwestern shore, before returning to Cataraqui.

Champlain was an accomplished cartographer who, during his numerous expeditions into the interior of North America, capably mapped out pathways for those who would follow him. He died on Christmas Day in 1635 at the age of sixty-eight from what is believed to have been a stroke. His death in Quebec, the city he founded in 1608, ended his thirty years of extending French possessions in America.[4]

This bronze statue, created by Vernon March of Ottawa's War Memorial fame, was erected in Couchiching Beach Park in Orillia, Ontario, in 1925 to commemorate Samuel de Champlain, the first European explorer to come to that area in 1615.

In 1663, Canada's French population was only three thousand, comprised mostly of fur traders, clerics, and government officials. The Iroquois-speaking people of the St. Lawrence area, earlier known as the Laurentians, were first mentioned by Cartier in 1534 and last mentioned by Roberval in 1543. By 1603, when Champlain arrived, they had vanished.[5] By then the Native population had been reduced drastically by warfare and disease, principally smallpox, carried to the New World by Europeans. The Onondaga fishing village at the easterly tip of Wolfe Island survived until 1675.[6] In 1664, Louis XIV had ordered his troops to eradicate the Iroquois Confederacy of Five Nations, which included the Onondaga nation. One of these French expeditions was likely responsible for the Onondaga being driven from Wolfe Island.

New France became a Royal Province in 1663 under Louis XIV, and in 1671 Rémy de Courçelles held a short tenure as governor. At that time Cataraqui (Kingston) had been selected as the seat of government because of its superb harbour. Charles Le Moyne, whose significance is discussed later, accompanied the governor from Quebec for the construction of Fort Frontenac at Cataraqui. But it was Louis Henri de Buade de Frontenac, appointed governor in 1672 at the age of fifty-two, who would go on to achieve considerable success for the French.

In July of 1673, after sending René-Robert Cavelier La Salle as emissary to pave the way, Frontenac held a meeting with Native chiefs to negotiate peace and establish a location for managing the now widespread fur trade. Accompanied by four hundred habitants, Native warriors, and soldiers, he sailed up the St. Lawrence, braving the rapids of Lachine and Long Sault, and on toward Lake Ontario. Upon arrival at Cataraqui, a three-day historic meeting ensued comprised of trade negotiations, feasts, and the exchange of gifts with the Iroquois. This meeting represented the first international peace convention to be held in Canada.[7] The agreement included the trading of liquor with the Natives to further the development of the fur trade, a provision that provoked disputes with the newly appointed Bishop de Laval Montmorency. Subsequent to this meeting, Frontenac had a palisaded fortification erected at Cataraqui, near the site of present-day Kingston.[8]

La Salle, a descendant of one of the most respected families in Rouèn, Normandy, had come to Canada in 1666 and was granted land near the Lachine Rapids, where he farmed and established a fur trading post. Eventually, La Salle sold this seigneury near Lachine. After providing considerable assistance to Frontenac, particularly in communicating with Native people, La Salle was awarded the seigneury of Cataraqui in 1675 by Louis XIV. Recognizing the significant potential of this region as a base of operations, La Salle returned to France to petition the king to also grant him Fort Frontenac at the mouth of the Cataraqui River. This patent of nobility and the acquisition of the fort would provide him with considerable responsibility and influence. On May 13, 1675, Louis XIV conferred title to this territory as a seigneury to La Salle, accompanied by the following mandate:

> To repay the 10,000 livres which the fort had cost the King; to maintain the fort on a self-sufficient basis creating a garrison equal to that already established at Montreal, employing fifteen to twenty labourers; to build a church when the number of inhabitants reached one hundred; to support

one or two Récollet friars and to form a settlement of domesticated native peoples in the neighbourhood.[9]

Fort Frontenac and its surrounding islands were granted to René Cavelier, Sieur de La Salle as:

> Four leagues of adjacent country along the lakes and rivers, above and below the said fort (Frontenac) for half a league into the interior of the said islands each league composed of two thousand toises, together with the islands Ganounkoesnot and Kaouenesgo and adjoining islets; with the right of hunting and fishing on the rivers and Lake Ontario.[10]

Wolfe Island, still called Grande Île, became part of La Salle's seigneury through this declaration, and so, historically, La Salle became the first owner of Wolfe Island subsequent to the French Crown. Other islands included in this acquisition were Amherst, Simcoe, Garden, Horseshoe, Howe, and Cedar.

The whole seigneurial territory was granted "by title and fief" to La Salle, his heirs, successors, and assigns, in return for his seven years of service in Canada on behalf of the king of France. La Salle returned to Canada from France in 1668, took possession of Fort Frontenac and his seigneury, and within two years had replaced the wooden palisades of the fort with a hewn stone wall about 550 feet long, three feet thick, and fifteen feet high. Portions of that original old stone wall were uncovered on two occasions, first in the 1930s and again in July of 1971, when repairs were being made to the sewage system of the present Fort Frontenac.

La Salle established a colony and built a shipyard to produce sailing vessels needed for transport and defence purposes. From here, he conducted a lively fur-trading business, having expanded it from a canoe operation to a schooner service.[11] As the first private landowner at the mouth of the St. Lawrence River, La Salle also counted a ten-mile strip of the mainland among his titled possessions. However, his dealings in the fur trade and his sudden rise to power caused personal enmity with the Jesuits, whose mandate it was to maintain the Catholic religion in New France and to convert the Native peoples to Catholicism. By this time La Salle had entered the realm of the great empire builders. Somewhat of a visionary, he was constantly dreaming of expanding New France by way of exploring those western lakes and rivers that he had learned much about from the Native people. Striking an alliance with Frontenac afforded him that opportunity to explore further afield. He was unsuccessful in his quest to find the mouth of the Mississippi River, but his dream was later realized by other explorers, including two of Charles Le Moyne's sons, Bienville and Iberville. Restless to explore the New World, La Salle spent his later years seeking the Mississippi, but was murdered in 1687 by a mutinous follower.[12] Admiration for this courageous, but reputedly arrogant, man bears testimony in the many buildings that honour his name in the Kingston area and beyond.

THE FRENCH SEIGNEURY

Many of the early French explorers and émigrés of noble background who came to Canada from Normandy were familiar with the seigneurial system in use in their homeland since the twelfth century and implemented the same method of land tenure in New France. Even the noble Grants, descendants of whom were in Kingston and on Wolfe Island in the late 1700s and early 1800s, were privy to the seigneurial system. Originally Scottish, the Grant family had lived in Normandy for four centuries. In 1700, when Louis XIV conferred the title of baron upon Charles Le Moyne, his seigneury at Longueuil, near Montreal became a barony. And when a Grant descendant was united in marriage with a Le Moyne, they brought the baronial title to Wolfe Island. Historically, the Longueuil lineage was Catholic until the first Grant appeared.

In the 1600s and 1700s, the seigneurial system became essentially the basis of law and convention governing the control of and payment for land. Many seigneuries near Quebec and Montreal were controlled by the Church and became part of the legal and economic framework of the community.[13] The seigneur in Canada was a vassal to the French Crown. As decreed by Louis XIV in March 1663, the seigneur was obliged to clear the land on his estate and parcel it out in tenure to the peasant farmers or "habitants" who cultivated the land as tenants of the king. In return, fixed dues were paid to the seigneur in kind, money, or services enabling him to repay the king for use of the land. If the tenant's property was not cleared within a certain time frame mutually agreed upon (usually six months), it was subject to forfeiture — a distinct feature of Canadian feudalism. These seigneurs were not rich, so many had difficulty meeting their obligations.[14] The manor house became an administrative and political unit usually under the charge of an intendant — an agent of the seigneur. This feudal system disappeared in France during the French Revolution, but remained in Quebec until the mid-1800s.[15]

JACQUES CAUCHOIS AND THE CUROTTE (CURAUX) BROTHERS[16]

On November 25, 1685, Sieur de la Forêt, lieutenant to and attorney on behalf of La Salle, confirmed a grant of the whole of Wolfe Island to Jacques Cauchois in accordance with the original terms and conditions as laid down by the king of France to La Salle. Because no price was mentioned, it is possible that La Salle granted the island to Cauchois in exchange for services rendered as a pilot on Lake Ontario and on the St. Lawrence and Mississippi rivers. Howe Island became known at that time as Île Cauchois, indicating that it too had been deeded to Cauchois in exchange for his service to La Salle. The actual passing of Wolfe Island from La Salle's ownership into the hands of La Forêt to Cauchois represents the first recorded private conveyance or land transfer of any part of Ontario from one person to another — a significant moment in the history of Wolfe Island.[17]

The Wolfe Island land conveyance occurred only two years after the marriage of Jacques Cauchois and Elizabeth Prudhomme at Montreal in 1683. Jacques, originally a native of Rouèn, Normandy, remained the owner of Wolfe Island's thirty-three thousand acres until his death in 1708 at Fort Frontenac, where some believe he is buried. However, author H.C. Burleigh's research concludes that although Cauchois's death was recorded at both Montreal and Fort Frontenac, he very likely was buried on Wolfe Island.[18]

Jacques and Elizabeth's daughter, Madeleine, inherited these islands upon her father's demise. When she married Martin Curaux (Curotte) in 1713 in Montreal, the couple became the owners of Wolfe Island, and Martin became a storekeeper at Fort Frontenac. Madeleine died in 1724 and her only son, Jacques-François Curaux, inherited all rights and title to the island upon his parents' deaths. Not being interested in land ownership as his desire was to enter the priesthood, Jacques-François conveyed this inheritance to his half brothers, Amable and Michel Curaux, in March of 1784.

Michel is registered as having been married at Montreal in 1766, but there does not appear to be any recorded ventures of these Curaux families to Wolfe Island. Their growing involvement in the fur trade may have deterred the Curaux brothers from taking up residence on Wolfe Island, yet it has been said that the initial settlement of unknown inhabitants on Wolfe Island was observed in 1780 on the site of the Old Survey, only three miles across the channel from Cataraqui. Fur traders from many points west and north used this busy channel in their commute to Montreal and a small community of fur traders living on the island could have been vulnerable to their competitors. Amable Curaux obtained a fur-trader licence for the Cataraqui region, dated September 24, 1781.[19] This transaction, and the fact that his father Martin worked at Fort Frontenac, would suggest that they were indeed living in the area of Cataraqui and possibly on their Wolfe Island seigneury at that time.

United Empire Loyalists did not begin to arrive on Wolfe Island until 1795 and yet the presence of pastures on the island was alluded to in the land grant given to Cauchois one hundred years earlier. An extract from the grant reads as follows: "we give and concede to the said Sieur Cauchois for himself, his heirs and assigns, the above named Grande Île, Islands and Islets, pastures and reefs adjacent to this said Grande Île."[20] It is possible that some early French settlers had already cleared some of the island of trees before any British had arrived, thus creating these "pastures" along the front road. Some clearing of the land may have been ordered by the Cauchois family during its early ownership as the seigneurial obligations were transferred from owner to owner.

Actually, Jacques-François Curaux's benevolent gesture created a double dilemma for his half brothers. Firstly, Amable and Michel were not interested in nor did they intend to fulfill the prerequisites stated in the original grant from the French Crown, even if it meant forfeiture of their ownership rights on Wolfe Island. Secondly, they anticipated difficulty in obtaining a clear title due to the fact that this was the first change of ownership since 1763, when the French Crown had ceded Canada to the British following the battle at the Plains of Abraham. However, anxious to test the validity of their title under those conditions, the brothers petitioned the governor-in-chief of British North America, Lord Dorchester, and the council setting forth their claim to title, asking that it be certified or confirmed by the British Crown. On three occasions their petition was referred to the members of the executive council in the province of Quebec and each time an affirmative report was handed down.[21] In 1788, after deliberation by the council and consultation with the attorney general and solicitor general, it was declared that legal title to Wolfe Island rightly belonged to the claimants — namely, Amable and Michel Curaux.

ÉGLISE REFORMÉE DU QUÉBEC (HUGUENOTS)

Records of the Protestant cemeteries on Wolfe Island abound with French surnames of people who were buried in the early 1800s. In our efforts to establish who some of the earliest French settlers might have been, and their places of origin, it became apparent that several were Huguenots. There seems to have been a preponderance of Huguenots emigrating from France to the New World during the years of their persecution at the hands of French Catholics. In the early seigneurial days of New France, there were reportedly 350 Huguenot habitants settled in the St. Lawrence Valley. Their initiative, economic expertise, and desire to found a colony loyal to the French throne, where they would be free to worship God as Reformed Catholics, melded with the Christian beliefs upon which Quebec and Canada were founded.[22]

Family names such as Daryeau, Cadotte, Huot, Bruyière, and Mosier, to mention a few, may be found in the Protestant cemeteries and are examples of names of Huguenots who fled to Wolfe Island during the late 1700s, or were descendants of earlier French dwellers.[23]

How many may have remained on Wolfe Island is unknown because, over time, there was intermarriage with Catholic immigrants as well as with the influx of the non-French United Empire Loyalists.

The earlier Wolfe Island settlers who homesteaded on the area of the original seigneury — or Old Survey, as it is also known — were predominantly French-Canadian. Dauzat's *Dictionnaire etymologique des noms de famille et prenoms de France* records the surnames of all the original French families who emigrated and settled in New France between 1608 and 1760, including Bezou, Brabant, Brenier, Cadot, DeRush, Devereaux, Dout, Ducey, Grindle, Joliffe, La Fleur, La Londe, Lambert, La Rush, Perregaux, and Rousseau. With the exception of La Fleur, families bearing all of the above names did at one time live in the Old Survey of Wolfe Island. Peter La Fleur apparently was a French naval officer who arrived on the island much later and settled on Holliday Bay in the Fourteenth Concession. Some, if not all, of the other families may have dated back to the 1700s.

THE FRENCH SETTLEMENT "OLD SURVEY"

Although it has often been speculated that Native people were the only inhabitants of Wolfe Island prior to the arrival of the United Empire Loyalists, there is much evidence to the contrary. During the Curaux ownership, there had been many recorded sightings of trees being levelled and wood being hewn. More importantly, La Salle granted Wolfe Island to Jacques Cauchois in 1685 under the original terms and conditions of the "grant" from Louis XIV. With the mandate to clear and settle some of the land within six months, or face forfeiture, it seems highly improbable that, during 110 years of French ownership collectively, no effort would be made by the Cauchois or the Curaux to live on the island and derive some benefit from it. Their very presence would certainly necessitate the felling of trees and chopping of wood. Furthermore, the farms on the narrow strip along the Front Road are typical of the French settlements that bordered the St. Lawrence River as far east as the Gaspé Peninsula. This is the only section of Wolfe Island ever to have been divided in this manner and has always been referred to as the Old Survey. However, there is no record at the land registry office for Frontenac County as to who actually created the Old Survey, when it was first surveyed, or who registered the survey or the date of the registration. As settlers who leased in this area acquired land that had evidently been farmed at an earlier date, it seems logical that the Old Survey dates back to the French-Canadian era of the 1700s.

Isabel O'Shea, a highly esteemed educator, now in her elder years, and descended from a Wolfe Island pioneer family, shared her speculation as to the origin of the island's first French settlers. Pierre Gaultier de Varennes, Sieur de la Vérendrye (1685–1749), a renowned French soldier and fur trader, spent many years exploring the west and establishing fur-trading outposts with his four sons and a nephew. As his headquarters were in Montreal, they would have passed Grande Île with frequency. In her opinion, la Vérendrye planted French settlers on this part of Wolfe Island during the Curaux seigneury period. This theory would substantiate the presence of pastures alluded to in the land conveyance as well as the presence of French settlers. She believes that by 1766, after the Treaty of Paris, some returned to France, some to Quebec, and some remained.[24] However, this has yet to be substantiated by historical research. When the earliest Loyalists, tenants of David Grant (who along with Patrick Langan would purchase Wolfe Island in 1795), were admitted to the Old Survey, indeed, some of the remaining French people worked for them.

On Wolfe Island, twenty-nine ribbon-shaped lots had been created. The eastern-most lot 1 begins at the western boundary of what is now known as St. Lawrence Street in Marysville. These lots extend numerically in a westward direction along a pathway that came to be known as the Front Road (land bordering a lake). Lot 30 on the west shore, irregular in shape, comprises Staley Point and the shoreline of Staley Bay, all of which are adjacent to lot 29. The lots varied in acreage due to the uneven shoreline, but the river frontage of standard-sized lots was approximately three arpents, or six hundred feet. Lot depths were generally thirty-three arpents, making the whole lot area approximately one hundred acres. However, Old Survey maps reveal interesting variations. The financial status of these tenant farmers may have been a factor in the determination of lot size as there appeared a variance of anywhere from fifty to 150 acres. However, the above changes may have occurred during the British period in the early 1800s, when Loyalists were being allotted land.

The third item of interest on the Old Survey is the seigneury house on the Front Road. Such a building suggests that either the Cauchois or Curaux families had tenant farmers in the area, as a manor house indicates the presence of an overseer and some kind of rental arrangement. In those times, dues were usually paid

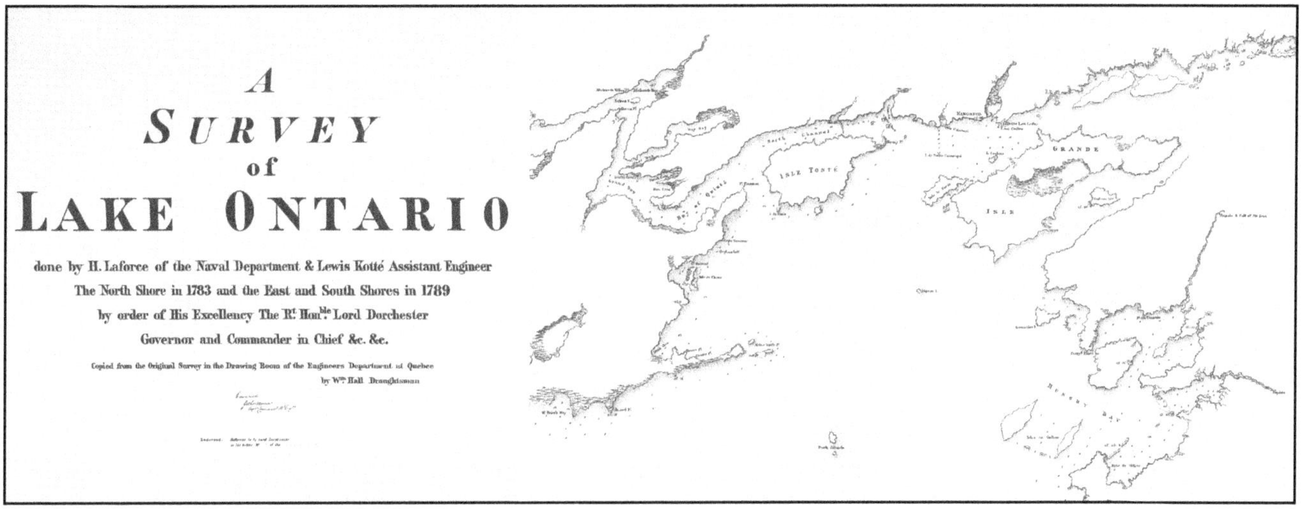

0021743-3. Description of Map with Surveyor's Name, N.M.C. 0021743-1.

Map 2: Wolfe Island and Surrounding Islands from a Survey of Lake Ontario, 1783, by H. LaForce and Lewis Kotté of the Naval Department, by order of Lord Dorchester.

with one quart of wheat per acre per year, delivered to the seigneury headquarters. The Wolfe Island manor still exists on the Front Road on lot 6, Old Survey. It has been known as Areson's for many years, having been purchased by a Dr. Areson of New Jersey, in 1927. Constructed of limestone, it could be the original building, but in all probability this elegant house was preceded by a log structure that served as the original manor house.

Another item of consideration regarding the seigneury is the nearby wharf. Early maps indicate that the first regularly used public docking place on the island's north shore was just east of Cone Point, there to serve this most important residence in this area. The substantial wharf existed in the bay until 1870 at the eastern boundary of the seigneury lot, now part of Peg and Ken White's property.

Bateau Channel, the waterway between Simcoe Island and the northwestern shore of Wolfe Island, by its very name conjures up an image of days long past. The bateaux, or barge-type ferryboats, were used to transport goods, as the waterway was the highway during this era. The name Bateau Channel appears on very old maps. This evidence of the French presence, as well as other vestiges in existence today, is a record of some activities of this tiny colony on Wolfe Island, the most westerly part of the seigneurial system of New France.

The general location of the Front Road has not changed since the late 1700s. It follows the northwest shoreline from the present Sixth Concession to Sand Bay Road at the head of the island and probably evolved from a bush trail in French-Canadian times. The Front Road and the Old Survey are closely related, as this seigneury land was designed to accommodate settlers along the road by providing farmland at the back and water at the front. In the mid to late 1700s, this roadway boasted no less than fifty-two dwellings — mainly shanties, all family-occupied. Seigneurs were obliged to build a gristmill for the use of the habitants, who would be charged a *banality* (fee for its use). The civil and moral duty of the seigneur was to erect a gristmill within a year of establishing the seigneury or he sacrificed banal rights.[25] The first gristmill on Wolfe Island was located on the shoreline near the manor's wharf in the area later known as Mill Point.

CHAPTER 4
Lineage of the Barony of Longueuil

The Honourable Charles William Grant, the fifth baron de Longueuil, was popularly known as Baron Grant. A descendant of the Le Moynes, one of the most influential families of New France, he played a vital role in the settlement of Wolfe Island. The story of the Longueuils begins along the St. Lawrence River on the south shore across the river from Montreal, some 150 miles east of Wolfe Island.

THE LONGUEUILS OF QUEBEC

Charles Le Moyne (later known as Charles the Elder) was the son of an innkeeper in Dieppe, Normandy. In 1641, at the age of fifteen, the adventurous Charles sailed with his uncle, a Quebec surgeon, to the growing colony at Ville Marie (Montreal). The following year Charles became an indentured servant of the Jesuits,[1] working as a *donné*[2] at the Huron Mission in the area of present-day Midland, Ontario, where he learned woodcraft, assisted the priests, and absorbed the languages of the Native people, an experience enabling him to become a skilled interpreter of Indian languages.[3]

Le Moyne soon acquired the reputation of being a fearless fighter and a singularly effective negotiator with the Native people, for which he was well-rewarded with land holdings assigned to him by Governor Maisonneuve.[4] In 1671, his language skills were required by Governor de Courçelles during explorations near the present-day city of Kingston, and Le Moyne became the interpreter during the building of Fort Frontenac. As shall be seen, the Le Moynes would frequently travel to the Cataraqui area for over two centuries.

Charles had married Catherine Thiery-Primot (also from Normandy) in 1654 and fathered a large family, including eleven sons — several of whom also figured prominently in the early history of French Canada. One of his sons, Pierre Le Moyne, recognized as an exceptional military leader, has been immortalized in early Canadian history as Iberville.[5] He and his brother Bienville were responsible for the French acquisition of the Hudson Bay region to the north and for claiming the region of Louisiana to the south for France.

The first auspicious mansion of the feudal period in New France was the château built by Charles, by then a successful fur trader. In 1668, he had been awarded a considerable parcel of land through the practice of letters patent of nobility, a reward for his continuing efforts in colonization. He named the land and his château "Longueuil" after a village in his native Normandy. This holding was declared a seigneury in 1672. A son, Charles Le Moyne (the younger), inherited the Longueuil seigneury upon his father's death in 1685. He added more property to the holding, encouraged French emigrants to come to his estate, and developed Longueuil into one of the most important centres in New France. By this time, Sieur de Longueuil had attained the status of a town "notable," sharing the same importance as the mayor, the notary, and the surgeon.[6]

After serving with the French army in Flanders, Charles returned to New France in 1683 when he was appointed the mayor of Montreal. For these services, the king rewarded him with the title *baron de Longueuil*. The patent for the barony was dated January 26, 1700, and included the king's wish that Charles receive the title *baron*. In 1724, having already served in 1720 as governor of Trois-Rivières, he became the first Canadian-born governor of Montreal.[7] The first baron de Longueuil was killed in action against the Iroquois in 1729 at the age of sixty-three.

Charles Le Moyne III (the second baron), while at the peak of his illustrious military career, married a Charlotte Catherine de Gray. Before long he, too, became mayor of Montreal in 1733 and later the governor in 1749. Charles-Jacques, their first son, entered military service at an early age and by 1754 had risen through the ranks, as had his predecessors. At the time of Charles's death in 1755 at the age of fifty, he was the governor of Montreal. His son, Charles-Jacques Le Moyne IV, inherited his father's baronial title to become the third baron de Longueuil — a title that he would enjoy for only eight months, as he died in battle in that same year. In January 1754, he had married Marie-Anne Catherine Fleury d'Eschambault, who was with child when he left on that fateful expedition. The following March the baroness gave birth to twin daughters: Marie-Catherine Josephe, who died at five months of age, and Marie-Charles Josephe Le Moyne.[8] Thus ended the illustrious Le Moyne name as attached to the barony; however, the famous French-Canadian family name of Le Moyne did not terminate with the early demise of Charles-Jacques.

In 1770, fifteen years after her husband's death, by licence of the British Governor Guy Carleton, the widowed Baroness Marie-Anne remarried in Montreal. She and her new Protestant Scot husband, the Honourable William Grant, deputy receiver general of the province of Canada, were united after he declared himself to be Catholic. A Jesuit priest, Pierre René Floquet, officiated at the marriage, which took place secretly at Montreal. The couple, in an unusual step for those times, then repeated their wedding vows in a public ceremony on September 11, 1770, over which David Chabrand De Lisle, a priest of the United Church of England

and Ireland (Anglican), presided.[9] Through this union, Grant gained considerably more seigneurial resources to manipulate at his discretion. His somewhat checkered history in real estate and business dealings were evident before, and after, the marriage with Marie-Anne. (He was also known to change his religious persuasion from time to time in order to suit his political needs.) During the late 1700s, William had entrusted some of his seigneurial duties in the Montreal area to the care of his nephew, David Alexander Grant, and had sold a major portion of his holdings to him. By then, the de Longueuil seigneury had grown to the status of a hamlet or small village.[10]

As no children were produced from the union of William Grant and Baroness Marie-Anne, the barony, upon her death, passed to her only child, daughter Marie-Charles Joseph Le Moyne. In 1778, a French court confirmed that Marie-Charles, by birth, was the rightful heir to the title "La Baronne IV."[11] The Honourable William Grant, however, had not become a baron, as he had envisaged, by his marriage to the dowager baroness, for the title could not be acquired by marriage.

The Wolfe Island connection to the barony de Longueuil began with the union of Marie-Charles Joseph Le Moyne, La Baronne IV, and Captain David Alexander Grant of the 84th regiment. He had met the young baroness while managing his uncle's business ventures in Montreal. Their marriage at Holy Trinity Church of England and Ireland Cathedral in Quebec City on May 7, 1781, created the significant link between the Le Moyne and the Grant families. Among the witnesses to this union was Frederick Haldimand, the formal governor of Quebec. (He would later be prominent in the history of Carleton Island, located in the St. Lawrence River between Wolfe Island and the United States shoreline.[12]) Through this marriage the barony de Longueuil, originally French and Catholic, segued into a Scottish Protestant line.

David Alexander Grant, a captain in the militia, fought for the British in Canada. His father, also a David Grant, was the seigneur de Blairfindie back in France. Indeed, the Grants' lineage was as illustrious as that of the Le Moyne family, and they too are credited with extensive military service, having lived in Normandy for over 450 years as nobles and knights. The Grant family's original titles came from Scotland circa 1350 when William Grant was sent to France as the Scottish ambassador. The family maintained Castle Grant in Scotland as well as residences in Paris and Quetteville, France.[13] Now, the Grant lineage, coupled with the distinguished Le Moyne lineage, perpetuated the Longueuil barony. The barony became the only hereditary French title to survive the British conquest of New France and be recognized by the British Crown, passing permanently into what became known as the new British aristocracy.[14]

THE LONGUEUILS (GRANTS) MOVE TO UPPER CANADA

Captain David Grant and his friend, Lieutenant Patrick Langan, were stationed with Sir John Johnson's[15] second battalion of the 84th infantry regiment, which operated out of Carleton Island during the American War of Independence. Exactly what stirred their interest in purchasing Wolfe Island is not known, but they had crossed it frequently en route to and from the military barracks at Fort Frontenac. In so doing they obviously became aware of the island's size, future potential, and strategic location. On May 6, 1795, Grant, in partnership with Langan, purchased the island from the Curaux brothers, as recorded in the deed located in the attorney general's office in Toronto: "Michel and Amable Curotte, for the consideration of one shilling per acre, Convey Grande Island to David Alexander Grant and Patrick Langan, Esquires."[16] This transaction proved to be a prudent decision as the thirty-three-thousand-acre island cost these gentlemen the mere sum of fifteen hundred British pounds.

THE SEIGNEURY ON WOLFE ISLAND

At this juncture, David Grant's uncle — the Honourable William Grant — and Marie-Charles' mother — the dowager baroness — were living on the de Longueuil family property on Île Ste. Helene, opposite the site of Montreal. It is possible that, after the purchase, David Grant and his wife may have lived on Wolfe Island after the turn of the nineteenth century. Indeed, they may have built the stone seigneury house, or perhaps a log structure — vestiges of which are still evident on the seigneury lot behind the stone house. A letter, dated September 29, 1800, at Montreal from Grant and Langan states:

> We purchased the Grande Ile on the 6th May, 1795, from Michael and Amable Curot, to whom the island devolved by right of Descent. Soon after we caused it to be surveyed, erected a Dwelling House and placed settlers on the island, who are now improving it.[17]

The statement from these joint purchasers that they had already erected a "Dwelling House" gives credence to this possibility.

Alternatively, a structure named Elmlodge could be considered as this "Dwelling House." It is prominent on early Wolfe Island maps including the 1861 Walling Map and the fortification survey maps. This house, which appears to be situated within lot 3 of the Old Survey adjacent to the old Catholic church property, is depicted as the "residence of Mme. de Longueuil." Although it has not been possible to determine the date that this building was erected, it may be the more credible "Dwelling House." In 1863, Elmlodge was purchased from the baroness by Father Stafford, the resident priest, along with its surrounding four acres, to serve as the second Catholic rectory after fire destroyed the original.[18]

The Honourable Charles William Grant, as the eldest son of the Grant-Le Moyne union, inherited the title as the fifth baron de Longueuil after his mother's death in 1842. He contracted a distinguished marriage with Caroline Coffin, daughter of General John Coffin,[19] a United Empire Loyalist and British officer acclaimed for his victories during the American Revolution. Upon the death of his father in 1805, Charles William assumed most of the baronial duties, which included managing the family estates and the seigneury on Wolfe Island in 1806. Two children issued from this marriage: a son, Charles James Irving Grant, and a daughter, Charlotte Grant.

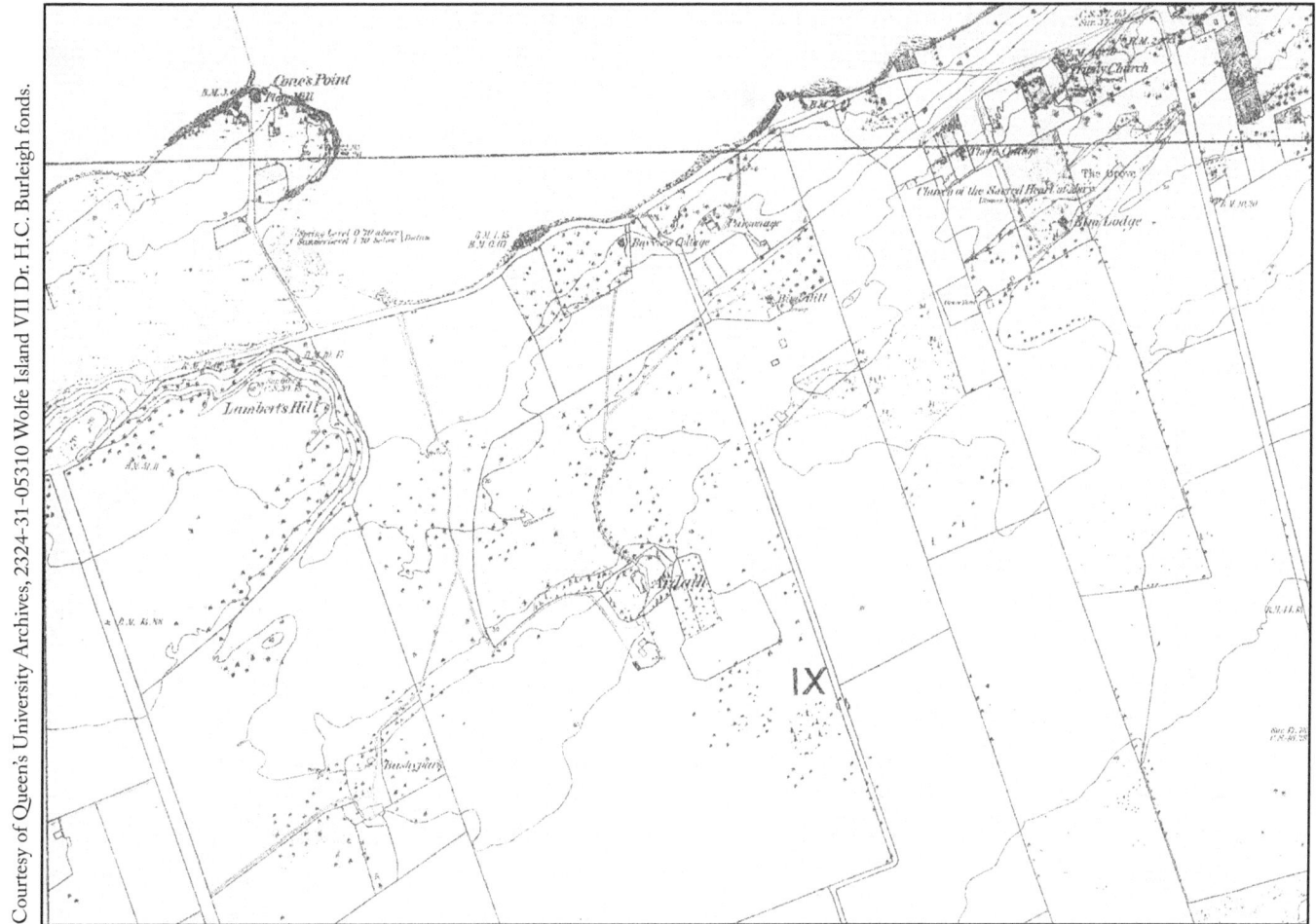

Map 3: Detail from the Burleigh Fortification Maps of 1869, showing the locations of Mill Point, Cone Point, Ardath Castle, Elmlodge, Bayview Cottage, Lambert's Hill, Sacred Heart Church, and Trinity Church. These buildings are all within the eastern section of the Old French Survey.

In 1819, Baron Grant had applied to the attorney general of Upper Canada to have the title of Grande Île (Wolfe Island) cleared on behalf of the heirs of the purchasers, David Grant and Patrick Langan, both of whom had died intestate. Ownership was finally settled in 1823. Two-sevenths of the island were reserved for the Crown as ordnance and Clergy Reserves. The remaining five-sevenths, including all adjacent isles, pastures, and islets, were divided equally among the Grant and Langan heirs. In 1822, the islands were surveyed by the government with concessions and lots marked; the Grant holdings were in the western half of the island. With the area now under British law, seigneurial tenure was no longer recognized — a disaster for the individual owners and tenants who no longer had title to any of the property they had previously occupied.

Charles W. Grant and his wife, Baroness Caroline, had moved from Montreal to Kingston and Wolfe Island in the early 1800s. Beginning round 1778, animosities between the French and the English-speaking minority were surfacing more frequently in Lower Canada. Discussions were underway in Britain regarding the possible division of the colony into Upper and Lower Canada, with a contemplated division just west of the barony of Longueuil[20] — the only Protestant barony in Quebec at that time. No doubt the escalating hostility was a factor prompting the Grants to sell their baronial property in Quebec and relocate to the Kingston area. The American Revolution was underway and large numbers of Loyalists were arriving in Canada. There was a need for land. With the Grant lands on Wolfe Island well positioned to receive newcomers, Charles W. built his new castle on Wolfe Island and a spacious home in Kingston.

His son, Charles James, born in Montreal in 1815, was first employed in the army where he served in the 79th Regiment. With his father's demise, Charles J. became the sixth baron de Longueuil, but did not acquire the seigneurial holdings. They went to his sister Charlotte. He lived at Alwington House in Kingston, the home built for his parents.

THE LONGUEUIL RESIDENCES OF KINGSTON AND WOLFE ISLAND

Charles W. Grant built Longueuil Castle (later renamed Ardath) around 1823, when the first limestone quarries were opened and shortly after the Grant family obtained clear title to their land on Wolfe Island. The castle was located west of Marysville, within the boundaries of lots 7 and 8 of the Old Survey, set on a higher level just west of the former seigneury property. The site afforded the Grants a picturesque view of Kingston and the St. Lawrence River's north channel. Prior to their taking up full-time residency at the castle, they used it as a summer home and farm investment.

Unfortunately, very few first-hand memories of the castle remain, as Château Ardath burned in 1935. However, a fairly accurate account, written in 1902 by historian Roy Fleming after he had taken a guided visit to the then-abandoned building, exists. In those days, Fleming could see Ardath from the south windows of the *Whig* newspaper building in Kingston.

Built along French feudal lines, the castle was a rambling twenty-five-room house constructed of dressed limestone from a local quarry.[21] The servants' quarters were confined to an area in the second storey at the back of the house, accessible only by a vertical iron ladder from the outside. The woodwork in this home was consistent with Old World castles even to the three-inch-thick carved oak-panelled doors that led up to trefoil-adorned Gothic arches and embellishments. Shelving in the wood-panelled library indicated the former presence of many books. An immense stone fireplace, blackened by much use, was the focal point for the manor hall, which measured twenty-five feet by thirty-five feet. Several other rooms were also dominated by the presence of vast fireplaces. The building's exterior was not adorned with turrets and towers as one might expect, but with stone-mullioned windows and gabled pinnacles, and there was a dungeon in the basement. It was a castle in every sense of the word, consistent with the seigneury manors of Quebec. Skeptics have speculated that the "dungeon" had simply been a wine cellar. The overall structure was small for a castle, only about one hundred feet in length, but it was a very large edifice for Wolfe Island in those days. The grounds were surrounded by a 425-acre farm comprised of its own outbuildings, a dairy, and an icehouse. Longueuil Castle was a focal point of activity in the early community as tenant farmers paid their tithes and dues there.

Picture a private fenced road (presently White's Lane) snaking up-grade between rows of sweet-brier and French lilacs, as it made its way from the Front Road toward what is now called Hillcrest Street, and further along to this splendid house no longer to be seen except in vintage photos. Ardath is remembered by author Katherine Hale as a "dream of beauty with terraced gardens and roses in summer."[22] At the lower end of the road the original frame gatekeeper's cottage still stands. Initially constructed of stone in 1830, and given the name *Bayview*, it was rebuilt and substantially enlarged by Gordon Roney, a Calvin Company shipbuilder, during the 1930s. After the castle was abandoned in the early 1900s, the gatekeeper's house was rented intermittently. One of its noteworthy tenants was Captain J.H. Radford, a Scot and a local real-estate speculator and owner of sailing vessels.

LEFT: *Ardath Castle as it appeared during its latter years after being abandoned. After the Allens, with their lively family and many servants, went to live at Alwington in Kingston, there were fewer social functions on Wolfe Island.* RIGHT: *Alwington House afforded the de Longueuils a taste of city living as opposed to the serenity of Wolfe Island.*

ALWINGTON HOUSE

In 1831 the Grants purchased an imposing waterfront site in Kingston, just east of the penitentiary on King Street West. The previous owner, Judge C.A. Hagerman, had finished only part of the house's foundation, but the Grants oversaw the completion and named it Alwington House after the Coffin family homes located in England, New Brunswick, and Massachusetts. By 1834 the house, constructed of limestone, was completed as a mainland residence for the baron and baroness. Its central, two-storey block was flanked on both sides by uniform one-storey wings, symmetry being the architectural hallmark of the period. In overall proportions, it became the largest mansion in Kingston.

Alwington's short life had a sterling history. From 1841 to 1844 the Grants leased Alwington for service as the viceregal house, the most important single dwelling in Kingston. In this official residence of the governor general of Canada, much of the basic structure of the Canadian government was mapped out in conversations on the cerise and white-woven satin of the sofa located in the state drawing room, or over the carved rosewood table in the governor general's office. Addresses were presented there and many political careers either established or lost within its walls.

While Charles Dickens was visiting America at the request of another noted writer, Washington Irving, Dickens and his wife had the occasion to come to Alwington House as dinner guests of Sir Charles Bagot on May 18, 1842. Dickens recorded his activities during his stay in North America in his journal, "American Notes." In spite of his own humble beginnings, it seems that Dickens was not impressed with Alwington: "The Government House is neither elegant nor commodious, yet it is almost the only house of any importance in the neighbourhood." Indeed, Dickens, in further notes, revealed that he was far more impressed with Kingston's penitentiary and penal system![23]

Baron Grant's family returned to Alwington from Wolfe Island and his issue continued to occupy the house until 1902. He died at his Kingston home in 1848 and his son, Charles James Irvine Grant, Baron VI, continued to live there until 1862 when he moved his family to France. The barons de Longueuil have maintained residences in Pau, France, and Surrey, England, throughout the ensuing years.

In 1863 daughter Charlotte and her husband Reverend Allen assumed residency at Alwington with their family, which included their sixteen year-old son — future novelist Grant Allen — and four daughters. Senator Henry Wartman Richardson purchased the house in 1910 and his grandson held ownership when it burned in 1958. The ruins of Alwington were finally demolished in 1959, allowing it also to fade into history. Only a historical plaque remains as testimony to the glory of its former existence.

THE FIRST ANGLICAN PARSONAGE

The first Anglican parsonage on Wolfe Island (later known as the Areson House), was built either before or, as some have speculated, at the same time as Trinity Church. The site of this house is indisputably that of the original seigneury manor, given the substantial evidence of the presence of a feudal seigneury before the de Longueuils purchased this part of Wolfe Island. The island's quarries were initially opened in the early 1800s, a fact that could justify the erection of limestone structure in the 1820s to replace a previous log cabin.

Lot 6 on the Old Survey is a seven-and-one-half-acre site on which the Areson house is situated. The house and lot were donated by the baroness de Longueuil in 1852 to the Church of England Incorporated Synod Diocese of Ontario. For the next fifty-seven years this house was used as the Anglican parsonage. However, in 1909 the diocese sold the house to George Friend (my great uncle), who in turn sold it in 1927 to Dr. William Areson and his wife Florence. Dr. Areson, a prominent surgeon from Upper Montclair, New Jersey, who was responsible for introducing pasteurization to the state, had sought Wolfe Island as a retreat, wanting to escape the nuisance of telephones — there was no such service on Wolfe Island until 1938. Canon Christopher Carr, whose mother was an Areson, inherited the house in 1997.[24] He has held the appointment of priest in charge of the Trinity Anglican Parish of Wolfe Island since December 2002.

A tour of this limestone residence, probably built by French stonemasons, was provided by Connie Carr, the canon's wife. A tall gothic arch peaks above an impressive front entrance flanked by stone-mullioned sidelights. The walls are about twenty inches thick, evidenced by very deep windowsills. Interior walls are of plaster and lathe construction with a dead space of two to three inches of air between them and the outer walls. This old-world method provides insulation and decreases condensation. Very high ceilings, original

Areson House as it appeared when Dr. and Mrs. Areson purchased it in 1927.

planked wooden floors, stone-mullioned windows, and coal fireplaces all give a French Colonial atmosphere to this imposing structure. The house is a very large square plan boasting a huge double living room and dining room opposite, with the kitchen traversing the back of the main level. The second floor contains a sizable master bedroom with original coal fireplace and walk-in closets, atypical of the 1800s. In addition there are four other bedrooms, one having been converted into a contemporary-sized bathroom. A carriage house was located at the back of this building during its early days. Originally, there was a verandah attached to the front of the structure and Dr. Areson extended it down the east side. This house, an elegant reminder of a period long ago, perches majestically on a rise with a commanding view of Kingston and the river. Although the identity of the builder is not known, intrigue surrounds the name "Emile Dionne," which was etched many years ago in the glass of a sidelight.

THE GRANTS AT KINGSTON AND WOLFE ISLAND

While Charlotte, Grant's daughter, was in Montreal to be educated, she met and married the aforementioned Reverend Joseph Antisell Allen in the latter part of 1843. They remained in Montreal until he was appointed incumbent to the Church of England Mission on Wolfe Island in 1847. Reverend Allen, born in Ireland in 1813, was a gentleman and financially at ease. Before their marriage he had had some connection with the Grant family and their holdings on Wolfe Island.

Mr. McDonald, the iceman, is making a delivery to the Aresons' side door. The little boys peeking over the ice cart are members of the Areson family. Photo circa 1930.

At that time he was living in St. Athanase in Montreal, while the baron and his family were living in the town of Dorchester within the barony de Longueuil. A legal document of the time cites the Reverend Joseph Allen as party of the first part, Charlotte Grant as party of the second part, and the Baron de Longueuil Honorable Charles William Grant and his wife party of the third part. This document signalled Joseph and Charlotte's marriage contract. As Howe Island was part of the original seigneury that Grant and Langan had purchased, another document shortly thereafter refers to land on the island that the Grants and Allens deeded in 1843 for the use of a common school.[25]

Some previously written historical accounts have speculated that the Reverend Allen superintended the construction of Longueuil Castle, but this was not possible as he would have been only ten years of age in 1823. The Grants moved back to their castle on the island in 1841 and the Baroness Caroline arranged for the building of Trinity Church of England and Ireland in 1845. By that time there were many settlers wishing divine office to be ministered on a regular basis. She donated the land and defrayed the entire cost of erecting this beautiful little French Gothic-style church — the first church on Wolfe Island. The cornerstone was laid on October 6, 1845, by the Venerable Archdeacon Stuart of Kingston in the presence of her son-in-law, the Reverend Allen, and other church dignitaries.[26] Construction of the limestone church, designed to accommodate three hundred parishioners, was finished within a year. The baroness, in a letter she had sent from Montreal, dated February 22, 1844, entreated Bishop Strachan (Toronto) of the Diocese of Ontario to admit her son-in-law to his diocese.[27] The bishop replied in March of that year, but declined to accept Allen. The problem cited was the dearth of funds held by the Clergy Reserves. A letter from Strachan to Allen dated January 25, 1847, expressed regrets about the limited money, but stated he would recommend that Wolfe Island be one of the first new missions established.[28] Despite Strachan's assertion that funds were in short supply, he and his diocese moved ahead during the 1840s with the construction of St. James' and St. Paul's, both in Kingston, St. Mark's in Barriefield, and St. John's at Portsmouth.[29] One wonders about Strachan's level of concern for the spiritual needs of Wolfe Island's Anglicans when the baroness had already defrayed the cost of church and land. However, shortly thereafter, Joseph did become the first incumbent of Trinity Church — a position he held until 1850. It is speculated that the baroness assisted with this particular incumbent's stipend.

After the seat of government was relocated to Montreal, the baron and baroness moved to Alwington and remained in Kingston until the baron's death on July 5, 1848, at the age of sixty-seven years, after a notable career in the legislative council. The baron was interred in the beautiful cemetery of Trinity Church, Wolfe Island, where a tall grave monument still stands not thirty feet away from where my father and mother were laid to rest.

Although Reverend Allen was reputed to be the incumbent of Trinity Church for a short period during the late 1840s, neither the duration nor the degree of involvement of his ministry are clearly defined. Exhaustive searches made at the Anglican Diocese of Ontario archives have not shed any light on his presiding over registrations of marriages or burials. The only baptism recorded as having been officiated by him was that of William Henderson on September 2, 1851.[30] Two of Allen's children (Dora Maude Carleton and Frederica Blanche Emily), born after this incumbency, were baptized at Trinity Church in 1852 and 1856 by

LEFT: *The de Longueuil tombstone, in Trinity Cemetery, was erected in 1848 upon the death of Baron Grant. Today, the inscriptions for the baron and baroness are still somewhat decipherable. Photo 2009.* RIGHT: *Trinity Anglican Church, Marysville, as it appeared in 1930 when Charles Wall was the lay pastor. It is located on the Front Road just west of Highway 95. Note the drive shed for horses and buggies to the left.*

the reverends Bousfield and Dobbs respectively.[31] A daughter, Caroline, had been baptized at St. George's Cathedral, Kingston, in 1845, before Trinity Church was built.[32]

While ministering at Wolfe Island, the Allens' affluence and station permitted them the life of the gentry. They provided much employment for Wolfe Islanders by hiring many servants, farmhands, and labourers, but did not remain aloof from them. Indeed, the Allen family was noted for the picnics and parties they provided for their staff. After her husband's death, the baroness returned to Wolfe Island and resumed living at the castle, and the Allens, having occupied the parsonage during Joseph's tenure at Trinity Church, moved in with her and in effect took possession of the castle.

Shortly after Reverend Allen's incumbency at Trinity ended, the baroness generously deeded the house and property of the parsonage to the Church of England Incorporated Synod Diocese of Ontario in 1852.[33] She split her remaining years between living at the castle with her daughter Charlotte and family and at Alwington with her son Charles and his family. She died in 1868 at the age of eighty-three. She, too, was buried in the Trinity Church Cemetery alongside her husband.[34]

One of the many views of Ardath Castle during the late 1800s.

Charlotte inherited her mother's property and holdings on Wolfe Island, and this land in time became known as the Allen Estate. Following the death of the baroness, Joseph Allen renamed Longueuil Castle with the Celtic name *Ardath* after his old home in Ireland.

The formerly handsome Ardath Castle was unoccupied for almost two decades after the death of the baroness and the departure of the Allens from Wolfe Island for Alwington House. The house was rented or owned by several people in its declining years and records are sketchy. The 1878 *Meacham Atlas* notes that Fred Whitmarsh, the son of English immigrants to Wolfe Island, occupied the land surrounding the castle at that time while Mr. Shirley Going owned the south portions of lots 7, 8, and 9 behind the castle property. It is also recorded that George Whitmarsh (1884–1927), Fred and Sarah's son, was born at Ardath in 1880. Fred and his wife died during the 1890s, and according to local lore, in the late 1800s a Mr. Bennett, reportedly a millionaire, came into possession of the old castle property.

The *Union Publishing Directory* of 1895 lists island residents George McRae and family — descendants of the original McRaes of Scotland — as living on lot 8 (Old Survey), part of the old castle property. Vincent Greenwood (related to the McRaes by marriage) recalled from his youth that the last regular occupant of Ardath was a Patrick Tobin, who died in 1912.[35] Unfortunately, lack of maintenance over an extended period led to decay and stone being hauled away for use elsewhere.

Patrick Hawkins, descended from early pioneers, owned some of the Ardath land in 1902, and he and son Oliver began to acquire more of the property by 1914. Oliver Hawkins operated a livery service in Marysville during the 1930s and later used the crumbling Ardath to store hay and farm implements. On a Sunday afternoon, February 24, 1935, fire of unknown origin demolished the castle remains, and Ardath passed into history. Seemingly, after the death of the baroness, no one was interested in preserving Ardath for its historical value, likely due to the lack of funding. Had its demise not occurred during the Great Depression, restoration might have been undertaken. Arguably, the site of the residence of the baron and baroness de Longueuil warrants a heritage commemorative plaque.

Another member of the Allen family is buried in the Grants' gravesite on Wolfe Island. As there is no grave maker evident, her relationship to the Grants or Allens remains a mystery. Eliza Josephine, wife of Henry F. Allen, was born in Ireland and died at the age of seventy in the same year as the baroness, according to the church cemetery records. Not having further evidence, it can be surmised that Eliza was a widowed sister-in-law of Joseph Allen.[36] Seemingly, Alwington was home to several of Reverend Joseph's kin during the early years after the Allens moved from Wolfe Island.

In the 1851 census, Joseph and Charlotte are recorded as being thirty-eight years and thirty-five years of age, respectively. Three young Allen adults, also born in Ireland, are recorded in this census. The twenty-three-year-old and the twenty-one-year-old were siblings of Reverend Allen; one, Dora Allen, spinster, remained at Alwington until her death in 1910. Her funeral was held there, after which she was buried at St. John's Anglican Church (Portsmouth).[37] The Allens' widowed daughter Caroline, Mrs. J. Maule Machar, mother of the noted Kingston novelist-historian Agnes Maule Machar, passed away in December 1923, and was buried at St. James Anglican Church in Kingston.[38] According to Agnes Machar, Charles Grant Blairfindie[39] Allen was born to Joseph and Charlotte on February 24, 1848, at Alwington, although it is more commonly believed that he was born at Ardath. Raised on the island and homeschooled until he was thirteen, Grant developed writing skills at an early age.

In addition to his clerical duties, Joseph Allen had some commercial dealings on Wolfe Island as he is credited with owning all the property in the Old Survey from the Fourth to the Sixth lines including Mill Point, with its gristmill and sawmill. Apparently, the gristmill, a two-section mill capable of grinding eight bushels per hour by steam and five bushels per hour by hand, was located in a frame-and-stone building on Mill Point. The hand-operated section was probably that which was started several years earlier by Alvah Bennett, one of the first settlers, and from which Mill Point derived its name. For a short period around 1850, Mill Point was referred to as Ledford Point after Captain John Ledford, who occupied three and one-half acres at the northwest end. Ledford, great-grandfather of Joan O'Shea, a current island resident, operated a scow service for Howe Island during the 1840s.[40]

Allen Street in the village, named to commemorate the Allens, appears not much more than a lane today. It runs from the northern boundary of the Catholic church property to the river, intersecting both Hillcrest Street and the Front Road. At one time, Reverend Allen owned three and one-half acres running the full length of the street's west side. An old deed describing the sale of three quarters of an acre of the Allen property to a Mrs. Sarah Blanchard, notes "Wolfe Street" as an earlier name for this street.

The Allens left Ontario in 1861 for a brief stay in the United States and then England to further son Grant's education. He attended a private secondary school in Kingston followed by university in Birmingham and Oxford. The early years in England during the 1870s were difficult for him as the economy of Wolfe Island had taken a downturn, causing some leaseholders to move from the island, thus impacting on his parents' income and consequently his stipend. During his last fifteen years of life, Grant was a prolific writer. His work *The Woman Who Did* was perhaps the most controversial, due to its inference of having a child out of wedlock. Grant's success as a crime novelist may have been initially inspired by living his childhood in close proximity to Canada's first penal institution at Kingston, however, while at university he became friends with the famous British crime writer Arthur Conan Doyle. Doyle's influence likely encouraged Grant's work. He is recognized as Canada's first crime writer. Grant died at his home in Surrey, England, in 1899.[41]

When Charlotte's brother Charles James (Baron VI) and his family moved to France in 1862, she and Joseph took up residence at Alwington the following year. During their ensuing years it is said that Reverend Allen held a brief tenure at a church in Kingston in 1884, and had a short-lived career lecturing in civil history at Queen's University. It would appear that he was discharged by the principal and an angry board of trustees following letters written in *The Daily News* (November 16 and 24, 1866). Allen was advocating political union between Canada and the United States.[42] Charlotte died in 1894, her husband in 1900. There are no known remaining Allen descendants in Canada.

In 1946, Baron X, Ronald Charles Grant, fifty-eight years of age, was living in Pau, France. He had served in the French Foreign Legion and the King's Own Yorkshire Light Infantry during the First World War. One of his sons, Lieutenant Raoul de Longueuil, was killed in action at the age of twenty-two during the Second World War. Another son, Raymond David Grant of Surrey, England, became the eleventh baron on his father's demise. The above rightful heirs, to this day, have laid no claim to any Wolfe Island property.

Retired Great Lakes captain and Wolfe Island ferry captain Richard F. Fawcett, a lifelong resident of Wolfe Island, recalled the 1993 visit to Wolfe Island by the son of the current baron de Longueuil. Apparently, Dr. Wallace Breck, who had written a paper for the Kingston Historical Society in 1989 regarding the de Longueuils, met Dr. Michael David Grant, a physician from Surrey, England, while the two men were in Montreal that year, and encouraged him to visit his ancestral home. Until then, Michael Grant had been unaware of Wolfe Island and the ancestral gravesite. While on the island he and his wife strolled through the grounds of the former Ardath Castle and visited the church and gravesite of his de Longueuil ancestors.

R.F. Fawcett and his wife, Marette, visited with Dr. Grant and his family over tea, and when interviewed, Marette remarked on her angst concerning what she should wear for tea with a baron's son. To their surprise, the Grants arrived in shirts and shorts, treating the experience as an informal summer outing. The visitor made no claim to any of the outstanding Allen Estate property and left Wolfe Island as unceremoniously as he had arrived.

Europeans have crossed many of the Thousand Islands since the early years of the seventeenth century, but doubtless, Wolfe Island has experienced the largest number of them, beginning with Champlain. Wolfe Island played host for many years to the ubiquitous de Longueuils, who will always remain a colourful part of its history. It should be noted that the barons de Longueuil possess the only noble title conferred by the French Crown that is recognized by Britain. By proclamation on December 7, 1880, Queen Victoria gave official recognition of this barony to Charles Colmore Grant, the seventh baron de Longueuil, effective January 1, 1881.

CHAPTER 5
What's in a Title?

The British government instructed Sir Frederick Haldimand, governor of Quebec from 1778 to 1786, to survey lands and incorporate a church glebe[1] of three to five hundred acres within each seigneury. Land was then allotted to militia settlers according to their rank and status. Non-commissioned officers received two hundred acres, and privates one hundred acres. All land grants were free and survey expenses were borne by the government. Settlers were established in these townships according to ethnicity and religion, as they had requested.

In 1790 La Salle's former seigneury was divided and granted to Loyalists who were flocking into Canada after the American Revolution. Sir John Johnson had petitioned unsuccessfully for the ownership of Wolfe Island, but with the executive council of Quebec upholding the title held by the Curaux brothers, he withdrew his claim. In lieu, he received a clear title to Amherst Island, which had never previously been sold by the French. Where there was no existing title, these islands were being appropriated as Crown land. The Curaux brothers later sold their interests in Wolfe Island to two army colleagues, Captain Grant of Scotland and Lieutenant Langan of Limerick, Ireland.

The change from French ownership occurred on May 6, 1795, when a deed was registered at York indicating that Amable and Michel Curaux had sold all their rights to Wolfe Island. This transaction set the stage for an infusion of United Empire Loyalists of varying ancestry into a unique community that would become known as the Township of Wolfe Island. Grant and Langan quickly put their investment to work. They had purchased approximately thirty-three thousand acres for one shilling per acre — the equivalent in 1795 of six thousand dollars — for the entire island. (Waterfront lots at this writing are valued at approximately $250,000 per acre). Shortly afterward they engaged a Kingston land agent to begin negotiating leases on lots of one hundred acres each, most of which were in the Old Survey.

Grant and Langan encountered frustrating surprises regarding their new ownership. Langan explained how they had been deceived by the Curaux brothers:

> Besides the consideration we paid to the former proprietors, Michael and Amable Curotte, we were compelled to pay Messrs. Watson and Rushley [merchants of London] a considerable sum of money [four thousand dollars] for a debt due them from Amable Curotte and for which those gentlemen had previously obtained a judgment of the court of Common Pleas in this Province; a circumstance carefully concealed from us at the time of our making the purchase.[2]

The Curaux brothers had established legal title to Wolfe Island under the British Crown without the necessity of keeping the original seigneurial obligations. Thus, the new owners believed they were entitled to receive clear title with no strings attached. This did not happen. Indeed, they and their heirs were caught in the midst of political change in the province, and the resultant issues would be problematic for decades to come.

The political climate in the province was mercurial in the early 1800s. Canada was still regarded by many as a French colony of Britain, but that status was changing quickly due to the influx of British Loyalists. In contrast to the French-Catholic liberal attitude, a strong Protestant conservative attitude, with deep-rooted loyalty to Lord Dorchester as the representative of the British Crown, was emerging. With the Loyalists pressing to be governed under British law rather than French civil law, Dorchester attempted to satisfy their demands in 1788 by dividing the western section of the province into four county-like districts bearing the names Eastern, Midland (which included Wolfe Island), Home, and Western. Three years later, the British parliament passed the Constitutional Act dividing Canada into two provinces separated by the Ottawa River, one predominantly French (Lower Canada) and the other English (Upper Canada). A lieutenant-governor was appointed for each province, while the governor general, usually at Quebec City, presided over both Upper and Lower Canada.

The Upper Canada administration, centred in York in 1793, became more self-serving and exclusive, ultimately evolving into a tightly knit group known as the Family Compact, which flourished from 1791 until 1837. This clique, their appointees, and friends, all of whom were conservative Church of England supporters, administered the affairs of Upper Canada to suit their own interests and to secure Upper Canada for England.[3] The ambitious Archdeacon John Strachan worked to institute the English parish system for the Church of England, with authority over the educational system in Upper Canada. By 1819, he had secured a Canadian Clergy Reserves Corporation to bring Upper Canada directly under the Church of England's administration. As a result, proceeds from Clergy Reserves' land sales were funnelled directly to this church. The leaders of the established Church of Scotland were irate at being cut out and not receiving some portion of this money for their church and educational purposes.

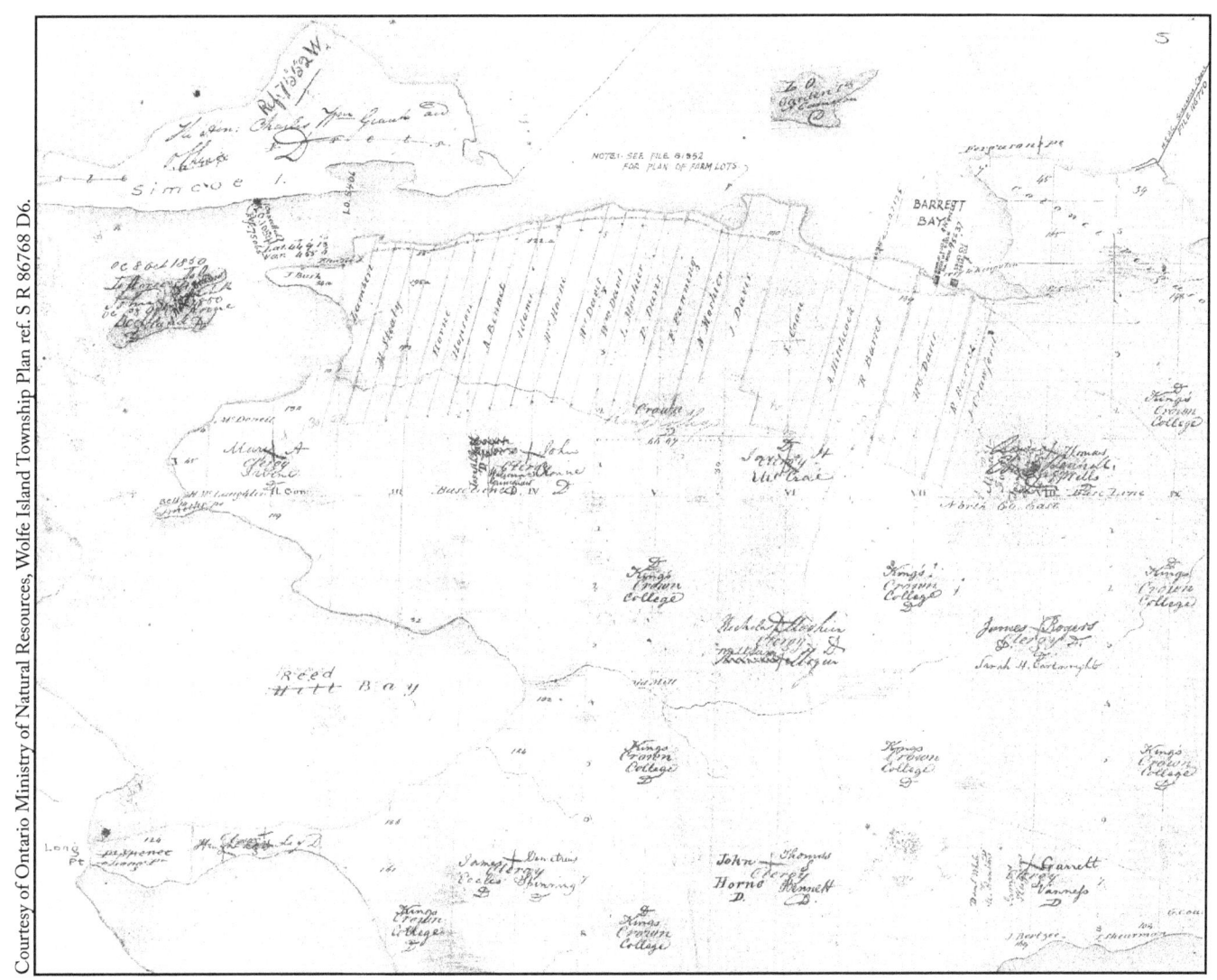

Map 3A: An excerpt from surveyor J.G. Chewett's map of October 6, 1822, illustrates the Head of Wolfe Island, including the Old Survey. The island at the time was part of the Midland District. This survey, designating the locations of the Crown and Clergy reserves, was completed after the Grant and Lagan heirs were finally granted clear title to Wolfe Island.

Other denominations joined in this foment. Ultimately, legislation was passed entitling all Protestant denominations to share in the reserves.[4]

Research of land titles on Wolfe Island shows a number of lots, registered as Crown land in 1828, being granted to King's College in York. When they were sold a few decades later, the seller was registered as University of Toronto on Wolfe Island — a sample of the Family Compact using its control of lands to generate revenue for their educational institutions. Strachan had used his influence to have King's College established by Royal Charter in 1827, with an endowment of Crown land and a stipend of one thousand British pounds annually for sixteen years. Faculty and students were exclusively members of the Church of England until 1843, after which other Christian faiths were permitted inclusion.[5] Later, he also founded the University of Trinity College in York for the education of Anglican divinity students.[6] Clearly, Strachan strove to keep Upper Canada British.

One-seventh of all lands granted in Upper Canada was to be set aside for the maintenance and support of the Protestant clergy. All land was under the aegis of the British Crown and was allotted gratis to Loyalists and the military, but all other land transfers required approval of the local colonial government. The Family Compact's control over land grants created major issues for Grant and Langan. They owned Wolfe Island, a very desirable piece of property, which had been granted by the French Crown rather than the English Crown, and the Clergy Reserves percentage on the island had never been set aside. That Grant and Langan were British subjects, had fought for Britain, were both members of the Church of England, and were gentlemen from reputable families did not enter into the equation.

The irony most evident in the whole affair revolved around the seigneurial mandate as stipulated in the original grant from the French Crown. Under the two-province system, seigneuries and their obligations were to continue only in Lower Canada. Three years prior to the Constitutional Act of 1791, the Curaux brothers had established, under the British Crown, that Wolfe Island was freehold and exempt. In 1795, when Grant and Langan acquired the island on the same terms the purchase was duly registered at York, but they never received a clear title. They were not in favour of the seigneurial system any more than the Family Compact, yet a move was under way to disenfranchise the partners because they were not fulfilling the seigneurial conditions as laid down in the original grant. It appears that the Family Compact was relying on loopholes within the Grant and Langan title in order to claim Wolfe Island as Crown land.

An example of just how far this government was willing to proceed in order to obtain possession of the island appeared in a proclamation published in 1805 forbidding Wolfe Island tenants from making further improvements to their properties.[7] In 1806, the problem was compounded when one of the partner-owners, David Grant, died intestate. The edict prompted two local yeomen, Samuel Cone (sometimes spelled Coan or Corn) and Samuel Hinckley, to forward a joint petition, dated November 27, 1805, to the council then assembled, praying "for a title under the Crown." They stated that they were willing to accept either a lease or deed so that they "may not be disinherited."[8] The following year Hinckley presented a petition signed by many inhabitants of the island. He received assurance from council that "in the event of title to the island being determined by the Crown," the lieutenant-governor would "deem it just to confirm to every person occupying a lot under the old title, to be a lot in his possession."[9] Hinckley was further instructed that everyone could pursue improvements with impunity. However, as land titles still had not been confirmed by 1815, he presented another petition, also to no avail.

An attempt to resolve the dilemma of ownership of Wolfe Island was initiated in July 1807 by Grant's widow, La Baronne IV, and Patrick Langan. This time the petition was addressed to Lieutenant-Governor Francis Gore at York.[10] It took Gore a year to act, but on July 30, 1808, he sent a letter to the secretary of state in England, mentioning that he was enclosing papers containing the statement of a matter of long standing. He concluded by saying: "I have taken the liberty of enclosing a copy of the Attorney General's opinion at Quebec, as well as the opinion of the Master of the Rolls … which is strongly in favour of those who derive their title from the original grant of the French King."[11]

During the confusion of the title dispute, approximately one hundred squatters had settled on Wolfe Island and were observed cutting timber recklessly. The Honourable Richard Cartwright, a member of the Land Board for the Midland District, in writing to Gore in 1808, mentioned the state of affairs and said that three of the offenders had been fined and imprisoned. The presence of squatters on the island spawned several theories, but the fact that British naval officers were privileged to seize white pine from Crown land for the masts of their sailing vessels may explain their unauthorized presence on this privately owned island.

Patrick Langan became intolerant of the delay and dispatched another letter to Gore on June 11, 1810, reminding him that this issue had been in continuance for fifteen years, and mentioning that he had served the British government for thirty-three years and had invested the best part of his savings in the Wolfe Island property. He also stated that he possessed the original reports together with the deeds and transfers deduced from the original grantor, the King of France, and, to substantiate his brief statement of the facts, he was providing "voluminous documents." A letter addressed to Gore from the Treasury Chambers in London on May 4, 1812, stated:

> The Lord Commissioner of His Majesty's Treasury having under consideration … confirmation of a grant of certain lands in Upper Canada, to the Baroness de Longueuil and Mr. Langan which were made by the French government, prior to the secession of that Province to this country … that under the circumstances stated and the legal opinions transmitted by Governor Gore … it would be advisable to authorize the Lieutenant-Governor of Upper Canada to confirm the original grant.[12]

In spite of these clear instructions from England to confirm the original grant, nothing was done.

The Family Compact proclamation of 1805 that forbade property improvements also offered grants of land on this island to suitable applicants. On July 18, 1813, Amos Ansley of Kingston Township petitioned Governor General George Prevost for a grant of "Wolf

Island including those Simco and Horsshoo Islands." Shortly thereafter, Prevost responded, suggesting "the expediency of reserving the said islands until after the war, in order to grant them to such deserving soldiers as may be disbanded in the Province."[13] On August 7, 1813, a committee from Toronto submitted a report to Prevost, stating, "That a Legal Title to Wolfe Island under French grant is claimed by Patrick Langan and asking until this claim is disposed of, is it needful to take up the petition of Mr. Ansley?" The report further stated, "no Islands are considered within the grant of the provincial government, without especial authority from His Majesty." The concluding remarks were "Lieutenant Governor Gore so far recognizes the claim of Mr. Langan."[14]

Soon after the Gore decision was handed down, Patrick Langan died, and his three daughters, Julia, Maria, and Charlotte, inherited their father's holdings. That same year, in spite of the formal recognition of Langan's claim, the government's determination to deal with Wolfe Island as Crown land became evident with regards to land at Brophy Point. Though Grant and Langan had purchased Wolfe Island outright from the Curaux brothers and had documents proving so, land registry office records erroneously show Brophy Point being transferred in 1813 from the Crown to Julia Leslie (Langan's daughter) and Charles Grant (later the baron de Longueuil).

At a lieutenant-governor's council meeting held on January 18, 1816, chaired by the chief justice, a brief was prepared and forwarded to Lieutenant-Governor Gore. Some of the highlights follow:

> On the petition of the heirs of Langan and Grant ... that since the grant to Mr. La Salle the (French) Crown has no interest in those lands ... every right granted stands unimpeached. This opinion is confirmed by Sir William Grant, the present Master of the Rolls ... we therefore are at a loss to discover why the representatives of the grantee have not had recourse to the courts of law to repel any obstruction to the enjoyment of their property, since the King's hand laid upon their estate by his military or civil servants in this Province might at any time have been removed on due application to the proper jurisdiction, as readily as any private trespass could have been punished on conviction. We ... humbly submit ... that the petitioners be referred to the courts of proper jurisdiction for redress of any injury to their title, or possession, either by individuals or the Crown.[15]

The statement "every right granted stands unimpeached," along with Gore's recognition of the claim, should have been sufficient to elicit a clear title, but still it was not forthcoming.

The next round in the long battle came from an unexpected source, and its outcome set the stage for the Grant and Langan heirs' next move. When Robert Gourlay attempted to set himself up as a land agent at Kingston in 1817, he soon found himself on a collision course with the Family Compact. As a result of opposition encountered, Gourlay circulated his soon-to-become famous questionnaire.[16] The paper, entitled "Principals and Procedures of the Inhabitants of District of Niagara ….," demonstrated that it was next to impossible for anyone to obtain an unclouded title to land under the existing system of government. Gourlay was arrested, tried for seditious libel, and banished from Upper Canada. The late Lois Darroch of Toronto so admired Gourlay, a Scottish radical idealist that, after writing his biography, she commissioned an artist to sculpt a bust of him. Ironically, the bust was placed in one of the gardens of St. James Cathedral in Toronto, overlooking the very cathedral of Bishop Strachan's former see and the site where his remains now lie.[17]

The heirs of Grant and Langan, determined to certify their continuing ownership of Wolfe Island, finally accomplished their goal by circumventing the Family Compact, and appealing directly to King George IV in 1819. Their petition stated that they were willing to forfeit all their rights on Wolfe Island to the king on condition that His Majesty would keep two-sevenths of it in lieu of his seigneurial rights and dues and regrant them five-sevenths in free and common tenure. The two-sevenths meant that one-seventh would go to the Crown and the other seventh to the Clergy Reserves.[18] This would indicate that there was no Crown land on Wolfe Island before this transaction was completed.

On behalf of the Crown, Earl Henry Bathurst, the colonial secretary, took the matter in hand. His letter of April 7, 1819, addressed to Sir Peregrine Maitland, the lieutenant-governor for Upper Canada, was forwarded for action to Attorney General John Beverley Robinson. An ardent champion of the Family Compact, Robinson's reply, finally dispatched to the colonial secretary on December 16, 1820, was an able, orderly presentation of the facts garnered from information and original documents provided by the heirs of Grant and Langan. His document provided indisputable proof with substantiating dates and particulars of every transaction that had taken place in the transfer of Wolfe Island from Louis XIV of France through La Salle down to the actual price that Grant and Langan had paid for the island. Yet Robinson's subtle, discreet remarks in the first part of the last paragraph of his covering letter would indicate that his Family Compact ideals superseded his decision as attorney general. After proving and presenting the facts in favour of the heirs, he injected his own opinion against granting a clear title. It would seem that Robinson's ambivalent remarks were intended to create a suggestion of doubt, as shown in this excerpt:

> Though I am not of the opinion that the memorialists (the Grant and Langan heirs) hold the estate in this Island according to the several degrees of interest which they conceive themselves to have succeeded to upon the death of the late joint proprietors; yet, as they undoubtedly possess …[19]

The facts, however, proved that the heirs of Grant and Langan were the rightful owners and had too long been denied certification by the clique in York.

By letters patent dated July 15, 1823, King George IV certified the land grant by allotting one-half of five-sevenths of the island to the Honourable Charles William Grant, the fifth baron de Longueuil, and the other half of the five-sevenths to the heirs of Patrick Langan.

The co-heir descendants of Patrick Langan were Julia Langan and her husband, the Honourable James Leslie, member of the legislature of Lower Canada; Maria Langan and her husband Archibald Kennedy Johnson, son of Sir John Johnson of the 84th Regiment of foot soldiers; and Miss Charlotte Langan.[20]

Only from this date onward (1823) did portions of Wolfe Island become Crown land, and these portions were gradually sold over ensuing years. The original parchment conveyance by which title to the land certified by Britain after France surrendered her foothold in Canada, was at one time in the possession of W.F. Nickle, K.C., of Kingston — a lawyer patronized by many islanders. Although the Crown did not certify the land grant until 1823, the work of surveying had begun in 1822 or earlier. It is likely that Henry Boulton of the surveyor general's office was in charge when Wolfe Island was mapped into concessions and lots to facilitate an equitable division of the land between the Crown and the estates of Grant and Langan. With some exceptions, Baron Grant acquired most of the western half of the island, including all of the Old Survey, and the descendants of Patrick Langan received most of the eastern half. The 1822 survey was neither the first, nor the last for Wolfe Island. The earliest, the Old Survey, dates back to the time of New France and was never altered in any of the subsequent surveys.

When the land grant was certified in 1823, Wolfe Island became officially freehold, thus terminating twenty-eight years of uncertainty for the lessees and landowners. By 1860 most of the island was occupied by ownership or lease. As late as 1894 at least twenty-five percent of Wolfe Island was still owned and leased out by descendants of the barons de Longueuil. By 1913 this had dropped to seventeen percent and, by 1980, none of Wolfe Island was owned by descendants of either Grant or Langan.

CHAPTER 6
Whence Did They Come

Generally, people who emigrate to new lands are seeking a better way of life. For those who came to Canada to settle on Wolfe Island between the 1700s and 1900s, this was particularly true.

Ships sailing from Holland, bound for America via England, brought scores of Dutch and English people to American shores. One of these ships was the historic *Mayflower*, whose passengers formed the core population of the thirteen British colonies situated along the Atlantic seaboard. Some of their descendants relinquished established homesteads and possessions to flee to Canada as United Empire Loyalists during the American Revolution (1775–83). They, along with many others, preferred to live under the stability of British rule rather than risk the uncertainties of the new American republic. It is estimated that between twenty-five and thirty thousand Loyalists were compelled to seek sanctuary in the Canadian wilderness.[1] Regardless of their status, aristocrat or pauper, they mobilized quickly for self-preservation, some travelling on foot carrying children and few meagre possessions.

FLIGHT TO CATARAQUI: THE ELLERBECKS

Extensive accounts of the experiences of Loyalist Captain Michael Grass, in his flight from America, have been recorded by historians.[2] Although he was indeed an important figure in the Loyalist development at Cataraqui, this story focuses on his lieutenant, Emmanuel Ellerbeck, a descendant of the Palatine Germans rescued from Catholic persecution by Queen Anne of England in 1709. Born circa 1748, he left his home in Yorkshire, England, bound for America at age twenty-seven. In preparing for life in the New World, he assembled a team of horses, a Black slave, a chest of tools, and sixteen guineas.³ After disembarking at New York, Ellerbeck attempted to settle at Poughkeepsie, but soon discovered that his arrival was ill-timed. Passionate protests against British rule of the colony led to his possessions being confiscated by the state, and the assets used to help finance their revolution.⁴ Bullied into joining the revolutionary army in 1778, he deserted shortly thereafter and moved to the British stronghold in New York City, where he joined the 84th Militia and earned a lieutenant's commission. By the time Ellerbeck acquired a house in New York, he had married Sarah (surname unknown) and they had their firstborn, Mary.

As Loyalists remaining in New York City at this time faced grave danger, British general Guy Carleton rounded up all available naval and commercial ships to transport them to safer shores. Although Carleton had arranged for safe passage to Britain and Canada's Maritimes, Ellerbeck's friend, Michael Grass, a fellow Palatine German and a captain in the militia, knew that the Cataraqui area would be amenable to settlers, having seen this neighbourhood while imprisoned by the French at Fort Frontenac during the Seven Years' War.⁵ He entreated Carleton to direct them to Cataraqui, and thus Lieutenant Ellerbeck and his wife Sarah sailed on Grass's ship, the *Camel*, at the head of a fleet of seven ships carrying sixty officers, enlisted men, and their families to safety in Upper Canada. Seventeen days later, after sustaining severe damage during a fierce Atlantic storm and rounding the Gaspé Peninsula into the perilous St. Lawrence, the *Camel* arrived at Sorel, Quebec — a British military station northeast of Montreal. The sick needed care, and with winter fast approaching, this contingent of originally well-to-do but now penniless refugees stayed at Sorel, during which time the Ellerbecks' son, Richard, was born. The more able-bodied men spent their time constructing bateaux for the three-week trip up the St. Lawrence River the following spring of 1783.

Governor Haldimand was aware that accommodation must be made ready for the Loyalists before they arrived. He ordered Major John Ross, commandant of the second battalion of the King's Royal Regiment of New York at Oswego, to advance to Cataraqui in July 1783. Ross's mission, with his soldiers, was to restore the French barracks, erect sawmills and gristmills, and prepare for the Loyalists' needs.⁶ The refugees' arrival at Cataraqui was timely as land surveys had been completed. Lot numbers were put into a hat, and Captain Grass drew the first, followed by Lieutenant Ellerbeck and so on, according to rank.⁷ Thus, these lots were settled primarily by disbanded Loyalist soldiers and their families, largely of German, French, Irish, and British ancestry. Ellerbeck drew the lot along King Street with a four-thousand-foot river frontage, site of the present St. Mary's of the Lake Hospital. After clearing some land, he and his family built a two-room log cabin.

In 1834, Emmanuel's eldest son Richard sold a choice portion of the property to Francis A. Harper, a cousin of John A. Macdonald, who, in 1836, built a very large, handsome house of limestone, quarried on the Ellerbeck site. The house, named Hawthorne, remains part of the St. Mary's Hospital complex. Many years later when excavations were underway to expand the hospital, it became evident that this former Ellerbeck lot originally contained not only the private family residence, but also a cemetery, as tombstones were found inscribed with their names. All of the Ellerbecks had large families, and, as descendants of the United Empire

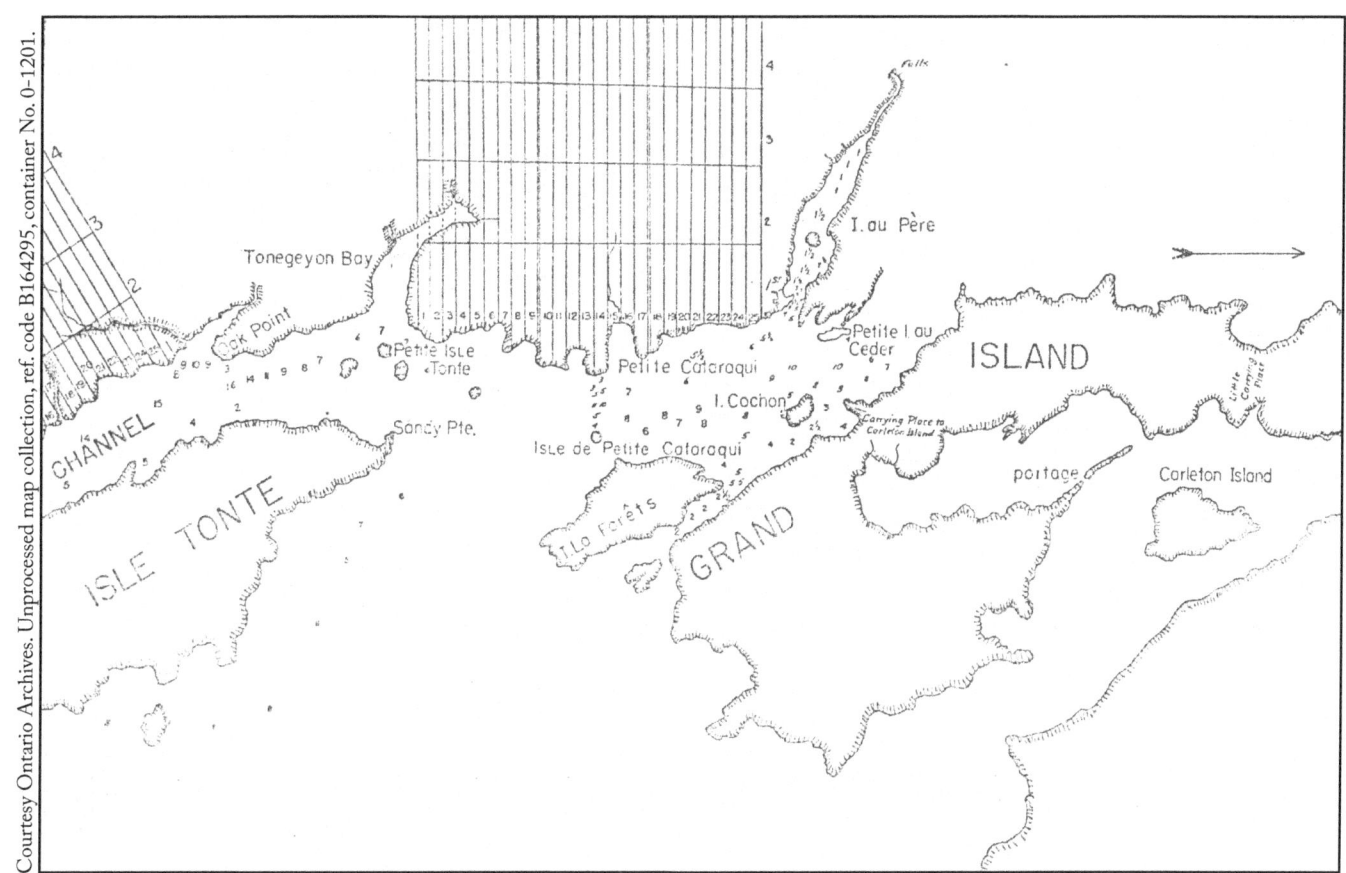

Map 4: The Township of Cataraqui (formerly the La Salle Siegneury) as surveyed and remapped in 1784 for the Loyalists' arrival. The survey, ordered by Governor Frederick Haldimand, was carried out by surveyors Lewis Kotté and James Peachey. Lieutenant Ellerbeck drew three lots within this survey.

Loyalists, each upon reaching the age of seventeen was granted two hundred acres. When the town of Kingston was laid out, a street bordering the west end of the property was named for the family.

Emmanuel's son, William W. Ellerbeck, spent his final years living on Wolfe Island with his daughter, Sarah Ann, and pioneer son-in-law, John H. Busch, who had lost his first wife, Arabella Hinckley, at the age of thirty. William's death on Wolfe Island is recorded but not the place of his interment.[8] He may be buried in the private family cemetery in Kingston. One of Emmanuel's four grandchildren, Richard Abbott Ellerbeck, married Sarah Howard in 1846. Having decided to begin their married lives on Wolfe Island, they rented a farm from the Grimshaw estate on Concession 5. They worked this land for twenty-three years, during

Whence Did They Come

which time they had ten children. Harriet Louise, the only female, died in 1858 at the age of four months after being accidentally thrown from a wagon. She was buried at the (Horne) Point Alexandria Cemetery. Eleven years later Richard and Sarah moved to Raleigh Township, Essex County, in southwestern Ontario to be closer to some of their family.

Other Loyalist contingents came to Canada on foot by way of the Adirondacks to Montreal, then acquired the bateaux necessary for travel up the St. Lawrence. Those who began arriving in Cataraqui's wilderness in 1784 were a mixture of families and Black slaves along with disbanded troops armed with lot-location tickets, their reward for army service. These novice pioneers, having to clear much land using primitive tools and build shanties for shelter, usually helped one another by working together in "bees."[9] As it would be another ten years before Grant and Langan came to open their newly acquired islands to immigrants, Cataraqui and the Quinte areas saw the first Loyalists.

UNDERGROUND RAILROAD

Some Black fugitives fleeing slavery in the United States found freedom when they set foot on Wolfe Island's shores, the island being one of the points of entry into Canada. One such Black family, the Sammons, chose to remain on Wolfe Island. Under the leadership of their patriarch, the older Uriah Sammons, they settled on fifty acres of lot 2 in the Tenth Concession. Uriah leased this lot from the Leslie Estate and made his home there until well into the 1890s. His sons, Matthew, Joseph, and Isaac, lived nearby and worked for other local families.[10] One of the lads lost his life in an unfortunate accident while working in a pine forest and was buried on the Sammons' property. Another family, the Jones, partially of Black ancestry, lived in the village of Marysville around 1900. According to the census records, Mr. Jones was a shoemaker.

James Allen, one-time captain of the passenger ferry *Pierrepont*, related how, while a young lad, he was asked by his father to surreptitiously row a skiff after dark from a pre-arranged spot near Cape Vincent to Wolfe Island. He picked up a passenger, a Black man fleeing captivity, and silently rowed him across under cover of night. When they reached Wolfe Island, the fugitive slave, upon having it confirmed that he actually was in Canada, knelt and kissed the stones on the beach.[11]

Among the profusion of Loyalists who used Wolfe Island as a crossover point, some of the more affluent brought their Black slaves with them and settled in Cataraqui or on the island. Although there are no other names of Black Loyalist settlers recorded as living in the immediate area, we do know that Wolfe Island was a route on the Underground Railroad — a clandestine system of assisting both fugitive slaves and free Blacks to safety in Canada. Safe houses were known to have been established at Ferguson's Point, Bayfield Bay, and, as some suggest, at the Villa St. Lawrence on Main Street. The French introduced slaves to New France in the early 1700s, but Upper Canada under Lieutenant-Governor Simcoe set the lead in emancipation in 1794. The British Act of Emancipation was passed in 1834.[12]

WOLFE ISLAND FOR LEASE

At the turn of the eighteenth century, one might envisage Captain David Grant (later followed by his son, Charles William) in company with land-sales agent John Ferguson at the northern access to Wolfe Island arranging leases for new settlers. Similarly, Patrick Langan or his deputy could have been stationed at the southern portal, Point Alexandria. In all probability, however, these business dealings took place in Kingston. Grant's and Langan's lands, surveyed and equally divided, were separated at a point just west of the canal. Perhaps the most impoverished of Wolfe Island's emigrants were the families ravaged by Ireland's Potato Famines of 1847 and 1849. In addition, scores of English and Scottish emigrants were enticed to the New World with promises of the proverbial "streets paved with gold." After the Napoleonic War ended in 1815, the depressed economy in Britain forced many more to emigrate.

England experienced such poverty during the latter part of the 1800s that multiple agencies actually removed children from their stricken families and sent them, along with orphans and street children, by the thousands to Canada, or to Australia. More than eighty thousand children fell into a class referred to as the little immigrants.[13] Several "home" children were sponsored by Wolfe Island farmers during this period and their descendants may be found on the island today. James Barrett was employed on the Briceland farm circa late 1800s. Tod Laverty, a Franciscan friar, was a descendant of Frank Laverty, another home child. Davey Crumby may have worked on the Scottish Settlement where he was known for his ability with the bagpipes. James and Henry Hulton were brought to Canada from Lancaster, England. James, a widower, with his nine-year-old son, Gene, was taken to work at the Peter McGrath farm, while Henry worked for George Greenwood. In later years they worked at the McRae place.[14] Other children were sponsored by the Catholic Church. Such was the case with Irish brothers John and Mike (O'Divilley) Devlin, whose families had survived the famine years. As teens they were sponsored by the childless Murphy family to help on their Wolfe Island farm.[15]

Whatever the cause for flight from whatever country, it appears that many newcomers to Wolfe Island were running away from intolerable circumstances. In many cases they fled with only the clothes on their backs, their hopes, ambitions, and a little money in their pockets after paying for their passage. The treacherous three- to six-week ocean crossing, often without sufficient provisions or fresh water, left many in a weakened state of health. Some came with skills, and many without, but for all the pioneer way of life would present many new challenges. Upon arrival, those sufficiently fit to continue their journey experienced stopovers at Quebec City and then Montreal before transferring to bateaux for the disquieting trip up the St. Lawrence River.

The bateau was the only river conveyance available in the 1700s and 1800s to transport groups of people, provisions, and cargo too large for a canoe. These flat-bottomed vessels, substantially constructed of fir planks and covered with birchbark to withstand the rigours of going upstream against the rapids, were built by the French craftsmen at Lachine. Gaps in the construction were filled with a spruce gum that hardened and rendered the vessels watertight.[16] Tapering to points at each end, the bateaux were open boats, forty feet long and six to eight feet wide, each with a lug sail set on a mast with about fifteen feet of hoist. The bateaux were navigated by powerful French-Canadian boatmen who entertained the passengers and themselves with traditional river songs synchronized to the pull of the oars. It took four men to row and one to steer. In Captain Thomas G. Anderson's words: "Their skillful exertion propelled the bateaux in defiance of the waves."[17] These vessels were often sent off in fleets of three or four, especially when large numbers of immigrants were en route to Cataraqui. On the return journey, these bateaux were generally loaded with fur pelts. At nightfall the voyageurs would cook and sleep on the beach while their passengers sought sheltered lodging. The less affluent, who had to cope with the damp and cold, huddled around campfires on the shore. The incredible feat of ascending five sets of rapids some 230 feet above sea level between Lachine and Kingston took about ten days.

As noted, the first settlers on Wolfe Island subsequent to the French were United Empire Loyalists. The vanguard in 1798 consisted of members of the Davis, Hitchcock, Hinckley, and Cone families (see Appendix IV for the Cone family). These families were joined by others of Dutch and Palatine German heritage in ever-increasing numbers.

POPULATION AND THE *PATRON'S DIRECTORY*

Wolfe Island was evolving into a microcosm of what was occurring throughout Upper Canada. My father did extensive research to trace the names of the earliest pioneers and their countries of origin and discovered inconsistencies with historical records. Statements contained the same errors — namely that the population on Wolfe Island consisted of only fifteen families in 1823 and fourteen families in 1835. The foregoing figures were traced to the *Patron's Directory of the (Meacham) Historical Atlas of Frontenac County*, published in 1878. My father determined the source of this inaccurate information. The *Patron's Directory*, as its name implies, was a list of paying subscribers. Anyone who lived on the island at the time could order a copy to have one's name and date of settlement included in the directory. However, the information thus recorded must not be confused with any independent statement of population statistics. A census taken in 1826, showed a population of 276 individuals residing on Wolfe Island. The *Directory's* unsubstantiated declaration that only fourteen families lived on the island in 1835 does not reconcile with census results taken the following year, which indicated a combined population of 346 people living on Simcoe and Wolfe islands. Many Wolfe Islanders either could not afford the subscription cost, refused for some other reason, or were not present when surveyed for the directory. When the atlas was published, approximately 230 farming families, living in various locations on the island, had not purchased a subscription and consequently their names were not included.

Baron Grant's land-sales book has also been quoted as containing an accurate list of the number of families who lived on the island at a given time. This assertion is also incorrect. The book did not include the names of people who had *leased* land from Grant, or the names of those who had purchased or leased land from Patrick Langan, the co-owner of the island.

Even though new laws, introduced after the War of 1812, provided that Americans must reside in Canada for a minimum of seven years before they were eligible to own land, they continued to arrive on Canadian shores. These laws meant little to those settling on Wolfe Island as most of the land on the island could be acquired only under long-term lease. The term *American* was perhaps a misnomer, as many of the immigrants from the United States at this time had been born in the British Isles.

Many Loyalists travelled as families. It is worthwhile to note that the Busch, Mosher (Moshier, Mosier), Orser, Sudds, and Huot families came to Canada as a group. Although these families originated from different parts of Europe, they had elected to move from the United States as a unit, and settled on Wolfe Island in close proximity to each other in the Reeds Bay area and on Simcoe Island. The Huot family, as well as brothers Nicholas, Lewis, and Reuben Mosher, were originally Huguenots who had come to Wolfe Island from Lansdowne, Ontario, in Glengarry County, after their journey northward prior to 1800.[18] Descendants of three of these families still live in the township.

Wells Bamford, Richard C. Irvine, Ebenezer Joslin, John Niles, and Sam and George Woodman, with their families, were also Loyalists. This group arrived at different intervals after 1800 and chose to live towards the foot of the island. Bamford gave his name to the bay and point near his home. Irvine similarly gave his name to the crossroads and bay adjoining his property. Irvine became a councilman and Joslin's son, Al, became the first customs officer at Port Metcalfe at the easterly tip of Wolfe Island. Those wishing to enter Canada after the War of 1812 were required to procure passports at Carleton Island, as the Americans had previously seized the island from the British[19] and it would remain American territory after the signing of the peace treaty.

Luther Harris, a member of the family who settled in the Twelfth Concession, became well-known as the proprietor of the Boxing (Boxen) Harbour Hotel,[20] which operated for many years. His hotel was actually a sixteen-room summer resort ideally situated on the bay east of Chub Point on the north shore of the Eighteenth Concession. In 1914, the hotel was destroyed by a fire of unknown origin.

Numerous homesteaders lacked the skills required for survival in their new environment, and many moved on to other locales. The Renshaw family was an exception. Originally from England, they had trekked with their fellow Loyalists from America. Matthew Renshaw had married Olivia Ecclemont while still living in the United States, but their children were born after their arrival in Upper Canada. A master craftsman, he was a cabinetmaker and copper worker and was able to produce various types of furniture, barrels, wooden pails, churns, tubs, butter bowls, and other household wares. It appears from the 1851 census that Matthew and John Renshaw were brothers. They and John's wife Mary were born in England and their mother Sarah came from Wales. This family, like many others, probably returned to the United States when peace returned.

According to the Chewett Map of 1822, most of the thirty lots on the old French survey were in the process of being developed. They had been sold or leased in the names of James and William Davis, Isaac T. Barrett, Samuel Hitchcock, Samuel Cone, Nicholas and Lewis Moshier, Thomas Davis, James Abbott, Morey Spoor,

Alvah Bennett, Mr. Adams, Frederick Fanning, Horne, Hopson, Lambert, Martin Staley (Stahl), and J. Busch. Other early settlers such as John Bassitt, Alex Hobson, William Marsh, Edward O'Conner, and Squire Hallas were community-minded citizens who took an active interest in shaping Wolfe Island's policies and welfare. Some of these prominent names appeared on petitions and the like in the 1830s. Interestingly, not one of these prominent colonists was cited in the *Patron's Directory*.

THE ENGLISH

English immigrants, intent on settling in Upper Canada, arrived in large numbers via the St. Lawrence River from 1820 to 1850. Records indicate that at least two Englishmen made their way to Wolfe Island during the early part of this period. Samuel Watts (1801–78) from County Kent and John Tarrant (1805–85) from Hampshire settled on the island as young men. It would appear that all of the Watts descendants have lived on the mainland since the 1980s, although the name Tarrant is still evident on the island today. Subsequent English settlers John Friend (1822–97) and William Bullis (1794–1871) set down roots some time in the 1830s.

The exact chronology of arrivals of immigrants from England is difficult to establish as they were interspersed with the mixture of people from all over Great Britain along with the Loyalists of English ancestry. Names of some early English settlers and counties of origin are listed in Appendix I.

THE IRISH

The Irish Potato Famine refugees during 1845 and 1850 were by no means the first settlers on Wolfe Island to come from Ireland. Indeed, at least fifteen Irish families had arrived during the preceding twenty years. Between 1815 and the start of the famine period, more than one million people left Ireland by choice in search of a more promising future. Many who came to Canada ranged in age from sixteen to thirty-four. After 1820, it was less expensive to emigrate as steamships were by then in operation.[22]

John and Mary Dawson, along with Michael and Catherine Baker, all born into the gentry in the late 1700s, were very early Irish immigrants. During the next few years, John Baker, a farmer, and John McCaul, a mariner whose wife and baby died in 1845, also settled on the island. Descendants from the above-mentioned families are not noted in present-day telephone listings, but those of Irish families who arrived later such as Bustard, Conley, Casey, Flynn, Holliday, Kyle, Murphy, O'Brien, O'Reilly, Hawkins, Hogan, Ryan, Devlin, Keyes, and others have persisted into the fifth and sixth generations.

The inscriptions on gravestones reveal much information about the deceased as well as past history. Appendix II lists the names of these earliest Irish pioneers who came to Wolfe Island and who represent eighteen of the initial thirty-two counties of Ireland.

THE PRELUDE TO THE SCOTTISH SETTLEMENT

The McDonells of Glen Garry and Invergarry Castle in Scotland were involved in the defence of Bonnie Prince Charlie in the 1745–46 war with Britain. The aftermath of their defeat at Culloden Moor and their resultant loss of lands, castle, and clan members left them destitute and scattered about Glen Garry. Three of the McDonell brothers — John, Allan, and Alexander — arranged for their Jacobite kin to sail to America around 1773.[22] They embarked from Fort William, Scotland, on the *Pearl*, a ship noted for having brought some early Scottish immigrants to the New World. Sir William Johnson's estate in the Mohawk Valley of New York comprised a huge tract of land, which he arranged to lease to them. Originally, George III of England had granted this land to Sir William for his assistance in capturing Fort Niagara in 1759. William's son, John, inherited the estate in 1776 upon his father's death. On this site, the younger Johnson created a colony called Johnstown for six hundred Jacobites who, by that time, had become fiercely loyal to Britain.[23] The Americans, bent on independence from British rule, did not trust him, believing that he was influencing Natives and other more westerly Americans against their cause.

When the Revolutionary War broke out, the male McDonells in Johnson's colony joined the British militia. An American plot to arrest Johnson was foiled when he outsmarted them by leaving for Canada early in 1776 with two hundred of his followers, largely of the clan McDonell. The perilous two-hundred-mile journey northward took nineteen days to reach Montreal.[24] Their next trek would be southwest to the area of Cornwall.

Father Alexander Macdonell[25] was the central figure in the McDonell clan for many years. Forced, because of his Catholicism, to leave Britain for Spain in order to be educated, he returned to Scotland after his ordination in 1790. He mustered the first Glengarry Fencibles Regiment for duty in Ireland during the Irish Rebellion of 1798.[26] In compensation for their service, George III arranged for Macdonell to take the five hundred soldiers and their families to Canada in 1804, and provided a grant for each of two hundred acres along the St. Lawrence River in the area that is known as Glengarry County today.[27] On arrival they would have been united with Sir John Johnson's Jacobite Highlanders from Johnstown, New York. A second Glengarry Fencible Regiment, comprised of the first generation of McDonells raised in Canada, served in the War of 1812 with their spiritual leader.[28]

Alexander Macdonell was consecrated the first Catholic bishop in Upper Canada in 1826.[29] His assistance with affairs of state was also rewarded by the king with a raise in salary and a seat in the legislative assembly in 1831.[30] An increase in his ecclesiastic responsibilities had already necessitated his move from Glengarry County to Kingston in 1821. He was involved in obtaining grants of land on Wolfe Island for his Gaelic-speaking kinfolk — a task facilitated by his influence with the government. A Loyalist to the end, he was well-acquainted with Bishop Strachan, who had arrived in Canada in 1799, shortly before him, and had taught in Cornwall during his early years in Upper Canada.

There are differing opinions as to the family relationship between the bishop and the Ban McDonells of Wolfe Island. Some early historians and local residents claim they were cousins,[31] and some have suggested that the bishop was a half-brother of Lieutenant Colonel Ranald McDonell, one of the central figures of the Scottish Settlement created on Wolfe Island for Glengarry highlanders. Although genealogical research pertaining to the Glengarry Scots would appear not to support any close relationship between the families, it is clear that the bishop was very supportive of the McDonells living there.

The tract of land established for the Glengarry McDonells consisted of approximately two thousand acres and encompassed the northeastern part of the foot of the island by Oak Point Road. Ranald McDonell, born in 1798, was raised in Glengarry County, became an ensign in the 2nd Glengarry regiment (according to the Upper Canada Militia Records), and advanced to the rank of lieutenant colonel in 1860 while with the Frontenac militia. His loyal service warranted him 180 acres on lots 14 and 15 of the Old Survey, a short distance west of Longueuil Castle. His deed to this land, dated February 20, 1830, designated him as one of the earliest landowners, subsequent to Baron Grant. By 1831, Ranald (or Ronald) had been appointed deputy to the surveyor general of woods and forests for the Crown on Wolfe Island. He was also a member of the first Wolfe Island Township Council in 1850 and remained an active, civic-minded member of the community until his death in 1862.

In 1823, McDonell had married Mary Brown, and they raised six children on the island. At some point he moved his family to the Scottish Settlement between the Tenth and Fourteenth concessions. The successful community of Gaelic-speaking Scots multiplied and many of their descendants still live on Wolfe Island today.[32] Although a few of the families allowed their name to morph into MacDonald over time, his tombstone reads McDonell, as is also the case with many of his kinfolk.

LOYALIST FAMILY ORAL HISTORY

Effort has been made to locate stories surrounding the flights of Loyalists who ended up settling on Wolfe Island. Whether the following tales are totally accurate or have been somewhat embellished over time, they nonetheless provide insight into the ordeals experienced by these families.

According to Isabel O'Shea, some of the O'Sheas in Virginia became United Empire Loyalists and fled to Glengarry County. Years ago her father related a tale to her family:

> He was told solemnly that his great-great-grandmother was carried as an infant from Virginia. They had to travel by night in order to stay under cover and so they slept in barns by day submerged in hay. The baby was fed sips of brandy so that she would sleep and not betray their presence. One day, Americans on patrol heard about the nearby presence of Loyalists. They went over the haymows with pitchforks but were not successful in finding this contingent of Loyalists because they had buried themselves so deeply in the hay.[33]

Mrs. Flora (McDonald) Devlin, when interviewed, shared more of these sagas. Her great-great grandfather was a McDonell from Glen Garry, Scotland. Mrs. Devlin's notable ancestor Flora MacDonald and her family fled to North Carolina after assisting in the escape of Bonnie Prince Charles from Scotland, subsequent to the Jacobites' defeat at Culloden Moor in 1746.[34] Flora was required to sign papers indicating that they would never raise arms against England again. During the American Revolution the Jacobites were not allowed to fight; their only alternative was to return to Scotland or to flee to Canada. Some did just that. Again, they travelled by night, trudging north through mountains, muck, and mire towards their destination — Glengarry County. It was not long before their provisions were used up and they were starving. One night, a white horse wandered into their camp. They killed it and survived on the meat. Mrs. Devlin's forebear was a babe-in-arms, being carried inside a covered wagon in this particular journey. The baby was likely Mrs. Devlin's grandfather's aunt, and possibly the same babe reported above to have tasted brandy at such a tender young age.[35]

Peter La Fleur was a French naval officer from Glengarry County who in 1804 married one of the clan's daughters, Mary McDonell. They, too, settled on Wolfe Island in 1817 and counted among their numerous descendants are John O'Shea, his siblings, and Flora Devlin. Although La Fleur's mother tongue was French, he very quickly learned to speak Gaelic. Peter later took to the Great Lakes as a ship's captain, making use of his naval background.

The cemetery records of the Church of the Sacred Heart of the Blessed Virgin Mary on Wolfe Island state that a Dr. and Mrs. McRae were among the early settlers on Wolfe Island. Originally from Scotland, they came by way of Glengarry circa 1830. This couple was likely Dr. John McRae and his wife Anne. After Mrs. McRae was widowed, she donated four acres of land for the first Catholic church and cemetery.[36] As this land lay within lot 1 of the Sixth Concession, this couple may have built the limestone house still known today as the McRae Place, believed to have been constructed shortly after the Hitchcock House. Apparently, the doctor had been granted two hundred acres in Quebec for services as a surgeon in the British army during the Napoleonic Wars. As the site of the initial grant was not arable, he was able to exchange it for two hundred acres on the Sixth Concession on Wolfe Island.[37] They may have chosen to come to the island because of other McRae kin — Duncan McRae and wife Margaret among others in Glengarry County — who also planned to move there. James Hector McRae and his wife Mary, also Catholic Scots, came to the island later in the 1840s and further developed the well-known farm with the stone house on the Sixth Concession. There were some Presbyterians from Glengarry County in addition to the Scottish Catholic United Empire Loyalists.

Another McRae family, seemingly unrelated to the above, was that of Weir McRae, born in Ireland, who embarked from Scotland and may have sojourned in Glengarry County on his way to Wolfe Island. He had two children by his first wife, Delila Ellis, who was born in Upper Canada. After she died, Weir married Irish-born Nancy McCready of Wolfe Island. They were both Presbyterian, but their lineage embraced Catholicism when son George McRae married Elizabeth McLaren.[38] Official records bearing Weir McRae's name spell it as such, but he persisted in signing his name as "Wier McCray."

SETTLERS FROM SCOTLAND

Wolfe Island's population was steadily increasing, but not just due to new settlers. Records indicate that, in 1851 alone, ninety-four babies were born. This census also shows that many Scots immigrated to Wolfe Island directly from their homeland in the early 1800s. The first known to have done so was William Henderson (1821–99). He arrived during the 1820s prior to the first Irish immigrant and settled on the Seventh Concession. Elizabeth and James Rattray, both born in the 1700s, emigrated from Scotland and set up farming on the Nineteenth Concession. Incidentally, James Rattray (1762–1859) is the oldest person buried in the St. Lawrence Cemetery, fondly referred to as the Loyalist Cemetery because of the many Loyalists buried there. Another Scot, John Horne (1798–1887), a farmer, settled on the Eighth Concession. Descendants of these pioneer families, in addition to the Berrys, Browns, and Kiells, still live on the island. Appendix III contains a list of Scots and their counties of origin (where known) as cited in cemetery records.

No other large-scale settling of specific ethnic groups occurred on Wolfe Island for about the next one hundred years. The increase in population, as recorded in the 1861 census, peaked at 3,601 and is attributed to the continuing influx of immigrants drawn there by the availability of work in lumbering, stone quarrying, and farming, and the presence of established communities.

Courtesy of Mable McRae, 1990.

Several generations of McRaes lived in this fine Scottish masonry limestone building, including Mable McRae. The house, built in 1838, is located on the Sixth Concession. Photo circa 1990.

Because lumbering and quarrying were phased out on the island after 1862, various newcomers chose to move in search of work. A depression, from 1857 to 1859, lowered the price of wheat and led to diversification in grain farming. An ensuing emphasis on dairy farming led to an increase in the size of farms rather than the expansion of population. As dairy farming expanded, cheese factories began to appear.

In the early 1900s, young people from the farms began to move to mainland cities and the United States in search of work with regular hours and steady wages. During the Great Depression and the Second World War, some farmers out of necessity abandoned their farms to find sustainable employment. The census figures that follow record the population shift from the bustling activity of earlier years:

Census Figures: Wolfe Island 1826–1971

Year	Population
1826	276
1831	531
1841	994
1851	2,654
1861	3,601
1871	2,737
1881	2,383
1891	2,654
1901	1,796
1911	1,612
1921	1,579
1931	1,378
1941	1,196
1951	1,102
1961	1,169
1971	1,212

DUTCH IMMIGRATION FOLLOWING THE SECOND WORLD WAR

Throughout the four-year post Second World War period (1948–52), about eighty families, comprising approximately 250 immigrants from Holland, settled on abandoned Wolfe Island farms. By the end of the war, Holland's infrastructure was shattered. Many of her natives, who chose to emigrate, came to Canada. The hardships of the resistance prepared these industrious people in large part for the arduous task that lay ahead.

The first to arrive were the Hasselaars, who settled on Wolfe Island in April 1948, followed by the Vollerings, who came later that summer. Soon after, families with names such as Posthumus, Van Strien, Broeder, Sjonger, and de Reuter appeared. These newcomers and those who followed brought uncultivated land back into production and updated farm equipment and buildings while raising families, all of whom have become an integral part of the community.

Dutch immigrant Gepke Sjonger indicated that her family actually emigrated from Freisland, a province on the north coast of Holland. They faced an additional challenge upon arrival in Canada as they spoke a different language than their Dutch compatriots. The Reverend J. Appelman of the Mill Hill Missionaries (St. Joseph's Missionary Society) was one of several priests from the Netherlands posted in areas where their fellow countrymen were living.[39] After serving a short time on the mainland, Father Appelman was appointed the incumbent priest at the Catholic church on the island for the period 1987–98. He often commented on the large variety of dialects he encountered among his Dutch communicants. Many of these immigrants from Holland left a positive mark on the island and then moved on, in many cases to occupations other than farming.

THE CAPE VINCENT CONNECTION:
French Activities in Northern New York

A half-mile excursion on Horne's ferry across the south channel of the St. Lawrence River from Point

Alexandria takes one to the American port of entry, Cape Vincent, New York. Champlain's early exploration of this area led to French settlements that would form a natural conduit for trade and communication with the north side of the river. The first settler on the shoreline opposite Point Alexandria was Abijah Putnam, who had come from Oneida territory near Rome, New York. In 1801 he established the settlement of Port Putnam, two miles east of Gravelly Point (Cape Vincent). Putnam operated a ferry service between this port and Big Bay (Bayfield Bay), Wolfe Island.[40] Peter Sternberg and John McComb purchased Port Putnam from Abijah in 1805, and Sternberg, after acquiring a licence from the American government, secured a ten-year lease, dated February, 20, 1867, to operate a ferry between Carleton Island and Wolfe Island via Bayfield Bay.[41] His ferry, based on Carleton just south of Bayfield Bay, served the island's growing community.

The two American ferries docked at a wharf on Bayfield Bay rather than Point Alexandria, possibly because Loyalist Samuel Cone of Wolfe Island controlled all of the point and spurned competition. In the early 1800s, an inn serviced by this wharf was established on the west side of the Eleventh Concession (the old turnpike) about one-quarter mile from the shore. In summertime, the inn, later known as the Halfway House, was considered to be halfway between Marysville and the foot of the island. In winter, by ice, its location was

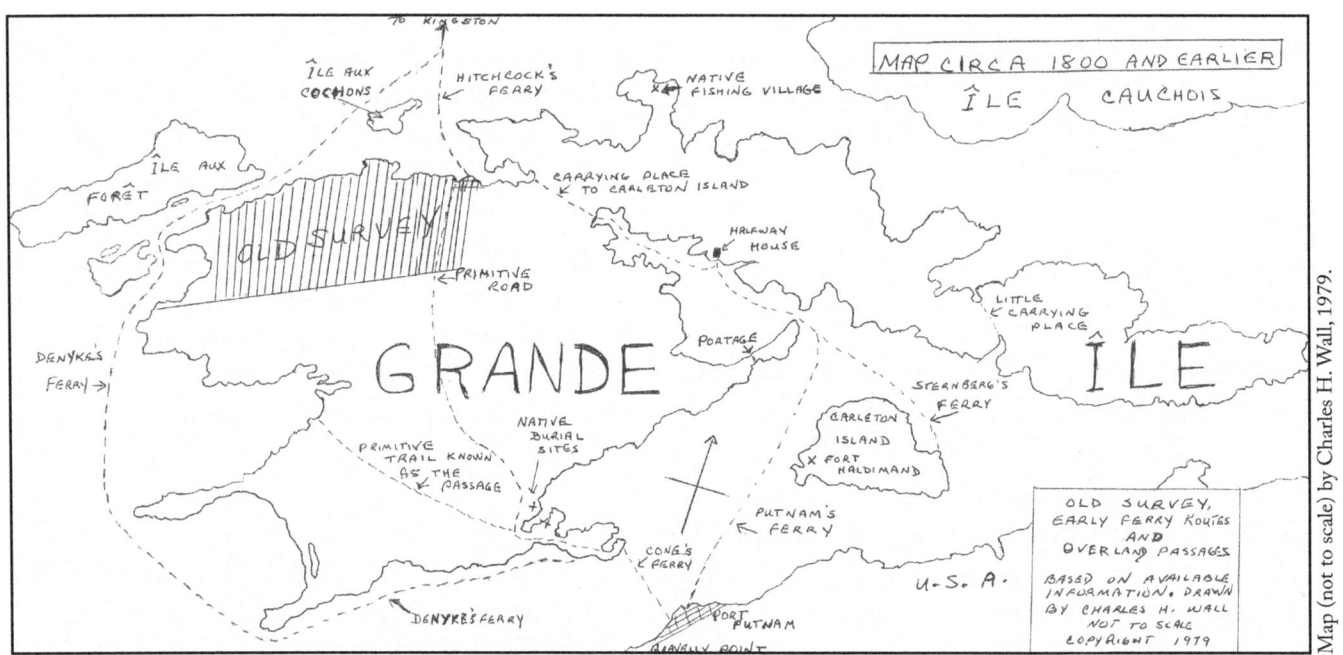

Map 5: *This map of Grand Île representing* circa *1800 or earlier has been adapted from a variety of sources to illustrate early ferry routes, Overland Passages, Carrying Places, Portages, Native Burial Grounds, and the Old French Survey.*

viewed as approximately halfway between Kingston and Cape Vincent. At one time in the 1870s, the hotel was operated by Johnny O'Shea's great-grandmother Louise (Horne) Smith. A large stable was available where stagecoach drivers would feed and change horses while the passengers rested at the inn. Dining was accompanied by spirits if desired, and lodging was available to overnight guests.[42]

After the Wolfe Island Canal was opened in 1855, the ice-stage route was across the river to Bayfield Bay, over the bay to the Eleventh Line, and on to the Halfway House for the usual stopover. They continued on the ice up the canal and across the river to Kingston. The return trip retraced this route.

Among other settlers at Port Putnam was Daniel Spinning in 1804. Daniel's first wife, Jerusa Standish, was a descendant of Myles Standish, who had come to America on the *Mayflower* in 1620. Humphrey Spinning, Daniel's ancestor, had first settled in Connecticut in 1637. Another Wolfe Island connection involves the Cone family. They too were already established in Connecticut by that date, after which both families moved to Jefferson County, and from there to Wolfe Island.

During the late 1700s, after more attempts were made at colonization in the present upper New York, French aristocrat and financier, Jacques Le Ray de Chaumont finally succeeded amidst the aftermath of the American Revolution. Chaumont, born in 1760 at the Château de Chaumont near Tours, France, had purchased large tracts of land in northern New York during his stay in the United States. He married Grace Coxe of New Jersey in 1790 and later returned to France. After his two children were born, he came back to America in 1807. He brought his son, Vincent Le Ray, to manage his affairs and they successfully established several French settlements in New York.[43] As some of these French immigrants had served as allies during the American Revolutionary War, Chaumont influenced the United States government into offering them land grants in Gravelly Point after 1776 — a reward for their loyalty to the American cause.

Vincent Le Ray deeded a water lot to R.M. Esselton in June 1809 for the exclusive right of running a ferry.[44] This may have been the second ferry service running between Gravelly Point and Hinckley's Point, Wolfe Island. Eber Kelsey, who had come to Gravelly Point in 1809, ferried from there to Wolfe Island while Samuel Hinckley ran a ferry service from his more northerly wharf on Point Alexandria (Hinckley's Point) to the Cape, both using rowboats and scows.[45]

Gravelly Point, later named Cape Vincent by Jacques Le Ray in honour of his son Vincent, was a bustling mercantile and lumbering centre in the early 1800s. Lumber from the clearing of the land was used in shipbuilding, potash production, timber rafting, and stave forwarding to Montreal. As this town prospered, Port Putnam faded and was eventually abandoned.[46] At that time, emigration to Wolfe Island was in its early stages and some of the new islanders took advantage of employment in Cape Vincent.

The American government, intent on ending the cross-border fur and lumber trade, imposed exorbitant tariffs on the Canadian merchants in the region south of the Great Lakes and along the St. Lawrence River.[47] The British, in turn, placed an embargo on American goods in 1807, an act that seriously affected the economy of the fur and lumber outposts on the American frontier. The resulting negative relations between the two countries contributed to the War of 1812.

Cape Vincent was one of the most vulnerable American settlements along the St. Lawrence-United States shoreline. The settlement required protection during the War of 1812, and members of the French troops who had previously seen action in the American Revolution were housed in the stone barracks near the shore.[48] Cape Vincent was besieged by the British on several occasions. In 1924 this old barrack property was purchased by the local township for board meetings. Since 1992 the building has been home to the Cape Vincent Historical Museum and contains countless artifacts of the 1700s and 1800s, one of which is a framed document regarding Swiss geodesist F.R. Hassler, who had worked for the United States government as superintendent of the coastal survey. After the War of 1812, he worked on the original survey that attempted to delineate the international boundary.[49]

In 1812, Bonapartist émigrés, mainly aristocrats, sought refuge outside France after the French Revolution and the subsequent fall of Napoleon. Large numbers of them settled at Cape Vincent and environs. Count Pièrre François Réal, one of the more notable in the above group, was Napoleon's prefect of police. When Napoleon was exiled to Ste Hélèna in 1815, Count Réal, became involved in a plot to rescue him. His ruse was exposed and he came to Cape Vincent in 1816 after being exiled from France.[50]

A house was built for Réal in Cape Vincent on land where the present waterworks powerhouse is located. Although he occupied the house, he had decorated it with many of Napoleon's possessions with the intent that it would become his friend's refuge should the latter escape from exile. Réal returned to France in 1818 after the house was completed, but alas, Napoleon died in 1821, never to see his intended abode. It ultimately passed into the hands of Réal's friend, Theophilus Peugnet, who lived there until it burned in 1867.[51] Evidently, Réal was back at Cape Vincent in March 1822, as his name is included in a list of charter members of the first Masonic Lodge of Cape Vincent. This lodge association may indicate that Réal was Huguenot.

In 1815 Vincent Le Ray built a stone house for himself facing the St. Lawrence River. Othniel Spinning, possibly Daniel's brother (also Hart Massey's[52] deputy customs collector), hauled limestone by boat from Carleton Island for Le Ray's house. It still stands after nearly two hundred years and is probably the oldest stone house in Jefferson County.[53]

The stone barracks at Cape Vincent, New York, built circa 1800, housed French-Canadian and American troops during the War of 1812. The barracks began a new life as a the Cape Vincent Museum in 1992.

That year, Chaumont's grandson, Jacques, was visited by a friend, Joseph Bonaparte, then King of Spain and brother of Napoleon I of France. Joseph had become accustomed to vacationing in the upper New York area and had purchased a large tract of land at Natural Bridge, near Harrisville. There, he built a well-fortified home and hunting lodge intended as a refuge for his brother should he be able to escape from Ste Hélèna, but his efforts on behalf of his brother were also in vain.[54] Joseph Bonaparte also visited Count Réal on several occasions at Cape Vincent. When the political tide turned after Napoleon's death, enabling the French exiles to return to France, Réal returned home where he died in Paris in 1831.[55]

Le Ray's effort to encourage more emigration from France to the Cape Vincent area finally materialized in 1830 with the arrival of a group, mostly from Rosière, France. By 1832, with Le Ray's financial assistance, they founded a village some ten miles from Cape Vincent and named it Rosière in honour of their old home. These newcomers were mainly Catholic. During the period before their church was built in 1858, Le Ray arranged visits from a parish priest in Kingston, Ontario, to minister to their spiritual needs.[56] The early French names associated with Protestant churches in the area were presumably those of Huguenots. Before there was an Anglican church on Wolfe Island, families at the Foot ferried to St. John's Church at Cape Vincent.

As evidenced from the foregoing, Cape Vincent possesses a rich French history. Annually, since 1968, on the Saturday contiguous to Bastille Day in France, the town swells, becoming alive with celebration as the people of the area commemorate their heritage. The popular French Festival is replete with barbecues, French breads and pastries, craft sales, French entertainment, and a street parade led by "Napoleon." The government of France takes this celebration seriously, and the French ambassador in Washington and the French consul in New York visit on occasion but never fail to arrange delivery of *petit-fours*. The festivities end with a fireworks display and, needless to say, the "Tricoleur" is displayed prominently.

Preoccupation with first families on Wolfe Island led to an examination of records at Cape Vincent where names, both French and British, duplicated those on Wolfe Island. Of the numerous French names on both sides of the border, it was possible to match only Docteur and Winborne (Wenborne), which would suggest that most of the French population on Wolfe Island originated from Quebec.

Martin Docteur, a Bonapartist who came to Cape Vincent from the province of Lorraine, France, via Algeria, settled in Rosière.[57] Alexander Docteur, his descendant, married Jane Monroe in 1869. They lived on Wolfe Island and had six children. Alexander and his descendants all farmed until around 1970 and Docteurs are still present on Wolfe Island. Less is known about the Wenbornes. Romaine Wenborne was a St. Lawrence River guide, and, as all the Wenbornes on Wolfe Island rest in Protestant cemeteries, they likely were Huguenots.

OTHER FAMILIES ASSOCIATED WITH BOTH WOLFE ISLAND AND CAPE VINCENT

According to local publications, Ida Fowler is believed to have been one of the cross-border teachers.[58] As there were no government grants available for the St. Lawrence School at the Eighteenth Concession of Wolfe Island, the people of this area hired teachers from the American side. The teachers were reimbursed with free board in local homes and small stipends paid by the students' parents. Although Ida's career spanned the river, she lived in and was buried at Cape Vincent.

The names Briggs, Davis, and Irvine appear in cemetery records in both places, but kinship could not be established. David Briggs apparently was among the early settlers who came to Cape Vincent in 1809. The Briggs surname was later present on Wolfe Island and subsequently on Simcoe Island. The Davis family, who were among the first United Empire Loyalist families to appear on Wolfe Island, owned the coal dockyard on the north shoreline of Marysville at the end of what is now called St. Lawrence Street. Richard and son James were known to sell coal and wood in the Cape Vincent area. This Richard Davis had been a drummer in Sir John Johnson's regiment, in which Patrick Langan had served as a lieutenant. The surname Cook (Charles and Robert) also appears in both Cape Vincent and Wolfe Island records; seemingly, descendants migrated easily across the border to the north.

EARLY SETTLERS OF POINT ALEXANDRIA

Points and bays all around Wolfe Island bear the names of people who owned land on or adjacent to them. None appears more beckoning to the American shore than Point Alexandria, Wolfe Island's gateway to the United States. The shoreline meets the seaway channel to the south and frames Button Bay to the north. The land area comprises lots 10, 11, and 12 in the Eighth Concession. Multitudes of people have travelled across Point Alexandria throughout the years, but Samuel Cone, a Loyalist who arrived before 1800, was its earliest recorded settler. On April 27, 1802, the Court of Quarter Sessions in Kingston granted him the first charter "to run a ferry from Wolfe Island to the American shore"[59] — the precursor of the ferry service still in operation today. The ferry vessel could be any type of watercraft from a rowboat to a scow, depending on the number of passengers and/or the amount of cargo.

It not known how much property Cone occupied, but he may have leased the whole 212-acre point from Patrick Langan, who owned that portion of the island. Little is recorded about his personal life, but his brother Darius Cone (Coan, Coon) is listed as being on the island in 1817. After Samuel sold the ferry franchise to Samuel Hinckley in 1820, information about the Cones ceases, suggesting they moved from the island. There are no Cones identified in any of the Wolfe Island cemeteries.

The Hinckleys, Samuel and Mary, had come to Wolfe Island from Pittstown, New York, as Loyalists. They began to establish their small dynasty on Hinckley's Point in 1801. Their two daughters, Mary and Minerva, and son Rodney came with them; all three had been born in Herkimer, New York. Three more children were born between 1802 and 1819.[60]

Mary "Polly," the eldest of the children, was born in 1789, and is still spoken of fondly today. The town of Marysville was named in her honour. Her first husband, Thomas Davis, died at a young age. Thomas, great-grandfather of Captain Leath Davis, had tended the lighthouse on Pigeon Island for fifteen years. On his final trip home to Wolfe Island, he drowned when a gale force wind blew up and swamped his boat.[61] Polly's second marriage, to Archibald Hitchcock Jr., united her family with the Hitchcock family of early Loyalist fame. The second child, Minerva, married Nicholas Mosher (Mosier), one of the three Huguenot brothers who, with the Davis family, were among the earliest settlers.

Between 1815 and 1818, the Hinckleys spent some time at Rome, New York, but Point Alexandria lured them back. When Samuel acquired the ferry charter from Mr. Cone in 1820, he initiated a family tradition that continued for the next sixty-five years, culminating in ferry ownership on the south shore and ferry management on the north shore. In 1826 he also leased the 212-acre farm on the point formerly leased by Samuel Cone. Hinckley must have been known for his engineering capability, as he was contracted by the American government for two hundred dollars to draw up plans for a bridge at Schenectady, New York. This was followed by a contract with the Canadian government for eighty dollars to plan a bridge between Kingston and Barriefield, Ontario.[62] Given the time frame involved, it would appear that the Penny Bridge, built over the Cataraqui River and separating the inner and outer harbours of Kingston (later replaced by the LaSalle Causeway) was designed by him.

Samuel built the Hinckley residence on the point near the ferry dock as an inn. After his death in 1849, his younger daughter Olivia and her husband Demetrius Spinning became the innkeepers. The Spinnings, originally from Scotland, had settled in the Cape Vincent area around 1800. As a young man, Demetrius had moved to Wolfe Island and settled on the Ridge Road. In addition to farming, he developed a talent for weaving, especially working with linen. He also served as the township coroner for some time. After Demetrius became an innkeeper, he and Olivia turned the running of the Spinning farm over to their son, Damon. Their other son, Edwin, began farming one hundred acres across the road from Damon, within the Fourth Concession.

Samuel's son Coleman, born in 1809 at the Hinckley farm in Marysville, was married in 1830 to Isabella Bradshaw of Quebec. Although Coleman's early pursuits were in farming, he was contracted by the Canadian government to build a road between Marysville and Hinckley Point. During his early years he also obtained his marine captain's papers, enabling him to operate steamships between Cape Vincent and Canada until he was approximately seventy years of age.[63] Upon Samuel's death in 1849, the Hinckley farm was divided between his son Coleman and son-in-law Demetrius Spinning. By 1857, Coleman's prosperity with the ferry franchise allowed him to make a successful bid to run the Wolfe Island ferry on the north shore for the next fifteen years. This lease was granted with the proviso that he would begin service when the ice broke up in the spring of 1858. Two years later, Coleman sold his rights in the Point Alexandria ferry franchise to Thomas D. Horne Jr. who, in 1851, married Angeline Spinning, Coleman's eldest granddaughter. Thus, to some extent, the ferry operation remained in the family.[64]

This ferry usually docked in the same general location where the Horne ferry docks today, but as Hinckley also owned several properties in Cape Vincent, the ferry docked at three different locations at Cape Vincent. The present Cape Vincent ferry wharf is either on or contiguous to what had been a shingle factory in the mid-1800s and later a coal dock. Rock-filled cribs from the old pier can still be seen just under the surface of the river, a few feet from shore. Some of the beams used in the cribs are about fourteen inches square by fifty or sixty feet long and serve as a reminder of the timber-trade days when the pier was constructed.

Coleman Joseph Hinckley (Coleman Jr.), born in 1841, provided mail service on Wolfe Island for many years. At the age of twelve he delivered American and Canadian mail on horseback, a role that he and, later, his sons would carry on for a total of seventy-eight years.[65] In 1855, he, in partnership with C.M. Kinghorn and Alexander Campbell of Kingston, was responsible for the dredging of the Wolfe Island Canal, an undertaking that cost their firm about ten thousand dollars but provided passenger steamers a much shorter route between Kingston and Cape Vincent.[66] The firm also built the steamer *Pierrepont* with wood from the Hinckley farm.

Later, the firm of Nickle, Folger, and Hinckley purchased another passenger ferry called the *Maude*, rebuilt it, and re-registered the steamship as the *America*. Coleman Hinckley Jr. was the captain of a succession of steam ferryboats of the time, under Kinghorn's employ. In 1872 the company of C.M. Kinghorn, Nickle, and the Folger brothers was purchased by the St. Lawrence River Steamboat Company. Captain Hinckley worked for this company until his retirement in 1905.

Coleman lived in Cape Vincent during his latter years and, after retirement, assisted in the preparation of *Evert's History of Jefferson County, New York*, published in 1878.[67] Hinckley's Point, the extreme easterly projection of Point Alexandria, and Hinckley Shoals Flats, to the east of the point, are named for his family. The original Kinghorn, Campbell, and Hinckley ferry from Kingston via the Wolfe Island Canal moored at Cape Vincent just north of the Watertown and Rome, New York railroad station. The ferry office was located at the river end of Hinckley's property on Murray Street.

THE HORNE LINEAGE

By the late 1820s, the Hinckley, Horne, and Spinning families had cleared their lands, leased from Patrick Langan's heirs, and settled into farming. As noted, it did not take long for these families to become linked by marriages, and there were similar links with other first families: the Moshers, Davises, and Hitchcocks. The Moshers can also trace their ancestry back to the famous *Mayflower* through to Francis Cooke, one of the passengers.[68]

In time, Alexandria Point's population grew. However, as the Horne family expanded, the number of Spinnings and Hinckleys diminished, some returning to the United States after the American Civil War (1861–65). Some Spinnings, Hornes, and Brownes (the latter being related by marriage to John Horne) had travelled to England to wait out the Civil War. Upon their return, the Hornes gradually increased their land holdings through inheritance or purchase until they owned all of Point Alexandria.

The Horne family had originated from the Scottish Hebrides, where they likely were crofters or tenants of small farms presided over by a laird. Scores of these families were evicted when lairds elected to use the lands for sheep-grazing.[69] The Horne family members immigrated to Canada via Quebec in the late 1700s, where Thomas D. Horne was born in 1801. By the time of the 1851 census of Wolfe Island, he was a widower with eight children, all born in Upper Canada.

Other Hornes, after sailing to Canada, settled in the Scottish community of Glengarry County late in the 1700s. Another, John Horne, born in Scotland in 1798, travelled to Canada where he married Jemima Browne of Upper Canada. Yet another Horne, Robert Sr., born in 1808, was living with his large family on the Old Survey at the time of the 1851 census. Likely the Loyalist Hornes of Glengarry were siblings or cousins, for when they moved to Wolfe Island they settled on farms in close proximity to each other around 1834.

The original hotel, built around 1835 by Samuel Hinckley and later known as the Spinning Hotel and Inn, faced the American shore. Thomas D. Horne rebuilt and enlarged the original to create this handsome structure in 1871. The hotel, sitting right at the point of entry into Canada, soon housed the customs office. This inn was a Wolfe Island landmark.

Courtesy of Tweedsmuir History, Wolfe Island Library.

Thomas Darrell Horne Jr. purchased the Wolfe Island-Cape Vincent ferry enterprise from his wife's grandfather in 1860, and he either replaced or added to the original two-storey frame Spinning Hotel in 1871. The much grander edifice, built close to the point facing Cape Vincent,[70] continued as a hotel, but now also contained a customs office. The contractor, a Mr. Hamnel, had constructed the building with one part providing living accommodation for the Horne family while the other part contained hotel rooms and a large ballroom. The lower fieldstone enclosure was tall enough to serve as the verandah railing and a foundation. The main body of the house was three storeys, with a fourth sitting atop the central section, somewhat in the fashion of a widow's walk. As well as being the hotel proprietor, Horne maintained the ferry operation and farmed with the assistance of his family until his death by drowning in 1884. The hotel was closed but his wife and son continued farming. At about twenty-four years of age, son William assumed the operation of the ferry for a number of years. When he died in 1945 at the age of eighty-four, he was succeeded by his sons William Jr. and Darrell. The first power-driven Horne ferry was put into service about 1910. It carried passengers but was also used to tow cargo-carrying scows. This operation could be hazardous, as revealed by the deaths of Rodney and Herman Moore, relatives of the Hinckleys and close friends of the Hornes.

The 350-passenger *Jacques Cartier*, put into service circa 1937, was the first motorized car-carrying ferry owned by the W.E. Horne Ferry Company. The intent was to shorten the trip between Cape Vincent and Marysville to one hour. After landing at Horne's Point, passengers would be bussed over the seven miles to Marysville while the craft sailed around the Head to meet them and carry on to Kingston. However, the operation was not cost effective and the township council was not in favour of the Horne's monopolizing the ferry trade. The service was discontinued and the *Jacques Cartier* was sold five years later.[71]

Sadly, the beautiful hotel cum customs office and home to generations of Hornes burned on Easter Day in 1944. At that time, G. Darrell "Dee" Horne of a subsequent generation was enlisted in the Marine Squadron of the Royal Canadian Air Force, which was engaged in the Second World War. He was able to arrange leave in order to attend to the disaster at home. The house was rebuilt of concrete with two self-contained apartments and is still the Horne's residence.

After the war ended, George Darrell and his brother, William Esmond Horne, farmed and ran the ferry.[72] By this time a motor-driven landing barge was in use. In time, the Hornes assumed the ferry operation running in both directions from May through to mid-October. The present vessel on this run, the MS *William Darrell*, built at Port Dover, Ontario, and named for the brothers, was put into service in 1950. This diesel engine-powered boat fairly flies across the channel with its cargo capacity of ten to twelve cars and passengers.

The brothers had a very substantial mahogany motorboat, constructed by Gordon Roney of Wolfe Island, that Dee's brother Bill used to run a government ship-piloting service. He guided foreign ships in the St. Lawrence through unfamiliar dangerous waters before the inception of the St. Lawrence Seaway. Following Dee's death in 1970, his sons Bruce and George took their father's place in operating the ferry service along

Horne's ferry the William Darrell *is being loaded with cars at Point Alexandria. Cape Vincent may be seen in the background. Photo 1970.*

with their uncle Bill. Now, many years later, George, who has his master seaman's papers, and Bruce, who has his captain's papers, continue operating this reputable ferry service while farming on Point Alexandria, now known as Horne's Point.

This port of entry to Canada has always been staffed by Canadian Customs. In the early 1800s, the customs house was located close to the ferry dock, with various islanders assuming the role of customs officer. The location of the customs house changed several times between then and the early 1900s, when the Hornes found room for this government office in their inn. After the demise of the hotel in 1944, room was made in the Hornes' new residence for a customs office and Dee Horne assumed the position of officer until his death.

The federal government subsequently erected a new customs building near the shore and constructed a new ferry dock. These were open for service in 1971, with a staff on duty at specified hours each day. As this area has always been notorious for smuggling, customs is a highly scrutinized operation. If people ever doubted the efficiency of the current border security at Horne's Point, they would have been quite shocked on September 11, 2001, the day of New York's twin-tower terrorist disaster. On that day more police and customs officials were observed on both sides of the channel than passengers.

The Hornes who settled on Wolfe Island came via Glengarry, or from the United States via Massachusetts and Cape Vincent, and were considered to be Loyalists. Rachel (Jamieson) Horne, now deceased, was the matriarch of the Horne lineage. She was a fine artist and designer of jewellery and her artistry may be found in many homes on and off the island. But perhaps her most popular work is the Wolfe Island map illustrated

Pictured here are Rachel Horne and her great granddaughter Rowen Edwards. Photo 2008.

with churches, schoolhouses, ferries, lighthouses, and other points of interest. The original of this map hangs in the waiting room at the Kingston ferry docks, beckoning the uninitiated to come and explore the island's hidden treasures.

CHAPTER 7
A Teapot in a Tempest

Before the arrival of the Europeans, Wolfe Island provided refuge for indigenous peoples and a forest sanctuary for wild game. Seasonal visits by nomadic Native people in spring and autumn continued throughout the 1800s. What could be envisioned as an idyllic locale on Wolfe Island gradually changed over the following decades.

During the Curaux ownership (1708–95) some notable Europeans landed on Wolfe Island's shores. Father François Picquet, a Jesuit priest, traversed the island in 1751, pursuing his missionary work with the Natives. In 1749 he had been responsible for building Fort Presentation as a mission station and fur-trading post at Ogdensburg, New York. The Marquis de Montcalm, the French defender of the Citadel of Quebec, while leading a military detachment, crossed the north channel of the St. Lawrence from Fort Frontenac to Wolfe Island on August 4, 1756. He, with his soldiers and Native allies, hid in the woods on Bear Point awaiting the opportune time to strike the British fort at Oswego, New York. The successful mission, known as the Battle of Chouagen (the Native term for Oswego), totally destroyed the town after a ten-day siege and brought all of Lake Ontario under French control.

For years both French and British had been attempting to gain control of the lake. On a larger scale, the concerted struggle between these European nations for control of the North American continent led to the onset of the Seven Years' War in 1756, when Britain declared war on France. Fighting on the local front saw British troops under Colonel John Bradstreet's command seize control of Fort Frontenac in 1758. The French abandoned the fort and retreated to Montreal. In 1759, the British captured Quebec City, where General Wolfe died in battle on the Plains of Abraham and General Montcalm expired from his wounds the following day. The leaders of French Canada were succeeded by British governors: Jeffery Amherst, Wolfe's commander-in-chief (1860–63), James Murray (1764–68), Guy Carleton (1768–78; 1786–91), and Frederick Haldimand (1778–86).[1]

The Treaty of Paris, signed in 1763 by Great Britain, France, and Spain, was a multifaceted pact, part of which terminated the Seven Years' War and established British rule in New France. The British Parliament passed the Quebec Act on June 22, 1774, which secured French civil law, British criminal law, and religious freedom for members of the Roman Catholic faith.[2] The French were allowed to maintain their roots and thus religion and patriotism of a local and cultural nature developed hand in hand.[3]

Not surprisingly, the Quebec Act became one of the factors leading to the American Revolution (1775–83). After the Thirteen Colonies won independence from Britain and became the United States of America, they were still engaged in disputes with the British government over their rights and the rights of their legislatures. The passing of the Quebec Act by the British Parliament further enraged the Americans as it allowed Quebec to retain its domain as far as the Mississippi River — territory that included the Native lands in the Ohio Valley,[4] which the Americans viewed as theirs by right.

Those loyal to the Crown had begun to flee the United States by April 1776. Many Loyalists went to the Maritimes,[5] followed soon afterwards by contingents to southern Ontario, including Wolfe Island. During the revolution, a British gunboat patrol from Carleton Island kept watch on Wolfe Island as the refugees passed to and from the outpost maintained at Cataraqui.[6]

The Constitutional Act of 1791 created the province of Canada (Lower Canada and Upper Canada). By royal proclamation in 1792, Grande Île was renamed in honour of General Wolfe, and similarly Île aux Forêt was renamed to recognize Lieutenant-Governor Simcoe. At last, Wolfe Island had a significant historical identity.

THE WAR OF 1812

For a short period prior to 1812, an air of prosperity pervaded most of Upper Canada and the Kingston area in particular, but the threat of war was never far away. Tensions heightened on October 31, 1808, when a party of American soldiers boarded a Canadian ferry as it sailed its route from Point Alexandria to Kingston. The vessel, owned and operated by Andrew Denyke, was proceeding about 120 feet off the south shore of Wolfe Island when the soldiers ordered him to stop and be searched. When he refused, the Americans threatened the captain and his passengers. Denyke complied and the ferry was towed to Sackets Harbor, where the passengers and crew were held in custody. That evening the crew of the ferry cut the chains holding their boat and escaped back to Canada. An American guard, who had fallen asleep on their vessel, was taken to Kingston as proof of the incident, and, on November 3, Andrew Denyke gave a sworn affidavit before Judge Richard Cartwright. The Americans, deluded by the notion that the Canadians were downtrodden and in need of help, thought that if they attacked the Canadians would gladly join them and help drive the British out of Canada.[7] How wrong they were!

American President James Madison declared war on Britain in June 1812. It was a war fought largely in the British colonies of North America and on the waters of the Great Lakes. The War of 1812 created a "tempest" in the vicinity of Wolfe Island. To the north were the British naval dockyards and garrison at Kingston, and to the south of the island were the substantial United States patrol at Cape Vincent and the naval base at Sackets Harbor. The following quote from "The Romance of Fort Frontenac" reveals the effect on area islands:

> Improvement in the defenses of Fort Frontenac and the town of Cataraqui were initiated late in 1812. Before the end of the following summer, trees and buildings were removed from the hills, heights, and islands overlooking the naval and military centres. Observation posts, known as signal telegraph stations, were established on Amherst, Snake, Simcoe, Wolfe, and Cedar Islands as well as Herchmer's Point and similar key positions on the mainland.[8]

This information brings to mind the Garrison House, as it has been known on Wolfe Island for many decades. It still stands, although much in need of repair, on the hilly shoreline between concessions Seventeen and Eighteen, overlooking Carleton Island and with an excellent view of the South Channel both to the east and west. As the architectural style of this limestone structure is totally out of character with other limestone buildings on Wolfe Island (it is elongated at both ends, barrack-like), it has been suggested that this may have been the original garrison or observation post built by the British at the time of the War of 1812. Records at Kingston's land office indicate that the British released this building and the Crown land on which it is situated in 1828. It was signed over firstly to King's College, Toronto (an entity on paper only until it was built in 1843), and then to the University of Toronto when King's College joined that institution in 1850. Seemingly, this property went through a few changes of ownership before George Woodman, an early Loyalist immigrant, was able to purchase it in 1861. The Crown and the Clergy Reserves Corporation also sold some of the lands to the Canada Company, a private land-development company incorporated in England in 1826. Further sales to settlers enabled these companies to realize profit.[9]

Although the United States' naval force used Wolfe Island as a screen when going up or downstream in the south channel, American citizens felt intimidated by the proximity of the island to Cape Vincent, only about a quarter of a mile away. Indeed, at the outbreak of war, the citizens of Cape Vincent fled inland, and shortly thereafter Commodore Isaac Chauncey wrote a letter to the secretary of state in Washington expressing his concern. He specifically noted that his squadron was frozen in the ice at Sackets Harbor, and that the enemy forces at Kingston were trained to walk with snowshoes and could easily cross the ice to Long Island (Wolfe Island) en route to Gravelly Point (Cape Vincent) and thence continue on to Chaumont Bay and Sackets Harbor. What Chauncey did not know was that, although all the soldiers at Kingston were trained in the use of snowshoes, there were not enough snowshoes to equip the entire force.

Although Wolfe Island's population was small, every able-bodied man was a member of the local militia

The Old Garrison House, currently owned by the Doyle family, sits on a hill by Concession Fourteen overlooking Carleton Island to the south as well as the American channel. The building was used by the British during the War of 1812 as a barracks and signal post. Photo circa 1975.

and was expected to defend his own holdings. However, two islanders signed up for active duty elsewhere — eighteen-year-olds Alvah Bennett and Thomas Davis. Bennett joined the Second Battalion of the Frontenac militia and Davis fought at Queenston Heights under General Isaac Brock. These young men were from two of the first Loyalist families to settle on Wolfe Island.

Early in the war a party of American soldiers invaded Wolfe Island. Native people who lived there and acted as lookouts for the British discovered the intruders and set up an ambush. A short skirmish ensued, leaving an American officer dead and sending the others back in quick retreat. During the summer of 1813, due to continued threats of an invasion in the Kingston area, a gunboat patrolled the wooded shores of Wolfe Island to guard against a potential invasion and reassure the loyal islanders of mainland support. No incidents occurred until later that fall.

The first took place on October 16, 1813, when a large flotilla of various sized vessels from schooners to bateaux set out after dark from Grenadier Island carrying seven thousand well-armed American soldiers.

Their mission was to capture Kingston, but they were defeated before they landed. Around midnight a storm of gale-force proportions accompanied by driving rain and sleet struck them unmercifully, swamping the ships. The following morning saw the mainland beaches and island shorelines strewn with wreckage. Fifteen larger vessels and several small boats were totally destroyed. To add to the disaster, several inexperienced pilots inadvertently took their vessels to shore on Wolfe Island for repairs, only to discover that they were in enemy territory. The wind continued to blow steadily for two days, leaving them stranded on enemy shores until they were rescued by the American schooner *Sylph* and taken to Cape Vincent.[10] A month later, seven American naval vessels fired on the British vessels and the batteries at Kingston during a twenty-four hour siege. The British were ultimately successful in fending off the enemy.[11]

Three deserters from the British forces in Kingston had made their way to Wolfe Island and, to satisfy their hunger, shot an ox. Alvah Bennett's younger brother was searching for their father's ox when he was captured by the deserters. They threatened to kill him if he did not lead them through the woods to the south shore. Apparently, the lad did some quick thinking, for after aimlessly leading them around, the deserters found themselves in a swamp (Black Pond) at the head of the island. The boy made a run for safety, leaving them to fend for themselves. Several days later one was shot, another was captured by Natives, and the third was never heard from again.[12]

According to R.M. Spankie's paper for the New York Historical Association, following the War of 1812, the *Kingston Gazette* carried the following notice:

Each soldier to receive one hundred acres of land; officers entitled in the first instance to 200; to receive provisions for themselves and families for one year, that is, those who had lost or require it on new land; implements of husbandry and tools to be supplied in sufficient quantities and other comforts according to necessity to cultivate the land, the land thus taken cannot be sold until after three years cultivation.

The above advertisement appeared on July 17, 1815, yet it was not until 1835, twenty years later, that Alvah Bennett would collect his one hundred acres of land. Possibly a combination of illiteracy and the lack of knowing how to communicate with the authorities stood between Alvah and a more timely receipt of his well-earned grant of land. At the conclusion of the war, he was paid his sixpence per day of service and his father received eighty dollars as recompense for the ox that had been shot by the deserters.

The ferry service from Point Alexandria to Cape Vincent, previously under lease to Samuel Hinckley, had been suspended during the War of 1812. Some time after the war's end, the ferry lease was again up for tender. Although there had been another competitor, the lease was reinstated with Samuel, due in large part to his previous experience and his loyalty to the Crown and Canada.

Skirmishes between the Americans and British occurred sporadically on Lake Ontario and down the St. Lawrence River as far as Prescott and the Crysler farm at Morrisburg, where Canadians were victorious. Both sides had suffered many casualties in the battles.

Settlers on Wolfe, Garden, and Simcoe, surrounded by gunboats and bateaux transporting infantry from both antagonists, must have lived in fear as the war continued around them. By 1814, many British troops were injected into the cause, forcing the Americans to retreat and, by 1815, after three treacherous years, war came to an end — a war that had been visible at times from Kingston and the Frontenac Islands, but never so much as scathed Wolfe Island.

The signing of the Treaty of Ghent in 1814 officially ended the War of 1812 (though skirmishes continued into 1815 as word of the treaty was slow to spread). Notwithstanding the determination of borders between the British and Americans on October 20, 1818, on-and-off boundary disputes over the status of Wolfe Island persisted during the next four or five years. The United States had assumed that the Holland Land Company[13] of New York State owned Wolfe Island. This particular dispute was ultimately settled in 1822 by trading this Grande Île for the Grande Île near Niagara. The latter, and other small islands near Cornwall, were ceded to the Americans. Carleton Island remained in American waters, with the international boundary being traced very close to Wolfe Island's south shores. Peace returned in 1815, during which period the latest private owners of Wolfe Island were in the process of securing their title to the land.

THE MACKENZIE REBELLION, 1837–1838

Part of the contention between the Family Compact and the Reformers stemmed from the former's power over some two million acres of the Clergy Reserves. This land, which, until 1825, could only be rented, was still standing dormant, separating communities, impeding the building of roads, and generally threatening the interests of the inhabitants and the general development of the province. "The existence of the Family Compact prevented the removal of this evil."[14]

The Reform Party, largely composed of sons and daughters of United Empire Loyalist refugees, grew out of their misery and frustrations concerning this situation. Their peaceful, but ineffective, revolt escalated into an open rebellion led by William Lyon Mackenzie[15] on December 7, 1837. The largely "farmer" rebels, many armed with only pitchforks, clashed in midtown York near John Montgomery's hotel, the rebel headquarters. Government forces burned the tavern and took prisoners, including Montgomery. Most of the rebels scattered, some to America where they were later pardoned and allowed to return home. The less fortunate in captivity were tried and some hanged for treason. Mackenzie and other rebel patriots also fled south of the border where, with some American assistance, they initiated turmoil at several border communities. He ultimately established headquarters in Watertown, New York, where he was able to muster arms and enthusiasm from the secret societies called Hunters' Lodges. They were dedicated to liberating Canada from British domination.[16]

Rebel prisoners from York were incarcerated at Fort Henry in Kingston. A volunteer company from Wolfe Island, under the command of a Captain Saunders, was placed on duty at Point Frederick to relieve experienced soldiers for duty at the front. While neither these volunteers nor the island residents were involved in actual fighting, the effects of war once again touched the island. The first recorded incident was on a Sunday night in May 1838. That evening a lengthy and violent thunderstorm struck the area, during which fifteen rebels, among them John Montgomery, the Toronto tavern-keeper who had been sentenced to death, made their escape. They tunnelled through a recently mortared four-foot wall of the fort and escaped via a subterranean passage. Thirteen of the group made good their escape to the United States after splitting into smaller groups.[17] One group of four located a rowboat, eluded the gunboat patrol, and landed on Wolfe Island where they soon perceived that they were unwelcome. The intruders evaded their pursuers and trekked across the island, carrying their boat to the south shore. Once in the water, they escaped to the American shore opposite Carleton Island and eventually to Watertown. John Montgomery, ultimately pardoned by Queen Victoria in 1843, returned to Toronto, set up another tavern on the original site, and lived to the age of ninety-six. Imagine the yarns he was able to spin during his latter years!

As the year wore on, Anglo-American tensions resulted in several border incidents with another American invasion appearing imminent. The mustering points opposite Wolfe Island were Cape Vincent and Watertown. The British at Kingston were speculating as to when and where the attack was going to take place — questions that may possibly have been answered had the Wolfe Island ferry not been detained by the Americans. The ferry (owned by Samuel Hinckley) was on its regular trip to Cape Vincent on a Sunday in November when it passed the steamer *United States* on its way downstream. The latter was unusually laden with male passengers and oversized packages of luggage — a dead giveaway that something was awry. To ensure that this news did not reach the Canadian mainland, the Americans detained the Hinckley ferry at Cape Vincent for some hours. By that time the *United States* had unloaded its passengers and cargo and the invasion was underway near Prescott. The passengers were members of the "Hunters' Lodge," and that landing initiated the historic Battle of Windmill Point. The British detachment sent from Kingston turned the tide on this bloody four-day siege. The surviving Americans, unable to retreat to the American shores, were captured along with their leader, Nils Von Schoultz — an American of Scandinavian heritage. In Kingston and the islands, the mood of foreboding gave way to the fervour of excitement on Friday, November 16, as the steamer *Brockville* sailed upstream to Kingston with the victors and the vanquished.

After the rebellion, the ongoing hostility between the Reformers and the Family Compact continued and led to a political crisis in Upper Canada. The Reformers, now supported by many prominent families, were still under the control of British colonial appointees, but they wanted more political power in the hands of the citizens. Lord Durham, sent from Britain as governor general from 1838, was aware of the issues blocking Canada's political progress. In his report he recommended limiting the clique's power and outlined the rationale for the Act of Union, which was proclaimed in 1841, uniting Upper and Lower Canada and creating the new province of Canada. By 1847, a form of self-government was in place.

PIRATE ON THE RIVER

During the Rebellion of 1837–38, one man became an enigma, known for his escapades along the St. Lawrence River. William "Bill" Johnston, a self-styled "Commodore of the Navy of the Canadian Republic," was surely more of a pirate than a naval officer. An islander, his exploits around Wolfe Island evoked both fear and respect from its residents. He was born at Trois-Rivières, Quebec, on February 1, 1782, and when he was two years old his family moved to Bath, Ontario, where Bill became a farmer and merchant.[18] He moved his business to Kingston, and, not satisfied with the profits of honest labour, turned to smuggling as a means of enhancing his income. From information shared with my father in the 1930s, it would appear that Johnston ran an illegal halfway house on Wolfe Island where he sold liquor to travellers who crossed the island. The property on which he had squatted was also a hideaway for his smuggling operations between Canada and the United States.

When the British authorities caught up with him, he was conscripted into the army at Kingston but conned his brother into taking his place. Shortly thereafter, his brother deserted and the British arrested Bill. The elusive Johnston escaped custody and went into hiding, whereupon the authorities confiscated the bulk of his goods and property. Irate at what he considered an injustice, Johnston moved to Sackets Harbor, bearing a grudge that would torment the British for some years to come.

Johnston went into action as a spy for the Americans when they declared war on the British in 1812. He and his buccaneers raided Canadian vessels and settlements along the St. Lawrence and robbed mails and military couriers on the adjacent roads.[19] At the conclusion of the war he settled at French Creek (Clayton, New York) and turned his attention back to smuggling and trading. The 1837 Rebellion gave him another excuse to return to piracy. He occupied a small island near the foot of Wolfe Island, which he named Fort Wallace, and continued his illicit activities from there.

Johnston was the most active in the year 1838. The then-fifty-six-year-old was strong, muscular, and agile, his massive frame striking fear into many. His "fleet" consisted of one twelve-oared boat, twenty-eight-feet long, capable of carrying twenty men, yet light enough to be carried by two men. Four sons and several Americans made up his "navy." They acted under the guise of Patriots but were in fact outlaws and criminals. Their exploits, though bold and daring, were typically of the hit-and-run variety to satisfy Johnston's personal revenge on the British. However, the nature of his raids at times also brought down the wrath of the Americans. When he was in trouble with the British, he hid on Devil's Oven or Whiskey Island in the United States, and, when in discord with the Americans, he hid on Hickory Island in Canada. All three islands were well-wooded and provided excellent cover.

By the time of the Rebellion, Wolfe Island had earned the title "Queen of the Thousand Islands" because of its beauty. Perhaps this inspired Johnston to boast that he would one day crown his beautiful pistol-packing daughter, Kate, "Queen of the Thousand Islands." Although Johnston's forays took him past Wolfe Island with frequency, he must have had fond memories of his earlier smuggling days there for he never attacked it.

In order to finance his escapades, Johnston raided and pillaged at will. One of his more dramatic antics was the capture and burning of the Canadian steamer *Sir Robert Peel* in the upper St. Lawrence River on May 29, 1838. Johnston had spotted the vessel docked at Wells (later called Wellesley) Island for fuelling. When the crew went ashore, Johnston, with a dozen Americans disguised as Natives, boarded. They awakened the sleeping passengers, ordered them ashore in their night attire, and moved the vessel downstream. There, he and his men plundered the possessions of the passengers and crew, stole the military payroll aboard the ship, and set the steamboat afire, allowing it to drift down the river.[20] A rescue ship, the *Oneida* arrived by dawn and conveyed the passengers and crew to Kingston. As a result of that episode, Governor General Durham offered a reward of one thousand dollars for information bringing conviction to any of the pirates, and the governor of New York offered five hundred dollars for the arrest of Johnston. His twelve men were apprehended shortly after this escapade and imprisoned for six months at Watertown, but once again, the wily Johnston eluded his captors.

Throughout June 1838 he plundered homes on Amherst and Main Duck islands and robbed the mails at Kingston. During a Fourth of July celebration at Fort Wallace that same year, parties of British and American soldiers made another attempt to capture Johnston and his cohorts, but were only able to seize two men. The captives and Johnston's boat were taken to Sackets Harbor.

Bill Johnston preferred to lead rather than to be led. At the Battle of Windmill Point on November 15, 1838, he departed early, leaving Nils Von Schoultz to his fate. But one of Johnston's men was captured and hanged publicly in Kingston. Johnston was finally apprehended by American troops and taken to Auburn for hearings, but in true character he escaped once again. He was recaptured at Rome and sentenced to one year in prison at Albany. After serving six months of the sentence he broke away and went into hiding until the heat was off, then made his way to Washington, where he presented a petition with supporting signatures for his pardon. President William Harrison granted Johnston a pardon in 1841.

Johnston returned to French Creek and a short time later was appointed keeper of the light on Rock Island, about four miles from Clayton, just off Fisher's Landing. He became a tavern keeper in Clayton, but local folklore indicates he continued to supplement his income with his first love — smuggling. While on his way to attend Rock Island one night, Johnston slipped and fell. He died at age eighty-eight, the victim of a fatal head injury.[21] At the time of his death in 1870, Johnston owned several islands in the St. Lawrence, three of which were named Ball, Shot, and Powder. Johnston's daughter, Kate, later married and lived a respectable life, and his son, John, became the president of the Exchange Bank of Clayton.

A plaque commemorating the notorious "Pirate Johnston," was erected in 1958 on the Bay Street dock in Gananoque by the Ontario Archaeological and Historic Sites Board. Annually, the town of Alexandria Bay, New York, enacts a "Pirate Invasion" complete with nineteenth-century pageantry. Bill Johnston and the era of pirates are gone, but not forgotten.

CARLETON ISLAND

Carleton Island lies snuggled in the south channel close to Wolfe Island with only the international boundary narrowly separating it from Canada. Earlier referred to as Buck or Deer Island, it was renamed by the British in honour of Sir Guy Carleton, governor from 1768–78 and 1786–91. This was the last French stronghold in Upper Canada, having been used in earlier years as a fur-trading post but latterly only as a stopover. After rousing British ire once again with the attack on Oswego, the French in 1757 stationed a guard of twelve men on the island in order to give warning of any approach of the enemy. August 27, 1758, was the fateful day when Colonel Bradstreet and three thousand troops, including Native warriors, proceeded from what was left of Oswego, rounded the head of Wolfe Island, and landed at and destroyed the French stronghold of Fort Frontenac.[22]

After the 1759 British victory in Quebec and the French retreat from the Kingston area, the inevitable happened. The British seized Carleton Island, where they built a fur-trading post and fortifications.[23] By 1771, the island had become a rendezvous for various Native allies to the British. The need to relocate their shipyards led the British to choose Carleton Island as opposed to Cataraqui. The island offered defence capabilities as well as the availability of wood for building. Other supplies were brought from Lachine by bateaux, and soon their shipbuilding was in full operation.[24]

Governor Haldimand, at British headquarters in Montreal, approved the construction of a fort on the island, which was subsequently named in his honour. Fort Haldimand was central to the marauding raids by the British and Natives against the Americans during the Revolutionary War.[25] The British military force on

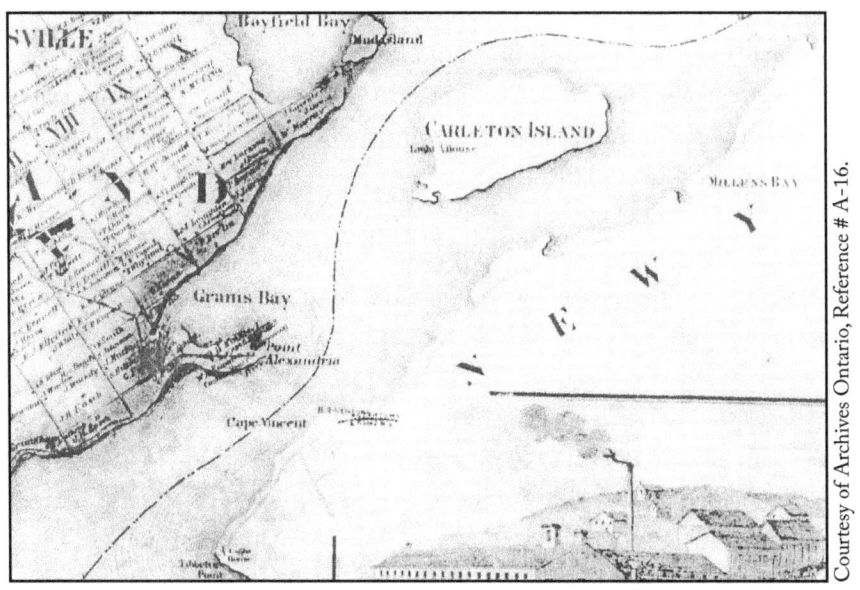

Map 6: A detail from the Walling Map 1860, showing Point Alexandria, Ontario; Cape Vincent, New York; Carleton Island, New York; and the International Boundary. Many United Empire Loyalists fleeing the United States found safety on Wolfe Island by crossing this narrow channel by scow or rowboat.

Courtesy of Archives Ontario, Reference # A-16.

the island in 1778 was known as the 84th or the Royal Highland Regiment.

Sir William Johnson, superintendent of Native Affairs in the province of New York, had "married" Molly Brant, a major leader in the Six Nations in 1759. A powerful and well-educated partner, Molly provided considerable assistance to Sir William's role in Anglo-Indian diplomacy. Johnson died in 1776, at which time Molly's function became much more significant with the outbreak of the American Revolution. Her fierce loyalty to the British Crown ensured assistance from Native allies, including the Iroquois, who believed that the Americans were a threat to their land and security. In 1779 she was forced to move from her estate in Mohawk County of upstate New York to Carleton Island, where she continued to exercise great influence on the Native warriors.[26]

Sir John Johnson, the son of Sir William Johnson by a previous marriage, commanded a detachment of the Royal Yorkers stationed at this garrison on Carleton. This was the period of time when Captain Grant and Lieutenant Langan, members of this detachment, forged the friendship that would eventually lead to their purchase of Wolfe Island. Molly Brant's brother, Joseph, a distinguished Mohawk leader well-known in Canadian history, was commissioned a captain in the British army by Governor Sir Guy Carleton. Joseph also held this position at Fort Haldimand during the Revolutionary War.[27]

Despite British promises, Native interests were not protected within the treaty of 1783 between the United States and Great Britain, when Native lands were divided between the two countries. Efforts made by the British to maintain their Native allies included compensating members of the Six Nations who were their faithful supporters during the war under the leadership of Joseph Brant. In 1783, Governor Haldimand arranged for land to be purchased from the Mississauga Nation and granted to the Mohawk and others of the Six Nations. The nations, who received this land grant, along both sides of the Grand River, in October 1784, comprised the Onondaga, Cayuga, Seneca, some Tuscarora, and Oneida.[28]

The previously established naval shipbuilding yard at Carleton Island presented a major threat to the Americans. The British fleet, operating on Lake Ontario out of Carleton Island during the War of 1812, was under the control of the Quartermaster Corps of the British army. This newly formed patrol, entitled the Provincial Marine, and its precedent, the French Squadron, were the forerunners of the present-day Canadian naval force.[29]

East of Cataraqui (Kingston) is the Barriefield Escarpment, which, in the 1800s, was a well-forested peninsula separating Haldimand and Hamilton bays. This peninsula points southward from the mainland. Over time the marshy lands had filled in, allowing the British to relocate their naval dockyards from Carleton Island to this location. Today, it is the site of Canada's Royal Military College, founded by the government of Alexander Mackenzie in 1870 on the site of Point Frederick, the former naval establishment.[30]

Around the 1890s, a man whose name seems to have been lost over time came to Wolfe Island from France, bringing a map of the area with him. He stated that a French payroll for Carleton Island was buried out around Button Bay. His attempt to locate the money, according to local lore, was unsuccessful.[31]

UNREST TO THE SOUTH

Concern around threats of invasions from the south continued during the course of Wolfe Island's rapid growth spurt throughout the period of 1812 to 1838. Despite the fact that Wolfe Island was vulnerable to attack, it was never fortified. Security was manifested by scouts, mostly Native, patrolling its shores, in addition to the British offshore gunboat. The actual fortifications for this area were arranged in a semicircle to the south of Kingston. The main installation was a stone wall that ran along Kingston Bay, west from Brock Street. New barracks were built to the east in 1824 and Fort Henry was erected during the period 1831–36. The Martello Towers were added in 1846. At this juncture, the island was mostly owned or leased, there being little Crown land remaining.

Wolfe Island's 1851 census lists the names of at least nineteen British soldiers living at the dwellings of the Dawsons, John Craine, D. Price, and Hiram Lathrop. The largest number, seven, were billeted at Spinning's hotel on the south shore.[32] The fact that the soldiers did not belong to island families, were mature men in their twenties and early thirties, and mostly lived in groups of three, would indicate that there was a specific reason for their presence. These men may have been outpost scouts charged with the responsibility of ensuring that Wolfe Island would not be victimized by a surprise American attack.

By 1861, when the island's population peaked, the United States was in the throes of its Civil War. Although the Americans were too busily engaged in fighting each other to attack Canada, new tensions and the issue of "skedaddlers" (draft dodgers) became problematic. Wolfe Island once more became caught up in the fray, but in a somewhat different role. Because both sides in the United States conflict were short on manpower, the Union of the North brought in a bill to draft males aged eighteen to thirty-five for a period of three years. One unusual exception was that a person could send a substitution in his stead. As substitutes were difficult to acquire, it was generally a case of their going to war or becoming draft dodgers. Records indicate that there were scores of the latter, and many made their way to Canada, some staying on Wolfe Island. The much larger exodus from Maine into New Brunswick gave rise to the Mapleton District of Carleton County becoming known as Skedaddler Ridge.[33]

Some wealthy Americans, desiring to have their sons exempted from war duty, paid Canadians to substitute for them in the Union Army. The go-between recruiter was called a "crimp." These brazen mercenaries, often in uniform, swaggered around Canadian border towns searching for young men and, using bribery or trickery, enticed them to enlist with the Union forces.[34] Many an intoxicated Kingston lad found himself across the border and a member of the Union army when he awoke.

According to island historian, Johnny O'Shea, islander "Dode" Briggs was also in on this ruse.[35] The monetary arrangement for substituting young Canadians was either a cash settlement to the parents or exchange for some cash and the labour of the wealthy American's son in the place of the Canadian's son. Duff Cosgrove, who moved to the island to begin a teaching career in 1902, told my father that he knew four or five Wolfe Island farmers who had actually received sums ranging from five to ten thousand dollars in exchange for their sons' service to the Union.[36] Such arrangements would have cleared the way for skedaddlers living with island families to return home to the United States. Seemingly to curb this practice, American and Canadian customs officers at Cape Vincent and Wolfe Island would exchange places on occasion. During the course of this war it was not unusual for Americans to come to Wolfe Island to buy horses and grain. They willingly paid one thousand dollars per horse and two to three dollars per bushel for barley or oats. In a small way, these transactions helped to boost the island's economy.[37]

FENIANS

Following the end of the American Civil War, there were mounting fears regarding Canada's ability to continue as a separate nation. A hostile American government was being urged from many quarters to invade Canada and incorporate it into a continent-wide United States. The unemployed Union Army, a well-seasoned fighting force, was desperately in need of work. Furthermore, the Fenians, a secret Irish revolutionary brotherhood established in 1858 for the purpose of freeing Ireland from British rule, were aiming to irritate the English by attacking Canada.[38]

The Fenians were no different than the Hunters' Lodge of 1837–38 or Bill Johnston's pirate gang. They were border bandits engaged in unauthorized warfare, despite their claims of wanting to wrest Canada from Britain and give it to the United States.

Noting that the threat of American invasion hung over Canada once again, the islanders rallied to the call by providing a company of fifty-five volunteers under Captain Shirley Going and Lieutenant George Murray. These men were posted at Kingston until the trouble passed. Every other able-bodied man on Wolfe, Garden, and Simcoe islands was part of the on-the-spot militia and expected to be prepared at any moment to defend their own with whatever they had. Moreover, the Garden Island naval brigade of forty-four men under the leadership of Captain H. Roney was primed to take to the water if necessary.[39]

The first Fenian raids into Canada occurred in June 1866, with the main attempts to capture Canada launched from Niagara and Buffalo. From that time on for the next four or five years there were sporadic raids along the Canadian border. During late summer of 1866, Fenians, intending to launch a surprise attack on the south shore of Wolfe Island while an annual party hosted by the Reverend Joseph Allen and family at Ardath Castle was in progress on the north shore, set sail from a point near Cape Vincent. Either someone learned of the intended attack or they were spotted by lookouts, because the approach of the Fenians was announced at the party. As word spread, every available island man raced on horseback, or by other means, to the south shore with guns at the ready. Needless to say, the Fenians withdrew when they saw the islanders lined along the shore ready to do battle.[40] If any good came of the Fenian efforts, most surely the feeling of nationalism among Canadians increased. Fear of invasion from the south was a unifying factor contributing to Confederation in 1867.[41]

BATTLE ON THE DOCK

The following incident, involving Wolfe Islanders, contained the components of war. There was a battle without a shot fired and it took place on the village dock around 1881. Three characters were involved in somewhat of an international confrontation.

Captain J.H. Radford, a Scot who had arrived on the island in 1852, lived up the Front Road in the Castle gatehouse. He was a real-estate speculator who owned 140 acres at Ferguson's (Livingstone's) Point, where he operated his vessels. Radford, albeit a marine captain, was also a military captain commanding No. 6 Company, 47th Battalion militia, and he took his job seriously. Edward Rousseau, a blacksmith who lived and had his shop on Victoria Street, was of French descent and not very keen on the British and royalty. On the day prior to the incident, Edward's son Peter had joined the militia for a three-year stint. The third participant in this event was Thomas Dawson, born on Wolfe Island and the son of John Dawson Sr., the proprietor of the Wolfe Island ferry and the Ferry Inn. Thomas, then forty years of age, had been reeve for seven years with the distinction of being the first to be elected by the people.

In 1878, Thomas was appointed sheriff of Frontenac County. Herein lay the difficulty. Captain Radford's mandate was to enlist islanders and maintain a company of militia on Wolfe Island — a task he found difficult. Apparently, he had encountered stiff opposition and Thomas Dawson had emerged as his strongest foe. The following is Captain Radford's account to the Honourable Oliver Mowat, attorney general of Ontario, of a serious confrontation on September 2, 1881, between himself and Sheriff Dawson:

> Yesterday, in my capacity as Captain of No. 6 Company 47th Battalion, I received as a recruit one Peter Rousseau over twenty-one years of age who took the oath of allegiance to Her Majesty and agreed to serve for the term of three years. I delivered to him a complete set of uniform clothing, a rifle, bayonet, belt, cross belt and haversack, all of which he took to his father's house where he was living. This morning, as I was going on the ferry boat to take passage for Kingston, his father Edward Rousseau, called me aside and after asking me why I had brought such disgrace upon him as to allow his son (who he declared to be of age) to join the volunteers, he told me I must at once dismiss his son from the service and come and get his uniform or he would burn it, rifle and all. I told him not to do so as I would have him punished severely. He then said he would pitch them out on the street as he would not allow them in his house. I again warned him not to do so and said I would have to take his son into camp and if any clothing was injured, he (the father) would have to pay for it and cautioned him of the danger of destroying the Queen's clothes. Whereupon,

Thomas Dawson, a magistrate, interfered and said he (Rousseau) had a perfect right to throw them into the street or anywhere else he wished, and that he the said Dawson, would not allow me to play any bluff game while he was around and he would back up Rousseau in what he might do. Considering that such conduct is prejudicial to the safety and well being of this country, I feel it my duty to lay this case before you, hence this statement.[42]

The outcome of that dispute is not known, but the account shows that the feelings for and against the military, in those days, were no different than today. Of course, Radford and Dawson were competitors for vessel cargo, and business animosity could have caused Dawson's open attacks on Radford's work in the militia.

BOOTLEGGERS, RUM-RUNNERS, AND SMUGGLERS

The attempt to control the distribution of spirits was a long, protracted venture. It began some three hundred years ago when Bishop Laval of Quebec tried, unsuccessfully, to have liquor excluded from the fur trade due to its corrosive effect on the Native peoples. The huge profits gained in trading alcohol with the Natives for fur pelts was much too compelling for the French to be dissuaded. Eventually, the marketing of liquor was available to anyone who wished a licence. The resultant abuse of spirits by 1860 had led to vehement objection by a growing number of temperance societies. Their goal was to moderate or eliminate the use of alcohol.[43]

Women's objections to the use of alcohol ultimately spawned the Prohibition League in Ontario in 1874 — a movement that continued to grow. The Ontario Temperance Act was passed in 1916, during the First World War, prohibiting both the sale and consumption of alcoholic beverages. The United States followed suit in 1919.[44] Rum-running from Canada to foreign ports was legitimate under this law, but smuggling it back for consumption in Canada was illegal. Merchants bypassed the law by opening sales offices and warehouses in Quebec. Ontario products were shipped to Quebec and sold back to Ontario buyers legally through the mails.[45]

Main Duck Island, which lies in Canadian waters of Lake Ontario due north of Oswego, New York, was bought from the federal government in 1905 by farmer and commercial fisherman Claude "King" Cole. This insular environment enabled him to haul large loads of booze to his island. Cole's cover as a farmer, but more importantly as a fishery entrepreneur, allowed him to earn a very substantial living. Several times weekly he hauled his catch to Cape Vincent for sale to Booth Fisheries. On his trips to Oswego or Syracuse in his large yacht, Cole was known to transfer crates of liquor, well-covered by loads of fresh fish.[46] Here was an expert smuggler, known far and wide in the territory; one who also helped many other fishermen achieve similar smuggling success.

By the end of the Second World War in 1918, total prohibition in Canada had ceased. However, the concerted efforts of prohibitionists succeeded in suspending the import of spirits into Ontario by July 1921.[47] The month of July, a year earlier, had seen the onset of prohibition in the United States. This opened a huge field of smuggling into the United States to all who were willing to risk their cargo and/or their lives. Within five years thousands were involved in the rum-running, and Main Duck Island was busier than ever as a stopover point for perpetrators attempting to outrun the American coastguard. Although Canadian schooners and steamers were off-loading whisky to smaller vessels (speedboats) on the coast between Boston and New York, the destination for most of the booze was within the Great Lakes due to the inordinate number of breweries and distilleries along the shoreline of Lake Ontario.[48]

What has all the above to do with Wolfe Island, one might ask? The answer lies in the fact that much of the Prohibition years, 1920–33, were a desperately hungry time because of the Great Depression. Farmers were poor and work was so scarce that moving contraband to the United States in rowing skiffs and speedboats became an exciting, as well as very profitable, way to augment income for many. Local rivermen (river pilots, commercial fishermen, and fishing guides) used their instinctive knowledge of the area waters to enter the dangerous game of rum-running. Many were seasoned mariners from Kingston and neighbouring islands.

Such was the case with Victor Sudds, an ex-fisherman from Simcoe Island. Sudds and his associates (largely family members) moved from Simcoe Island to operate out of Kingston, where he eventually teamed up with the notorious smuggler Bruce Lowery from Prince Edward County. A Syracuse bootlegger handled the purchase and distribution of booze, which the well-armed Sudds and Lowery transported in their contractor's thirty-five-foot speedboat *Blackjack*. This invincible pair ran booze mainly to Sackets Harbor and Oswego.[49] To avoid the law, Sudds' team camped out periodically on Main Duck Island. Victor Sudds achieved wealth and notoriety and was known for his generosity, but died from cancer shortly after the end of Prohibition in 1935.

All ages were involved in the illicit activities and other islanders cooperated by permitting storage of the liquor in their barns. Orville "Tricky" McDermott, then in his forties, was wily and inventive in his money-making schemes. One of the wisest and most experienced, he sometimes worked with fellow Wolfe Islander Norman Conley running whisky to the United States. Tricky was once caught by the Ontario Provincial Police on the Wolfe Island ferry while carrying fifty-three bottles of liquor. In spite of pleading not guilty, he was fined $172 or five months in jail.[50] Obviously, he chose freedom. Tricky also had the advantage of being an excellent swimmer — a skill that enabled him to evade capture on numerous occasions. Although most Wolfe Islanders were cognizant of who among friends were smuggling liquor to eke out a living, no one ever reported any misdoings to the authorities. Even priests remained neutral, neither condemning nor condoning the activity.

Wolfe Islander Norm Conley was a different story, however. He disliked school so intensely that his teachers gave up on him. His parents, similarly, could not discipline this free spirit. Norm was of the fifth generation of Conleys who had sailed from Ireland in 1826 to work on the canal near Oswego. They soon settled on Wolfe Island's Long Point.[51] Born in 1907, he was a teenager just in time to participate in rum-running during Prohibition. Well-versed in the wiles and skills of the fishing guide, as were his ancestors, Norm had an abundance of knowledge to apply to the illicit trade. While in his mid-teens he met, by coincidence, a Cleveland racketeer who had accidentally moored his boat on shoals just off the point. The man went by the nickname "Sinbad the Sailor." Conley was so impressed with the gangster's boat and revolver that he went to work for him.[52]

By the age of eighteen, Conley was driving thirty-five to forty cases of whisky per trip from Quebec to Kingston in his 1920 Dodge. Before long he had a Lincoln and continued to flourish in his chosen career. He transported the booze on the Wolfe Island ferry to the head of the island, then rowed his cargo across to Cape Vincent. From that point, Sinbad arranged for its shipment to Cleveland.[53] These transactions made Norm Conley a rich and respected smuggler, but suddenly and without notice, Sinbad disappeared.

Conley decided to go into business for himself along with a man from Syracuse and an American pilot. Their contraband was loaded onto a pontoon aircraft on Long Point then flown to Oneida Lake in New York.[54] His illustrious rum-running career ended when Prohibition ended; he was just twenty-three and one of the more colourful figures of the era — a smuggler who lost many loads and was shot at but never spent a day in jail.

Bootlegging and rum-running were at their apex when my father was working on Wolfe Island. He knew some of the people involved in this risky business, but never talked about it until much later. It was common knowledge across the island that some big names from Chicago participated in the action around Wolfe Island. The following is an extract from my father's original manuscript:

> Let me tell you of an experience I had one day in the autumn of 1930. At that

Captain Charles Wall wore the Church Army uniform during his tenure at Trinity Church from 1930–31. Although he doffed his cap for this portrait, perhaps there was a similarity to the provincial police uniform when he wore the cap.

Courtesy of C.H. Wall Collection 1930.

time, I was wearing the Church Army uniform complete with cap, which looked similar in colour and style to those then being worn by the Ontario Provincial Police. I had borrowed an old Chevrolet 490 from Howard Tarrant and was on my way to visit Charlie Gillespie at the Foot. As I turned off the Seventeenth Line, a gear in the differential snapped and I coasted to a stop at Volty Bamford's gate. Mr. Bamford came down his roadway to greet me and while we were discussing my predicament, a car sped up the roadway from the Foot and stopped opposite us. The driver, red in the face, perspiring heavily and puffing, jumped out of his car and told Bamford that someone had given him a message that Constable Club of the Provincial Police was on his way to the foot. And then, turning to me, he exclaimed "and it was only you." Upon our asking what the problem might have been, he exclaimed that his car had been full of bottled liquor stashed in potato bags and he had just dumped the whole lot in the river! He had been transporting the liquor for transshipment to the United States.

CHAPTER 8
Establishing Roots

Many of the Loyalist pioneers fled from estates with sizeable homes. Now they faced the daunting task of clearing the land, constructing a shelter, and beginning again. Families helped one another through community "bees" — a co-operative approach to accomplishing major jobs like barn-raisings while allowing for socializing. The work was usually followed by supper provided by the women.

Wolfe Island, covered in timber, provided an abundance of logs for the early dwellings. Larger log cabins measured approximately twenty by sixteen feet and were generally six logs in height with sloping roofs made of tree bark and held up by poles.[1] Those dwellings, hastily constructed for shelter during the early stages of clearing, were approximately half the dimension of the above cabins, and were called "shanties."

Shanty Creek, so named in pioneer days, is a silent reminder of the time when its shores were lined with shanties, their locations providing easy access to potable water. The source of the creek, now indiscernible in places, was the large inland pond in the region of Big Sandy Bay. The creek wound its way across the island in an easterly direction and eventually emptied into Bayfield Bay. In more recent years the creek has been known by different names in different places, but its full length and route, which crossed the Fifth Line about five times, can be seen on most early maps, including that of Wolfe Island in the *Meacham Atlas* of 1878.

In 1851, almost eighty percent of the dwellings on Wolfe Island were constructed of logs, shanty style. The balance consisted of nine limestone and approximately seventy frame houses. These buildings were home to 2,600 people, comprising 422 families. The 1851 census figures suggest an average of six plus people per dwelling, including family members, unwed adults, and in some cases, servants. Initially, blankets suspended from hooks served as privacy screens until improved means allowed for a larger home and saws were available to fashion conventional doors.[2]

Each house had a stone fireplace that served for both heating and cooking. Initially, a simple hole in the roof provided ventilation, but in time proper chimneys were installed. Windows were holes in the wall, covered in winter and during stormy weather with whatever was available. To get a measure of light during the daytime, some of the pioneers used shorn sheepskin that could be drawn taut across the opening. By the early 1800s, glass manufactured at Mallorytown, Ontario, was in great demand for windows. Until outbuildings could be constructed, tools, harvested produce, and seed for next year's planting were stored in the living quarters, sometimes shared with livestock.

The many crevices in these log houses were filled with a combination of wood, water, and limestone. Small pieces of limestone would be thrown into a large bonfire, and once the embers had cooled, the lime was gathered and stored in a dry location. When required, a paste of lime and water was prepared, which, when applied to the chinks, rendered them waterproof. This limestone paste was also used between stones in the fireplaces and chimneys and other locations where a more durable binder was needed.

Wolfe Islanders were soon in the lime kiln business. A kiln was set up just west of the limestone quarry on the main road at Barrett Bay, close to the source of the raw material. This commercial kiln, itself made of limestone, is believed to have been a batch-operated pot kiln constructed so that the ingredients would come into contact with the flames. The cup-shaped shaft is believed to have been five to ten feet wide and eight to ten feet deep. John George owned the property where the kiln was located. He lived at the southeast corner of Main Street (as it has been called for more than 150 years) on the Seventh Concession where he had plied his trade as a cobbler since settling on Wolfe Island in 1811. The remains of another commercial kiln are evident on the north shore of Ferguson's Point in the Seventh Concession, as shown on the 1869 Burleigh Fortification Survey Map. Some farmers, such as John Holliday on the Sixteenth Concession, maintained small kilns for their own use. Usually, these kilns were used only in the fall or early winter to produce sufficient lime for the season's needs.

The pioneers continuously sought to improve their living conditions and planked houses began to replace the log cabins. The new type of construction was more efficient, but the "planked house" was cold and drafty in winter. Homesteaders soon learned that an inside wall attached to the studding helped overcome some of the draftiness. Sawdust, economical and readily available from the local sawmill, was used for insulation, loosely stuffed between walls and above ceilings.

Survival in the wilderness was demanding. It was usual to rise at dawn and retire at sundown unless a little tallow could be spared to burn a wick in a shallow dish to provide some light. A few families had been able to bring a primitive lighting device when they emigrated. The early Scottish grease-burning cruse lamp had been developed in the early nineteenth century. James Berry, an early settler, had brought one from Scotland. Two ladles, the upper one spouted, formed the basic structure. A wick was placed in the bottom ladle and oil put in the top. The angle of the top ladle allowed the oil to gradually feed into the bottom one. These cruse lamps were double or single and equipped to hang on the wall for safety purposes. Elaine Berry, whose recently deceased husband was the great-great grandson of the original James Berry, permitted a detailed examination of its operation.[3]

Robert Hitchcock, born on Wolfe Island, invented the Hitchcock Lamp, a model of which is shown here. Robert used a clockwork mechanism and fan to force atomized fuel upward to the burning wick. It was the safest illuminating device of the time and was used on the noted Greely expedition to the Arctic in 1881.

By 1835 commercial candles were being sold. Kingston boasted no less than four candle factories in 1850 and the island stores were kept well-stocked. The kerosene lamp was about to make its debut.

Methods of lighting advanced at even a faster pace once Wolfe Islander Robert Hitchcock invented a lamp. The son of Loyalists Archibald Hitchcock and Mary Hinckley (Davis), he was born on October 20, 1832, at Hitchcock House, the inn built by his father. After living with his parents for his first sixteen years, Robert went to work as a jeweller and watchmaker in Watertown, New York.[4] While there he conceived the idea for this lamp and had it patented in 1868. The Hitchcock Lamp Company was incorporated on April 19, 1872, in Watertown with one hundred thousand dollars capital, the company's chief stockholder being Governor Roswell P. Flower. Hitchcock supervised the construction of the factory and machinery.[5] The steady glow produced in the chimneys of the Hitchcock lamps was achieved by a wind-up fan mechanism in the base. Animal, fish, or vegetable oils, less flammable than kerosene, were used and the fan forced air upwards, carrying the atomized fuel to be burned. This lamp was an instant success and soon could be found in homes, factories, railway cars, and ships throughout the world.

Edison had perfected the incandescent electric lamp by 1879, and electricity was available in Kingston a short time later. However, like many other more rural Ontario communities, Wolfe Islanders did not acquire electrical service until 1938. In the meantime many islanders purchased gasoline-powered generating equipment to supply energy for lamps in their homes.

FURNITURE

Although serviceable, the early bunks with tick bags stuffed with straw or leaves for mattresses and pillows were not very comfortable, and many settlers made more permanent ones by stuffing them with feathers and down. Most of the bedding was homemade from store-bought cloth or used cotton sugar or flour bags. After bleaching, a single bag would be stuffed to form a pillow, or four would be opened and sewn together to make a sheet. Recycling was a way of life, with sugar bags also being fashioned into table covers and aprons, and brown burlap bags made into horse blankets or doormats.

Many immigrants of the early 1800s brought furniture from their native country only to learn that much of it was impractical as the limited space in the cabin only allowed for bare essentials. Most pieces were rough-hewn from timber on the property, often crafted of split basswood if carpenters were available.[6] Shelves, fixed to walls, sufficed for bureaus, and beds were built into walls supported by poles. Benches invariably served as chairs in order to conserve space, and furniture not in use was, if feasible, suspended from pegs attached to the wall.

The pioneers brought a few practical utensils, mostly of iron, when they emigrated. The most popular were the bake kettle, frying pan, teakettle, and skillet, which could be used for cooking in an oven or over an open fire. Dishes brought from the Old World were supplemented with pottery from the local Mississauga. Other household items, such as brooms, baskets, hats, and axe handles, were also obtained from the enterprising Natives. The British government provided hammers, saws, basic farm implements, and seeds gratis to Loyalist homesteaders, enabling them to get crops started.[7]

Garbage disposal was not an issue. The kitchen scraps and waste were fed to the pigs and chickens, or buried to enrich the soil. Waste fats were used to make soap, and dripping from roasts was spread on bread. Wood ashes from the fireplace and stoves were leached for soap making or sprinkled on the land for fertilizer. Worn clothing and cloth scraps were used to make quilts and carpets. Nothing was wasted. Mabel Eves, in discussion with my father, recalled how her parents saved wood ashes in a barrel or similar container and ran water through the ashes to make lye. The liquid was retrieved, brought to a boil, and waste fat was added to make soft soap.[8] With the necessity of daily recycling as practised by the pioneers, the land remained fairly pristine. Now, in the infancy of the twenty-first century, we are reaping the havoc created by a "disposable" way of life built up over many decades.

FOOD

The dream of every pioneer was to own livestock. No one was deprived of meat. The island abounded in deer, rabbit, squirrel, beaver, muskrat, bear, and a variety of wild fowl and birds was also available for food. The pioneers enjoyed beaver meat in particular as it tasted similar to wild duck and could be fried, roasted, or stewed. As late as 1974, beaver meat could be purchased at Murphy's Lake (Murphy's Seafoods in Kingston), where connoisseurs could obtain excellent fish and swap choice fish stories.

At times the hunt for food was turned into a sporting event. This was the case on May 4, 1827, when the islanders organized a "squerl" hunt. There were twelve men to a side, with Jeremiah Orser acting as captain for Simcoe Island and Nicholas Mosier captain for Long Island (Wolfe Island). The Simcoe Island team won with a total of 1,045 squirrels killed.[9] This was not a pointless slaughter, as the meat was used for food. Squirrels, especially the black ones, were eaten roasted, stewed, or baked in pies. Partridge, quail, ducks, and geese were in abundance, in addition to wild turkeys and passenger pigeons. These pigeons, native to the North American continent, far outnumbered all the other species. During their spring and fall migrations, they were so numerous that they "blackened the sky and could be knocked down with a pole," as Sheriff Justus Sherwood observed in his memoirs.[10]

The beautiful passenger pigeon was adorned with a bright dark-blue head, back, wings, and tail, and a bright, wine-red breast. Its tail was long and its overall length was about seventeen inches. Silent in flight, it could travel at a speed of sixty miles per hour. The abundance of nut trees on Wolfe Island attracted these birds — nuts were a staple in their diet, adding a special sweetness to their flesh, and enhancing the flavour whether roasted or in pot pies. Passenger pigeons had commercial value and were sold at the market in Kingston and in surrounding towns. However, the slaughter of these birds, from 1858 to 1875, was so uncontrolled that the passenger pigeon became virtually extinct by 1880. The last authenticated nesting on the continent was near Kingston in 1898.

The feathers of fowl were a bonus and seldom thrown away as they were ideal for stuffing pillows and mattresses. Sleeping on a down-filled mattress was one of the few luxuries of pioneer living. The following excerpt describes an experience my father recorded in his manuscript:

> I shall never forget the few occasions that I had while staying overnight at the old Montgomery homestead on the Sixteenth Concession. John Montgomery, a staunch churchgoing pioneer had settled at the Foot and had long since passed away but his daughter, Edith, was carrying on in true pioneer tradition. She was a kind, gentle person who, though never married, was very motherly. When I knew her in 1930 she was aging, but was young at heart. To every incumbent of the Anglican Church she was "Aunt Eadie" because of her warm welcome, summer and winter. When one could not return to the village because of nasty weather, the guest room was made available. What a treat for a twentieth-century city slicker! The bed was a four-poster and the mattress was a beautifully homemade, hand-sewn, down-filled creation that literally gobbled me up when I lay on it. A down-filled pillow and a homemade comforter, also padded with down, made me feel as though I were sleeping with the angels!

Fish was an alternative to meat and fowl. Rock and black bass were in abundance near the shore and muskellunge in deeper waters. Eels were plentiful and the Native people taught the islanders how to smoke the delicacy immediately after the catch to preserve it for future consumption. Atlantic salmon were the prized catch and, until 1840, were still plentiful in all the waters surrounding Wolfe Island. In winter, the pioneers fished through holes cut in the ice.

The natural surroundings provided the early settlers with a variety of desserts and snacks in the form of berries, nuts, and maple syrup. The "berryin'" season was ushered in by wild strawberries when all one wanted could be had for the "pickin'." Wild raspberries in greater excess, followed by black caps (blackberries) that were fewer in number but more popular because of their delicate sweetness and preserving qualities. Cranberries were still being gathered as late as 1875 near Reeds Bay and in the marsh area around Black Lake (Black Pond), as well as other marsh areas on the island. There were great quantities of plums and, for the settler who made his own liquid refreshment, there were chokecherries and wild grapes.

Hickory, butternut, beechnut, and black walnut trees were spread over most of the island with a large concentration of hickory trees in the vicinity of the Old Castle and a group of beechnut trees in the Spook Hill area near Holliday Point. Hickory trees and the butternut that was at times called the white walnut, or oil nut, existed in quantity until about 1900. The butternut cake, a favourite dessert, was plain but so tasty that it did not require fruit to complement.

The Mississauga, who were still coming to Wolfe Island in 1825, taught the islanders how to make several maple products: syrup, sugar, butter, and maple vinegar. It is said they had developed a method of producing a refined sparkling white maple sugar they sold to the pioneers for use as a sweetener. Sugar was also made from the sap of the black walnut trees, and though tasty, was not popular with the pioneers.

WATER SUPPLY

Water wells were practically non-existent, but there was no scarcity of water as the river ran fresh and clear. A water yoke enabled the carrier to transport the water hands-free. Islanders recall water yokes being employed as late as the early 1900s. In winter, water was hauled through holes in the ice. Blocks of ice covered with sawdust were stored in specially constructed sheds to help preserve perishables in summer, a practice that continued into the 1920s. In time, wells were dug for water but with varying success. In more recent years, Dan Lacey, a retired Wolfe Island farmer, used a dowser (divining rod) to avoid unnecessary digging. His instrument was a forked branch, usually from an apple, willow, or peach tree, which, when held over the ground, would move if there were water below.

CLOTHING

Initially, the pioneer settlers had to make do with the clothing brought from their native land. In exchange for furs, shawls, and similar items could be obtained from the Native women, who also shared their expertise in sewing clothing from the more durable deer skin.

Although moccasins were not popular with the newcomers, the pioneers did adopt the snowshoe, a boon for travelling through the winter wilderness.

Vests and similar clothing for men and women were often made from burlap and raw wool. The burlap could be a used feedbag and the raw wool required no spinning or weaving. Once the burlap had been cut to the size desired and sewn to shape, the edges were secured to avoid unravelling. Wool that had been lightly washed was pulled and rolled evenly by hand to form ten- or twelve-inch lengths, ready to be pulled through the burlap with a hook similar to a crochet hook. The method was similar to rug hooking except that the wool tufts were spaced four or five holes apart to allow room for settling. Such vests, usually sleeveless and worn in cooler weather, were wind- and water-resistant if a minimum of lanolin had been removed during the washing of the wool. Clothing could be purchased in Kingston, by those who could afford to do so.

WEAVING

Though originally a means of providing clothes and other necessities for the family, weaving became a way of earning income that flourished until 1870. Wolfe Islanders primarily used flax for weaving. With a great number of sheep being raised locally, wool was also plentiful. The raw product was spun into yarn to ready it for weaving. Linens and woollen carpets were produced, but the two main products were fulled cloth and flannel. Fulling was a process of shrinking and thickening of wool, accomplished by dancing on the wool that had previously been placed in water. The resultant wool was rendered more windproof.[11] The 1851 census indicates a prolific output of woven materials such as flannels, fulled cloth, and linen, with special credit given to the Weir McCrae family, Robert Gillespie Sr., and Demetrius Spinning.

Mary and Robert Gillespie Sr. emigrated from Ireland in 1838 with their two sons, Robert and Andrew. They lived in a log house on the Old Survey, where Robert Sr. and Andrew plied their craft as weavers. Andrew had brought a shuttle from Ireland, with which he wove woollen blankets for sale. This same shuttle was later owned by Mrs. Rodney Pyke (Mary), a relative of the Gillespies. She inherited the shuttle and for many years was known for her weaving expertise.

Laurinda Whitmore and her daughter, Mina, were weavers who lived on the Thirteenth Concession circa 1875. Their specialties were woollen carpets and woollen cloth for dresses and clothing. Working in their own home, they would sell from the premises. Other known weavers, from 1850 to 1875, were Sarah Ann Baldwin, Perthinea Sherman, Susan Buckley, Marianne Berry, and Ellen Flynn, the daughter of Foot resident Michael Flynn.

Another home enterprise closely related to weaving was the making of rugs and carpets from old clothing cut into strips. Mary Quigley, born in Ireland, was brought to Kingston in 1847 at the age of three by her parents, Mr. and Mrs. Patrick Quigley. After they moved to Wolfe Island in 1853 and settled along Reeds Creek, Mary developed a fine talent for weaving carpets on the loom. If the colour of the strip cut from old clothing was not suitable for her pattern she would dye the cloth accordingly. The products of her craft were so beautiful that people often bought them as gifts for weddings.[12] A spinster, Mary died in 1939 at the age of ninety-five.

OTHER CHALLENGES

As time progressed the settlers increased their earning power by adding cows, sheep, and pigs to their holdings, which enabled them to pay their rent or mortgage. So successful were these early pioneers that, by 1850, the island boasted nearly 1,000 dairy cows, almost 2,000 sheep, 1,200 pigs and 600 horses. The islanders were producing about 45,000 pounds of butter, 12,000 pounds of cheese, 5,500 pounds of wool, 600 pounds of maple sugar, 200 barrels of beef, and 650 barrels of pork per year.[13] Produce not required for home consumption was sold in Kingston and Cape Vincent, a practice that continues to a smaller degree today. Garden Island also created a ready market for much of Wolfe Island's produce once the shipbuilding company was in operation.

In addition to filling the ice house, the winter-work program for most pioneers consisted of hunting and trapping the plentiful rabbit, fox, mink, muskrat, beaver, and bear. There were so many foxes on the island in the early 1800s that one map-maker designated the island's name as "Fox Island." As time passed they were killed off for their fur, and although the fox population did increase from time to time, they did not cause concern until the early 1950s. During that era they were so numerous that the township council offered a bounty of three dollars per fox. The pelts were delivered to the clerk with an affidavit certifying that the animal had been killed in the township within the stipulated five days from the date of the bylaw (January 14, 1952). Fifty-eight fox pelts were recorded that year. Many more islanders were paid the bounty the following year.

Mink were plentiful at the foot of the island until 1875. Bears were killed for fur and in times of necessity their meat provided food. Most of the furs were sold or traded with the Natives. From the earliest days, wolves were a menace for sheep farmers. By 1837 the animal had caused such havoc that the islanders organized hunting parties to eradicate them. Armed with shotguns, muskets, and noisemakers, the hunters would spread across the island until they reached Big Bay. Ultimately, the wolves disappeared.[14] There is no record of any having been seen on Wolfe Island in recent times, although there are coyote sightings.

LONGEVITY

The general practice among Wolfe Island pioneers was for close neighbours to help one another, and pioneer activity required boys to work along with the men. One such boy was John McGlynn, who was born in 1852 on Wolfe Island. His father, Patrick, had settled on the Seventh Concession about 1850. John learned the rigours of pioneering from his earliest days and by the age of sixteen was a skilled ploughman who had won first prize in a match on his father's farm. As the years passed his ploughmanship was such that, in 1925, at the age of seventy-three, John won two silver cups and eight special prizes at the Frontenac County Ploughing Match. The Township of Wolfe Island presented him with an award at a banquet held in his honour. A member of the township council for several years, he died at the age of eighty-nine in 1940.

Several decades ago my father acquired an interesting list of names of settlers and native-born islanders. The list, assumed to be complete, contains the ages at death of those who lived on the island all of their lives and died during the years 1937–39. The average age at death was seventy-eight, two living to be ninety-five. The figures, well beyond the national average at the time, indicate the longevity of Wolfe Islanders. Considering the heritage and different inherent family tendencies, it would appear that Wolfe Island's air, soil, and general living conditions contributed to those long lifespans. Perhaps one of the best testimonies to longevity on Wolfe Island was Elsie Keyes, for many years the matriarch of the current Keyes family. She lived until shortly after her 107th birthday, remaining incredibly lucid and with a prodigious memory. A few weeks before she died in 2004, Elsie assured me that hard work was the secret to longevity!

CHAPTER 9
Early Industries and Livelihoods

Timber and limestone presented early Wolfe Island settlers with resources for at least two major industries. Although the fur trade began to diminish around the Great Lakes after the merger of the North West Company with the Hudson's Bay Company in 1821, the economic shortfall was offset by the rapid growth of the timber trade. One of the finest examples was the Calvin timber and shipbuilding enterprise on Garden Island.

FORESTRY

By 1806, during the Napoleonic Wars, all Baltic ports were closed to English trade, causing the British to look to the New World for timber.[1] Locally, the virgin forests of Wolfe and neighbouring islands were dense with old-growth trees, some of enormous girth. Timber, as a basic national commodity, produced more revenue than the fish and fur trades combined.

The timber and stone quarrying industries were closely allied as land had to be cleared to access the limestone. Settlers would fell trees and sell the timber to acquire farm tools, seeds, and livestock. The timber trade was the primary industry driving Wolfe Island's economy between 1840 and 1873. Many of the Highlanders from the Scottish Settlement were involved, even to the extent of building and operating their own sawmills near the shore at the Twelfth Concession. Daniel Cook's steam-driven sawmill on Wolfe Island was located on Reeds Creek in the Fifth Concession at the head of the island. It boasted of three employees, and could turn out an average of three thousand linear feet per day. After 1873, timber as a business or source of income slowly declined as the supply of trees diminished.

The Calvin Company on Garden Island was the first commercial enterprise to remove timber from Wolfe

Island. Initially, most of the timber was square-cut and held in booms in Garden Island's back bay until it was lashed together into rafts to be moved down the St. Lawrence River. Timber from the northern half of Wolfe Island was delivered to the shore and floated across the water or delivered over ice in winter. Timber from the southern half was delivered overland and floated to Oak Point or to the Calvin shipyard at the foot of the island. Wood rafted from Oak Point was mostly oak and elm, much prized in the European building trade. By 1850, most was being sawn into three-inch planks.

The Garden Island operation was also a ready market for cordwood fuel, delivered over the winter ice from Wolfe Island. Rathbun and Company[2] of Deseronto, Ontario, operated a lumberyard in the village of Marysville on the river side of the main street, halfway between St. Lawrence and Cross streets. Around 1900, this business was referred to as "Allinson's." At that time, W.L. Allinson was the yard manager. When Ken Keyes, a retired educator and politician born on Wolfe Island, bought the house and office building on this site several years ago, he did extensive work on the interior and, to his surprise, he found Rathbun work orders and sales receipts in the walls.

By 1847, the economy had slowed and timber sales were falling off at Quebec, seriously affecting production at both Garden and Wolfe islands. Later, the depression that affected Europe in 1873 virtually decimated Canada's international trade, and exports were depressed well into the 1890s.

This former Rathbun Lumber Company site was sold to Vincent Greenwood in the 1890s. Just prior to this photo being taken in 1991, the boathouse collapsed, but the Greenwood garage remained standing. The entire property was later sold to and restored by Ken Keyes. The water, between the former wharf and the tiny isle, was deep enough for early steamers to moor. Note glacial striae in the foreground. Photo 1991.

Courtesy of Mable (Greenwood) McRae.

LIMESTONE QUARRYING

The outstanding quality of Wolfe Island's limestone made it a sought-after commodity for building the Welland and Rideau canals. As much of it was found lying horizontally near the surface along the north shore, it was economical to quarry and readily accessible to water transportation. Alexander Mackenzie, an accomplished Scottish stonemason worked on some major contracts in the Kingston area. In 1843, with his own team of stonemasons, he built an explosive-proof arch as a memorial to the fallen that still stands today at Fort Henry. At a later date he dressed the limestone on the front doors of St. Mary's Cathedral in Kingston. Mackenzie, a Baptist openly opposed to Strachan and the Clergy Reserves system, would periodically find that his craftsmanship had been defaced.[3]

Mackenzie's experience in constructing locks along the Lachine Canal led to his being made foreman in charge of enlarging the Welland Canal in 1845. As Wolfe Island limestone had been chosen for the contract, Mackenzie returned there for the winter of 1844 to superintend the extraction of limestone for use the following summer. This must have been a pleasant winter for Alexander as he is recorded as courting a young lady of Wolfe Island.[4] He later took on more work at Fort Henry and the Martello Towers at Kingston.[5]

Mackenzie's liberal, progressive political leaning had inspired Reformers, and resulted in his election to the Legislative Assembly in 1861. With the establishment of the Dominion of Canada in 1867, he was elected to the first House of Commons and became Canada's first Liberal prime minister after the fall of John A. Macdonald's Conservative government in 1878. Mackenzie retained his seat in Parliament until his death in 1892. He took great interest in military matters and was instrumental in establishing the Royal Military College. His aim was to educate young men to be officers competent in training volunteer forces as required to protect the country.[6]

During the construction of the Rideau Canal (completed in 1832), many islanders worked on scows transporting the stone and the stonemasons. Not surprisingly, new settlers were enticed to Wolfe Island throughout this period. In addition to providing stone for large buildings, the fine texture of the island's limestone made it desirable for lintels, sills, caps, and mouldings, all of which were fashioned by artisans on the island. Wolfe Island limestone was also used for the tower of St. Mary's Cathedral in Kingston, Fern's Point Lock, piers and abutments of Kingston Mills, the Grand Trunk Railway bridges, and heavy base courses on several public buildings.

Stone from the Davis Quarry, located along the northwestern shoreline at the Head, was used to build the Kingston shipyard and line the dry dock, and was also used in the construction of the Kingston Penitentiary. Buildings of major historic note on Wolfe Island, fashioned from locally quarried limestone, include Trinity Anglican Church, Longueuil (Ardath) Castle, Areson House, Sacred Heart Catholic Church, the Town Hall, Hitchcock House, Christ Church (Anglican), and the Keyes' schoolhouse. Remnants of the historic wharf from which this stone was shipped are still evident in the water in front of Edward and Gail Kenney's property on lot 25 of the Old Survey.

Will Dignem at Breakey's Bay ran a large stone quarry on the east side of the bay. As a stonecutter, he also worked in the Calvin shipyard at the foot of the island. In 1862, stone drawn from this quarry was used in the construction of Christ Church on the Fifteenth Concession at the foot of the island. Dignem's limestone was also used to line Farrow's Point Lock, one of many locks that disappeared with the opening of the St. Lawrence Seaway in 1959. The Breakey quarry was reopened in the 1930s by the MacFarland Company of Kingston for the extraction of crushed stone used to construct island roads. At its peak, limestone quarrying also supported the creation of jobs in other occupations, since boats, scows, and wharves had to be built and operated to accommodate the stone trade. A combination of work in the mining and timber trades caused Wolfe Island's population to peak at 3,601 in the 1861 census.

In 1921, George McDonell's limestone quarry in the Eleventh Concession was productive enough to be listed in the statistical review of the National Department of Mines. Quarries were open-pit mining with all the work being performed by hand with the assistance of a steam-engine crusher. According to Captain R.F. Fawcett, Paddy McDermott was one of the many men who drew stone for McDonell. In time, the combination of increased use of poured-concrete foundations for buildings, the use of steel for lintels and girders, and the general use of bricks for buildings and permanent dwellings led to the decline of stone quarrying and the exodus of Scottish and French artisans from the island.

Wolfe Island, however, is still rich in quality limestone. Quarries presently in use are the Greenwood Quarry (formerly the Lambert Quarry), just west of the village, and

The village (Greenwood's) quarry behind Lambert's Hill is still active. Photo 1973.

Courtesy of C.H. Wall collection.

that of the former Vincent Alarie, purchased by McKendry Quarries of Kingston in 2000. Surveys indicate these two quarries will be productive for many years.

SAND-GRAVEL PITS

Two pits located on the south shore near the end of the Sixth and Seventh concessions have been productive for almost as long as these properties have been owned. Another is located about one-half mile west of Port Metcalfe. The gravel sections are more of a sand-gravel combination, the gravel being finely grained, a mixture proven to be ideal for sanding the island roads in winter.

John A. Busch was the first pioneer to own the south shoreline lots, replete with sandpits. According to a descendant of William Stevenson, the second owner of this 360-acre farm and a Scot born in Ireland, he farmed this land and made good use of the sand. The soil was ideal for growing asparagus and strawberries, and the pit afforded him extra income. He would dig and haul sand to Cape Vincent, over the ice by horse and sleigh in the winter or by scow during the summer, where it was used in road construction. William was busy at these operations in the early to mid-1800s when he and his wife Margaret were raising their children, Eliza and Andrew Craig, in the 1840s. He subdivided the farm into two lots: one that became known as the Russell farm (Eliza's married name) and the other for his son Craig. This combined area became known as the Craig-Russell farms. A descendant, Donalda Parkes, stated that when her great-grandfather Andrew Craig died, her grandfather Clifford Andrew had to take over his parents' farm at the age of thirteen with assistance from his uncle.[7]

The Pyke family had settled on Wolfe Island by 1850, and, according to the 1851 census, owned lots adjacent to the Stevenson farms. Their shoreline lot was also blessed with a sandpit and, before long, grandsons of Grant and Dexter Pyke were hauling sand over to Cape Vincent. They created a "trolley cart on track" system to move the sand to the shore, then empty the load directly into their barge. In the late 1800s, Grant was contracted by New York State to deliver his sand to Cape Vincent, much of which was used to build the concrete road between the Cape and Watertown. Grant went on to other ventures when his son George H. took over the farm. By 1954, he had bought the Stevenson 360 acres. Descendants of William Stevenson still live on Wolfe Island.

FISHING

Initially, fishing was an essential to the pioneers' food supply, but as Wolfe Island's population grew, it evolved into a profitable mainstay. By 1865, several islanders were listed as fishermen, many of whom in earlier years had been enumerated as farmers or tradesmen. Among many reasons for this shift — including the depression of 1857 and the decline in the timber and quarry industries — was the ever-increasing market for fish in Kingston.

A petition from freeholders and inhabitants of Wolfe Island addressed to Sir Francis Bond Head, the lieutenant-governor, dated July 25, 1836, indicates a fairly well-organized fishing industry on the island:

That your Petitioners are all natural British Subjects on the said island, the majority of whom served in the Army, Navy and Militia during the last war. That they all for many years prosecuted the Salmon and other Fisheries in Lake Ontario in the neighbourhood of Kingston and have erected Houses and other Conveniences for the Salmon Fishery on Pigeon Island a barren rock of about Four Acres totally unfit for cultivation situated about Fifteen Miles South West of Kingston and about Five miles from Long Point, on the South Westerly End of Wolfe Island. That your Petitioners are desirous for their mutual benefit, as well as that of the other British Subjects engaged in the Fishery in the neighbourhood that the same Privileges they have hitherto enjoyed on the same island might be preserved to them.[8]

This petition was to offset an earlier one presented by James Eccles who had settled on Horseshoe Island about 1833. The island, shaped as its name suggests, lies just off the northeasterly tip of Wolfe Island. Eccles, although not personally involved, knew that Wolfe Island fishermen, after making a catch on the lake, landed, cleaned, and cured their fish on nearby Pigeon Island. In an attempt to capitalize on a good business opportunity, he submitted a petition requesting that Pigeon Island be sold or leased to him, thus enabling him to collect a docking fee from all fishermen using Pigeon Island.

The Wolfe Island fishermen, aware of the purpose of Eccles' petition, submitted their own counter petition asking that the land be granted or leased to them. They pointed out that James Eccles had only been settled in the neighbourhood for about three years, while they had been landing their catch on Pigeon Island since time immemorial. These fishermen also drew attention to the fact that Eccles had no investment in the island, but they had erected houses and other conveniences for the salmon fishery. Eccles had offered to erect a wharf for the purpose of creating a small harbour in which to secure the boats against bad weather. The fishermen countered this proposal by saying it had been attempted in the past and was not feasible as waves broke completely over the island during violent storms. From their perspective, Eccles intended to make all fishermen pay annual tribute for their privilege of landing or curing their fish, a monopoly that they felt would ruin their trade and prejudice the general public.

Thirty-three Wolfe Island fishermen, some of the more prominent surnames being Davis, Busch, Hoover, Barrett, McDonell, Chisholm, Lambert, Horne, McRae, Staley, Mosier, Hopson, and Archibald Hitchcock, signed this counter petition. They had the support of seven eminent Kingstonians whose names accompanied their petition with a recommendation and their signatures: W. Macaulay; Thomas Markland, J.P.; J. MacFarlane, J.P.; David John Smith; A. Manaling, J.P.; H. Cassidy; and W. Gildersleeve.

On August 25, 1836, the executive council recommended that no action be taken on either petition. The fishermen continued to use Pigeon Island, and James

Commercial fishermen are cleaning the day's catch on Pigeon Island, circa 1920s. The man to the right is Jim Davis.

Eccles' reputation and prestige did not appear to have been damaged, since he later became a councilman and subsequently, in 1864, deputy reeve.

From the earliest times, Kingston provided a ready market for island fishermen, and, by 1840, the popular partners Henry Smith and Cecil Nichol, along with other islanders, were transporting their catch to Kingston on a twice-weekly basis. The fish market was located on the shoreline at the foot of Brock Street, where customers came directly to the fishermen, whose twenty to thirty boats were drawn up on the shore. The usual price for a twelve- to fifteen-pound salmon was twenty-five cents. By the 1850s, government regulations forced the fishmongers to conduct business within set boundaries of the general Kingston market area, where, it has been said, a good day might see over two hundred farmers' teams serving customers. Transferring the fish trimmings and accompanying stench uptown caused much consternation.

Further regulations, coupled with the growth of large commercial fisheries, brought about a change in the industry that benefited the island fishermen. Their entire catch could be sold at one time to such firms as Booth Fisheries, who not only retailed the fish through their Kingston store, but also packed and shipped to other centres. Around the early 1900s, John H. Davis, the lighthouse keeper for Pigeon Island, ran a large fishing operation. His employees fished for salmon in-season and sold their catch to Booth Fisheries in Kingston and Cape Vincent. Allan and Clarence Davis carried on this business until fish quantities began to shrink some thirty to forty years later. The three Belyea brothers, Fred, John, and Bert, who operated out of Simcoe Island in the 1920s and

30s, were among the last to engage in commercial fishing in this region.

Fishing evolved into a sport during the past century as the quantity and quality of fish diminished, decimating commercial fishing. Fishing for bass, pickerel, and lake trout with a guide became popular. However, the guiding enterprise dwindled once the waters became infected with sea lamprey, toxins and alien scavenger fish discharged in the ballast from cargo ships.

CHEESE FACTORIES

The Wolfe Island Cheese Factory[9] was the first to be established on the island. In 1865, while on a visit to Theresa, New York, islander Truman S. Bennett witnessed the production of cheese and decided to try his hand at it when he returned home. From his first trial run in 1866 sprang one of Wolfe Island's most important export products. Although it has been asserted that the Ingersoll Cheese Factory in Oxford County was established at approximately the same time, the Wolfe Island factory was the first in Ontario to produce cheddar cheese. Bennett financed his cheese operation by offering share subscriptions. The factory was strategically located on the west side of the Sixth Line Road (Highway 95), placing him primarily in a location with an excellent water supply, in the midst of several dairy farms, and on the main north-south road with a ferry available at each shore to take his products to Kingston and Cape Vincent.

Between 1870 and 1880 the American Republican government introduced high tariffs on goods entering the United States. This and other factors led to a serious depression on both sides of the border. Wolfe Island's population decreased significantly and Bennett's cheese factory was forced to close. Eventually, Coleman Hinckley bought and relocated this factory to the other side of the road and re-established the business. According to island historian Johnny O'Shea, Hugh Horne, a local farmer, bought the outstanding shares and asked Johnny's father, who at the time was working at the Gilt Edge Cheese factory on the Thirteenth Line, to buy the former Bennett factory from Hinckley. Tom Hutchinson, a friend and businessman, loaned Johnny's father money to buy the cheese factory and Dr. Spankie, the island physician, advanced him funds to buy the farm. Hence, the operation became known locally as O'Shea's Farm and Cheese Factory.[10] In 1924, J.D. "Duff" Cosgrove assumed the position of secretary. The business was purchased by the Ault brothers and the factory closed in 1955.

The Silver Springs Cheese Factory,[11] the second to be established on the island, was still listed as a business in 1878. It was located at Cold Springs near the northeast corner of the Eighth Line Road and Main Street. Charles Greenwood, its owner, established the factory on farmland leased from the Allen Estate. At some later date this factory became shareholder-owned and evolved into one of the largest cheese-producing factories in Frontenac County. In 1940, Claytus Gurnsey, the cheesemaker there, won the Whig-Standard Trophy and the Frontenac County Award for the factory manufacturing the largest number of highly rated cheeses. The following year, beginning on May 1, 1941, for a six-month period, Gurnsey produced 3,439 boxes of cheese that scored ninety-four points or more in the

Central Ontario District of the British Empire Show held at Belleville. In 1943 he became a three-time winner of the Whig-Standard Trophy for the highest-scoring cheese in Frontenac County and, thus, permanent possessor of the award. John Keyes, a member of the cheese board, was listed as president of the factory in 1951; his co-shareholders were Robert Horne, Thomas Connelly, and Claytus Gurnsey. The Silver Springs Cheese Factory closed in June 1956.

The Ontario Cheese Factory,[12] considered the third on Wolfe Island, was located on lot 24, Old Survey, opposite Simcoe Island, probably due to the considerable number of dairy farms in the vicinity. The long-time cheesemaker of this shareholder-owned factory was Charles Price. Duff Cosgrove looked after their accounts for many years. A fire that destroyed the first factory also took the life of one of the island's nurse-midwives, Mary Horne. The second building was demolished after the company had ceased operations. Records indicate that Harold Gurnsey was the last person to make cheese at the Ontario Cheese Factory.

Dairy farming also gave rise to two other cheese factories at the foot of the island, circa 1897. The original St. Lawrence Cheese Factory, owned by Harold Burke, employed George Jones as cheesemaker. On July 26, 1924, the boiler blew, causing a fire that destroyed the building. Remnants of the foundation may be found north of the present factory, which opened in 1929 on George Rattray's land. The new St. Lawrence factory,[13] henceforth known as Rattray's, was located on the east side of the Seventeenth Concession. With prices at ten dollars each, many local farmers purchased stakes in the enterprise, the largest shareholders being William Dignem, John and George Niles, Joseph Woodman, William and Charles Gillespie, and James Keogh.[14]

Although George Rattray had learned cheesemaking early in his life, he also employed other cheesemakers through the years. One of note was Charles Price, formerly at the Ontario Cheese Factory. Rattray's factory and its produce always had a good reputation. Coal, used to fuel the water pump and the boilers for the hot water and steam necessary in the cheese production, was brought in from Clayton, New York.[15] In addition to running his own business, Rattray sold cheese for the Cold Springs Factory and was a cheese buyer on the Kingston Cheese Board for fifty-four years. Throughout the 1920s he also operated Marysville's general store, presently known as Fargo's. The St. Lawrence Cheese Factory has been idle since 1944, after which time local milk was trucked to the Gilt Edge Cheese Factory.

The Gilt Edge Cheese Factory,[16] erected in 1897, was owned and operated by Arthur Henderson. When he retired, his son took over the business. Henderson had learned the art of cheesemaking in Pittsburgh Township at the Granite Hill factory. At the age of sixteen he became a resident of Wolfe Island and went on to become one of the oldest cheesemakers in eastern Canada. His factory, located on the Thirteenth Line Road, ceased operations when the Kraft Company opened a plant near Cold Springs in 1955.

By 1946 only three factories were still in operation: O'Shea's, Cold Springs, and Henderson's. These factories yielded an average of four hundred pounds of cheddar per week. As long as milk was being produced locally and directed to these factories, the dairy industry was economically sound. In separate and individual transactions the Ault Brothers Milk Company

 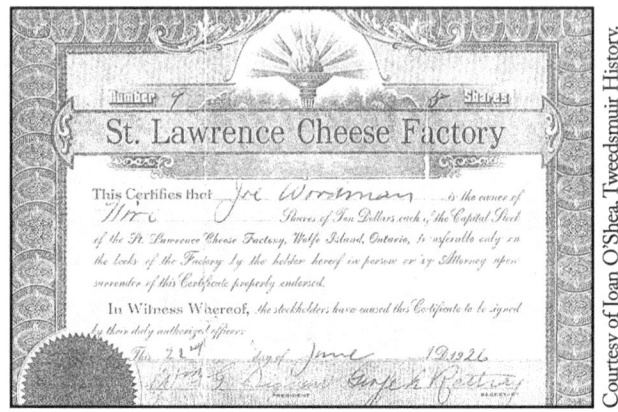

LEFT: *The St. Lawrence Cheese Factory, formerly owned by George Rattray, still sits on the Seventeenth Concession. The first floor is poured, paved concrete. Cheese production ceased in 1944.* RIGHT: *The St. Lawrence Cheese Factory operated on a shareholder basis. A shareholder's certificate is shown here.*

purchased each one and built a new factory on the main road near Cold Springs. The smaller plants were closed, marking the end of the pioneer cheesemaking industry on Wolfe Island.

Approximately two years later, the Kraft Company bought the Ault operation and developed a thriving business based on output of thirty dairy farmers and twenty-five employees, largely from Wolfe Island. In the 1970s, Kraft switched from the production of cheddar to mozzarella cheese. At one time their output of mozzarella was nine million pounds annually.[17] By 1980, the Kraft plant was handling about eighty-eight million litres of milk per annum, procured from twenty-four local Wolfe Island dairy farms. To make up the daily shortfall from island farmers, the factory trucked in thirteen thousand litres per day, five days per week from the mainland.

An ominous period began in July 1985 when the plant manager, Bill La Rocque, announced the impending closure of the Wolfe Island operation. Twenty-eight employees were given the option of moving to Ingleside, Kraft's larger plant near Cornwall, as the company intended to reduce local production to a three- or four-day week. Twelve employees remained, and, by 1987, under foreman Alex Quist, the variety of cheese being produced was altered to feta to satisfy the increasing taste for Greek cuisine. The plant reverted to a five-day, full-time employment pattern for eleven employees. Shortly, they were producing one million pounds of bulk feta cheese per year under the Ainos brand label. The feta was shipped to Montreal for distribution across Canada.[18]

Alas, this was not to last. In February 2000, Kraft closed the plant permanently and transferred its Wolfe Island operation to Ingleside. The closure was a blow to the island's economy, creating not only job loss but impacting on other businesses that had benefited from the patronage of these Kraft employees. Initially, dairy farmers were not affected by the plant closure as the Ontario Milk Marketing Board handles the distribution of milk. Today, milk is being trucked off the island to the mainland, a reversal of the previous practice.[19] The twenty-four prosperous Wolfe Island dairy farms in the prime of the Kraft production days have dwindled to four. Some farmers have converted to beef cattle, one even to bison.

Eddy Taggart, a sixth-generation Wolfe Islander who worked for Kraft in the capacity of pasteurizer-operator for thirty years, provided background on Kraft's operation on Wolfe Island. In June 1997, prior to the plant's closure, he retired from his position, along with cheesemaker Albert Martin. Currently, another Wolfe Islander, Randy Rixton, trucks the milk, daily, from the remaining local dairy farms to the plant at Ingleside.

BEEKEEPING

Honey has always been one of nature's more nutritious foods, and bee culture has been one of the means taken by some to obtain the bread on which to spread the honey. Yet honey has also been used to some degree in winemaking. Beekeeping was initiated on the island by some of the earliest settlers. Mead has been produced extensively throughout Ireland for many centuries. The secrets of its production were, no doubt, brought to Wolfe Island by early Irish or other old world pioneers.

Beekeeping was common throughout the 1800s. William G. Woodman and his wife Mary pictured here, kept bees until 1908.

Courtesy of Della Bullis, from the C.H. Wall collection.

133　Early Industries and Livelihoods

Father Thomas Spratt, seemingly the first beekeeper on Wolfe Island, arrived as pastor to the Catholic community in 1872. His bee assistant, Bruno Spoor, was a native islander of pioneer heritage. Records in the Baker store ledger shown to my father indicated that Father Spratt was also involved in the production of eggs and butter, commodities that he used along with the honey to pay his accounts at their store. When Spratt left, his successor, Father J.P. Fleming, carried on with the bee culture.

Bruno Spoor continued as apiarist, then was replaced by Gordon La Rush, a local man wishing to learn the art. Some time later, his brother, Richard "Dick" La Rush, with money given to him by his mother, bought ten beehives from Father Fleming and joined Gordon to establish a large beekeeping operation. The success of the venture and the quality of the La Rush honey is demonstrated by the many ribbons won at the Canadian National Exhibition in Toronto.

John Kingsley, the son of William and Mary, was well-known for the many hours he spent as township councillor and manager of the ferry. His fame, however, came through his bee culture, which brought him praise and business from across Canada and in England. John died in 1933 at age seventy-three. His son Wilfred continued the production of honey in the Kingsley tradition.

BUILDING TRADES

By the mid-1800s, the island was experiencing a building boom. While there were several stonemasons and at least eight resident carpenters at that time, apparently there were only two painters: John Craine and his son, Joseph. The Craines had recently moved back to the island. There was only one bricklayer, but that was not a detriment to the island, where wood and stone were used for most of the building. George Marsh, who lived in the village, was the only tinsmith. For anyone wishing to have custom-built furniture and built-in cupboards and doors, there were two brothers who were cabinet and door makers. The only other men whose names have been recorded from the early building trades include the following carpenters: Michael Turcotte, James Murphy, John Johnson, and James Livingston. No specific record of their work could be found.

TRAPPING AND ICE HARVESTING

The abundance of fur-bearing animals on Wolfe Island and the surrounding area enticed trappers until the early 1900s. According to island historian Johnny O'Shea, one of the early French Canadians to live on the island was a trapper named Pierre who lived by the creek in the Scottish Settlement. Some farmers trapped during the winter months, but landlocked mariners, deprived of income during the freeze-up, became the main trappers. Some set their traplines on or around the island while others set theirs throughout the smaller islands downriver. Bears lived on Wolfe Island during the 1800s, but the animals mainly sought were fox and mink. In the late twentieth century, muskrats were trapped in the island marshlands and around the old canal.

Ice harvesting around Wolfe Island employed over six hundred people in deep winter to cut ice for storage until spring. Much of this work was done by mariners who found employment at Cape Vincent or with the Calvin Company of Garden Island. They would fill the holds of vessels tied up for the winter with the harvested river ice. From about 1875 to 1900, as soon as the lake and river ice broke in the spring, these ships set sail with the first cargo of the season, usually to Lake Erie where they unloaded the ice into large commercial icehouses to sell locally. Island men also filled private ice houses on Wolfe Island with ice cut from the clearer sections of the frozen river when it had reached a thickness of at least twelve inches.

CHAPTER 10
Down to the Sea

Wolfe Island, like most other island communities, provided employees for vessels plying the waters of the Great Lakes. Indeed, it was sometimes a matter of sailing or starving when there was insufficient work for the able-bodied. The various ships built and operated by the Calvin Company of nearby Garden Island during its boom in the 1800s provided steady employment for Wolfe Island labourers and mariners. Many also worked on vessels locally owned and operated from Wolfe Island.

MARINERS

Census records, from 1851 to 1881, list many islanders as mariners, but no information as to their seafarer status or names of their vessels. Information from Calvin Company records cite certain names of Wolfe Island seamen hired at the turn of the century: John Flynn, James Davis, and William Kelly on the schooner *Norway* in 1896; Matthew and Thomas Flynn, along with William Kelly, on the steamer *Augustus* in 1898; and Rodney Yott with John Todd on the steamer *Simla* in 1910. John Gray, a fireman on the *Simla*, later worked in the same capacity on the first Wolfe Island ferry. Matthew Dorey, the chief engineer on the original *Wolfe Islander*, had previously been chief naval engineer for the Calvin Company.[1]

Among other Wolfe Island mariners were two families, each of which produced three men, all obtaining their captain's papers. They were the Davises of Victoria Street and the Kenneys, who lived opposite the town hall on Division Street. The earliest Davis family to come to Wolfe Island was United Empire Loyalist. Originally from Scotland and Wales, they emigrated from the United States in the early 1800s. Brothers William, Oliver "Chuck," and Henry Leath Davis of the early

1900s generation all became Great Lakes steamer captains. Captain Leath Davis, son of Henry, followed suit. They all had varying employment with the Keystone Line, the Quebec & Ontario Line, and the Hall Shipping Company of Montreal. Leath spent his last fifteen years on the water as the director of Marine Tourism for the Ontario Northland Company.[2]

Captain James Kenney became a Great Lakes marine captain and engineer who worked for many years for the Calvin Company of Garden Island. In the late 1800s and early to mid-1900s, he was reputedly one of the finest tug captains on the lakes. His sons, Clarence and George, followed in his path. Clarence, known as "Ginn," was the youngest Wolfe Island sailor to obtain both his mate's and captain's papers during the 1930s and 1940s. He also held his coastal waters captain's papers. At that time it was necessary to attend the navigation school at Queen's University, Kingston, to obtain certification. In the early 1940s, the school was moved to Lakeshore Boulevard in Toronto and renamed the Dominion Marine School.

Both Clarence and his brother, George worked for the Keystone Steamship Line. During the course of the Second World War, Clarence piloted trial runs on corvettes built in Kingston while George sailed on the *Cedarton*, owned by the Gulf and Lake Navigation Company. They, along with many other Wolfe Islanders, including Gene Hulton, R.F. Fawcett, and Vern Yott worked in Canada's Merchant Marine transporting supplies and munitions to coastal naval bases such as Cornerbrook, Newfoundland, and Halifax, Nova Scotia.[3] George attained his captain's papers in 1939, and his son Edward received his navigational status papers for inland waters from St. Lawrence College in Kingston.

The class of 1927 School of Navigation, Queen's University, is shown here. The gentleman standing at centre back is Captain Henry Leath Davis, father of Leath Davis.

Courtesy of Captain Leath Davis.

SHIPBUILDING

Nine Mile Point lighthouse is located at the westerly tip of Simcoe Island. Although the lighthouse was erected in 1833 and operated manually for more than a century, it is now controlled electronically by federal authorities from Prescott, Ontario. All ships approaching the St. Lawrence from Lake Ontario would be guided by this beacon.

Although Garden Island was the hub of the Wolfe Island Township's shipbuilding industry, Wolfe Island shared in this business. In the early days, most individuals on the island built the type and size of craft according to their individual needs and skills. In time, businesses were established specifically to produce seaworthy watercraft. Some built smaller craft, such as pleasure boats, shooting skiffs, and rowboats, along with oars, skulls (spoon-bladed oars), and paddles. Others specialized in larger pleasure craft and custom-made, freight-carrying schooners. The fact that three steam ferries were constructed on the island in 1836, 1850, and 1857 by local craftsmen with local materials indicates that these men could build most anything that could float. C.W. Cooper, a Kingston barrister-at-law, wrote an essay on Frontenac, Lennox, and Addington counties, published in a Kingston newspaper in 1856, wherein he called Wolfe Island, "somewhat famous for the build of its boats and small vessels."

It is believed that early ships were built at Point Alexandria, Reeds Bay, and Ferguson's Point. At a later date, much of the work was carried on at the Foot, where the Calvin Company operated a shipyard under the name of Calvin, Breck and Rees, specializing in schooner-type vessels. An 1870 tabulation of cargo carriers on the Great Lakes indicated that schooners far outnumbered barques and brigs. The Calvin property on the south side at Port Metcalfe included houses to accommodate workmen, sheds to hold tools, and a large wharf. Sunken cribs from the wharf as well as remnants of wrecks that can still be seen offshore when the water is low, presented a danger to shipping for years.

Sailmaking, and its companion flag-making, were part of shipbuilding. John Dixon, an expert sailmaker, lived and farmed close to the Calvin shipyard and probably custom crafted sails for these vessels. His son, John Jr., became a ship's carpenter and likely worked at the shipyard, which continued to operate until circa 1890.

My father reviewed some old Calvin Company accounting books and gleaned interesting data for the 1896 season regarding the schooner *Valencia* and the steamer *Reginald*. Monthly wages ranged from seventeen dollars per month for a deckhand to fifty dollars for a first mate. Some of the prices paid for provisions taken on board that season were: milk, ten cents per gallon; bread, twenty cents per pan; butter, twenty-nine cents for two pounds; bacon, ten cents per pound; berries, fifty cents per pail; and apples, thirty cents per bushel. At one time or another, Wolfe Islanders Anthony Deforge, Frank Lawrence, William Hawkins, George Cadotte, George Miller, Dexter Lewis, William Canada, Preston Raymond, and cook Mrs. Fertian sailed on these two vessels.

SHIPWRECKS

Shipwrecks were the result of storms, collisions, stranding, and fire. Wolfe Island itself has, no doubt, been a factor in causing many shipwrecks because of its size, geographic location, and the numerous shoals surrounding its shores. The earliest recorded vessel wrecked off Wolfe Island was the French-owned *Le Blanc Henri*. She was bound upstream on June 17, 1764, when she hit a spit off Wolfe Island and sank. The ship was carrying one hundred thousand dollars in gold, silver, and other valuables at the time of the accident. Interestingly, there is no mention of a map identifying any narrow extension of land from Wolfe Island as a spit, yet every long, narrow reef, shoal, or sandbank extending out from the Wolfe Island shoreline is a spit. Discover the right spit and one could become rich! It has been rumoured that Wolfe Islander Norman Conley, an expert swimmer and diver in his youth, stated that he discovered the location of the sunken treasure ship during his "bootlegging days" in the era of Prohibition. Norman revealed this shortly before his death, but did not divulge the location. Alas, the secret of *Le Blanc Henri*'s resting-place died with him![4]

Another vessel, the *Globe*, grounded in Bateau Channel during a snowstorm in December 1851, apparently without casualties. As the *Globe* was well down the channel between Simcoe and Wolfe islands, its cargo was removed by Calvin Company employees and stored in their sheds on Garden Island. In 1857, a steamer by the name of *Montreal* burned in the St. Lawrence River with a loss of 250 persons. Although this accident happened just off Wolfe Island, further details are lacking.[5]

Late in the fall of 1870, an unknown schooner is said to have disappeared mysteriously. Seemingly, the vessel was blown into Big Sandy Bay where she hit bottom. When it became evident that the ship could not be moved, she was abandoned with the intent of refloating her in the spring. However, when the crew returned, their vessel was nowhere to be seen. Old-timers living in the area reportedly saw the schooner slowly disappear below the surface during the winter. It was assumed that she had grounded in a bed of quicksand.

Sarah (Kemp) Michea's family Bible and an eyewitness provide details of another disaster that took the life of one of my great uncles. The 142-foot, 305-ton, three-masted schooner *Jessie H. Breck* sank on May 17, 1890. She was Calvin-owned, in her seventeenth year of service, and freshly laden with timber at Toledo, Ohio. Before leaving port the captain had telegraphed his superiors at Garden Island to advise them that he preferred to not pull out as the ship was taking on too much water. Despite his request, he was told to proceed to Garden Island. To exacerbate the situation, the vessel was buffeted by heavy winds throughout the journey. Just as she approached better sailing conditions past Horseshoe Island, disaster struck, and the *Jessie H. Breck* capsized with the loss of all hands. An eyewitness to this disaster was a young lad named Lewis Orr (later Captain Orr). He was in his elder years when relating the following details to my father:

> This is the story of the *Jessie H. Breck* as I saw it. I was at Snake Island Lighthouse with my sister Sarah. It was a nice day, but the wind was southwest hard. My sister said, "There is a vessel coming off the head of Simcoe! When it gets down here, tell me," so I sat on the doorstep and watched the ship, and all at once she disappeared, and I told my sister that the vessel had gone behind Simcoe [down the Bateau Channel]. My sister said, "Oh now, she would not do that," so that was when she was upset. We did not know what had happened till the next day when my brother came to the lighthouse and told us that a vessel was on her side at the head of Simcoe Island, and all were drowned. That day there was a funeral for a Mr. Busch, who had died on Simcoe, and, after Captain Charles Staley [another seaman who lived on Wolfe Island close to the site of the tragedy] had taken the funeral attendees on his small steam barge to Wolfe Island, he came back and took us all to see the *Jessie Breck* on her side at the head of Simcoe Island. As the vessel was lying port-side down, with the gale coming from the southwest, this would seem to indicate that her cargo had shifted, probably due to the amount of water she had taken on.[6]

Of the *Jessie H. Breck's* eight-member crew, seven were from Wolfe Island, four were of the Michea family raised in the Reeds Bay area at the Head. Thomas Michea, aged thirty-five, was captain, his brother Joseph, thirty-one (my maternal great-uncle), was mate, their sister Miriam, thirty, was the cook, and James, twenty-six, was a crewman. The other islanders who died were William Mullin, aged sixty, and his son John, twenty, as well as Donald McDonald. The eighth victim was Frank George, fifty, of Kingston. When the storm had subsided, another great-uncle, William "Willie" Kemp, used grappling irons trying to recover crew members but was only able to retrieve Joseph's body.

Joseph Michea was honoured at a funeral service attended by hundreds of people, and conducted by the fraternal Ancient Order of the United Workmen (AOUW). His sister Miriam was found on May twenty-second, two miles off the head of Simcoe

Island. Miriam and her brother James were interred in the Point Alexandria Cemetery.[7] On June 16, Captain Thomas was found five miles from the site of the tragedy at a point below Cedar Island where the current had carried him. A home funeral, also conducted in the AOUW tradition, was followed by burial in Trinity Cemetery.[8]

Young Donald McDonald, a twenty-year-old crew member, was discovered near the foot of Amherst Island the following day. Finally, the body of John Mullin was located by fishermen near Simcoe Island.[9] (It is believed that John and father William were predecessors of the respected Buck Mullin of Wolfe Island). The diverse and distant locations where the victims of the disaster were found are testimony to the strength of the currents and undertow in the area. The *Jessie H. Breck* was later re-floated and converted to a tow barge bearing the name *H.M. Stanley*.

The *Jessie H. Breck* was named for Ira Allen Breck's second wife. Ira was a partner in the Calvin and Breck Shipbuilding and Lumber Merchant Company headquartered on Garden Island. The schooner had been constructed at Port Colborne, Ontario, in 1873, for the Garden Island firm of Breck and Booth.

The Michea family was related to the Grimshaws, Gillows, and Kemps, and like Captain Charles Staley, they were sailors. One wonders whether Captain Staley, as he surveyed that tragic scene, remembered the day twenty years earlier when he was involved in a similar situation. It was November 17, 1869, and he was master of the 352-ton schooner *George Thurston*. His mate, another islander, was Robert Andrew Horne. Both lived

The Jessie H. Breck, *watercolour, Captain George N. Henderson, artist, circa 1880s. This vessel capsized on May 17, 1890, losing all hands on board.*

Courtesy of Ben Holthof, curator/registrar Marine Museum of the Great Lakes, Kingston.

along the Front Road. The vessel was loaded with wheat and headed for Oswego, New York, when it ran into heavy seas off Nicholson's Island. Conditions worsened to the extent that the ship sprang a leak and ran aground on the Prince Edward County shoreline. As the ship settled underwater, Captain Staley and his crew clung to the rigging until they were rescued.[10]

In addition to these disasters there were those American ships wrecked during the War of 1812, along with the "unknown soldiers" lost at sea in vessels that possibly hit shoals and just disappeared. In his *Great Lakes Shipwrecks and Survivals*, William Ratigan alludes to the "probability of eight hundred million dollars worth of salvageable shipwrecks lying on the beds of the Great Lakes, containing fortunes in copper ingots, prize lumber, beverages, cheeses and the like."[11]

Statistics regarding the excessive number of shipwrecks and loss of life on the Great Lakes are overwhelming. In 1855, 118 lives were lost, 407 in 1856, and an unknown but much larger number in 1869, when ninety-seven ships sank during a four-day hurricane.[12] Various Wolfe Islanders sailed the Great Lakes at that time and likely many of them were lost in these disasters. A tombstone in the old Sacred Heart Church Cemetery indicates that three members of one family died by drowning. From the dates given on this grave marker it is likely they were mariners who sailed out of Garden Island on Calvin-owned vessels. Two brothers, William and Thomas Snell, drowned on November 7, 1880, the same day that all hands were lost when the schooner *Norway* capsized. The third brother, John Snell, at the age of twenty-nine, drowned on May 27, 1889. This date coincided with the day that all aboard were lost off the schooner *Bavaria*.[13]

Drowning was not the only fate a sailor might encounter, as revealed in the 1861 census that states, "John Crawford, husband of Susannah Crawford, was killed on board the steamer *Hercules* by a blow from a rope." A grave monument erected by fellow Orangemen in Trinity Church Cemetery indicates that Crawford, thirty-seven, was killed on June 8, 1860. The *Hercules* and the large tug *Highlander* were destroyed by fire on the night of December 9, 1871, at the Garden Island dock, with the loss of one life. Captain James Dix, witnessing the catastrophe from Kingston, recounted that the conflagration appeared to engulf the entire island.

TRIANGLE OF DEATH

Does Lake Ontario have a triangle similar to the Bermuda Triangle where vessels and men mysteriously vanish? Mystery shrouds a triangular area of eastern Lake Ontario whose corners are located at Wolfe Island, Mexico Bay (northeast of Oswego, New York), and Point Petre. There has been speculation that paranormal events within these boundaries cause ships to crack up or be pulled to their doom. The area, where an exorbitant number of ships have gone down or been afflicted, has been referred to as the "Marysburgh Vortex" by Toronto author Hugh F. Cochrane.

All the waters of the Great Lakes system flow into this triangular configuration east of the Oswego-Point Petre line. As the waters of Lake Ontario approach the St. Lawrence River, the flow becomes more and more constricted, acting as a massive funnel. The waters ingress at the surface while also moving in an upward

Map 7: The Marysburgh Triangle (or Vortex) location is shown on this map of the eastern end of Lake Ontario. Historically, most of the sailing mishaps during the days of sail and steam occurred within this triangle.

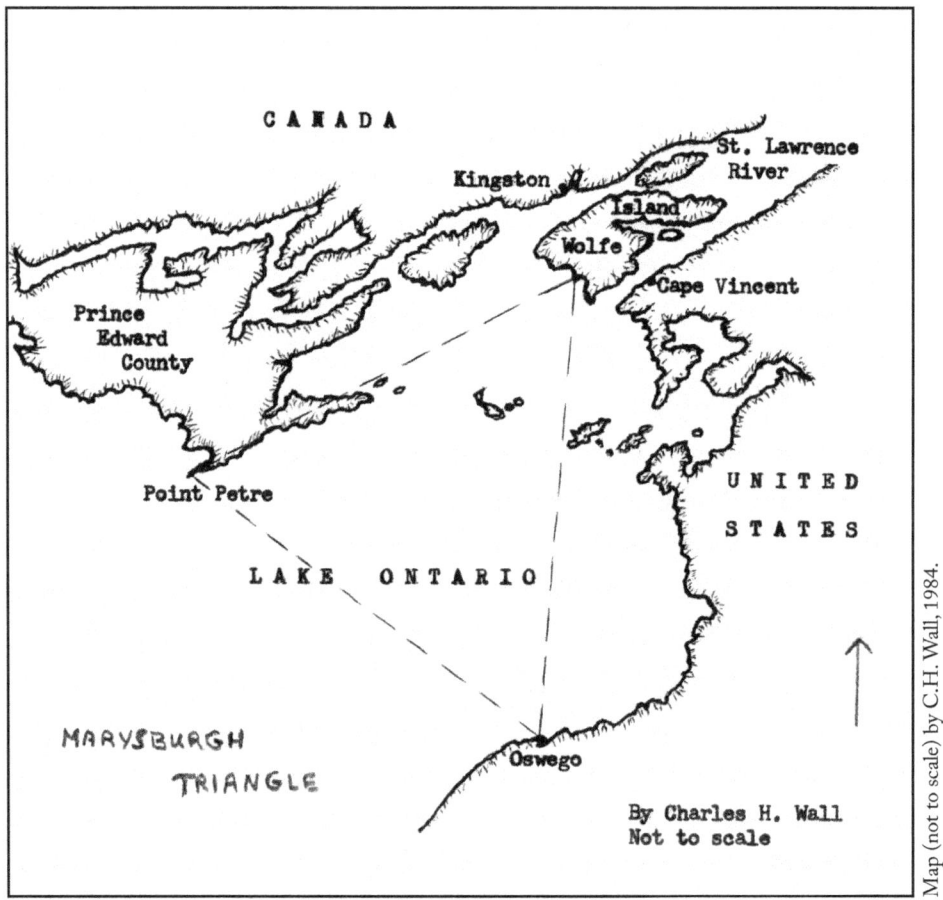

vortex from varying depths of six hundred feet to no more than three to ten feet in many places, thus making it a treacherous area for all navigation. Wolfe Island simulates a stopper in this furious flow of water, splitting the river into two channels as the water commences its long trip down the St. Lawrence River.

There have been hundreds of shipwrecks within this funnel. Willis Metcalfe has stated that two thirds of all shipping losses on the Great Lakes have occurred in the eastern end of Lake Ontario. In 1883, forty vessels and 672 lives were lost, mostly in this particular area.[14] Wolfe Island mariners received their initiation while sailing within these confines and would have set sail from Wolfe and Garden islands for practically every Canadian or American port within the funnel and far up the Great Lakes. Although many ships have been wrecked and an unknown number of mariners have lost their lives here, in no instance is it recorded that an unnatural attraction contributed to their misfortune.

Many brave men drowned after casting off in unseaworthy vessels, bad weather, or a combination of both. Added to known hazards were the unpredictable shifting cargoes, snapping masts and booms, lost sails, fires, and crewmen being washed overboard. Men endured the constant uncertainty of elements such as fog, frost-fogs, snow, ice, rogue waves, waterspouts, gales and gusty winds, and the omnipresent danger of colliding with hidden reefs, shoals, or being spiked on submerged vessels or juggernauts, those runaway logs from timber rafts.

RHYTHMIC FLOW

Information concerning vessels known to have been wrecked during the 1800s in the area of the so-called Marysburgh Vortex reveals that half of them went to their graves during or near the seven-year "rhythmic flow" water level. Rhythmic flow of water levels in the Great Lakes is an unusual occurrence recognized by the Native people for centuries but only taken seriously by the Europeans since the mid-1800s. This phenomenon could occur simply by coincidence, yet it is thought to be influenced largely by the amount of precipitation compared with the degree of evaporation in any one season. Precipitation, snow, or rain, occurring with little or no break, does not permit dry-out and, because sufficient evaporation cannot occur without dry spells, water levels naturally will rise under these conditions.[15] The cycle tends to last about seven years, with more amplified fluctuations at approximately thirty-five year intervals. This observation offers an environmental alternative to the Marysburgh Vortex theory, as wrecked vessels could easily have met their fate by hitting submerged objects that in normal or high water years would have been well below their draft.

MAGNETIC ANOMALIES AND WEATHER PATTERNS

My father's sense of logic spurred him to find explanations for these mystery-shrouded "triangle" occurrences. His study indicated that the presence of magnetic materials might interfere with the integrity of a ship's compass, causing loss in the sense of direction, but early mariners may not have been aware of the presence of iron deposits in the lake bed or the earth's crust.

Edward Kenney, a Wolfe Island native and resident for more than sixty years, is also a seasoned navigator of these waters. He had never heard of the Marysburgh Vortex, although he knew there were more shipwrecks at the eastern end than elsewhere in Lake Ontario. When magnetic fields were mentioned, he agreed that a line of iron-ore deposit in the lakebed and riverbeds exists, marked on the river navigation charts — fields that intensify as one travels eastward near Fort Henry. This vein of iron ore is referred to as a magnetic anomaly and is powerful enough to pull a sailing compass off ten to fifteen degrees, requiring mariners at the wheel to compensate for the interference. This hazard increases if navigating in the fog. Edward learned early in his navigation career from another trusty island mariner, "Buck" Mullin, how to execute this manoeuvre. With the advent of more weather warnings and sophisticated electronic navigational equipment such as radar, sonar, and especially GPS (Global Positioning System), these potential hazards no longer pose the same threat.[16]

Late fall, especially November, has always been the most brutal season for shipping. Lake Ontario boasts some of the deepest waters of all the Great Lakes, causing, in rare instances, waves that can exceed fifteen feet. November and December can produce icing with strong winds, high waves, and thick fog. As the days shorten in the fall and the air temperature cools, the lake water is still relatively warm by comparison, providing heat and moisture to fluctuating air masses. At this time of year, warm air masses from the United States collide with Arctic air from Canada and the more thermally unstable these air masses become, the greater the potential for them to turn into cumulus clouds as they rise. These clouds eventually produce heavy snow showers over the lake and some surrounding shoreline areas, especially downwind at the eastern end of the lake. It is probably safe to assume that this entity, referred to as "lake effect," has always been a potential nemesis for mariners.

The following is a quote by James Foster Robinson from a 1970 *Whig Magazine*: "[T]here is a backwash, in Eastern Lake Ontario from Kingston that apparently deposits many of the wrecks in a huge hole southeast of the Main Duck Islands."[17] Here may be found most of the sunken ships of the area. Such foregoing conditions could motivate belief in strange inexplicable phenomena in this eastern triangle of Lake Ontario akin to that of the Bermuda Triangle.

BALLADS

Sailing, ballads, and taverns were closely associated during the 1800s. Indeed, happy occasions, at home or in the tavern, usually inspired a singalong, when ballads, especially those incorporating everyday experiences, were sung. While at work, sailors generally preferred rhythmic shanty songs to help them get through their day.

The following are lyrics to a ballad that originated in the 1800s, and although there are other versions, this one could easily have been sung on Garden Island or Wolfe Island due to the number of French-Canadian residents. As there was only one farm on Garden Island, it is possible that the last two lines of the first stanza referred to Wolfe Island.

> Now all good woodscow sailor mans,
> Take warning by dat storm,
> An' go marry nice Islan' girl,
> And live on one beeg farm
>
> Den de win' can blow lak hurricane,
> An' spose she blow some more;
> You can't get drown in Lak Ontair'
> So long you stay onshore.[19]

While immigrant seafarers from France, Britain, and Ireland brought their own songs and tunes, new ones were always being introduced — some to commemorate catastrophes. One such ballad was written about the ill-fated schooner *Jessie H. Breck*. Eyewitness reports, other than Captain Orr's, have been recorded regarding this tragic incident. A local balladeer portrayed the events in a song that my father often heard sung at house gatherings by islander Nellie Bolton in 1930, but his quest for a copy of the lyrics was without success.

Simcoe is a small island off the northwest shoreline of Wolfe Island, separated by a short ferry ride across Bateau Channel, in which the *Jessie H. Breck* capsized. In the history of Simcoe Island written by Sanford Eves, he includes poignant poems that he has written, and mariners' ballads. The following stanza of his "Ballad of Nine Mile Point" refers directly to the unfortunate demise of the *Jessie H. Breck*. The lighthouse on Nine Mile Point, the westerly tip of Simcoe Island, was a welcoming but warning beacon for vessels approaching the St. Lawrence.

> The *Jessie Breck*, with timber on deck
> Capsized in a summer squall
> The Captain and all the crew were lost
> The waters claimed them all
> It was eighteen ninety in the month of
>   May
> When normally peaceful waters play….[20]

The *Jessie H. Breck* has been immortalized in this and other ballads, imprinted in the minds of the families and friends of the beloved crew members, allowing them some sense of closure. Other families suffering similar losses have not been so fortunate.

CHAPTER 11
Garden Island: One Man's Empire

Garden Island's original sixty-five acres of limestone lying in the St. Lawrence River, slightly to the northwest of Wolfe Island's village of Marysville, has been reduced through erosion by ten acres since first surveyed. Although small in comparison to Wolfe Island's thirty-three thousand acres, its historic period is worthy of note. The island, previously part of Wolfe Island Township, became a member of the Township of Frontenac Islands in 1998.

Seemingly, Captain Grant and Lieutenant Langan were the first owners of Garden Island subsequent to La Salle. During the French regime, the island was referred to as "Île aux Cochons" or "Île du Porcs," likely because La Salle's men kept swine there. Upon his initial sighting in the mid-1700s, Reverend Pièrre François Xavier de Charlèvoix called it a "very pretty island, in the middle of the river, inhabited by swine."[1]

According to Marion Calvin Boyd's account of the history of Garden Island, the first letters in D.D. Calvin's possession, authenticating ownership of the island, were written in 1823 and state that Garden Island was, at that time, in the possession of a number of Montreal men.[2] As this date coincides with the date of the patent for Wolfe Island in the names of the heirs of Grant and Langan (Grant was from Montreal), they are likely the persons referred to in the letters.

When their title to the islands (Simcoe and Garden) was certified in 1823, the Grant and Langan heirs chose to surrender Garden Island to the Crown in accordance with the Clergy Reserves' mandate, the area of that island representing the approximate "one-seventh" in relation to the area of Simcoe Island. Angus Cameron, a lately discharged captain of the Fourth Battalion of Incorporated Militia, petitioned for a grant of Garden Island on October 16, 1830. Like Grant and Langan, he had served earlier in the 79th Regiment of Foot Soldiers, more commonly known as the 79th Highlanders or Cameron Highlanders. His success in apprehending deserters eventually led to an honourable discharge with distinction upon his retirement from the service.

After acquiring the island, Cameron settled toward the western end where he maintained a fifteen-acre farm for several years. Although the 1851 census records his dwelling as a one-storey frame house, he actually built the only brick home on the island. At that time Cameron, a Scottish immigrant, was single and fifty years of age. He became the first reeve of the Township of Wolfe Island in 1851, a position he held in seven elections over the following ten years. After selling his interests in Garden Island to D.D. Calvin in 1862, Cameron moved to Wolfe Island.

Dileno Dexter Calvin, and subsequently his heirs, became the next and final owners of Garden Island. The surname Calvin had its origin in the Noyon-Picardy area of northern France, where the French Calvinist movement of the 1500s, named for John Calvin, one of the dominant Protestant reformers, spawned many Huguenots. It is likely that D.D. Calvin was of Huguenot Calvinist ancestry.

Born in Vermont, he was only eight years of age when his father died with little provision having been made for his education. In 1798, at the age of twenty, Calvin left for New York State and within seven years had become a successful lumberman near La Fargeville. His early success with timber rafting of oak and pine down the St. Lawrence to the Quebec City coves for transshipment to British markets[3] inspired him to move to Clayton in 1825 to better concentrate on this expanding enterprise.

While still maintaining an interest in his Clayton business, D.D. Calvin leased the eastern section of Garden Island from Angus Cameron in 1836. He partnered with another American, Hiram Cook, and with John Counter of Kingston to form the Kingston Stave Forwarding Company in 1838. That same year, this partnership initiated their first shipbuilding enterprise on Garden Island. Their first sailing vessel, the schooner *Queen Victoria*, was launched in 1839.[4] Calvin soon began hiring tradesmen and building vessels for gathering and transporting timber from various ports within the Great Lakes basin, a move that strengthened his position in the British market.

Logs, unloaded from the timber-carrying barge Burma *shown at the left, are formed into a log boom.*

Courtesy of Maurice Smith, curator emeritus, Marine Museum of The Great Lakes.

Timber, once loaded onto Calvin vessels, was shipped to Garden Island where it was unloaded and held in booms between piers in a sheltered back bay waiting to be assembled into rafts. Calvin's team lashed the timber into cribs measuring forty-two feet by sixty feet. Four or five cribs were joined together to become 240 foot drams.[5] Each dram contained fourteen thousand cubic feet valued at nine pence per cubic foot. A complete raft consisted of nine drams, each with its own sail, appearing like a small village of huts on the larger raft. These huts provided sleeping and cooking quarters for crews of about twenty raftsmen. A steam tugboat guided the rafts until near the rapids, at which point the tug would disengage. The crew then separated the rafts to shoot the rapids. Thirty-foot oars, fastened at the bow and stern of each raft, were used for steering.[6]

After navigating the rapids, the crew would reassemble the smaller units and resume travelling in the second tug's tow until they reached the next set of rapids, where the process would be repeated. Between Prescott and Quebec City, five sets of rapids had to be negotiated. Timber rafting down the St. Lawrence, largely dependent on the expertise of these French Canadians, was a major enterprise for most of the nineteenth century. Much of Calvin's success can be attributed to his chief raftsman, Aimé Guérin, who worked for the Calvin Company for thirty-four years. Upon completion of the 350 miles to Quebec City, the Calvin Company representative would collect a fee as they were essentially operating a forwarding company.

Calvin and Cook formed another partnership in 1851 for the purpose of acquiring more ships. A self-contained village soon evolved at the eastern end of the island, which served as headquarters for the company as well as home for families of the employees. The village also possessed facilities for educational and recreational activities.[7] By 1862 Calvin had purchased the western half of the island, becoming sole owner. Ira Breck, Calvin's brother-in law from his second marriage, became his partner for a new company called Calvin and Breck.[8]

The workers constructed many buildings to accommodate the diverse trades involved in shipbuilding, including the essential sawmill (which, by 1870, was steam-driven), a carpenters' workshop, a joiner-shop, a blacksmith shop, a machine shop, and a boiler shop. A warehouse was added for storage, along with four barns and stables for horses used in the shipyard. Sails were constructed, repaired, and stored in the sail loft, which, having been replaced in the late 1800s, is the only workplace structure still evident today.

These shops buzzed with activity for seventy-five years. The 1851 census enumerates seven shipwrights, four sawyers, twelve carpenters, nine blacksmiths, five boilermakers, one engineer, two sailmakers, and one foreman in the employ of the shipbuilding division at Garden Island. A private lighthouse was erected on top of the first sail loft. As this location was opposite Wolfe Island's Ferguson's Point, the lighthouse assisted with the safety of all watercraft at the western end of the St. Lawrence.[9]

Coal used to produce steam power for the sawmill and the steam vessels was shipped to Garden Island from a variety of locations on the Great Lakes, including Ohio and Pennsylvania. Calvin and Company became well-known across the Atlantic as well as throughout the Great Lakes basin. Knowledge of Garden Island as a port of entry to Canada became widespread.[10]

Calvin had formed other joint ventures during the 1870s with the inclusion of his son Hiram A. Calvin.

Partnerships and offices existed in Quebec City, Kingston, and Hamilton, as well as Clayton, New York. Twenty acres at the foot of Wolfe Island became the site of another timber-rafting yard in the name of Calvin, Breck, and Rees. Using much the same method that the American magnate F.W. Woolworth employed while founding his famous "five and dime" chain, Calvin extended partnerships even to foremen in his timber-cutting camps.

During Calvin's peak business years, his enterprises supported in excess of one thousand employees, no less than seven hundred of them living and working on Garden Island. In its latter years his company was known as Calvin and Son and, after the founder's death, as Calvin Company Limited (run by Hiram and his two sisters). By 1865, Calvin's firm was one the biggest timber dealers in Canada, controlling the largest single timber operation in Quebec City's timber coves.[11]

To complement the timber business, the Calvin Company engaged in related ventures such as shipbuilding, salvage operations, warehousing, and forwarding. They bought and sold commodities such as flour and salt and, between 1858 and 1874, gained a lucrative return from their government contract for the operation of a tugboat service on the river west of Montreal.[12] The freight business covered the Great Lakes basin and the tug service operated on the St. Lawrence.

During their three quarters of a century in business, the Calvin ventures were estimated to have owned more than sixty vessels, with a maximum of twenty in any year. They chartered many ships and built many others, from schooners, barques, brigantines, river barges, steam barges, lake tugs, and river tugs, to side-wheelers. With the exception of those vessels manned exclusively by French-Canadian crews, Wolfe Island mariners frequently worked in various capacities on Calvin vessels.

My father's review of the Calvin papers containing examples of Wolfe Island-mariner involvement found that Thomas Dawson, a Wolfe Islander, was the master of the schooner *Robert Gaskin* in 1877. A manifest, dated November 18, 1867, indicated that the cargo loaded on board the schooner *Laura E. Calvin* at the Port of Chicago consisted of 13,435 bushels of corn weighing 217 tons. The corn, shipped by John L. Rainny of Chicago, bound for the port of Toronto, was consigned to Gooderham and Worts, a major distillery company in Toronto. Her master was Anthony Joliffe of Wolfe Island.

Another manifest of the *Laura E. Calvin* shows that, on July 7, 1868, she was loaded at Bay City, Michigan, and bound for Garden Island with 169 pieces of square timber occupying ten thousand cubic feet, with the value at that time of one thousand dollars.[13] Each piece of timber bore the letters "L.E.C." (the vessel's initials) as identification for quality and protection against theft or loss. George Dawson, another Wolfe Islander, was master of this vessel.

The Calvin Company kept up with technology, shifting from sail to steam and building the type of vessel needed as the occasion arose. Their first steamer, the *City of Kingston*, was built for lake duty as early as 1841.[14] Forty years later, when they needed their own ocean-going vessel to carry timber to Britain, the Calvin Company built the full-rigged barque *The Garden Island*, which was launched from the north side of the island on May 8, 1877. Many of her years of service were spent sailing the open seas. On one of her longest voyages she sailed from Cardiff, Wales, loaded with coal

The barque Garden Island, *shown under construction on the island, was launched on May 8, 1877.*

for Ceylon and returned with a cargo of rice.[15] *The Garden Island* had become a "tramp ship" — visiting many international ports for trade purposes — unlike her sister ships that plied only the Great Lakes. A Norwegian company acquired *The Garden Island* in 1884 and re-registered her as the *Trio*. Lost at sea in 1906 after a commendable service of twenty-eight years, she was a notable credit to the Calvin Company and perhaps the finest achievement of those master shipbuilders.[16] The company's first steam timber drougher, the *D.D. Calvin*, was launched in 1883 and assigned to carry timber from Illinois to Garden Island. Her colours of bright green with white upper parts were subsequently carried on all Calvin vessels.

At the peak of Calvin's business undertakings, the winter population of Garden Island was about 450 people. In the summer, this rose to over 750 due to the influx of French-Canadian raftsmen from Lower Canada and seasonal workers from Wolfe Island and elsewhere. Inhabitants were also of Scottish, English, Irish, and American origins. During the Calvin era, many of the island's permanent families could boast of three generations.

Dileno Calvin personified the work ethic and lifestyle instilled in the people of Garden Island at the time. Clearly a self-made man, his ambition and entrepreneurial nature drove him to create a lucrative empire including contacts in Scotland. As he was strongly opposed to organized labour, such as the Seaman's Union[17] of the late 1890s, he imported sailors from Glasgow.[18]

A portrait of Calvin, painted in his latter years, depicts a white-haired man of youthful appearance exuding an aura of success. He apparently was always clad in a black suit and a white shirt and tie. In spite of his ardour for America, the land of his birth, Calvin became a naturalized Canadian citizen in 1845, and eventually a monarchist; ultimately, he was commissioned a magistrate. He retained his large land holdings in the United States, which included the Calvin homestead at La Fargeville. In 1844, at the age of forty-six, Calvin was influenced by a religious revival and was baptized into the Baptist church, a religious persuasion he followed for the rest of his life. Absolute temperance was the rule on Garden Island.[19] The island settlement that evolved with Calvin at the helm has been likened to a fiefdom and his employees referred to him as "the Governor." He dominated the community he had created and demonstrated a paternal approach to his workers during the recession following the panic of 1873 by reducing wages temporarily in lieu of laying off workers.[20]

Over the years yet more houses were required on Garden Island. Three roadways were laid out. Broadway Street was the main thoroughfare, while Fancy Street ran a short distance to the southwest off Broadway. Blanchette Avenue ran south from Broadway and turned east and parallel to the south shore, within view of Ardath Castle on Wolfe Island.[21] In contrast to Wolfe Island's log cabins and shanties, Garden Island had only frame buildings (except for Angus Cameron's brick house), often referred to as planked cottages. Most were two-family dwellings.

To provide services for that large a number of people, there had to be other buildings, such as a general

Dileno Dexter Calvin built his empire on Garden Island amidst the timber trade.

Courtesy of Maurice Smith, curator emeritus, Marine Museum of The Great Lakes.

store. Like all other buildings on Garden Island, the store, replete with a butcher section and bakeshop, was company-owned. Kept well-supplied, it was operated by Hiram Cook during the 1840s. The store was destroyed by fire in 1897.

The Calvin Company had their own currency system, called the Calvin Company scrip, which the workers used to purchase goods at the Calvin store.[22] The senior storekeeper doubled as postmaster and, after the telegraph was introduced in 1867, the junior clerk became the telegraph operator. The tenant farmer at the head of the island provided much of the fresh produce and dairy products. In winter he drove a daily stage over the ice to Kingston, charging the regular fare for his services. During the sailing season the Wolfe Island ferry stopped four times daily at Garden Island. The farmer and the schoolteachers were the only people working on the island who were not employed by the Calvin Company, although the school was subsidized by the firm. The part-time customs officer was a government employee.

Calvin's store catered mainly but not exclusively to Garden Islanders, Wolfe Islanders, and the Wolfe Island Ferry Company staff. Practically everyone had a running account and transactions were handwritten in a ledger. But this thriving community on a tiny island had more than a store and a schoolhouse; they also had a hall that opened at night. Known as the Mechanics' Institute, it had been established by Calvin in 1869 and became one of the foremost institutes in the province, complete with papers, periodicals, and books, and equipped with tables and chairs. Between 1881 and 1906, its nineteen hundred volumes had expanded to over six thousand.

The institute was actually an early version of a public library, an entity that Wolfe Island did not have officially until 1984. By 1906, the Garden Island Public Library, as it was then known, was receiving government grants under the public library system.[23] When Andrew Carnegie, the famous Scottish-American steel magnate-cum-philanthropist, provided funds through endowments for scores of public libraries in the United States, Great Britain, and other English speaking countries, this Mechanics' Institute met the criteria for subsidy from the Carnegie Endowment.[24]

The Garden Island Naval Company, organized during the 1860s, was another group requiring a meeting place. The Fenians, intent on liberating Ireland from English rule, escalated their raids in 1866 and posed a serious threat to Canada. Garden Island, a strategic post for British militia presence, as was Wolfe Island, had its own naval brigade and an improvised gunboat, the steamer *Watertown*, on river patrol. They stopped all suspicious craft observed crossing from the New York shore at Cape Vincent.[25] By 1866, a volunteer association of about forty men, most of whom had seen action in previous wars, was prepared to do their part against the Fenians or any other threat to Canada and was ready to mobilize upon the indication of any threat. The association's captain was Henry Roney, foreman of the shipyard; Abraham Malone, the accountant, was the first lieutenant; and William Marshall, the shipping agent for the Calvin Company, the second lieutenant.

It had not been necessary to build a church on Garden Island, as close proximity to Wolfe Island allowed easy access to the four established churches. As well, clergy from the Anglican and Presbyterian churches came to hold services in Garden Island's schoolhouse on Sunday evenings. Dedicated islanders also conducted afternoon Sunday school on a weekly basis in this well-used schoolhouse.

Garden Island had the reputation of being a model community. There was work for everyone and social activities for relaxation. Despite the diverse religious backgrounds of these inhabitants, Calvin's Baptist influence pervaded the atmosphere of the community. His absolute rule of temperance, good order, and united endeavour based on Christian principles resulted in a closely knit society that avoided religious conflict. Whatever the compelling force, during the Calvin regime Garden Island became a popular place to work. There doesn't seem to have been a resident physician, but due to the proximity of the island to Kingston, it may be assumed that illnesses not resolved on the island would have been treated at the Kingston hospital.

Politically, it was almost an unforgivable sin to vote other than Conservative as Calvin was a personal friend of John A. Macdonald, the popular leader of the party. Calvin was elected in 1868 and again in 1877 as the member for Frontenac County in the Ontario Legislature. An eccentric individual in many ways, well-known for his disdain for short men and dogs, Calvin was a colourful figure already in his seventies when he participated in provincial politics.[26]

On January 26, 1866, the Municipal Corporation of the County of Frontenac passed bylaw 14, incorporating the island community of 750 persons, and for the next fifty-four years it was known as the Village of Garden Island. Indeed, D.D. Calvin was Garden Island's first and only reeve until his death in 1884. At the time of his passing, Calvin owned ninety-two percent of the company. His funeral procession consisted of a flotilla of vessels from Garden Island, joined by other vessels from Kingston. They sailed down the river to Clayton, New York, where Calvin's body was interred. Apparently, all the members of his family were not buried in the same locale as grave markers in Trinity Church Cemetery on Wolfe Island indicate the dates of death of certain of his offspring.

Although son Hiram Augustus succeeded his father and the Garden Island operations did continue, a steady reduction in the timber trade, coupled with changing conditions in shipping, brought about a gradual decline. The extent of that recession is evident in the population data from census records. There were 762 people in 1871, 242 people in 1901, and only four residents left in 1921. The company's last rafts were floated down the St. Lawrence in 1914 at the onset of the First World War.

Lasting but a lifetime, the company had fulfilled its obligations in an exemplary fashion, but by 1915 the war was exacting a toll and other enterprises were becoming competitive. Seeing only a questionable business future under these circumstances, the corporation shut down operations. In 1920, the village corporation's charter was annulled and Garden Island was once again annexed to Wolfe Island. Garden Island remains Calvin Company-owned and no one is permitted to buy land there as long as the Calvin family is in control. The family and their friends have used the remaining cottages as a private summer retreat since the 1920s.

Over the ensuing years the waters have given up relics from Calvin's industries. A handmade shovel with the wooden handle still intact was found lying in the water just offshore. Hand-forged timbering spikes with rings through the top, once used in tying rafts together, have been discovered. Timber markers and blue oak staves have, from time to time, washed ashore. Only vestiges of the cribbing in the shipbuilding bay are still visible, although divers have indicated the presence of shipwrecks in the back bay.

Discussions with Duncan McDougall, a retired professor from Queen's University, provided much about the summer Garden Island community during the 1930s and onward. Duncan's father, also a professor at Queen's, and his mother rented one of the cottages on the island while Duncan was growing up. He remembered playing with many children while their parents, largely university faculty members, enjoyed each other's company in the solace and tranquility of this island. Duncan recalled the arrivals of "old Mrs. Calvin" (Hiram A.'s widow) being chauffeur-driven off the Wolfe Island ferry in an open landau-type McLaughlin Buick, accompanied by her son, as they approached their white frame cottage that was referred to as the "big house."

The Calvin house was a typical Victorian structure with fenced-in property, but the beautiful, fret-worked verandah was long gone. The Calvins, Duncan observed, were very conscious of their wealth and station, but few were aware of their philanthropy. To the eyes of a child, Hiram Calvin appeared to "lumber around like an old professor. He was a tall man, lugubrious and not convivial."[27]

Duncan and his family continued to vacation on Garden Island until more recent years when they

The Big House was the initial Calvin home on Garden Island. Its original Victorian fretwork deteriorated with time. Names of adults (l–r) are Mrs. Catharine (Wilkinson) Calvin, Mr. and Mrs. Hiram A. Calvin, and three of their children. Photo circa 1890.

purchased land on nearby Simcoe Island. Property on Garden Island, in this twenty-first century, is still not for sale. Duncan noted that Angus Cameron's brick house was history by the 1930s and very little evidence remains of the original Calvin operations. Fire destroyed the machine shop in the early 1980s and the pattern shop no longer exists. Aside from several remaining cottages, only the sail loft is still visible.

A frequent passenger aboard the old *Upper Canada* ferry when it was in service and making regular stops at Garden Island (1960s to early 1970s) was the well-known Canadian literary figure Arnold Edinborough. He would always disembark with his bicycle at Garden Island. Only recently, in discussion with Duncan McDougall, did I become aware of the reason for Edinborough's attraction to Garden Island. He had come to Canada from England to assume a post at Queen's University as an English professor. In addition to writing books and being an arts advocate, he wrote regularly for the *Kingston Whig-Standard* and was the publisher of *Saturday Night* magazine. He and his wife became members of this Garden Island literary community, having learned of it from other faculty members. They spent their summers at a house on the northwest shore of the island but moved some time prior to his death.

John Kinnear d'Esterre, a retired jeweller, and his wife Meg, a descendant of the Calvin family, retired to Garden Island from their home and business in Kingston in the late 1980s. They built their house around the old foundation of the pattern shop. John engaged in building ketches and schooners after learning to weld, and resurrected the old marine railway that enabled him to launch boats. Fifteen to twenty years ago, he custom-built steel-lined vessels with wooden interiors for consignees. John received a prestigious award from the Kingston Historical Society in 2004 that honoured his work in preserving the physical and archival records of the D.D. Calvin Company. For many decades he has served as an untiring member of all groups marine and historical in the Kingston area.[28]

The Wolfe Island ferry no longer stops at Garden Island. The *Upper Canada* was decommissioned and replaced by the new and much larger *Wolfe Islander III* in 1976. Passengers on this ferry may sight glimpses of a handful of cottages among the trees as she slips by the former industrial beehive. Those cottagers, who still come to Garden Island, do so by their own means. Gone is the era when these waters were full of sailing vessels, barges, salvage tugs, and small steamers — many built at the Calvin shipyards. Now the waters are dappled with small sailboats, motorboats, and jet skis that bounce to and fro in the ferry's wake.

CHAPTER 12

The Lifeline: Wolfe Island Ferries

Waterways were the principal routes of transportation for the early settlers throughout the French regime. Some form of boat was essential to obtaining supplies from Kingston or even to visit other parts of the island because of the poor condition of or lack of roads. Until roadways were in place, each man, from his own imagination or previous experience, built the boat best suited to his personal needs. Many simply improvised rowboats or roughly fashioned canoes.

FIRST LICENSED FERRY FROM WOLFE ISLAND TO KINGSTON

The enterprising Loyalist settler Samuel Hitchcock, believed by some to have initially settled on Cone Point (Mill Point), owned and operated the earliest known officially licensed public ferry between Wolfe Island and Kingston. It was actually a bateau-type flat-bottomed vessel built of pine, held together by wooden spikes,[1] and was equipped with a sail, pike poles for manoeuvring in shallow water, and oars to be used as need arose. The dimensions were twenty to thirty feet by ten feet with a depth of three feet, making it capable of carrying extensive amounts of freight and passengers.

The legislative act governing this ferry was set down by the Court of Quarter Sessions held at Adolphustown in January 1802. Hitchcock was granted permission to operate his ferry for a period of seven years as of May 1, 1802. It was to be somewhat of a water taxi on call, with the fares set at five shillings per person; seven shillings, sixpence, man and horse; five shillings per cow, horse or ox; thirteen shillings for man, horse and carriage.[2] Considering the size of Hitchcock's boat, as dictated by the number of people and amount of freight he was expected to be able to carry, it would appear that there were more than only a couple of families living on Wolfe Island circa 1800.

The first condition of the act also stated, "Samuel Hitchcock shall keep a regular ferry from his house on said island to Kingston."[3] If this phrase can be taken literally, it can be assumed that the ferry was initially landing somewhere in the vicinity of Leander Street. In those days Hitchcock owned the whole village area from the middle of Leander to the Sixth Concession. The log structure at the shoreline to the west of Leander Street had been built a year or two earlier by Samuel and his father, Archibald Sr. Their first home is reputed to be the oldest, longest-standing building on the island, an edifice worthy of heritage designation. Despite facelifts through the years, its size and location are essentially the same as originally erected.

In 1809 the ferry lease was renewed with Hitchcock for a further seven-year term. He then sublet his ferry for a span of three years to his friend and neighbour Alvah Bennett, who had settled on the island about two years earlier. Under Alvah's control, "The ferry then landed further up the island near Mill Point."[4] Bennett moved the docking site to a wharf in the bay east of Cone Point, which was closer to the gristmill he was establishing.

FERRY LEASE GRANTED TO THOMAS DAVIS

It is likely that Samuel Hitchcock Sr. had died by 1816. When the ferry lease came up for renewal that year, Thomas Davis, who had arrived about the same time as the Hitchcocks, made the successful bid. His lease, drawn up at York, stipulated:

The first Hitchcock home is the oldest house on Wolfe Island. Built circa 1800, it still stands intact at the north end of Leander Street. Currently, this log cabin is owned by David Helwig of Prince Edward Island. Photo 1972.

Courtesy of the C.H. Wall Collection.

Thomas Davis, his executors, administrators and assigns were to … keep and use a common public ferry … across the River St. Lawrence … for travellers and their stores, cattle, carriages, and property … from the 25 March, 1816 … unto the full end and term of seven years … paying therefore yearly rent or sum of one pound and five shilling of lawful money of Upper Canada, in half yearly payments … provided always … Thomas Davis is hereby firmly bound and enjoined to carry across said ferry, Indians or soldiers with proper passports or under command of their officer or officers without fee, toll or reward.[5]

Davis was the only Wolfe Island ferry operator to lose his life while in the business of ferrying. He drowned in the St. Lawrence River in November 1821 when his small boat capsized in a gale while returning from the Pigeon Island lighthouse. His wife, Mary (Hinckley) Davis, carried on with the ferry until the lease expired. In order to support her seven young children, she applied for a renewal in her name. The petition was granted by Lieutenant-Governor Maitland and the lease was extended for another term from March 25, 1823. In the summer of 1824, the widowed Mary Davis married Archibald Hitchcock Jr., the son of Samuel. Thus, the ferry business returned to the Hitchcock family and the landing place that they had built on their property at the north end of the turnpike.

During the time this ferry from Wolfe Island to Kingston was owned and operated by Wolfe Islanders, a second franchise, monopolized by mainlanders, had been operating from Kingston to Wolfe Island. Initially, it was licensed in 1787 for service between Kingston and Point Frederick, having evolved from a personal convenience for Richard Cartwright Sr., a Kingston merchant involved in the forwarding trade. He held a land grant on the base of Point Frederick and a shipyard near the foot of Gore Street in Kingston. The ferry likely accommodated mainlanders as well, and Wolfe Island was added to that franchise when the lease was renewed by Captain Andrew Denyke in 1802. One of his destinations may have been the south shore near Point Alexandria, as that was the area where, in October 1808, while carrying passengers, he was accosted by an American patrol boat.[6]

CONTRABAND AND ABNER IVES

Bill Johnston has been described as a smuggler, but he was not the only participant in this lucrative business. The Thousand Islands area was ideal for smuggling and rum-running, and Wolfe Island was used as a go-between point. The passing of the United States "embargo on non-intercourse" laws of 1807–09, coupled with weak border patrol on the Canadian side, turned the trickle of goods moving illegally into a flood. In one instance, even the government of Upper Canada was embarrassed when it inadvisably or unwittingly leased a ferry to a known smuggler.

It was the ferry run from Kingston to the island that posed the problem. Andrew Denyke possessed the

Kingston ferry lease for the seven year term beginning March 25, 1816. Two years later, he sublet to Daniel Brown who in turn assigned the lease to Abner Ives, a smuggler. When the lease expired, it was advertised by tender to go to the highest bidder. There were four bids, the lowest for fifty dollars per year and the highest (Abner Ives's) $125.10 per year.[7] Ives's bid was only $5.10 above the third bidder, suggesting that he may have had some insider information. According to the rules, the lease went to Ives.

The outcome created a storm of protest and Attorney General Robinson was brought into the picture. In answering a request for information about Ives, someone in authority in Kingston, who indecipherably signed himself "W.A.M.," provided Robinson with some details. Apparently, when he heard that Ives was to get the lease, he considered it his duty to inform the government of Ives's character in an official letter dated March 2, 1827, and addressed to Major George Hillier, military secretary to Lieutenant-Governor Peregrine Maitland:

> [T]he fact is that the man (Abner Ives) came to this place (Kingston) a few years since and established himself here as a professed smuggler which business he continues to follow and earns his bread by it. There is scarcely one engine in ten made of smuggled goods in which he is not engaged and the quality of contraband and other articles which he clandestinely brings are for the ship makers here…. I therefore could not help thinking it highly improper to place in the hands of such an individual, the control of a ferry situated in the ferry highway of smuggling and which would, if possessed by him, materially assist him in his illegal pursuits.[8]

He concluded by writing that Mr. Ives was morally disqualified.

Yet, on February 7, 1827, it was ordered that Abner Ives "shall receive" the lease, and the attorney general was requested to require from Mr. Ives a bond with ample security to ensure that, during the period of his lease, he would not commit any breach of the revenue laws.

EXPANSION OF HITCHCOCK LANDING

Archibald Hitchcock, although not able to sign his own name, was a highly motivated man. To encourage travellers to use his ferry to and from the United States, he built a larger loading area and provided a tavern for weary travellers. He also spent upwards of one hundred pounds for repairs to the turnpike leading across the island. By Order-in-Council, the lease was granted to him for another term at double the previous rent plus the expense of the lease.

Hitchcock erected his now-famous Hitchcock House. Built in 1832 of locally quarried limestone, it became one of the early landmarks on the upper St. Lawrence to be pointed out by tour-boat guides.[9] Although the inn has had several owners, a few minor construction changes, and has been known by other names, the basic limestone structure remains intact. This historic tavern — or "summer hotel," as it was called for many years — reached the apex of its popularity under Allan McLaren, who took it over in 1904. During McLaren's regime a frame section was added to the back to accommodate the increased patronage. There were times when the overflow of summer guests had to be bedded down next door in the upstairs portion of the Masonic Hall, also owned by the hotel proprietors. Meals were served in the dining room located in the main building. As an added attraction in the 1900s, an outdoor dance floor was constructed over the water with music provided by bands hired from Kingston. Island groups often rented the main floor of the Masonic Hall to hold dances, bazaars, and other social events.

After McLaren's death in 1934, the business was carried on by his wife, Emily, and son, Mac, until 1951 when it was sold to N.A. Landry of Detroit, Michigan. The hotel was sold once again to Dr. R.J. Livesey of Kingston and Professor Brooks of Queen's University, at which point it was known as the Inn on the Island. When Jan and Mae Hasselaar of Wolfe Island purchased the inn in 1975, Hitchcock House regained its original name. The Hasselaars were well-acquainted with the hotel business on the island, having managed the General Wolfe Hotel for several years.

On April 7, 1834, after a meeting of the Court of Quarter Sessions, James Nicholls, justice and clerk of the peace at Kingston, addressed the following letter to the clerk of the executive council in Toronto:

> I am directed by the Chairman of the Sessions to say that Archibald Hitchcock, applicant for a Licence for the Ferry between Kingston and Wolfe

The limestone Hitchcock House Hotel, which underwent expansion in the early 1900s, was originally constructed in 1832. The patrons, mainly fishermen, were provided with fishing guides and St. Lawrence skiffs. The hotel was closed to the public in 2007 when it was purchased by an American family. Photo circa 1900s.

Island; appeared this day before the adjourned Sessions; and exhibited the plan and description of the Steamboat he proposes to replace on the said Ferry line; and that the Magistrates are satisfied with the plan and details thereof; that the same when completed will be a great public convenience.... The engine contracted for to be equal to eight miles per hour; and the whole to be completed in four months.[10]

It appears that a lease was not negotiated, but a recommendation made that Hitchcock be allowed to operate a ferry in both directions on condition that a steamboat of the dimensions exhibited to the magistrates be completed when the 1835 sailing season opened. His steamboat was built and readied in time, but the engine was not installed until the summer of 1836, giving him only two months of operation before *The Wolfe* was laid up for the season. Hitchcock applied the next year to ferry in both directions with the renewal of the Wolfe Island to Kingston lease, but asked to be relieved of the responsibility of providing a steamboat, as he had lost money operating it the previous season.

RETURN TRIP FERRY SERVICE

Hitchcock ferried in both directions, without the steamboat or competition, but under the watchful eye of the customs officer. Several mainlanders presented their petitions, knowing that a firm lease had not been negotiated. Some sought the privilege of ferrying one way, while others requested both directions. Abner Ives, the former lessee of the Kingston to Wolfe Island run, presented no less than three petitions in as many years. The delay in granting him ferry service between Wolfe Island and Kingston stemmed from the desire to appoint a loyal subject of good reputation. Deserting British troops could find a way out of Canada from the Kingston area without much difficulty, due to the number of vessels. The government was anxious to license only persons willing to check for deserters. The ferry carried soldiers gratis, and each prospective lessee was required to be recommended by several influential persons and two additional individuals who would act as bondsmen. As a result of pressure exerted by the various petitioners and the need for ferrymen with special qualifications, the executive council dispensed with the procedure of granting leases to the highest bidders and recommended that all ferrymen be appointed by the lieutenant-governor.

Realizing that the ferry between Wolfe Island and Kingston was the lifeline to the island, and that it should be run for the convenience of the islanders, T.W. Kirkpatrick, the collector of customs for the Port of Kingston, addressed a letter to the lieutenant-governor in Toronto, dated June 20, 1839. Kirkpatrick strongly recommended Archibald Hitchcock as the most appropriate person to hold the lease. Enclosed with the customs officer's letter was a certificate signed by prominent persons at Kingston, who attested to Hitchcock's character and loyalty with the suggestion that he should be the lessee.[11]

THE *STRAWBERRY* AND JOHN DAWSON

Archibald constructed his new two-masted sailing vessel, named her the *Strawberry*, and put her into service in 1841.[12] After his death in 1842, John Dawson acquired ownership of the ferry and continued to operate her from the Hitchcock wharf. Shortly thereafter, Dawson constructed a clinker-built vessel (one whose sides were built with overlapping boards) to replace the *Strawberry* in 1844. This may have been the paddlewheel steamer called the *Raftsman*. He made arrangements to operate this ferry alternating weekly between the Hitchcock dock and his Dawson dock, located in the village directly opposite his hotel (presently the General Wolfe Hotel). Dawson could now share in the summer hotel trade that the Hitchcock House had previously monopolized. Soon afterward, Dawson renamed his hotel the Ferry Inn.

UNDER NEW MANAGEMENT

Within a few years, John Dawson leased his ferry to John and George Ives of Kingston, and they in turn sold the lease to Thomas Kirkpatrick. During this period of revolving ownership, the ferry service deteriorated to the degree that, by 1850, the township council was desperate for change. At a meeting in March of that year, Reeve Angus Cameron was asked to draw up and forward a petition to both the lieutenant-governor and the county council suggesting that ferry charters be discontinued and that the responsibility for ferry service be given to county council.

A year later, on February 20, 1851, Absalom Briggs of Wolfe Island petitioned the lieutenant-governor with a memorandum from the township council regarding the ferry, which apparently resolved the matter. On June 17, the council received an official communication stating that control of the ferry service had been given to the municipal council of the United Counties of Frontenac, Lennox, and Addington. Two days later bylaw 28 was passed, setting forth regulations for the ferry service:

> [T]hat, until steam conveyance can be procured to the satisfaction of this Council … the said duties may be carried on by sailboats and rowboats … in the space of time not exceeding one hour and not more than eighty minutes between the city and Wolfe Island … the lessee must have a boat capable of carrying at least twelve full grown oxen at a time and a cabin for passengers.[13]

There were exceptions to the fare schedule. Her Majesty's troops and militia men on duty, and clergymen, with their horses and carriages were entitled to a free passage on the ferry.[14]

THE STEAMERS: *Maude* and *Maud II*

Thomas Davis Jr., an islander and the son of Thomas and Mary (Hinckley) Davis Hitchcock, was well-acquainted with shipbuilding and understood the council's requirements. He had seen the Calvins of Garden Island inaugurate several steamers, including their first, the *Prince Edward*, in 1838. He set up shop on Wolfe Island. In 1852 he launched his new vessel, known as *Maude*. She was a great improvement over the previous sailing ferries, being capable of providing four regular trips daily.

The council of Wolfe Island was granted control of the ferry and Coleman Hinckley Sr. was granted the lease. That year Thomas Davis sold his ship to Messrs. Kinghorn, Campbell, and Hinckley, and the Wolfe Island Canal opened for service.[15] At the end of the 1857 season, the *Maude* was taken off the Wolfe Island run and placed on the Kingston to Cape Vincent route. After some years of service she was retired or renamed, as a second *Maud* — with a different spelling — was launched in 1871 in Kingston for politician and financier Charles Gildersleeve, and named for his daughter, Maud. Gildersleeve, not happy with its service, sold the ferry to the Folger brothers (Americans living in Kingston) in 1872, and she sailed under the Folger flag from 1872 to 1892 on the Kingston-Cape Vincent run via the canal.[16] In 1895 the vessel was sold to the Thousand Islands Boat Company and enlarged. The increase in size enabled her to be used as a tour boat with a capacity for 650 passengers. She was later sold to the Georgian Bay Tourist Company of Midland and renamed the *Midland City*.

Coleman Hinckley Sr. had successfully bid on behalf of his company, Messrs. Kinghorn, Campbell and Hinckley, to lease and operate the ferry between the island and Kingston. A warrant issued by Her Majesty, Queen Victoria, allowed him "to conduct a ferry service in Her Majesty's waters," and a ten-year lease was granted by the township council on December 22, 1857. This date also marked the beginning of the St. Lawrence Steamboat Company owned by the Hinckley partnership.

The passenger steamer Maud *plied the waters between Kingston and Cape Vincent via the Wolfe Island (Bateau) Canal, around 1872 to 1892.*

Courtesy of Bessie (Holliday) Kenney), from the C.H. Wall Collection.

COLEMAN HINCKLEY AND THE *PIERREPONT*

The *Pierrepont* was put into service in 1858. She was built at Point Alexandria of timber cleared from Coleman Hinckley's farm and milled at Edward Grindle's sawmill near Reeds Bay.[17] Coleman Hinckley Jr. was her first master, and the steamer was the first vessel to pass through the canal. Although the *Pierrepont* was engaged to transport islanders to and from Kingston, the scheduled four trips daily to the island allowed its owners time to serve Garden Island and also make regular trips to Cape Vincent. Finally, Wolfe Island was linked to the Canadian and American shores by a direct route.[18]

By 1861, the year of Wolfe Island's largest resident population, business was so brisk on the ferry that a second vessel, the steamer *Gazelle*, was put into service with Captain Coleman Hinckley Sr. at the helm. Advertisements appearing in *The British American* during the seasons 1861 through 1864 indicate that both vessels were calling at Wolfe Island and, in addition, the *Pierrepont* was on a schedule to Cape Vincent morning and night, while the *Gazelle* made extra trips to Gananoque. The *Pierrepont*, built hurriedly with unseasoned timber to meet a launching deadline, experienced difficulties during the 1864 season. To remedy the dilemma, both vessels were replaced by the larger steamer *Watertown*. The *Gazelle* was put on another run and the *Pierrepont* was retired to occasional use, but ultimately sank at the Hitchcock wharf circa 1870.

THE *WATERTOWN*

The *Watertown*, which tied up nightly at Cape Vincent where Captain Hinckley Sr. lived, provided service for eight years, during which time it attained publicity in connection with two marine fires. The first incident was on September 9, 1865, when she suffered a disastrous fire at the Cape Vincent dock with loss of one life. The second occurred on May 22, 1867. A fire aboard the *Wisconsin* gutted the vessel so completely that it sank off Grenadier Island, taking many lives. When news reached Cape Vincent, the *Watertown* sailed on a rescue mission but recovered only fourteen bodies. On December 20 of that same year she is reported to have assisted her ailing sister ship, the *Pierrepont*, through the ice.[19] The *Watertown* was retired from service in 1872 and is known to have passed through the Wolfe Island Canal on her way to Cape Vincent in 1874, probably her last trip.

In 1872, the St. Lawrence River Steamboat Company (owned and operated by the Folger brothers — Benjamin, Fred, and Henry) purchased the firm of Kinghorn, Campbell and Hinckley, and, after negotiating with the township council, obtained a seven-year renewable lease.[20]

PIERREPONT II AND THE *WAUBIC*

The new 130-foot steamer *Pierrepont II* was launched by the Folger brothers on September 2, 1871. She was a walking-beam sidewheeler, built in England and shipped in sections to be assembled at the Kingston shipyard.

An old sailor, who loved this vessel, told my father that he could always recognize her in the dark by the peculiar tone of her whistle. In 1913 the St. Lawrence River Steamboat Company merged with Canada Steamship Lines and sold the *Pierrepont*. Canada Steamship Lines continued the service to Cape Vincent.

In 1918 the Rockport Navigation Company Limited (owned and operated by John and Robert H. Carnegie of Rockport, Ontario), took over the Kingston-Cape Vincent run with their ferry, the *Waubic*. Built in Collingwood in 1919, it had a capacity for 450 passengers and twelve cars. In addition to operating on a twice-daily schedule from Kingston to Cape Vincent, making connections with the New York Central Railroad she sailed moonlight cruises among the Thousand Islands, with special excursions to Wolfe Island. The Kingston-Cape Vincent trip was discontinued in 1937 when the Thousand Islands Bridge at Ivy Lea was built.[21]

After some thirty years of service, Wolfe Islanders were expressing generalized dissatisfaction with the ferry runs. The *Pierrepont II* was American-owned and American controlled by the Folger brothers of Kingston. Frequently, the ferry schedule from the regular Kingston-Wolfe Island run would be changed for more lucrative cargo-paying stops elsewhere in the area.[22] In May 1903, frustrated Wolfe Island landowners went to the polls and voted overwhelmingly against the renewal of the ferry lease that was to expire on July 4, 1904. Subsequent to the expiry date, the *Pierrepont II* bypassed Wolfe Island on its route between Kingston and Cape Vincent.

THE FIRST *WOLFE ISLANDER*

The May 1903 vote galvanized islanders into exploring the purchase and operation of their ferry, but a major challenge would be the financing of the venture. Council voted to issue twenty thousand dollars in debentures. When tenders were opened, the lowest bid was ten thousand dollars over budget and the council was compelled to order downsizing of the proposed vessel

The Pierrepont II *swings around a Martello Tower in Kingston Harbour on its way to Garden and Wolfe islands circa late 1800s.*

to meet the available financing. By November the contract was let to the Bertram Engine Works in Toronto and the first township-owned ferry, registered as the *Thomas Fawcett* in honour of the reeve,[23] began service on August 3, 1904. A steel sidewheeler with a wooden superstructure, the ferry could accommodate the passenger and freight needs of the island community. She served admirably for the following forty-two years.

In 1905 this ferry was given a new name — the *Wolfe Islander*.[24] In addition to a regular schedule involving round-trip stops at Wolfe Island, Garden Island, and Kingston, she made Thursday afternoon trips to Breakey's Bay, where there were a shipyard and a brickyard, and lay over for the night before visiting Howe Island the next day. Later, Saturday trips to Simcoe Island and the head of Wolfe Island in Bateau Channel augmented her schedule. Farmers rounded up their cattle and loaded them onto the *Wolfe Islander* in the spring to be taken up the channel to Horseshoe Island where they would pasture until fall. The ferry master would unload the cattle into the water to swim ashore. The trip that followed was a pungent experience.

The *Wolfe Islander* was licensed to carry 304 passengers plus crew. The first crew consisted of captain, James Crawford; mate, Michael O'Shea; purser, Lloyd Card; fireman, Robert Berry; engineer, Robert Tetro; two deckhands; one cook. Like many ferries, the *Wolfe Islander* experienced her share of unusual events, some interesting and some frightening, but all were part of the saga of sailing. One early adventure occurred at night during a heavy snowstorm when the vessel was literally lost for over two hours. She was finally guided to the Wolfe Island dock by islanders who had set gasoline-soaked straw ablaze onshore. During another storm she was blown onto rocks at Howe Island, where she remained for two days before being set afloat. Seemingly, in December 1923, she almost sank at the Howe Island dock. A stranger incident, however, occurred on a Saturday night when she was spotted off the Kingston Yacht Club shoreline, drifting unmanned toward Lake Ontario. Her dock lines had been untied — by whom and for what reason was never established.

The first Wolfe Islander *was upgraded circa 1920s. She is shown pulling away from the Kingston Harbour with the former Richardson grain elevator silo in the background.*

Special trips, tours, and excursions were added to her regular schedule to increase revenue. The *Wolfe Islander's* service came to an end when she was condemned or, more gently, retired, on July 1, 1946.[25] The township council empowered Reeve Craig Russell to sell her for not less than four hundred dollars. Another islander, Oscar McCready, bought the vessel and had it towed to Button Bay where he beached it, intending to use it as a cabin for duck hunting. Unfortunately, it was unusable because of high water levels. The longest standing captain of this first Wolfe Island ferry (1914–1934) was Allan MacDonald, a native Wolfe Islander.

During the *Wolfe Islander*'s last four or five years of service, some people severely criticized the vessel as unseaworthy. However, she was inspected yearly, and, as Captain Ross Carnegie said in 1941, "She is an old boat and old boats have to be treated as such. If I thought she was unsafe, and I know she is not, I certainly would not be in command."[26] After the *Wolfe Islander* was retired, the islanders were without a regular ferry for over four months.

FILLING THE BREACH

Nineteen forty-six was a sobering year for islanders. Their lifeline had been severed. Fortunately, Buck Mullin and his father Rollie began using their fishing boat, *Sadie*, as a water taxi. The non-stop demand for service created an urgent need for a larger boat. The *Rebola*, a fine wooden craft measuring thirty-two by ten feet, was built for the Mullins by Gordon Roney of Wolfe Island. They named her after Buck's sister, Reba, and his

TOP: *Gordon Roney, a Wolfe Island boat builder, repairs one of W.E. Horne's boats. Pictured (l–r) are: (unknown), Louise Hawkins standing on crate, Gordon Roney, Arnold "Cricket" Hawkins, (unknown), and Sadie McDermott. Note the label on the crate. Gordon's father, Henry Roney, was a shipbuilder for the Calvin Company.* BOTTOM: *The* Wolfe Islander (2), *put into service in 1946, is seen approaching the island wharf. Photo 1973.*

mother, Ola Hinckley. During the open water season, she served as a water taxi on a daily twenty-four hour basis. Buck also provided winter service with his powered-up ice boat, *Saucy Sally*, driven by a large airplane propeller likely obtained from the War Assets Corporation. A Studebaker engine provided its power. In 1938 Councillor Craig Russell had spearheaded a campaign to obtain a new ferry for the island. As township reeve during 1945 and 1946, he continued to pursue this project. In August 1946, the council voted unanimously to ask the provincial government to supply one. That fall the Honourable George Doucett made the presentation.

During the breach the islanders' lifeline was also supported by two Second World War landing barges loaned to the township through the efforts of Dr. H.A. Stewart, a member of parliament for Lennox and Addington counties. The barges were able to make the crossing in less than twenty minutes. Although their capacity was limited, they bridged the gap. My grandfather, Captain James Kenny, piloted one of them for a short time when he was in his eighties.

WOLFE ISLANDER (2)[27]

This vessel, originally named the *Ottawa Maybrook* and built at the Collingwood shipyards for use in China's coastal waters, was in the hands of the War Assets Corporation. C.D. Howe, federal minister of transport, arranged for its release to be converted to ferry service.[28] Constructed of steel with a market value of $250,000, the new ferry, like its predecessor, was named the *Wolfe Islander*. However, there was a big difference in their power plants: the first was a coal-burning steamship and the second a motor ship powered by a diesel engine. With George Bates as her first captain, the second *Wolfe Islander* began regular service on November 18, 1946, with a capacity of twenty average-sized cars and 190 passengers. But running this new ferry was an expensive operation. In spite of efforts made to break even, on February 20, 1948, council passed a resolution to notify the Ontario minister of highways that the Township of Wolfe Island could no longer finance the ferry. This was not resolved until 1964 when the provincial government finally assumed responsibility for the operation of the *Wolfe Islander*. During the period before this decision, a plan was underway wherein the provincial government attempted to replace the *Wolfe Islander* (2) with two smaller ferries from Sault Ste. Marie. An ironic twist of fate had this plan reversed when the two ferries sank in a storm in Lake Huron.[29]

A government tugboat tows the Wolfe Islander (2) *toward the Kingston wharf. Because of the buildup of ice in the channel, this was a familiar sight during the January to March period. Photo 1972.*

THE *UPPER CANADA*

The free service on the *Wolfe Islander* (2), the ever increasing tourist traffic, and the fact that Wolfe Island has been a natural crossing point since the 1600s, made it necessary to augment the service with another vessel in 1965. Thus, the motor ship *Upper Canada* was put into service. Formerly the *Romeo and Annette*, she had begun her life as a ferry in New Brunswick before being purchased by the Ontario Department of Highways to serve Wolfe Island. She was scheduled to run on the same timetable as the *Wolfe Islander* (2), but would leave Kingston when the latter was departing the island dock.

The island had never experienced year-round ferry service and emergency service contact with the mainland had always been weather-dependent. In the fall of 1965, the provincial government provided an ice-breaking tug to break a channel through the ice and attach a towline to the *Wolfe Islander* (2) when necessary. Although this did help to provide the much needed safe, daily crossing during the winter months, ever-changing ice conditions and mechanical breakdowns played havoc with the schedule. In 1970 the Ontario government conducted studies of alternative routes that were less expensive for the taxpayer but very inconvenient to islanders, especially in winter. The favourable aspects were the building of two new docks and the provision of an end-loading ferry boat. Various proposals ensued, resulting in divisiveness among islanders and with the department, but ultimately compromises materialized.

The Upper Canada *was added during the tourist months to ease the wait time for the larger ferry. Photo 1968.*

BUBBLE SYSTEM

In preparation for the new ferry under construction in Thunder Bay, a bubble system was installed on the channel floor between Kingston Harbour and the Wolfe Island winter dock at Dawson's Point. Wilfred "Billy" Bolton of Wolfe Island, who worked for the Ministry of Transportation, was the bridge-crew supervisor responsible for the installation of this new-fledged system.[30] Various ice-density tests were conducted over the winter of 1971–72. During the next winter, steel pipe was welded together on top of the ice to the length of 17,525 feet. In the spring, once the ice was manageable, the pipe was put on the riverbed along the 3.3-mile ferry route from the dock in Kingston to Dawson's Point, marking the beginning of what would become the world's longest bubble system.[31]

The pipe, varying in width from three to six inches, is equipped with nozzles at fifteen-foot intervals throughout its length. Four compressors, located in a station in Kingston, pump warm air steadily through the pipe at about three hundred pounds pressure per square inch. As the warm-air bubbles leave the nozzles they cause an agitation, forcing the warmer water at the bottom to rise towards the surface. This motion in turn helps to keep the ice thin enough for the vessel to push through.[32] It sounds simple enough, but the total cost of the project was five hundred thousand dollars. To complement and assist the bubble system, five current inducers are used in the docking areas — three at Kingston and two at the Dawson dock. The inducers are capable of producing sufficient current to keep the dock areas relatively ice-free, eliminating the need for tug intervention.

END-LOADER — *WOLFE ISLANDER III*

The new ferry to be known as *Wolfe Islander III* was built at Thunder Bay by the Port Arthur Shipyards of the Canadian Shipbuilding and Engineering Company of Collingwood. Her plate shows "Ship No. 128, 1975." She was officially launched and christened on August 15, 1975, by Molly Apps, wife of then-retired Kingston and the Islands MPP, Syl Apps.[33]

The *Wolfe Islander III* requires a crew of only five. The trip from Port Arthur to Kingston took seven days under the watchful eyes of three local captains: senior ferry captain R.F. Fawcett, Howard Hogan, and Lewis Kiell. On the first trip were two mates, two deckhands, three engineers, a cook, and three representatives of the ship's designers. The inauguration ceremonies took place on February 5, 1976, at the new Barrack Street ferry terminal.

The total expenditure for the new ferry, docking terminals, and other costs was approximately seven million dollars, considered a worthwhile investment. The *Wolfe Islander III* provides the essential link between the highways of Canada and the United States. It furnishes round-trip conveyance for hunters, fishermen, and tourists. Most importantly, this ferry accommodates Wolfe Island foot passengers and all vehicles with daily year-round toll-free service to and from the island. The stated capacity is fifty vehicles and 338 passengers. The *Wolfe Islander III*, with a length of 205 feet and a width of

After being launched in 1976, The Wolfe Islander III *still functions today as the primary means of transit to Kingston. Here she is seen approaching the island dock in mid-afternoon. The school buses are bringing Wolfe Island students back from their secondary school in Kingston. Photo 2000.*

sixty-six feet, is the largest vessel to serve Wolfe Island. Four diesel engines, one toward each corner of the vessel, drive the Aquamaster propulsion units, enabling the wheelsman to guide the vessel in any direction. A major inconvenience is experienced when the ferry is in dry dock for servicing as there is no backup service.

Two end-loaders arrived at the Kingston berth in 1982. The *Saguenay* was soon sold, but the *Charlevoix* remained for several years. Her name was changed to *Frontenac* after being refitted for use at Amherst Island.[34] The retired *Wolfe Islander* (2) was purchased by the Comet Foundation in 1985 and towed to a location just northeast of the dock at Dawson's Point that September. She was sunk to be become a diving site.[35]

MOMENTS OF APPREHENSION ABOARD WOLFE ISLAND FERRIES

The *Wolfe Islander* (2), like its predecessor, experienced some "interesting" moments. The most spectacular was on January 14, 1950, when she went on a wild, nineteen-mile dash down the north channel of the St. Lawrence River. The ferry, carrying ten passengers, nine crewmen, Captain Joseph Sisty, and mate Harold Cosgrove, was blown off course, with the stern headed into the mouth of the river. Captain Sisty later said, "It was take a chance and put to open water or see the *Islander* batter herself to death against the concrete dock in port."[36] So, down the river she went, lashed by wind and waves, the captain looking for a safe haven to anchor until the storm abated.

When he realized he could not anchor behind Brophy Point, Sisty took her down to Quebec Head, the most easterly tip of Wolfe Island. After five attempts, he was successful. Six hours later he brought the vessel back up the same channel and berthed her safely. Observers onshore estimated the waves to have been fifteen to twenty feet high at the height of the storm. Because the wind gusted at ninety miles per hour, telephone lines were down and the vessel lost contact with land and caused great anxiety onshore, where concerned people were trying to catch sight of the ferry. Just when they surmised she had sunk, *Whig-Standard* reporters about two and one-half miles west of Clayton picked her up in high-powered lenses and let everyone know the good news.

I recall as a youngster hearing the foregoing spine-tingling tale told in retrospect by mate Harold Cosgrove in our kitchen in Toronto. No laughter had occurred on board during the storm's onslaught, and many Hail Mary's were offered up until they finally anchored. The Cosgroves were great friends of my parents, and to hear "Skee" (as he was nicknamed) tell the story with the twinkle in his eye was quite riveting. "Why," he exclaimed, "the local news had reported the ferry missing and likely sunk with all aboard." Fortunately, these trusty seamen resolved a very precarious situation. To get some idea of the power of that storm, according to local farmer George Pyke Sr. it blew the whole end out of a large barn on his farm, scattering the sheet metal over eight hundred yards. It also ruined a large double barn on Allan MacAdoo's Wolfe Island farm, killing four head of cattle.

Elwood Woodman is one of a host of mariners raised on Wolfe Island over a span of two hundred years. After gaining experience on the Great Lakes, he attained his mate's ticket in 1957 and his captain's papers at the

Dominion Marine School in 1963. His career spanned thirty years from 1963 on the *Wolfe Islander* (2) to 1993 when he retired from the *Wolfe Islander III*. Elwood talked about irregular events, some humorous and some nerve-racking, that can occur during a regular watch on a ferry. Early in his career he was sailing with Captain Ferguson of Garden Island. One day the captain's son, Father John Ferguson, boarded the ferry with his dog. During the crossing the playful animal goaded Elwood into tossing a stick for it to retrieve. Weary of playing the game, he flung the piece of wood over the side and, lo and behold, the dog followed. Elwood raced to the wheelhouse to advise the captain that the dog was overboard. Captain Ferguson, with some reservation, turned the ferry around and retrieved the dog.[37] This type of sport was summarily banned.

Babies have been known to enter the world unexpectedly. Several, over time, have been born in transit to Kingston while on the ferry, but, in winter conditions, ice floes could complicate the safe journey of the expectant mother. In one situation, while Captain R.F. Fawcett was piloting the *Wolfe Islander* (2) through the ice, he advised islander Pauline Edwards to keep her legs crossed until they reached Kingston![38]

Incidents of this type are legion, but another story came from Elwood's days as a deckhand. One winter, when the water level was particularly low, a stone-crusher transport boarded. The driver was required to park the vehicle in jackknife manner so he could back off upon arrival. Elwood had forgotten to double up the ropes to compensate for the vehicle's extra weight and ensure that the ferry would not move when the truck came aboard. Suddenly, all hell broke loose. The stone-crusher approached the ramp cautiously, but as soon as his vehicle hit the ramp, the driver applied the brakes, the force of which broke every line securing the ferry to the dock. The ferry, then in motion, was connected to the dock only by the back end of the truck, as the front end was on the boat. Fortunately, the *Salvage Prince* was nearby. When Captain Bates saw the incident, he put the steel nose of the tug against the side of the ferry and shoved her back into the dock. Had George not saved the day, one very large, heavy stone-crusher would have ended up in the drink.[39]

WOLFE ISLAND FERRY DOCKING FACILITIES

Captain Shirley Going emigrated from Ireland in 1848. He lived in the village and set up business as a real estate broker (listed as real estate speculator in those days). In May 1857 the township council loaned him twelve hundred dollars for a term of ten years for the construction of a steam gristmill and took a lien on the property and machinery. By November it was ready.[40] Going's office and mill were located in the village close to the water opposite the present Going Street (named in his honour). The road leading to the mill was in such poor condition that council allowed him to use ten days of his 1858 statutory labour to make improvements. From that beginning, Going became a prosperous man. At the height of his career he owned the flour and gristmill in addition to a large storage shed and office building on the property. According to the Allen's Survey there was a wharf stretching 250 feet from the shore out into the bay, at the end of which was a covered warehouse thirty feet by sixty feet. It was at that wharf that the *Pierrepont* would moor. By comparison, the Hitchcock and Dawson wharfs were each approximately fifty feet by 135 feet. Shirley Going's other holdings at that time included five village properties and at least seven farms toward the head of the island.

Around 1900 the Wolfe Island ferry began to land at Cummins' Wharf, owned by Charlie Cummins, the proprietor of the general store at the northwest corner of Main and Centre streets (now Fargo's). The wharf occupied approximately the same location as the present village dock, but also had a large warehouse on the water end. Grain was stored in the loft and hay on the lower level until there was a sufficient quantity to ship.

In early days, ferry docks and landing places were the property of the ferry owners except for the wharf near Cone Point, which was likely owned by the seigneury. The Hitchcocks, Dawsons, Goings, and Cummins each owned their docks. The present village dock and water lots were purchased by the township council in the early 1900s, and sold to the government of Canada for one dollar when it undertook to rebuild and maintain the wharf.

The waiting room that stood on the village dock was sold to Richard La Rush after the council agreed to accept his offer to purchase on May 16, 1947, on condition that he would remove it before work began on the dock. The building now stands on La Rush property on the north side of Main Street in the village. After being operated for several years by Mrs. La Rush as Marie's Dinette, it was closed then reopened for a short period as an antique shop. The building remains the property of the La Rush family.

WATER LEVELS

George Copway, an Ojibwa missionary and author, wrote in 1850, "Lake Huron is of great depth. Its waters are known by their beautiful clearness and the fact of their rise and fall once every seven years."[41] This natural fluctuation has since been proven to actually occur in all the Great Lakes within a six-to-nine-year period rather than the former seven-year rhythm. A more drastic alteration in water levels has been measured at approximately thirty-five year intervals, as discussed earlier.

Before 1976 and the launching of *Wolfe Islander III*, the changing water levels created problems as the older ferries required compensation at the ferry docks for safe mooring and loading. Very high levels would obliterate the sight line of the wharf's edges and temporary ramps of planks and cinders had to be used for vehicles and passengers until the water level receded. An exceptionally high level compared with an inordinately low level can mean the difference of between five and six feet. As a rock ledge close to the Marysville dock posed a serious threat to ferries, the provincial government built another dock at Dawson's Point, where the water is much deeper. This dock is used in the winter and year-round, even in gale-force winds.

This historic overview of approximately two hundred years of Wolfe Island's lifeline to the mainland includes the many vessels and technological advancements of the period. It is difficult to imagine improvements of the same magnitude in the near future.

CHAPTER 13
Coping With the Hazards of Isolation

There was a great demand for transit between Cape Vincent in the United States and Kingston via Wolfe Island during the 1800s. A number of enterprising individuals took on the challenge.

Wooden springless wagons covered with canvas provided the earliest mode of land travel between Kingston and Bath.[1] By 1846, these wagons, drawn by oxen, had evolved into the horse-drawn stagecoach — a simple wooden enclosure containing passenger seats suspended by leather straps. Travelling over rough roads, circumventing tree stumps, and sometimes sinking to the axles in mire when crossing streams or muddy roads could be an unnerving experience for the passenger. As lacking in comfort as this may seem, the stage gave ferry travellers a connection between the Hinckley wharf and the wharf at Marysville. The first commercial stage would run in conjunction with the schedule of the new steamer *Islander*, piloted by Captain H. Ives.[2]

Once winter set in, settlers could access the mainland with relative ease because the frozen river formed a natural bridge. On good ice, one could walk from Wolfe Island to Kingston in about one hour. Poor or slushy ice lengthened the trip to five or six hours. Ice, ten to twelve inches thick, would withstand horse and cutter, stagecoaches, and, in time, motor cars.

ICE PUNTS

Ice punts or ice boats, used extensively in the spring to cross the north and south channels, also navigated the less stable ice with relative ease as the wind in their sails propelled them over the dangerous areas. The larger punts were twelve to fifteen feet long, four to five feet wide, and equipped with runners, oars, poles, and ropes, all available for pushing, pulling, or rowing should a mishap occur. Ice punts carried both cargo and passengers. The men were often called upon to assist navigation.[3] The township owned an ice punt primarily used to transport the daily mail. The earliest ice punts and ice boats in Canada were created in response to inter-island transit needs within the Kingston region of the Thousand Islands.[4]

STAGE EXPRESS LINES

By 1860, primitive methods of transit were replaced by Coleman Hinckley's Kingston and Cape Vincent Express Company. As advertised in Kingston's *The Argus*, Hinckley promised "a new outfit of ice boats, covered sleighs, spring wagons and the like, the best accommodation for travellers anywhere in Canada and low rates for safe transfer of freight." "Partway" or "through" tickets to Albany and New York City could be purchased at the railway office on Ontario Street in Kingston.[5] This stage line made use of the Wolfe Island Canal, but when that ice was poor they crossed Brophy Point to Cedar Island and thence to Kingston. The Hinckleys had been transporting the mail on horseback across the island for many years. As the island's population swelled they simply expanded their services. Although the ferries were licensed and controlled by some level of government, the stages were not. Consequently, the ferry owners' stage line usually had competition.

A rival father and son team of George and Absalom Briggs outdid the Hinckley line by providing two return trips daily and one on Sundays. Their Briggs

LEFT: Two Hinckley Express stagecoaches are shown at the Cape Vincent railroad station ready for a return trip across the ice to Kingston via the Wolfe Island Canal, February 15, 1898. Each coach had two drivers: Dexter and Henry Hinckley for one , and Jack Kirk and Tom Muckian for the other. RIGHT: The Hinckley winter Ice Punt Express also operated on a regular schedule. Photo circa late 1800s.

Courtesy of Norman Horne, from C.H. Wall Collection.

Daily Express was a passenger-and-freight conveyance connecting the Grand Trunk Railway at Kingston to the Watertown and Rome Railroad terminus at Cape Vincent. In their advertisements the patrons were assured of a comfortable journey and safe passage for livestock.[6]

FOLGERS' WINTER STAGE-LINE

After the St. Lawrence Steamboat Company (Folger Brothers) took over the ferry service in 1872, they too ran a winter stage line comprised of two horse-driven sleighs, one carrying passengers and the other freight. Their stages, painted black on top and yellow on the supports and runners, became a familiar sight. A schedule called for a departure from Wolfe Island to meet an eight a.m. train in Cape Vincent and return to the island to clear customs at Horne's Point. The stage then took passengers across the island and frozen river to arrive in Kingston at about eleven o'clock a.m. The return trip leaving Kingston at one o'clock p.m. would meet the four p.m. train leaving Cape Vincent. One of the better-known drivers was Tom Muckian, but Dexter Hinckley — the company manager on the island — his son Henry, William "Bill" Horne Sr., and Bert Watts were equally reliable. Their reputation was that they never lost a passenger, horse, nor piece of freight, despite poor ice conditions.

THE ICE BRIDGE

Until sometime in the 1940s, the ferry always had a winter layup, the length determined by the severity of the weather and the amount of ice. The longest was from December 20, 1904 to April 10, 1905 — a total of 115 days. The shortest was three days in March 1953.[7] The density of the ice always dictated the weight of traffic and, with the exception of a long cold snap, had to be under continuous surveillance. Old-timers knew that the state of the ice was ever-changing with the temperature, wind, precipitation, and water currents. Ice considered to be safe one day could be extremely hazardous on the following one.

A multitude of sleighs, cars, and trucks rest at the bottom of the St. Lawrence to prove the point, and indeed, not a few persons and horses drowned due to discrepancies in the ice. Some, fortunately, only received a frigid dunking. It was customary, as a rescue precaution, to leave the horse's halter rope in place and a second rope hanging loosely around its neck. If the horse fell into the water, one would grab the rope, push the horse down into the water, and, as it resurfaced, pull the rope to help the horse back up onto the ice.

Once the ice was safe to walk on, a route was "bushed" by a row of evergreens from the island to Kingston to serve as markers to guide travellers on the right route. A blinding snow squall could disorient and throw any person dangerously off course. Bush locations were altered according to ice conditions.

To overcome the unsafe spring and fall conditions presented by the ice bridge, a tugboat, the *Salvage Prince*, owned by Captain Grant Pyke of the Pyke Salvage and Towing Company of Kingston, was used to break ice during the 1940s and 50s. Her steel hull would forge a channel between Kingston and Garden Island where passengers from Wolfe Island with sleighs, coaches, or on foot would meet the tugboat.

Grant, a native Wolfe Islander, was the father of George Pyke, who owned the well-known Pyke farms on the southwest shore of the island. George Bates, the tugboat's captain, would ferry passengers to Kingston during periods when the *Wolfe Islander* was in dry dock for repairs. Captain Bates, Francis Woodman's half brother and the husband of Margaret Hawkins, has often been referred to as the islanders' guardian angel, as he and the *Salvage Prince* have rescued many.

THE BIG CRACK

The "Big Crack" was a fissure that occurred in the ice every year in a different site, but usually about midway between Garden Island and the mainland. The crack was carefully scrutinized throughout the winter season because, contrary to common belief, its condition did not change due to wind and water pressure. It buckled and shifted due to temperature fluctuations, even when below freezing. Loud rumblings caused by the movement of ice below could be heard in the vicinity of the crack. For pedestrian traffic to cross the rift, which usually heaved a few feet, several long wooden planks were placed side by side lengthwise to it. Someone usually stayed at the crack in the daytime to monitor its condition and to ensure safe passage. People usually gave the attendant a small fee to compensate for his time and for the planks provided. Periodically, the township purchased the lumber

and appointed Patrick "Paddy" McDermott, a man well-versed in the idiosyncrasies of the crack, as keeper of the bridge. On several occasions when crossing during the winter of 1930–31, my father used Paddy's advice especially when driving a horse and cutter.

Captain George Bates, Mable McRae's uncle, was legendary for his remarkable seamanship on the Great Lakes and his many feats of rescue.

Orville "Tricky" McDermott, a respected riverman, is especially remembered for his chestnut mare, Minnie. For about eight winters prior to reaching twenty-one years of age, Minnie had crossed the ice under safe conditions, pulling a sleigh loaded with produce from the island to Kingston. Once the sleigh was reloaded with provisions for her return trip, off she went without a driver! Orville would start Minnie on her way and drive his car across to wait for her. At times, Minnie was known to enter the car path rather than the sleigh path. At the sight of car lights she would turn around, go back, and resume the proper course without the aid of a driver.[8]

Island lore has it that, during the 1940s, Tricky was known to charge a twenty-five-cent toll to motorists who wished to cross the ice by his route. He would barricade the entrance until a motorist paid him, then would throw in particulars about the route and tips about weak spots for good measure. The local police did not know whether the toll was legal, but there was no other way to drive across. For many years, even into the 1940s, knowing the safety of the ice highway was essential for island farmers.

EMERGENCY AIRLIFTS

The sense of isolation was felt most acutely during those winters when crossing was not only perilous, but at times impossible. At one point in 1951 it was necessary to fly bread to the island. During the 1959–60 winter, native Wolfe Islander and former RCAF pilot Gene Manion provided air service with his own plane. As recently as 1963–64, planes replaced the ferry service when the channel was impassable. The township arranged to retain a four-seater aircraft through the Kingston Flying Club with Douglas Wagner as pilot to operate on a demand basis.[9]

ACCIDENTS AND TRAGEDIES

One of the earliest recorded mishaps involved my great uncle, John Kemp, and six friends: Nathaniel Orr, John Wall, G. Wilson, Leo Cadotte, Albert Davis, and J.C. Daryeau. These men worked farms on Simcoe Island, and, on January 12, 1886, boarded Kemp's sleigh for a trip to Kingston. Although they were careful to use the bushed track, the ice gave way under the load and carried horses, harness, and sleigh to the bottom. Fortunately, the men were saved.[10]

On March 18, 1946, four of Wolfe Island's sons perished in a disaster. The victims were two young Alarie brothers, Gerald and George, along with thirty-eight-year-old Clarence Adair and Howard Cummins, recently discharged from the United States Marine Corps. The young men had crossed to Kingston earlier that day in an ice punt — a flat-bottomed, pointed-nose craft known as a "sharpie." On their return, observers noted that the boat was overloaded. Four survivors were rescued off Brophy Point, where the punt had capsized: Leon McDermott (the boat's owner), Keith McCready, John Lacey Sr., and Robert White. Witnesses to the accident, W.J. Hogan and C.F. Gurnsey, were responsible for their rescue.[11]

In spite of the availability of a tug, accidents continued as people persisted in striking out across ice on foot or in vehicles. New Year's Eve, 1955, was the fateful day for Mrs. Marion Fox. She lost her life while attempting to walk to Kingston unaccompanied. About three weeks later, Clarence Ogle, a Wolfe Island hardware merchant, drowned when he and his truck went to the bottom of the river.[12]

Perhaps the worst near-tragic incident involving some Wolfe Islanders occurred on Christmas Day, 1955. Fern (Fawcett) Small, her husband, Lieutenant (later Major) Darrell Small, and their four young children left the married quarters at the Barriefield Military Base to embark on the *Salvage Prince* for Christmas dinner with family on Wolfe Island. Their trip to the homestead was uneventful, but the joy of their revelry turned into terror on their return journey. My cousin, Gary La Rush, had readied a horse and hayrack bobsled for their trip across the ice to where the *Salvage Prince* awaited them at Garden Island for the transfer back to the city. The following eyewitness account was recorded by Darrell Small, a near victim:

> Seventeen of us boarded the sleigh sitting on butter-boxes and wrapped in blankets. Fern and Aunt Mae Pyke sat at the left front holding Holly (two years old) and Leslie (a four-month old babe). Carol sat on the tail-board of the sleigh loaded with our gifts. I knelt between Fern and her aunt. Off we trotted with sleigh bells, a typical Krieghoff scene. As we neared the tug, the rear bobs broke through the ice. To seek thicker ice, Gary swerved away from the *Prince* which put us parallel to a fillet-crack, cutting the corner of the ice slab where the boat-track met the river flow. The sleigh tilted left and slid into the water. Those at the rear had time to scramble onto the firm ice, our eight year old Carol among them. Aunt Mae, a veteran in ice crossings, calmly turned up her butter-box, dropped in her purse and gifts and shoved the box across the sleigh onto the ice. She then turned heroine, grabbing an eighty year old Dutch lady by the collar of her lamb coat and dragged her to safety. In the openings among the ice cakes were Gary and the horse, Fern, myself, Holly, Leslie, Shirley Marlow and her two little girls. Mercifully, the horse died of shock and dragged the sleigh down with him.... Treading water, I managed to hold up Holly and a Marlow child, until they, Shirley and her baby were rescued. Fern was holding our baby, Leslie. She had an elbow on the ice edge and caught one of the kapok jackets that were tossed into the fray, still tied up as they were stored, tucking one under her fur coat, she was able to pass Leslie to a rescuer. No longer able to tread water, I gave up and began to sink, saying farewell to myself or was it to my angel?... Once on board I became aware of a lot of screaming and yelling from the excited passengers on the tug. A saintly girl named Gertrude

Hogan gave her fur coat to wrap Holly. Tommy Crumpet, the engineer, took Baby Leslie and laid her on the rocker arms of the diesel engine to warm her. He undressed and wrapped her in his woollen shirt. Capt. Bates got under way and set a record for the one and one-half mile crossing; some say we were at the Brock Street dock in six minutes. There an ambulance waited and the children were loaded into it and taken to Kingston General Hospital.[13]

Although each passenger had assisted however possible, the real heroes were Captain George Bates on the *Salvage Prince*, his crew, and Gary La Rush. The crew tossed life-saving devices to the soaking frigid commuters while Gary made desperate but futile attempts to free his horse from the doomed sleigh. Finally, he was forced to let them go down and turned to rescuing passengers with Captain Bates and crew. Miraculously, all were saved.[14]

Most of the accidents and deaths by drowning throughout the years have been due to people gambling on the ice being thick enough to carry the weight entrusted to it. It has been estimated that one person walking on ice should have a minimum of four inches of ice under foot and a two-ton vehicle some twelve inches of ice. It became generally accepted that a slow sleigh was safer than a fast car. In 1965, with the aid of a tug and a towline, *Wolfe Islander* (2) operated dock-to-dock all winter and continued to do so until her retirement. The vessel was not always on schedule, but the service remained constant. Despite this daily, safe, winter-ferry service, many residents persisted in crossing the ice in four-wheeled vehicles or by snowmobile. Kingston ultimately passed a bylaw in 1985, after the Murphy tragedy, forbidding any crossing of the ice by vehicle or on foot.

CAPTAIN GRANT PYKE AND THE *SALVAGE PRINCE*

One of the few clues to Kingston's industrial past is a grey, barn-shaped building at the foot of Gore Street just east of the Marine Museum of the Great Lakes. This building was the headquarters for the Pyke Salvage and Towing Company from the late 1920s onward. Grant Pyke Sr., a descendant of one of Wolfe Island's pioneer families of the early 1800s, owned this company for twenty-five years. In the early 1920s, Captain Pyke, requiring improved docking facilities for his slowly expanding fleet, established his base on the Kingston wharf.

The Kingston harbour, and indeed the three-and-one-half mile stretch of water to Wolfe Island and surrounding islands, usually froze deeply in winter, causing the frequent stranding of vessels, including the Wolfe Island ferry. Captain Pyke proceeded to remedy the problem. Frustrated by the ongoing lack of a boat with ice-breaking capabilities, in 1924 he commissioned a shipbuilding company in Selby, England, to construct such a vessel. The new ninety-two footer, christened the *Salvage Prince*, was a handsome, 450-horsepower, steam-driven tugboat capable of carrying four tons of cargo. The *Salvage Prince* had a huge cast-steel propeller

The tugboat Salvage Prince *with Captain George Bates at the helm is towing the much larger Canadian Steamship Lines passenger ship,* Rapids Prince, *after freeing it from a shoal at Lachine Rapids. This feat was one of many successes for native Wolfe Islander Captain Grant Pyke and his Pyke Salvage and Towing Company of Kingston. This same tugboat would transfer islanders who had travelled the ice by sleigh or on foot as far as Garden Island on to Kingston*

Courtesy of Grant and Margaret Pyke.

and stowed a one-ton anchor.[15] The vessel's steel bow, which could crush ice up to a depth of twenty-four inches, enabled her to function year-round. She repeatedly paved the way through the ice for the Wolfe Island ferry, but Captain Pyke could not envision that one day this very vessel would rescue his *Prince* from the treacherous ice.

The *Salvage Prince*'s propeller, an artifact on the Pyke property, gives some perspective as to the tug's size. Grant's son had measured the propeller diagonally and found it to be eight feet, three inches from tip to tip. The cast-steel prop, estimated to weigh a ton, gave credence to the boat's power.[16]

On one occasion Captain Fawcett recalled rescuing the *Salvage Prince* from one of her ice-breaking sorties during the winter of 1958–59 while he was at the helm of the *Wolfe Islander* (2) on a routine trip to the island, following the icebreaker. The *Prince* would thrust up onto the ice and her very weight would crush it, thus creating a pathway for the ferry. This time, the ice was so dense that, when she forged up onto the ice, she was unable to break it and subsequently rolled on her side like a beached whale. There she was, all ninety-two feet of her, the rescuer in need of rescue! Captain Fawcett manoeuvred the ferry close to the *Salvage Prince*, enabling his crew to hook onto her with a cable over her stern. This exercise righted the *Prince* and freed her from her perch.[17]

THE ICE STORM — JANUARY 1998

Wolfe Island has often encountered weather patterns that differ from those of the mainland. This was not so on January 7, 1998. The severity of the storm warning that had been issued was underestimated. Heavy freezing rain during late afternoon covered the island and

Leaning against this tree is the propeller from the famous tug Salvage Prince, *the size of which suggests the tugboat's strength. Pictured (l–r) are: Captain R.F. Fawcett and three generations of Pykes: Grant Jr., son Jason, and grandson Jack, photo 2006.*

parts far down the river to the east, paralyzing towns and bringing cities like Montreal to their knees. Within twelve hours island trees were so densely coated with ice that branches broke off and tree trunks split. Then lights began to flicker — an omen that the worst was yet to come. By Thursday evening the relentless freezing rain had produced such thick, heavy icicles clinging to hydro wires that the hydro poles surrendered. One by one they toppled. Many roadways were blocked by fallen trees and branches while power outages were being reported throughout the island.

Flora Devlin's observation that "each blade of grass was like a spear that did not break when stepped upon" characterized the density of the ice on the most delicate of objects.[18] She also remarked that her beautiful cherry tree had split in all directions, resembling an inverted umbrella. The weight of this heavy covering of ice was even too much for the CKWS television transmission tower to bear and, of course, telephone lines and poles did not escape. With utility poles, wires, and tree branches scattered askew following the storm, "Wolfe Island looked like a war zone," according to island resident Walter Knott. Within forty-eight hours the island was without power. Never were they more isolated. The ferry had continued to run on schedule, Mr. Knott observed, but the boat could not dock without the ramp mechanism being plugged into a makeshift power source.[19]

After the initial shock, islanders began to mobilize. Dairy farms were the highest priority as cows' needs had to be met in a timely fashion. Until generators could be activated, cows waited to be milked and watered. Temperatures of milk coolers could not be maintained nor equipment cleaned.[20] As the dairy farmers' herds are their livelihood, they rallied to assist each other by milking each cow by hand, the old-fashioned way, until all systems were functioning again.

It was not long before Mayor Jan Haesselaar declared a state of emergency, raising awareness of the needs to the broader community. It seems that Wolfe Island shared the brunt of a storm that was declared the worst in Kingston's history.[21] Some of the islanders' necessities included generators, lamp fuel, matches, candles, batteries, water, and patience. Steve Fargo and the Mosiers, local merchants, did an exceptional job of searching out emergency supplies and foodstuffs not requiring cooking. Those lucky enough to have wood-burning stoves fared somewhat better. The abundance of wood fuel allowed many to maintain a modicum of warmth and prevented water pipes from bursting in their homes. The irony was that young families, dependent on electricity, had to move in with parents or in-laws for warmth from old-fashioned wood stoves, as in the case of Lois and Sidney Eves.[22]

As the freezing rain persisted, basements were flooded and the longer the power outage, the more foodstuffs in freezers were at risk of putrefying. Wilf Brown, Danny Mosier's garage mechanic, visited homes with generators to pump out basements and help keep freezers operating.[23] An emergency shelter was established at the fire hall by island volunteers, and detachments of OPP officers transported supplies of meals, flashlights, batteries, flares, and traffic-barrier tape to Wolfe and Howe islands. Islanders, assisted by reserve soldiers from Thunder Bay, delivered bottled water and thermal packs while checking dwellings for owners' needs, especially those of the elderly.

The need to restore hydro poles and lines was addressed by truck crews from as far away as northern Ontario and New York State. Teams not already involved with repairs in the pathway of this deleterious storm mobilized as early as possible because close to four hundred disabled poles had caused three weeks of silent cold darkness on the island. The earlier efforts of volunteer firefighters to clear much of the tree debris

The Simcoe Island ferry is seized in the ice of Bateau Channel. The air boat in foreground is indigenous to the St. Lawrence region. They are commonly called "Scoots" in the Georgian Bay area.

Courtesy of Anne Taggart. Photo 1995.

and pull-downed hydro lines out of the snow saved the hydro workers at least two days of work. During the crisis, electricians from Belleville donated their time, along with a hydro crew of seventeen from Kitchener.[24] Area by area, power was restored within seventeen days.

How did islanders in remote areas cope? They cut holes in the river ice for water. They kept their fireplaces stoked and confined their living space to one room if possible. If they were fortunate like Flora Devlin, isolated at the Foot, young people came to stay with them. She noted that two men, who had come to hook up a generator for her, were from a town near the Ontario-Manitoba border.[25] Royal Military College students came to help remove broken branches from road arteries and dispose of them through the chipper.

All in all, the highlight of this disastrous period was the surprise visit of the Honourable Prime Minister Jean Chrétien and provincial dignitaries. They surveyed the damage and greeted many residents at the fire hall, which had been converted into a temporary shelter. Their very presence and concern and the outside assistance boosted the spirits of all who had struggled with the storm. Once again, Wolfe Islanders had overcome a seemingly insurmountable hazard of isolation. Their special ability of drawing together and working as the tightly knit community they have been for many decades saw them through this natural disaster.

CHAPTER 14
Establishing Transportation Links

This heavily wooded island was used as a route between Cataraqui or Fort Frontenac and points south by Champlain, Frontenac, La Salle, Joseph Brant, Montcalm, and countless Native people, explorers, friars, surveyors, and pioneers. A 1784 map by government surveyors Lewis Kotté and James Peachey illustrates that at least two routes had been well-established. The one most frequently travelled was across the neck of land that links Barrett Bay to Bayfield Bay. It is identified as the "carrying place" to Carleton Island. A portage between the presently named Carpenter Point and Bayfield Island, necessary because the point and the island were not yet completely separated by water, is also specified. The second route, designated "little carrying place," crossed the narrow section in the Fifteenth Concession. Canoes were carried or bateaux transported on small wheels over these portages.[1]

When the Wolfe Island shoreline was surveyed in 1816, the second portage was no longer necessary as a new island had been born. From that point on, this little island and adjoining water were named Bayfield Island and Bayfield Bay after the the Royal Navy hydrographic surveyor Admiral Henry Wolsey Bayfield. Between 1816 and 1856 he surveyed the shorelines of the Great Lakes and Georgian Bay, the St. Lawrence River, and the Gulf of St. Lawrence.[2] Bayfield Island (previously called Mud Island) was once part of Wolfe Island, but over a period of years gradually separated.

ROAD CONDITIONS

Surveyors descended on Wolfe Island in 1836 and began their work. The whole township, with the exception of the Old French Survey, was to be reassessed into lots approximating one hundred acres, and the need for roads was apparent.

When homesteaders needed to travel within the confines of the island, they used the most expedient method available — usually a rowboat or horseback, depending on their destination. Some pioneers chose the horse-drawn rough wooden box on runners called a "jumper." Two-wheeled carts succeeded the jumper before wagons came into general use in the 1850s. Wooden sleighs, drawn by oxen, were used both summer and winter to carry passengers and supplies.

As lots were cleared and neighbours settled closer to each other, fences were built to keep cattle from straying through crops. Tree stumps, the natural by-product of clearing the land, were converted into fences. Roots were turned outwards to hasten the drying process and, when it was time to replace the stumps, any dried-out, unsaleable timber was split lengthwise and built into split-rail or snake fences. While early barriers served useful purposes, the varying widths at the base of fences, and the fact that many early survey markers had been lost or destroyed when timber was removed, led to boundary disputes between neighbours. As this problem worsened and became widespread throughout Upper Canada, the government passed legislation in 1834 to establish the role of "fence viewer," who was required to examine and make a determination in disputed situations. His decision was final. Fence viewers are still employed in many rural areas, primarily where there are livestock. The Township of Frontenac Islands continues to budget for the financing of fence viewers to mediate such occurrences.[3]

Roads were desperately needed, but the funds to build them were not available. As the number of settlers increased, the need expanded. By 1825, the crossover route was no longer adequate. Conditions worsened to the point that Samuel Hinckley, operator of the ferry between Point Alexandria and Cape Vincent, let his lease expire with the explanation, "the road across the island being in a very bad state, and the ferry thereby becoming unprofitable, your petitioner did not apply for a renewal of the lease."[4] Travellers from Kingston were cut off from the United States, and Sam Hinckley and his fellow residents on the south shore were isolated from the north part of the island and mainland Canada.

Although he had given up the ferry service, Hinckley was not quitting. If the Quarter Sessions could not or would not do something to improve road conditions on the island, he would. He journeyed to Kingston and Cape Vincent, soliciting assistance from those who would benefit most, and he undertook to build a road. The cost of construction was upwards of fifteen hundred dollars — a major sum for the time. So determined was Hinckley to build the road that he contributed his own labour and undertook three quarters of the cost.

Hinckley petitioned for a renewal of the ferry lease and at the same time presented the facts concerning the new road to the magistrates. He asked to be reimbursed for his financial outlay. Two years following the completion of the work in 1829, a three-man panel was convened by the Quarter Sessions to examine the road and determine the value of the work with a view to awarding Hinckley a sum to cover his investment. Their report stated, "it remains a good firm road, well drained and passable at all times and as a consequence of its improved state, we would remark that the mail is conveyed with great regularity and dispatch across the island and a public stage now runs from Cape Vincent to Watertown three times each week."[5] After assessing the length of the road (seven miles) and the value of the work, they reduced the requested amount "to the sum of $1,280 as the lowest sum that Samuel Hinckley ought to receive."[6] The committee's closing remarks were, "the judgement, enterprise and public spirit displayed by Mr. Hinckley on this occasion is uncommon, as it is praiseworthy."[7] The workmanship was deemed the best quality of road work in the Midland District. Hinckley's route traced what was then called the Old Cone Road and the turnpike.

When Sam Hinckley was re-granted the ferry lease, the terms were for seven-year renewable periods with the proviso that he would receive reimbursement for the road work "from the rents of the ferry alone." The rent payable for the lease of the ferry was about six dollars per year! It has also been said that Hinckley's road work also cost him three daughters — some of the men who assisted him in the task proved to be worthy suitors.[8]

In winter the so-called main roads were covered with snow. Homesteaders along the main roads, working cooperatively, were responsible for ploughing sections from their home to their neighbours' place. "Ploughing," then, was dragging a log behind a horse or two shorter logs side by side behind a team. On the return trip the path would be widened enough to permit sleighs to get through. Those living close to the river usually made their pathway to the river ice.

The first sleighs were flat wooden platforms attached to runners and, when metal runners were not available, two straight boughs with the bark removed were used. Because of the island's inordinate snowfall, the all-purpose horse-drawn bobsleighs were used; their box-like frames could ride atop the snowdrifts. In sub-zero weather, brick-sized pieces of stone were heated in the fireplace, wrapped in cloth and placed on the floor of the sleigh for warmth.

The British term "turnpike," as applied to the Sixth Line, was used loosely, as Wolfe Island never had a toll road. (The word was taken from an earlier road that had served islanders since the 1700s.) This primitive road, called the "turnpike" and drawn on a map in 1836 by Publius V. Elmore, a surveyor from the Quinte area, is shown running to the west of the newly surveyed Sixth Line.[9] As shown on the map, it began at the village dock (Hitchcock's) and, after veering through the woods in an arc to the west, swung back to connect with Button Bay Road. At the time, the road was also known as the Old Cone Road after Samuel Cone, who had operated the first ferry from Point Alexandria to Cape Vincent. At least six log cabins were built on the west side. Three were occupied by members of the Mosier family and one by James McRae.

As late as 1845 there was another winding primitive road known as "The Passage."[10] This one began at Reeds Bay and extended to the Old Cone Road near the island's south shore. Although its purpose is now obscure, it may have served the mills, fishermen, and early travellers. Button Bay Road, the former Old Cone Road, and Button Bay, previously called Granis Bay, were named for the great number of button bush shrubs that once lined the shores of the bay.

The north end of the Sixth was opened to the north shore, intersecting the Front Road at the eastern boundary of lot 6, Old Survey. The seigneury wharf was located at the north end of the road (Mill Point). When the ferry docks were moved to Hitchcock's landing, travellers persisted in using the more convenient old turnpike road. When the north section of the turnpike was

TOP: *The old* Wolfe Islander *is moored, facing west at the former township wharf located at the north end of the Third Concession between lots 23 and 24 of the Old Survey. A St. Lawrence skiff in the foreground is manned by John Taggart, a fishing guide. Photo circa 1900.* BOTTOM LEFT: *The Commercial Hotel was possibly the W. Davis Hotel shown on lot 24, Old Survey, of the 1878 Meacham Atlas map. This lot is actually labelled Davis Hotel on the 1860 Walling map. It may have been built to accommodate the Davis quarry workmen, circa 1850s.* BOTTOM RIGHT: *Dode Briggs's Channel Grove Hotel on Simcoe Island attracted patrons from far and wide, including high-profile business tycoons and government officials. The ladies pictured here (l–r) were Simcoe Islanders, circa 1910: Nora Sudds, Anna Sudds, Mabel Woodman, and Eva Sudds.*

incorporated as part of the Sixth, the newly surveyed road to the north shore was closed. The new roadway, which included portions of the old turnpike, the Sixth Line, and the Old Cone Road, became the main route across the island linking Kingston and Cape Vincent.

It is unlikely that new roads would have been opened for any other reason than to serve homesteaders, as the total allocation for roads in the township budget was only $160 per year. The actual expenditures for road maintenance were $171 in the year 1848, while more than a century later, in 1967, operational costs for roads exceeded $49,000. Current budgets for road maintenance on Wolfe Island approximate $763,000.[11]

The Old Survey had not made provision for roads running north and south. Morey Spoor and others who lived up the Front Road had petitioned in the previous year (1844) for a road between the Third and Fourth concessions of the new survey. According to bylaw 32, passed in 1844, the new survey provided for a road allowance between the concessions using the westerly limit of lot 23 in the Old Survey as a line. The road to be opened was to stretch from the north shore to the Base Line, allocating eighteen feet from lot 23 and forty-two feet from lot 24. When the contract was awarded, the sum of $180 was allotted for the work. This road work would allow access to the Staley Wharf, a nearby cheese factory, and the Davis Quarry from the interior of the head of the island. Farmers finally had a route for transporting hay to waiting ferries or scows, and milk to the cheese factory. This wharf at the north end of the Third Line became township property for public use.[12]

THE ROAD TO THE FOOT

With the population of the Foot (east of the canal) ever expanding, the need for a good road from the Seventh Concession to the Twenty-First Concession became a priority. In those days settlers had to petition the governing body for a new road or any changes to an existing one. In July 1841, fifteen eminent freeholders attached their signatures to a petition and report of the surveyor of highways, along with the proposed roadway map, to be presented to the justice of the peace of the Midland District's General Quarter Session.[13] Their names are shown as follows: Hugh McDonald, Lewis Mosier, Nicholas Mosier, John Horne, Thomas Sluman, Charles S. Davis, James McRae, Thomas Horne, George Marsh, John Cameron, Peter C. Davis, Alex Campbell, Archibald Hitchcock, J.J. Barrett, and Lewis Mosier Jr.

In the centre of this map is a structure marked "McDonalds." Research by Brian McDonald, a direct descendant of the island's Scottish Settlement, suggests it may have been a hotel at one time, referred to as the Blair Hotel on the 1878 Meacham map. As it was situated on the northwest corner of lot 1, Concession Eleven south of the Base Line, it may have been a focal point for the Scottish Settlement.[14] The requested roadway did indeed come to be, but it followed the village road east and traced a somewhat different route from the Eleventh Line through to the Seventeenth Line than is depicted on this rudimentary map.

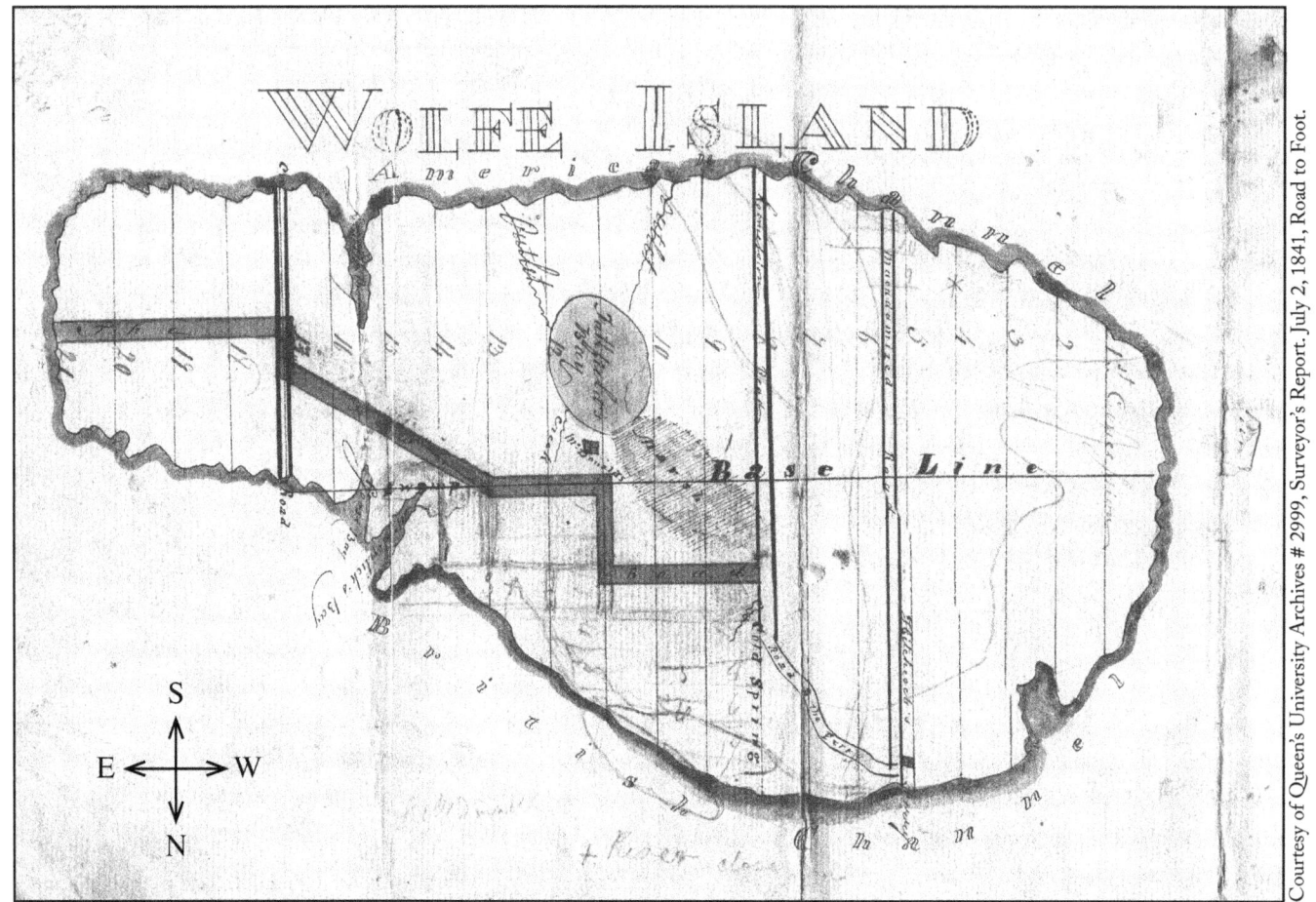

Map 8: Influential landowners on Wolfe Island petitioned the government for the road to link settlers at the foot of the island to the village and ferry service, shown in this map dated July 1841.

PATHMASTERS

A poster dated May 5, 1879, contained a copy of bylaw 150 for the Township of Wolfe Island regarding statute labour and the role of pathmasters, who were instituted by Upper Canada's first parliament, in 1793, as overseers of highways to ensure that roads were clear for travellers.[15] As Wolfe Island would not be developed for some time, this bylaw was not enforced until nearly ninety years later. It stipulated that the requisite duties of this appointment were:

> take out their road lists without delay and notify all persons within their

respective districts or bounds, liable to perform statute labour [road work], that they are so liable, the amount of labour for which they are respectively liable, the time(s) and place(s) when and where the said labour is to be performed and it shall be the duty of each pathmaster to make his return on his road list of the statute labour completed and the work done under his supervision, to the Clerk of this Council, on or before the fifteenth day of August each year.[16]

Pathmasters were required to work along with those whom they were overseeing. Among Wolfe Island's earliest pathmasters (1819) were Frederick Fanning and Thomas Davis.[17] Fanning was appointed to look after the Front Road, which at the time may have included intersecting roadways between Sand Bay Road and the Eighth Concession. Davis was assigned to the crossroad (the turnpike and the Old Cone Road) probably because he operated the ferry between the island and Kingston while his father-in-law, Sam Hinckley, operated the ferry from Point Alexandria and Cape Vincent. The crossroad connected the two ferries as it does today. Section 10 of the above cited bylaw stated, "All persons liable for statute labour shall perform the same for which they are so liable under the instruction and direction of their pathmasters when duly notified to do so."[18] However, there was a provision that only applied in certain instances whereby a person liable for statute labour could pay a sum of fifty cents per day in lieu of work.

If an appointed pathmaster, or person subject to perform labour, refused or was negligent in his duties, he was fined up to five dollars and costs. Non-payment would land him in the common jail for a period not exceeding ten days. The bylaw governing the above was signed by Reeve P. Dawson, H.O. Hitchcock, clerk, and was peremptory effective May 5, 1879. The amount of statute labour required of anyone was determined by the value of his property, or, if he was not a property holder, by his age or whether he owned a cart and horses or oxen to draw it. The usual work requirement was from two to twelve days per year.[19]

The statute labour bylaw's main concern was the repair of roads rather than the construction of better roadbeds, thus later generations inherited older roadways that would continually need repairs, rather than newer, improved roads. The first real move towards actual improvement did not come until 1924, when the Ontario government assumed responsibility for twenty-eight miles of the island's roads, consisting of one on the Sixth Concession and its feeder road to Point Alexandria, both now known as Highway 95. The Front Road on the north shore extended from the head of the island through the village of Marysville and eastward in a zigzag fashion to Port Metcalfe at the Foot. This twenty-one mile stretch is now known as Highway 96. My father recorded some personal travel experiences in his original manuscript:

> [B]ut even the takeover by the Ontario government did not bring an overnight change in road conditions. As late as 1931, driving conditions to the Foot were perilous, especially after

rain or snow. My work during the fall and winter of 1930–31 required my visiting people at the Foot of the island two or three times a week. This responsibility enabled me to become acquainted with the road conditions and alternate routes.... Let me share one vivid recollection. It was a rainy Sunday in November and I was on my way on the Fifteenth Concession to Christ Church for the afternoon service. I drove a horse and buggy and had reached the Thirteenth Concession, where I encountered the Rev. William Halpenny, who was returning from a service at the United Church on the Eighteenth Concession. We stopped to greet each other and exchange remarks regarding the weather and then we attempted to move on. As we made the effort to depart, I looked down and noticed that we were not going anywhere! Both our buggies were stranded in about ten inches of a thick, soupy quagmire. This was not a pothole! The same circumstance extended all along the main road to the Foot. I yet can hear my thoughts concerning the condition of that road being translated into very colourful language by some of the islanders!

When the snows came, we organized our horses, cutters, and sleighs and took to the fields.... The main route was to follow the roadway to Frank Fawcett's, on the south side near the Twelfth, and turn into his gateway. From there we followed a track that had been marked out from field to field. The route followed the path of least resistance and only touched the roadway where it crossed over.... As winter progressed and the ice became safe to ride on, we turned onto the river ice just east of the village. We rode under the old wooden bridge that had replaced the swing bridge over the canal, and travelled the length of the canal out onto Big Bay. We headed back onto the south shore of the island anywhere between the Fifteenth and Seventeenth concessions, depending on the condition of the ice. This route was so expedient that it surpassed in time and ease our navigating the roads in summer....

The section of the road leading to Livingstone's Point (Ferguson's Point) was a one-lane causeway across the marsh, which was covered with three to six inches of water. The Livingstone, Smither, Hall, and Cleary families, who lived on this point, crossed the water-covered section with apparent ease. On the contrary, I was terror stricken when I crossed — probably because I could not swim. Most of the other roads were not much better than laneways.

Aside from the sharp curves on the road to the Foot being softened about twenty years ago, there have been no major road improvements since highways 95 and 96 were paved in 1934.

THE WOLFE ISLAND, KINGSTON, AND TORONTO RAILWAY COMPANY INCORPORATED[20]

Who, today, would imagine Wolfe Island as the starting point for a Canadian railway that would run to Toronto and beyond? Yet this plan, spearheaded by John Counter, the mayor of Kingston, was initiated more than a century and a half ago. While the ultimate purpose of the proposed railway was to connect the growing cities of New York and Toronto, the immediate concern was to extend the trade route from Rome, New York, where the Erie Canal and the Great Western Railroad intersected, to Kingston, at the time a gateway to the quickly expanding western Canada.

The prospectus, engineer's report, provisional committee, and act to incorporate are contained in a fifty-four-page booklet.[21] Mayor Counter was chairman of the Provisional Committee, and a partner in the Calvin Company's stave-forwarding enterprise. The first four members of the committee were: John A. Macdonald, MPP, Kingston; Henry Smith Jr., MPP, County of Frontenac; Benjamin Seymour, MPP, Lennox and Addington; and T.W. Robinson of Kingston.

The financing of this project appeared to have been established with the responsibility for the cost of the portion of the railway from Rome to Kingston to be assumed by American interests, a third of the debentures to be endorsed by those living along the right of way. The total projected six–million-dollar[21] cost of the Canadian portion to Toronto, of which $5.5 million was pledged by England, left a reasonable balance of half a million dollars to be subscribed in Canada. As the provisional committee agreed to a contract for four hundred thousand dollars, this left only one hundred thousand dollars to be invested by the general public and people who lived along the rail line.

The proposed route for the Wolfe Island, Kingston, and Toronto Railway across the upper St. Lawrence required determining sites for bridges to cross the north and south channels — a first. The mainland terminals were to have been at Cape Vincent and Kingston, with Wolfe Island as the crossover point. William Dewey, a civil engineer and secretary of the Watertown Railroad Committee, surveyed the route across the island in 1836. Although three lines were surveyed, the engineers' report provided more sound reasons for recommending the third. All three lines were identical for the first mile, which began at the shoreline at Hinckley's ferry on Point Alexandria and proceeded to an area near the Seventh Line, where it would cross Button Bay inlet. (The railway was to have an embankment here.) From the north shore of the Button Bay crossing, three surveys were made. The map illustrates all three, but the focus here is on the favoured, the Red Line.

The Red Line would run diagonally from Button Bay to the shoreline of lot 10 on Mill Point. This route crossed the turnpike about one-half mile south of the Base Line and skirted the foot of Lambert's Hill. Engineers recommended this route as it crossed the Ridge

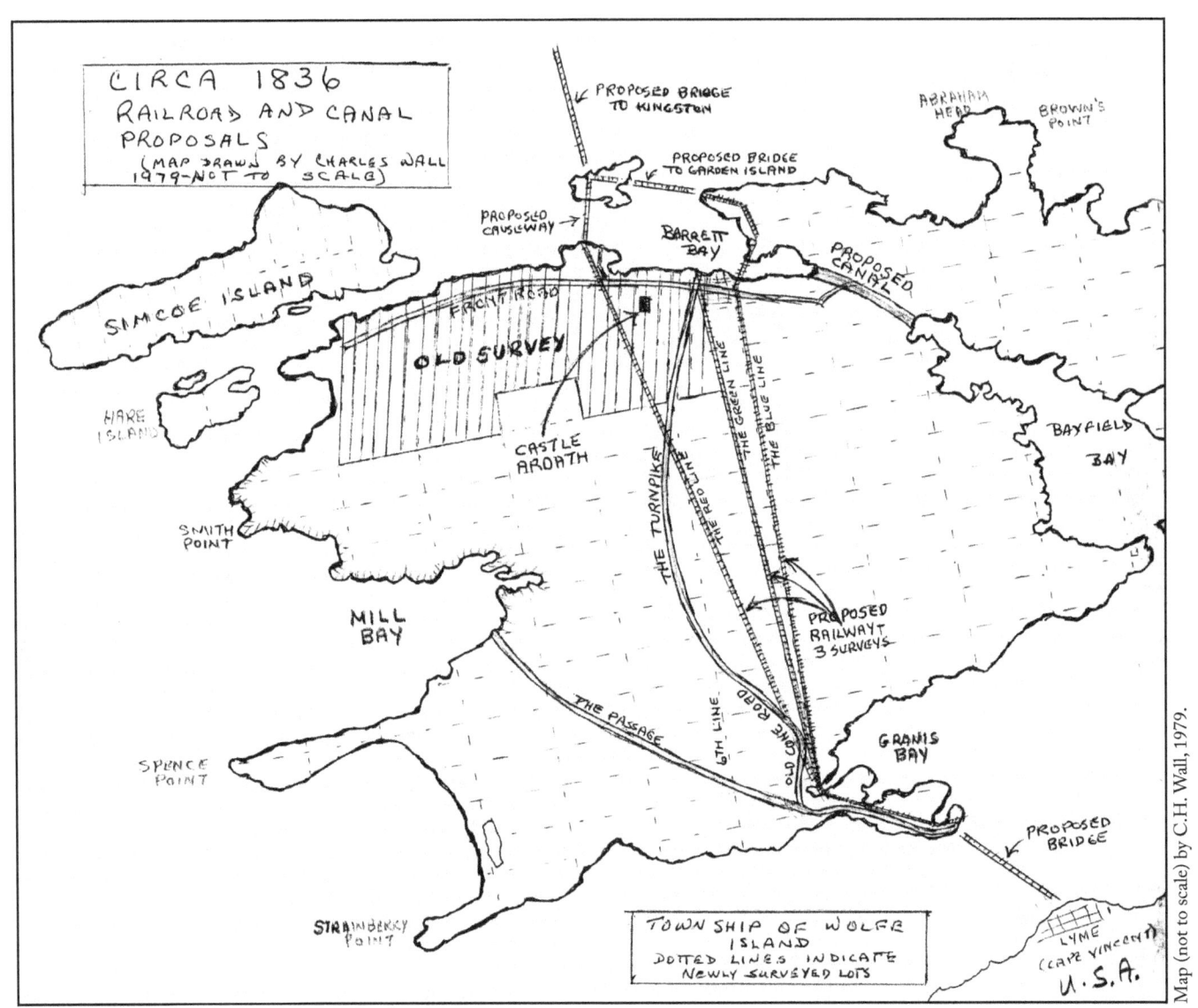

Map 9: This map has been adapted from specs presented in the 1836 railway and canal proposals for the Township of Wolfe Island.

at a point forty feet lower than the others and there was less rock to clear from the proposed line. At Mill Point the line would cross the river channel to Garden Island by means of an embankment, leaving one or more bridged openings to allow scows to pass and to prevent a rise in the water level during strong westerly gales. D.D. Calvin had agreed to cooperate in the Garden Island section where there was to be a terminus. The survey plan also called for a bridge a mile and a quarter long to span the north channel to Kingston.[23]

The prospectus and engineers' report were published at the office of the *Kingston Daily News* in 1846, ten years after the Wolfe Island survey. In the interim the survey was being conducted between Kingston and Toronto. One section of the report dealt with traffic across Wolfe Island from Cape Vincent to Kingston and projected thirty thousand passengers and forty-five tons of freight per annum. This volume may have generated eighty-six thousand dollars in annual revenue. The minutes of the Wolfe Island council indicate that, for a considerable time, the proposed rail line was a hot topic requiring much discussion. The issue was finally brought to a head on December 2, 1851, when it was moved by Mr. Cameron and seconded by Mr. Boyes:

> that, should the Municipal Council of Wolfe Island subscribe stock by issuing debentures or other, toward a railroad or canal, connecting the City of Kingston with the terminus of the Rome and Cape Vincent Railroad; this Council considers it would be equitable and just to look upon such subscription as a portion of their subscription, (as a part of this Council) in the great line of Rail Road contemplated and agreed to, by the Municipalities between this place (Wolfe Island) and Toronto.[24]

Apparently, the above motion was agreeable to all concerned, because two days later bylaw 38 was enacted, providing for debentures to be issued in the denominations of one hundred dollars to a total of four thousand dollars, to be redeemed at the rate of eight hundred dollars on the first day of January in each of the years 1857 through 1861. While Wolfe Island was spared the noise and pollution that accompanies a railway, one wonders what happened to so ambitious a project that it literally vanished into thin air except for the odd prospectus gathering dust in a public library.[25]

THE WOLFE ISLAND CANAL

Kingston, in its prime, had been the depot for the transshipment of cargo from lake schooners to riverboats navigating the St. Lawrence River. With a west-to-east transport system successfully in place, a north-south trade route was sought. The American railroad system, designed to access lake and ocean ports in the 1840s and 1850s, meant that shipping on the Great Lakes was largely directed to American ports, causing a gradual decrease of eastbound vessels on the St. Lawrence. The result was a reduction in calls at Kingston's port and the consequent loss of revenue. An alternative route emerged in the form of a charter granted, in 1836, to the Wolfe Island Railway and Canal Company. Its chief director was the Honourable Charles William Grant, the baron de Longueuil.[26]

The canal was to create a shorter water route between Kingston and Cape Vincent. Its proposed path was a straight line through the island from Barrett Bay on the north shore to Bayfield Bay (Big Bay) on the south shore. The length would be approximately two and one-half miles with a depth capable of accommodating vessels with a draft of no more than six feet. As time passed, construction had not begun on either the rail line or the canal.

When the railway charter expired in 1851, John Counter was a director of the new Wolfe Island Railway and Canal Company in partnership with other entrepreneurs — Henry Gildersleeve and future prime minister John A. Macdonald. Likely aware of improbability of the railway plan, he anticipated carrying fully loaded rail freight cars through the canal on barges towed by the ferry he had built at his Marine Railway works in Kingston. Named the *John Counter*, the ferry also carried passengers.[27] It ran between Kingston and Cape Vincent, but apparently was replaced after only one season, 1853–54.

In 1851 the county council authorized the purchase of four thousand dollars of stock in the new company. When construction lagged under the supervision of Kinghorn, Campbell, and Hinckley, the Gildersleeve interests in Kingston, which held a large block of stock in the proposed canal project, gave a construction contract worth fifty-six thousand dollars to Joseph Milner of Kingston.[28] The slow-moving project was finally completed in 1857. Every inch of the way was dug with

The New Island Wanderer, *a passenger ferry, circa late 1800s, was one of several that used the Bateau Canal en route between the north and south channels.*

Courtesy of Bessie (Holliday) Kenney, from the C.H. Wall Collection.

horse-drawn, hand-guided steel drag-scrapers capable of scooping only two and one-half bushels of earth or stone at one time. Islanders such as Alex Fawcett and John Gibson were foremen while local and transient labourers completed the work.

The only roadway over the canal was located where Highway 96 now crosses. In earlier days the crossing was made on a swing bridge attended by Joseph Kyle, whose property abutted the north shore of the canal. When boats approached the bridge, the boatman tooted and Kyle would leave his farm chores to swing the bridge. Records indicate he was paid for his service from the Gildersleeve office in Kingston. The canal, officially known as Bateau Canal, was a boon to shipping and was used by both cargo and passenger vessels. Increased traffic and use by larger vessels led to the canal's being dredged to the depth of seven feet in 1868–70. Kinghorn, Campbell, and Hinckley paid the ten-thousand-dollar cost.

In 1872 the St. Lawrence Steamboat Company, owned by Folger Brothers, purchased the island ferry business and the operation of the canal, but did little to maintain the canal as a functional waterway. Weeds and silt slowly filled the canal until, in 1892, its use by steamboats and larger vessels was abandoned. Thus, the "Big Ditch," as it was named by many (its sides were not lined with stone), ceased to be an active waterway. Today, large mounds of grass-covered earth line both sides of what remains of the canal.

From the time the canal fell into disuse until 1913, landowners whose property abutted the channel were puzzled as to the ownership of this waterway. With the death of Lucretia Gildersleeve, the mystery was solved. She had held all of the Wolfe Island Canal stock. James P. Gildersleeve, her brother and executor of her estate, surrendered the stock and filed a quitclaim, which stipulated that, as of that date, the Gildersleeve family would have no further legal or other entitlement to the property marked and known as the Wolfe Island Canal.[29] Seemingly, the canal property reverted to the original owners and their successors.

Private property aside, there has been intermittent agitation throughout the years to have the canal reopened, especially when dredges were working within a short radius of the unused ditch. Just two years after the property reverted to its original owners there was foment over dredging the canal because the government was deepening the channel at the foot of the island in preparation for building a new dock. During 1920 and 1921 citizen groups in Kingston and Cape Vincent mounted pressure to persuade the government of Canada to re-dredge and reopen the canal for navigation. In spite of its years of silt-fill and deterioration, a spokesman for the federal government declared in 1936 that the canal was a navigable waterway. However, the provincial government replaced the old wooden bridge with two three-foot culverts, making the canal non-navigable, yet groups still persist in trying to have some action taken.

Sporadic peaks of interest in reopening the canal lead to heated discussions at the township level. Apparently, the land owners along the canal route would still have the final word as to whether they wished the canal opened up to navigation or just sufficiently to help flush out the pollution that continues to build up in Barrett Bay and along the shores. The most recent efforts to bring this conundrum to the table occurred early in the new millennium, but efforts are currently stalled. Many believe that this area warrants recognition as a historical site with a designated plaque.

The first vessel to use the canal was the *Pierrepont* and the last, we have been told, was the *America*. The *America* and the *Island Wanderer*, both owned by the Folger brothers, made daily trips through the canal between Kingston and Cape Vincent. After the canal was closed, they and other larger vessels sailed around the head of the island unless forced by bad weather to go by way of the Foot. Until 1915, most of its length was still wide enough for two motorboats to pass with ease, and for a time it was used by the Edith Line and other sightseeing tour boats. About 1900, one enterprising islander, Allan McLaren, then owner of the historic Hitchcock House, built a shanty on the canal shore, where he ran a line of muskrat traps. Today, the canal is used only by a few fishermen in the spring, who claim that it abounds in bullheads.

THE BRIDGE —
"To Be or Not to Be"

The dream of a bridge connecting the island to the mainland is older than most of the residents. The earliest plan located, dated November 1955, was a drawing by David Humphries, a Kingston surveyor, of a proposal for Kingston Harbour submitted to the city's planning officer. The survey shows a bridge from Carruthers Point on the mainland to Snake Island, then across the foot of Simcoe Island and over to Wolfe Island to link up with Highway 96 at the head the island. This was to be a road-and-railway bridge and was accompanied by a suggestion that, when completed, industrialists could look to Wolfe Island for business sites. While most islanders agreed a bridge was needed, no one thought that their island paradise should be subjected to industrial pollution.

In 1958, New York State's Thousand Islands Bridge Authority proposed a toll bridge across the St. Lawrence between Cape Vincent and Kingston. The New York firm of Madigan-Hyland issued a 130-page study, prepared for the Thousand Islands Bridge Authority, in 1959. It mentioned that such a bridge would open up inland Wolfe Island to suburban land development to the estimated extent of 730 new homes in a span of sixteen years. It also noted that the five-hundred-acre waterfront tract at the southwest corner of the island (Big Sandy Bay), owned by the St. Lawrence Parks Commission, would come into its own as parkland serving a possible eighty thousand visitors per season. It predicted highway tolls of $1.50 per passenger car and forecast 729,000 cars would use the bridge during the first year.

In October 1970 the United States Congress approved the Cape Vincent-Kingston bridge and authorized the Bridge Authority to contract with the Canadian government to build the bridge. The United States stood behind the project with twenty million dollars in revenue bonds, but the Canadian government had not committed itself to any details regarding its role in financing its portion. Wolfe Island's long-time reeve, Tim O'Shea, once said that the bridge would bring tourist gold to Frontenac County. He had been a strong supporter and chairman of Frontenac County Council's International Bridge Committee for many years.

Regardless of the fact that Wolfe Island has been a crossover point for centuries and that the proposed bridge would be international in ownership and scope, many residents believe that the bridge would be more detrimental than beneficial. Their main opposition has centred on a combination of perceived access difficulties caused by long ramps, the impact of tolls on islanders, no controls on the number of vehicles accessing the island, and the possibility of undesired commercial enterprises destroying the tranquility of the countryside and ecologically sensitive areas.

During 1974, when individuals and groups were proposing alternatives to the ferry, a suggestion involving two bridges came from a special citizens' committee. This committee, chaired by Dr. W.R. Ghent of Kingston, met with John Rhodes, minister of Transportation and Communications, to discuss their idea. They advocated a permanent "bridge link" between Howe and Wolfe islands and the mainland. The proposed route was a bridge from the mainland somewhere in the vicinity of the present Pickett's Ferry to Howe Island and another span to connect Howe and Wolfe islands. The committee also recommended that there should be a controlled access spot bordered by a parkway along the route. To offset the cost, the committee advocated a toll of fifty cents, which they estimated would finance the cost over the ensuing ten years.

Although the "bridge link" idea had merit, major winter snow or ice storms would also indicate that bridges of any sort would prove no better than the ferries. Although each of the ferry routes serving the islands of Amherst, Howe, and Wolfe is equipped with a lakebed bubble system, the Amherst and Howe ferries had to discontinue service during a storm in 1977, while it took the *Wolfe Islander III* about two hours to make what is normally a twenty-minute trip. The culprits were not the bubble systems, nor the ferries, but the continuous fall of snow that created slush about five feet thick in each of the ferry channels. The Thousand Islands International Bridge at Ivy Lea was passable during the course of this storm, but barely usable because the U.S. Interstate 81 to the south was closed. Huge snow blowers from Trenton Air Base were used to clear the roads on both Amherst and Wolfe islands before the inhabitants could get to their respective ferries. The same difficulty would have been encountered had there been bridges. The fact that the residents of Howe and Wolfe islands are presently serviced with excellent ferry systems suggests that no high-rise international bridge or low-level bridge-link system will appear in the foreseeable future.

CHAPTER 15
Marysville Comes Alive

Wolfe Island's village was named Marysville before Mary Hinckley's death in 1877, in recognition of her contributions to the island. Endowed with the same humanitarian spirit so evident in her father, Samuel, she was, in turn, and frequently simultaneously, mother, ferry operator, tavern keeper, postmistress, and midwife. A woman busy with the chores and concerns of daily living, she was never too occupied not to assist others. Widowed early, she competed in a marketplace dominated by men, and was well-deserving of the title "Aunt Polly" so affectionately bestowed upon her.[1]

Mary was born in Oneida County, New York, in 1790, and later moved with her Loyalist family to the south shore of Wolfe Island. In November 1807, she married Thomas Davis in St. George's Church, Kingston (later the cathedral). In November 1821, Thomas drowned, leaving Mary with seven young children. Three years later, the young widow married Loyalist Archibald Hitchcock Jr., who had come to Canada via the United States. This second union produced four additional offspring.

THE VILLAGE OF MARYSVILLE

Three of Mary Hinckley's children, Tom Davis by her first marriage, and John and Oliver Hitchcock by her second, controlled all the property in the proposed village development site. Tom Davis's holdings to the east comprised all of lot A and part of lot 1, Old Survey, while the Hitchcock brothers' land to the west was the balance of lot 1 and all of lot 2, Old Survey. Leander Street divided the two properties.

Angus McLeod surveyed the whole area into village lots and completed his work mid-fall 1857. The following year, William Percival, P.L.S., planned the street

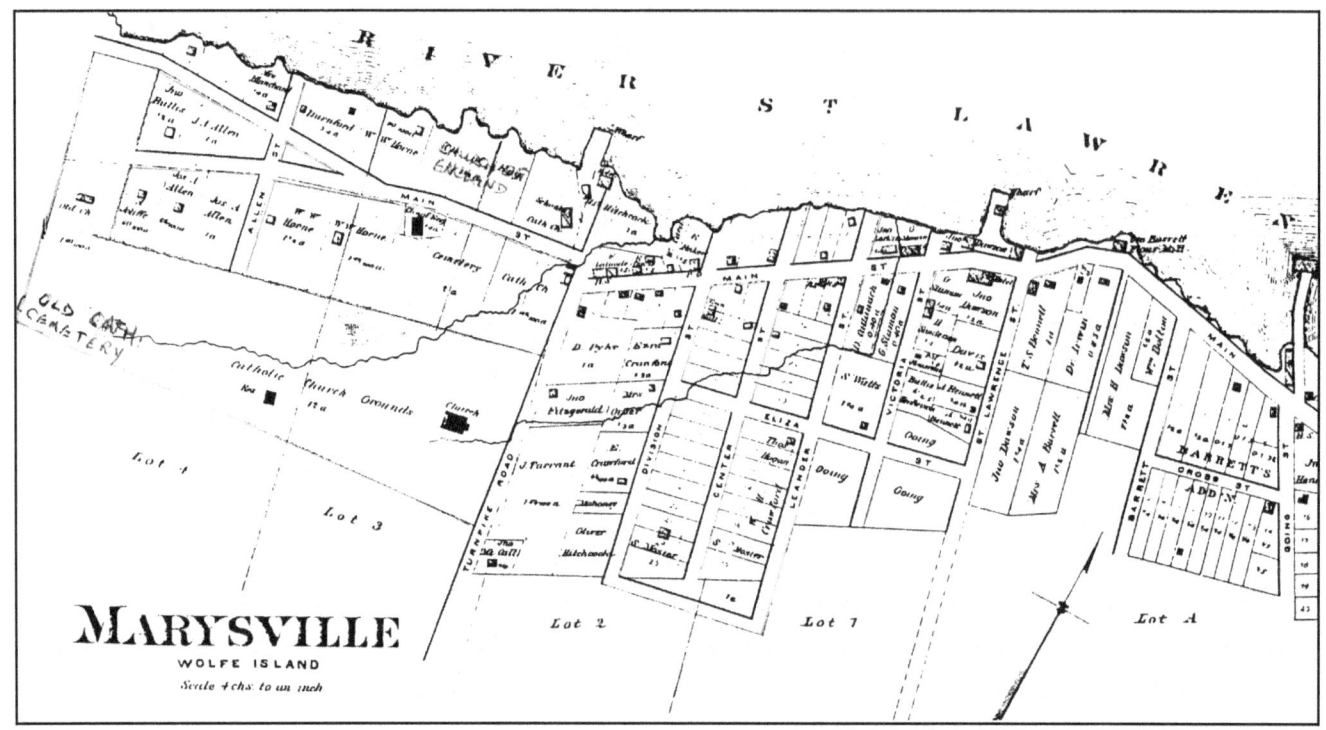

Map 10: The Village of Marysville, Wolfe Island, from the 1878 Illustrated Historical Atlas of Frontenac, Lennox and Addington. *This map shows the village's development by 1878, when the whole island was owned or leased. Original lots 1 and 2 are noted in the map's foreground.*

layout of the village, which was registered on December 7, 1858. The Marysville map was drawn from actual surveys by and under the supervision of C.R. Allen[2] and represents the village at that time. The transformation from the log-cabin era to village was easily accomplished. Most of the newer buildings were constructed of readily available timber, which was cheaper than brick or stone. Both Baker's brick store and Mullin's brick house on Main Street were built about 1878 by a Kingston contractor named McGraw. The bricks, made by Breck and Booth of Kingston, had been hauled across the ice the previous winter. Around 1900, a detached four-room house in the village equipped with an outhouse and well rented for from $2.50 to three dollars per month. At one time Marysville boasted far more buildings than at present, as many have succumbed to fire.

My father wrote about a fire in the village, one he did not witness but one that evoked many memories:

> I was at our home in Toronto on the night of January 30, 1977, when I was awakened from sleep with the

awareness of a fire on Wolfe Island. I could see the flames … but I could not envision what was burning. Our house on Leander Street came into view but it did not seem to be involved. As the picture disappeared from my mind, I noted that the flames were to the north of our house. The next morning at breakfast, I related the incident to my wife.… (She) phoned her good friend, Marie Baker, to inquire whether all was well with her and the family. To my amazement we learned that fire had destroyed Sid Fawcett's store and Ross Bustard's home [the former Tarrant store and homestead]. Both buildings were located at the corner of Main and Leander streets, several yards north of our island home. That was a melancholic moment for me because during my stay on the island in 1930–31, I had lived with the Tarrants. Hattie Tarrant had been like a mother to me in my home away from home. I can still see the pot-bellied stove in the middle of the store with men sitting around swapping yarns. Out front to the west was a gasoline pump and to the east was a hitching post, because times were changing and horse-drawn vehicles were giving way to motor cars. The stable at the back had been converted into a garage and it was there one day that a runaway car pinned me to a beam. Dora La Rush, standing in the doorway of the house later occupied by Antoine, saw what had happened and screamed to her son, Harold, to rescue me. In addition to physical injury and pain, I was on the verge of total collapse. Fortunately, the affable resident Doctor Spankie and I had our first meeting. His home and office were in the house which Ross Bustard had owned. Those were just a few of the many things that passed through my mind, and, not surprisingly, had helped me to fall in love with Wolfe Island and its people.

The building that housed Fawcett's Red and White store (presently the Island Grill Restaurant) was erected circa 1873, and throughout the years had been occupied on separate occasions by six owner-merchants, the earliest being John Larkin. The store was painted red and trimmed in white with the typical Victorian fretwork. Larkin was a commercial fisherman who operated the first grocery/dry goods business at this location. He was followed by T.A. Hatfield, a popular merchant. Business successors were John Friend and Son. Thomas Friend took over when his father died in 1887, occupying the premises for about thirty-eight years. A devout Anglican and church warden, Tom Friend is said to have lived his life as he professed. His nephew, Harold Friend, ran the business for a brief period in 1926. When Tom retired in 1927, Howard Tarrant became the new proprietor.[3] In 1950, after twenty-three years as a successful operator, increasingly poor health forced him to sell to Ross Bustard. Sid Fawcett acquired the property and business from Ross in 1975.

TOP: The store on the left, at the north end of Leander Street was erected in 1873. John and Thomas Friend owned it at the time of this 1918 photo. The building on the right was owned by merchant T.A. Hatfield. Later, for several decades, it functioned as Ernie's Lunch. BOTTOM: This is the same store and residence on Leander when it was owned by Howard Tarrant. Charles Wall lived there in 1930–31 when he was in charge of the Anglican parish at Trinity Church and Christ Church. The congregations included residents of both Wolfe and Simcoe islands. The store, later known as the "Red and White," was destroyed by fire on January 30, 1977. Photo 1930.

Courtesy of C.H. Wall collection.

THE BAKER DYNASTY

On New Year's Eve, 1977, the door was locked for the last time on Bakers' store. It had operated continuously under the family's ownership for more than 140 years. With no descendants to carry on the family tradition, the brother and sister team of Arthur and Marie Baker reluctantly closed their doors. The store had been founded in 1836 by their Loyalist great-grandfather, Michael Baker. His first shop had been located near the river on the west side of Leander Street, in the old log house later occupied by Tyner La Rush until his death.

As business increased, the Bakers acquired property at the northwest corner of Main and Division streets and built a frame building in 1851, large enough for more store space and living accommodation. A drive shed for customers' horses and rigs was built behind the store.[4] In the 1970s its walls were covered with the remains of notices proclaiming coming events and items for sale from distances as far away as Belleville and Brockville. One, from Gananoque and dated 1872, offered ten thousand pounds of wool in tweeds and flannels and declared that the company did custom spinning. Another notice, dated April 20, 1878, advertised a sale of household furniture belonging to a Sarah Ann — time had obliterated the surname.

As recorded in the *Canada Directory* 1857–58, Michael Baker was still the sole proprietor, with his family assisting in the business. By 1865, he, then eighty years old, had arranged a partnership with his son, Edward, who was actually running the establishment at the time. Upon his father's death, he became the owner. Born at Pillar Point, New York, Edward was brought to Wolfe Island when his parents emigrated in 1836. He married Eliza, daughter of Morey Spoor. By 1878 the business had outgrown the frame structure. In order to accommodate expansion and provide more living quarters, Edward Baker had an adjacent two-storey brick building erected. Little did he know that this structure would remain the home of the Bakers' family business for the next one hundred years. Although the store presently flies the Mosier sign, the original buildings remain intact.

While reading a customer's account in an old ledger, my father found a sampling of the variety of merchandise sold by Edward Baker and the prices charged in 1872. Most foodstuffs sold by the pound. Butter varied in price between fifteen cents and twenty-two cents throughout the year, bread was fourteen cents per loaf, tea fifty cents, sugar eleven cents, and cheese thirteen

The frame building that housed Baker's store was built in 1851. Note the sign at the top right corner of the original frame building — J.S. Baker, furniture dealer and undertaker. Photo circa 1880.

Courtesy of Theresa Broeders, from the Briceland Collection.

cents. Salmon and whitefish sold at fifteen cents and pork at ten cents. The best brandy was priced at fifty cents per pint and proof was one dollar per gallon. Chewing tobacco sold at twenty-three cents per half-pound, smoking tobacco fifty cents per pound, and matches seventeen cents per large box. Dressmaking supplies, hosiery, hair necessities, men's braces, boots, and polish were available along with household needs. Thirty years later house-building and repair items had been added to inventories, although prices had not increased appreciably. Bakers' store accepted subscriptions to the *Family Herald* for one dollar per year and the *Daily Whig* for $2.50 per year. By comparison, a 1978 subscription to the *Whig-Standard* was fifty-two dollars while current annual subscriptions exceed two hundred dollars. Furniture could be ordered from manufacturers' catalogues kept on the counter. Accounts at the store were payable by cash, produce, or work. Some individuals bartered honey, eggs, or butter. Others received allowances for hauling freight, while another was credited for mending a store awning.

Businesses on the island had always required goods shipped from Kingston and the proprietor was solely responsible for removing his cargo from the vessel and transferring it to his workplace. With no ferry service in winter, a depleted item remained out of stock until spring, when service resumed. These difficulties motivated enterprising islanders to earn credits on their store accounts by meeting the boat in summer to remove the supplies. In winter they would assist by hauling the freight from Kingston on ice punts or sleighs.

After Edward Baker's business opened in the new building, the family converted the old store into additional living quarters. Sometime later Tom Hutchinson rented the store section and converted it into a harness shop where he sold and repaired buggies. The next occupant was Harry Card, the liveryman, who operated the place as a garage for repairing cars. About 1920, George Rattray, the general merchant at the corner of Main and Centre streets (presently Fargo's), rented the space for displaying and storing new washing machines and small farm implements. Consecutively, the building was used as a dwelling, a Royal Bank branch office, a dwelling again, and a branch office of the Bank of Montreal. Monsignor Charles E. Baker returned to the island and lived in this building until his death in 1988.

Joseph Stafford Baker, Edward's son, grew up in the family business but, early in life, established himself as an independent agent for several mainland firms, using the family store as his point of contact and sales outlet. Joseph married Margaret Payne and they had four children: Charles, Sadie, Arthur, and Marie. When the children were still young, tragedy struck the family. Joseph's promising career came to an abrupt end when he was stricken with an illness from which he never recovered. It seems that he was also involved in undertaking and the sale of coffins, and it is said that he pricked himself with a needle and subsequently died of formaldehyde poisoning. His widow met the challenges of the ensuing years with determination. Eliza Baker, the children's grandmother, managed the store while Margaret raised her children. Sadie, Arthur, and Marie remained single and gave their lives to the family business, and Charles entered the priesthood. Sadie assumed management of the store with Arthur and Marie sharing the workload. After her death they became the joint owners and continued until their retirement.[5]

Charles, the only male in the Baker line not to follow in the grocery business, ministered in parishes at

Cornwall, Belleville, Stoco, and Tweed. He was referred to as the "Vicar General of the Parish" by the parish of St. Michael the Archangel in Belleville where, for over twenty years, he had assumed administrative and parish duties during Monsignor Nicholson's long siege of ill health. Father Baker's dedication was legendary, and upon completing fifty years in the priesthood, he was honoured with the title *monsignor*. In 1975 he retired from active parochial work.[6]

The lovely little house that sits on the Baker property near the river originally occupied a lot on the south side of Main Street next to the town hall. The house was moved to its present site during the 1970s when its original lot was sold to the township.

VILLAGE STREET LAYOUT

The Baker family's industry and influence in the community lives on. Michael Baker served as the township's first clerk and his daughter-in-law gave her name to Eliza Street, which runs east to west between Division and St. Lawrence streets. Other street names also carry little messages from bygone days. Leander Street commemorates the death of the seventeen-year-old Leander Davis, who drowned after falling through the ice off Wolfe Island. Whatever the reason the unusual name was given to the boy, it proved portentous; in Greek mythology, a lover named Leander drowned one stormy night in the Hellespont.[7]

When the village was mapped out and streets named, Queen Victoria was twenty years into her long reign. Thus, Wolfe Island obtained its Victoria Street, on which Alberta Victoria Boyd lived. It would appear that her parents named their daughter for both the queen and her consort. Wolfe Island's Division, St. Lawrence, and Main streets have no historical significance. Centre Street appears on the original survey as a line drawn down the middle dividing the village equally, east from west. This street, named long before the village was laid out, was the location of the first village schoolhouse where social and religious gatherings were also held. Now a home, this much-altered building still stands on the original site.

Barrett, Going, and Cross streets in the east end of the village are closely connected historically. Barrett Street obtained its name from S.T. Barrett, who operated the earliest village flour mill opposite what is now called Cross Street. Going Street was named for Captain Shirley Going, who built and owned the first steam-powered gristmill, situated near the water opposite the street bearing his name. The narrow, unnamed lane, later called Cross Street, lay between the properties of Dr. Irwin and Mrs. Dawson. This roadway was opened by the Dawsons to allow the Barrett family, living to the south, easier access to Main Street. Allen's Survey Map of 1878 depicts Cross Street running east and west between Barrett and Going streets.

Hillcrest Street begins just west of the Anglican Church as a fork from the Front Road and is aptly named as it runs along the crest of a hill. At present it is a short dead-end street, but at one time extended right across lots 5 to 15 in the Old Survey to enter the Fourth Line Road opposite John Craine's property. As the road was established in the mid-1800s with its entire length on property belonging to the Reverend Joseph Allen, it may have been a private road to accommodate the castle, as well as the Healeys, who lived south of Lambert's Hill, the McCullochs, who lived in the stone house just west of the Fifth Line Road, and any other tenants along its route. It was also used by parishioners of the first Catholic church, then located in the middle of a field that now adjoins the dead end. There is no mention of the road in council minutes and it never appeared on local maps. But many old-timers can still remember it, and from time to time portions of the road are uncovered when land is being tilled.

GROCERY, BUTCHER, AND DRY GOODS STORES

Apparently Bakers' store (established 1836) enjoyed little or no competition until after the mid-1850s when the island's population was at its peak. At that time the village was inundated with stores selling both groceries and dry goods — they were not called general stores unless they sold hardware and other non-food items for the home and farm. Various amenities, clothing, food, household, farm, and livestock necessities became so readily available that islanders were becoming less dependent on the mainland.

Some of Bakers' early competitors were Thomas Wills, William Allen, Samuel Maitland, and Orin Horton, all of whom had disappeared by 1865. Amelia (Darby) Coxall, a native of Bedfordshire, England, opened a small grocery business in a room of her home in order to support her five children after she had become widowed. Her son Johnnie, when he was thirty, started a men's ready-to-wear and shoe business — a line he probably chose because the island's only tailor,

The Cummins General Store, circa 1890, was and still is located at Main and Centre, the street that leads to the ferry wharf. The step at the side of the store has always been a place to "hang out and chat."

Courtesy of Theresa Broeders, from Briceland Collection.

Henry Sandieson, was about to retire. For thirty-five years Sandieson had run his business so successfully that he watched all of his competitors come and go.

About ten or twelve years later, when John Larkin began his business at the corner of Main and Leander streets, James McRae was opening his general store at the northwest corner of Main and Centre streets. He later traded under the name of McRae Brothers. Sometime after 1850, Gilbert Sluman of English parentage and Charles Cummins of Loyalist background set up a grocery store. Sluman, Thomas Keyes, and then Robert Payne (all grocers) in succession occupied a frame building on the lot adjoining John Larkin's place. Theresa Fargo, whose son Stephen now owns the original McRae establishment, showed me an insurance policy James McRae placed on the store and attached living quarters. The Insurance Company of Canada issued the policy on July 28, 1882, which covered "the cream two-storey shingle roofed dwelling and store on Main Street occupied by the insured." McRae's premium of ten dollars insured the above property for $2,500.[8] The policy had been discovered by Mildred and Keith Walton when they occupied McRae Place in the 1970s. In 2005, Joan O'Shea found more history concerning this building. After selling the house and store property to Charles Cummins, James McRae retained a mortgage. An indenture dated June 19, 1901, six months after McRae's death, discloses that Cummins paid the balance of the mortgage called upon by McRae's heirs in three instalments totalling eighteen hundred dollars.[9]

In the early 1900s, Charles Cummins was succeeded by his sons. Hugh Horne and later John Weir followed at the same location. In my family's lifetime, the business has been operated in turn by George Rattray, Charlie Coffey, then Clifton and Theresa Fargo. Clifton was descended from pioneer Loyalist Merritt Fargo, who earlier settled and farmed on the east side of the Seventh Concession just north of the Base Line. Theresa's son, Steve, presently operates the store, supplying services to islanders year-round and the cottage trade in summer.

According to available information, Frederick Whitmarsh opened the first exclusively meat shop around 1890, located on the site of the current General Wolfe Hotel marina. Subsequently, this building was used by grocers Oliver Davis and Ernie Whitmarsh, who also marketed fresh meats. A frame structure on the north side of Main Street, directly across from the present Wolfe Island Bakery, was O'Brien's butcher shop. This building stands today. Further west on Main Street, the neatly painted yellow-and-white building opposite the post office was, around the early 1900s, Philip Ryan's butcher shop. Of Irish ancestry, Ryan (1862–1931) was in turn a farmer, a butcher, and a carpenter. He occupied the house he had built abutting his shop. Ryan built several houses in Marysville and one on Howe Island, the materials for which he rowed across the channel from Wolfe Island.[10] George "Butch" Whitmarsh took over the business after Ryan retired. On the west side of Ryan's house was another butcher shop owned and operated by Frank Briceland. A shed at the water's edge served for slaughtering and dressing meat, and it has been said that on many an occasion the river ran red with blood. The only other known butchers operated in the frame building on Main Street. It was demolished in 1970 to make way for the present post office. Ernie Whitmarsh, the son of Butch Whitmarsh, was the third generation of the family to operate an island butcher shop.

The early ice cream parlours were known for a product yet to be surpassed. Delicious varieties, unique to each storekeeper and made without additives or preservatives, were never equalled by mass production. Among the island's first and last entrepreneurs was Mrs. Harriet Winbourne (also Wenbourne). Known as "Aunt Hattie," her father was Thomas Davis, a son of the early pioneer family. Her mother was none other than Mary "Polly" Hinckley. After establishing a successful business in Fred Whitmarsh's abandoned store, she moved to a shop further west and thence across Main Street to the store known, for decades since, as Ernie's Lunch. She remained at this location for many years. My father, during his incumbency at Trinity Church, visited her frequently to savour the excellent quality of her ice cream.[11] Two other islanders who made and sold fine ice cream were Norah Greenwood and Mrs. David Adair.

Early in the 1850s about three thousand pairs of shoes were being worn out annually. The need was met by nine permanent-resident shoemakers. The longest established was John George, who lived at the east end of the village, but the most popular shoemaker was John Webster, who worked out of his home on the Sixth Concession near the corner of Main Street.

The island's population dipped to approximately two thousand by 1870, but this does not appear to have affected the businesses significantly. The village still had three general stores, one merchant miller, one carriage maker, one wheelwright, four blacksmiths, two lumber merchants, two carpenters, one builder, one boat builder, one mechanic, two real estate brokers, two proprietors of vessels, one summer hotel, and at least three taverns or saloons. According to the 1871 census, there were also two doctors (one a surgeon) and four resident clergymen ministering to the Catholic, Methodist, and Church of England and Ireland congregations.

The expansion of farm operations generated larger incomes and increased the farmers' purchasing power that in turn helped sustain the village businesses. By this time, many farmers were raising and marketing turkeys, geese, guinea fowl, and wild pigeons at the Kingston market.

John O'Shea recalled the "turkey drill" of his youth. Domestic turkey farmers during this period would drive their turkeys across the island to Horne's Point. American buyers would choose them at the roadside, then bag and load them onto their boats and cross over to Cape Vincent where the turkeys would be sold.[12]

BLACKSMITHS

Most blacksmith and carriage-making businesses catering to the horse were located in Marysville throughout the 1800s. Although they worked independently, blacksmiths, harness makers, and wagon builders found it useful to be near one another as their finished products were interrelated. For instance, the blacksmith, in addition to forging horseshoes, nails, and all the fittings for harnesses and wagons, would make axe heads, hoes, forks, scythes, and a variety of other tools and implements for farmers. He also accommodated carpenters by manufacturing spikes, hinges, latches, and the like. Harness makers also crafted saddles, belts, hats, and even the leather apron worn by the blacksmith.

The earliest of several blacksmith shops well-established before 1850 included François La Londe

James O'Brien's blacksmith shop, circa early 1900s, was located on the river side of Main Street across from the Woodman House Hotel. Children used to stop there to warm up on their way to school. Vincent Greenwood owned the property in the background where the coal sheds were originally located. He was a descendant of the initial Greenwoods (Boisverts) of Wolfe Island.

and pioneer James S. Bennett. They were joined later by Patrick McAvoy, Edward Rousseau, and Gillison Davis. French blacksmiths such as François and Alfred La Londe were considered to be most competent at this craft. Their shop was at the northeast corner of Main Street and the Sixth Concession on property later owned by the La Rush family. The last blacksmith at that location was a Mr. Briceland.

Many were in business during Wolfe Island's zenith years of population, 1850 to 1875. Brothers James and John of the pioneer Bennett family conducted their rural smithy at the northeast corner of Concession Six (Highway 95) and Reeds Bay Road. Shipyards required the services of a blacksmith, and the Bennett brothers did work for the Reeds Bay shipbuilding concern. Many nautical needs such as propeller parts, gears, and the like would have been fashioned by these smithies. Patrick McAvoy's shop was originally situated at the site now occupied by the Wolfe Island Post Office. James McKenna, and to a lesser degree Pat's brother Conn, worked for him. This enterprise spanned about twenty years before it was bought and operated by Fred Crawford. So great was the need for blacksmiths during this period that another, unidentified shop existed immediately adjacent to McAvoy's at the southeast corner of Leander.[13] During the 1850s another blacksmith, possibly Tom O'Reilly, had located opposite Baker's store at the southwest corner of Division. James McKenna's grandson Joe Hawkins may have inherited the blacksmith's talent as he was known to have done horseshoeing at his home on St. Lawrence Street.[14]

Two more village blacksmith shops were situated almost back to back. One was owned by Edward Rousseau, who lived on Victoria Street, and the other by Gill Davis on St. Lawrence. Rousseau's shop, later owned by James Matier, previously stood on the lot where James

Flynn's (deceased in 1980) former house stands. Gillison "Gill" Davis was the grandfather of Clarence and Allan Davis who, for twenty some years, tended the Pigeon Island lighthouse.[15] Of a later date, and still within the recollection of some, was Griffin's blacksmith shop at the southeast corner of Main and Going streets. This business was founded by Ed Griffin in the 1870s and, at his death, was carried on by his son Isadore until it closed. Wilson Taylor's shop could be found at the corner of Main and Barrett streets. Apparently, Wilson was assisted in turn by each of his three sons — Peter, Ambrose, and George — early in the 1900s, following which time the shop was operated solely by Craig Russell for a time before its demise.[16] The decline in the number of blacksmith shops was largely due to the introduction of the motor vehicle.

Although Volty Bamford did some "smithying" and Henry Holliday had a forge, Jim O'Brien appears to have been the main blacksmith at the foot of the island. He even specialized in custom work.[17] John "Jack" O'Brien, Jim's son, was practising his skills in the early 1900s at his shop on the same lot on which Ken Keyes presently resides.[18] Other blacksmiths are recorded in the 1851 census, two of which, Benjamin Longueuil and Joseph Beaver, were located on lot 30 of the Old Survey. Oliver Hitchcock (Mary Hinckley's son) plied his trade where he resided on Concession Five (south of the Base Line). During the 1800s, the Calvin Company steadily employed four or five resident blacksmiths, but Wolfe Island smithies also did custom work for the Garden Island firm.

CARRIAGE BUILDERS AND HARNESS MAKERS

Inquiries in numerous places and the examination of eleven directories listing the occupations of Wolfe Islanders over the period from 1840 to 1900 turned up the names of only two harness makers: R.J. Kelly in 1889 and Andrew Ryan in 1900. What about all the earlier years? With some one thousand horses and approximately fifty working oxen on the island, it may be assumed that one of the better blacksmiths and possibly some shoemakers could have had harness-making skills. The earliest village wagon maker was Oliver Bruyière (sometimes Bruyere, Brengear, or Brewyer). His shop was on the west side of Division Street next to the unidentified blacksmith shop at the corner of Main, where he and his wife Margaret lived. The only other early wagon builder seems to have been John Bullis. Bullis (sometimes Bullers or Bullars) had his workplace at the northeast corner of the Base Line and the Eighth Concession (Cameron's Corners). Bruyière, who also did custom carpentry, and Bullis were each listed as "Carriage, wagon and sleigh builder."

In the early 1860s, David Cattanach (also listed as Cattanagh or Catniff) set up business as a wheelwright. Along with manufacturing and repairing wheels and wheeled vehicles, David and Donald Cattanach built and repaired carriages, wagons, and sleighs. Their residence and workshop were at the southeast corner of Main and Leander streets, which in recent years was Mrs. Dorothy White's property. In the latter 1800s, Joseph Davis opened a specialty wagon-making business, and about ten years later W.H. Bolton began a carriage-building trade that grew and became known as

"Bolton and Bolton, Wheelwrights" by the early 1900s.

Towards the close of the nineteenth century, three more establishments opened: Clench and Crawford, wheelwrights, then Andrew J. McRae and Malcolm McDonald, both wagon builders. In fact, McDonald, who lived on Leander Street, operated a carpentry shop for years at the corner of Main and Leander. He is credited with building many of the cottages west of the village, and worked as a maintenance man for most of them. By 1900, the versatile Philip Ryan was also in business as a wagon maker.[19]

LIVERY SERVICE

During the 1800s, a livery stable was established in the village. By 1895, the business was in the hands of William "Billie" Card and his two sons, Richard and Harry. Their stable was located near the water on property immediately west of Bakers' store on the main street of Marysville. The Cards catered to every need: a horse-drawn carriage for travellers, a flat wagon for freight, and their own unique oil wagon. In fact, Billie Card was the first to service the whole island with kerosene from an oil drum attached to his modified horse-drawn wagon. Harry Card later updated the business by adding two "Flivvers" (Ford touring cars) to the livery service.

Besides transporting passengers across the island from the village ferry wharf to the ferry bound for Cape Vincent, the livery was available day and night for salespersons, doctors, and all manner of emergency calls to any part of the island. Harry Card also operated a large motorboat as a water taxi. The livery was acquired by George Woodman and later sold to Oliver Hawkins and his family, who carried on until 1939. Oliver and his son, Arnold "Cricket" Hawkins, then branched out into horse racing with some of their fine standardbreds. Maxime Greenwood Sr. (known as "Max"), who lived in the old schoolhouse on Centre Street, also ran a livery business during Bill Card's early days. As times changed, the livery service became redundant, and Cricket Hawkins converted the building to a service garage and gristmill, which were later destroyed by fire.

THE EVOLUTION OF GOVERNMENT OF THE FRONTENAC ISLANDS

When the province of Canada was divided into Upper and Lower Canada by the Constitutional Act of 1791, it was stipulated that the land in Upper Canada would become freehold, while Lower Canada would remain seigneurial. John Graves Simcoe, appointed lieutenant-governor, arrived from England with the mandate to govern Upper Canada according to the terms of this act.[20] His first proclamation in 1792 divided Upper Canada into four districts, each having two counties. Kingston became the centre of Midland District with its two counties, Frontenac and Ontario. As the county of Ontario, at the time, encompassed all the islands between the mouth of the Gananoque River and Point Pleasant, Wolfe Island became part of that county.[21] This edict also named the islands in honour of recent British military heroes: Amherst, Gage (Simcoe), Wolfe, and Howe. When the county of Ontario was abolished in

1798 a bill was passed to determine the boundary lines of the townships. Wolfe Island then was included in the Township of Frontenac, along with Simcoe, Garden, Horseshoe, and Bayfield islands.

During his term, Simcoe attempted to develop a society based on a British style of aristocracy. The plan failed, due probably to the egalitarian sentiment emerging among the Reformers and the predominantly Loyalist population. Prior to 1840, political authority for the Township of Wolfe Island rested with the administrator responsible to the Court of Quarter Sessions on the mainland. He was assisted by road overseers, assessors, pound keepers, fence viewers, and other officials selected at annual assemblies held in Kingston.[22] Any interested parties could attend these meetings, which were usually held in taverns possessing adequate space to accommodate larger audiences and the ability to provide food and lodging.

As this was the era of the Family Compact and rampant political patronage, people most likely to be appointed to office would be Protestant, likely of Anglican persuasion, and holding views sympathetic to the governing clique. Should an islander not be in attendance at these meetings, non-residents unacquainted with the needs of the islanders were often appointed. This usually meant that improvements to the island's essential services would be on hold for many years, forcing islanders who could do so to finance upgrades themselves.

One such session, advertised in the *Kingston Chronicle*, stated that on December 22, 1826, a meeting would be held in Petrie's Tavern at the ferry dock at Point Frederick.[23] The dock mentioned was the last stop on the ferry's round trip out of Kingston and across to Wolfe Island. There was no bridge from Kingston to Point Frederick over the Cataraqui River until 1829, when the "Penny Bridge," (so-called because the toll was one penny) was built.[24] Islanders, no matter how anxious they were to attend these meetings, were hampered by the uncertainty of the scow-ferry crossing, always at the mercy of the elements. As well, the possible inconvenience and expense of having to stay overnight in Kingston contributed to their reluctance to attend. Yet some, such as Samuel Hitchcock, did attend — he was the first to hold office and use his influence on behalf of Wolfe Island.

QUARTER SESSIONS

The Court of Quarter Sessions, initiated in Kingston in 1789, sat quarterly, as the name implies. Islanders would appear before this court when their cases could not be tried or settled by the resident justice of the peace.[25] The quarter judge came to the island regularly to check the local magistrate's records and make comments concerning the judgments handed down. It was the duty of the local justice of the peace to prepare an accounting of all cases heard before him, with notations on settlements and judgments passed.

The earliest justice of the peace to live on Wolfe Island was Morey B. Spoor, a United Empire Loyalist whose family had come from the United States along with the Turcotte family, who settled on an adjoining lot. Morey married Turcotte's daughter, Harriett. Morey's home, built on lot 25, up the Front Road, was a modest Tudor-style frame building later covered with wood siding. Although his livelihood came from farming and selling lumber, he also engaged in sports and politics. In his early years, he was a fine athlete and, among other honours, became chief oarsman for the Wolfe Island Rowing Club. Morey's work as a justice of the peace prepared him for a political career. In 1857 he was elected to the township council and, over the next twenty years, was re-elected township reeve on seven occasions.

Some years ago a friend of Morey Spoor told my father that, upon his reading the records of Morey's judicial proceedings, he believed that Spoor was a good man suited to the office of magistrate. Spoor's prime concern was reconciliation, and he mediated with the accused and the accuser. Judgment was passed only when a reasonable solution could not be reached. On one occasion, after having heard the dispute concerning a fence and having the one party agree to erect a fence and the other to keep his animals at home, Morey sentenced both men to a handshake!

Morey was born in 1820 and died in 1903. His grave marker is in Trinity Anglican Church Cemetery where his mother, the former Olive Davis, was also buried. It is said that Morey had engaged in a dispute with the Catholic priest concerning his request to be buried in the Catholic cemetery where his wife Harriet would ultimately be buried. But, as he had not embraced Catholicism, his request was denied.

The local justice of the peace had authority to sentence an accused to prison in some cases, but the condition of the prison left the magistrate reluctant to do so. The jail used by Wolfe Island Township was at Kingston. A report of a grand jury of the Quarter Sessions in April 1844 said "that idleness and drunkenness were the most prolific sources of crime" and that the "crowded state of the gaol led to bad ventilation."[26] The prisoners registered complaints about the well water and the lack of adequate lighting at nighttime. The jailer informed the grand jury that "the meat furnished by food contractors contained excess amounts of bone which he was obliged to serve the prisoners as food."[27] The water and lighting problems were corrected by 1850, when bylaws were passed providing for "a continual supply of water to be delivered into the gaol by the water works company" and "lighting to be installed by the gas light company."[28] The jail system has not changed; prisoners from the island are still held in the Kingston jail. Policing of Wolfe Island was done by Bruce Woodman for about seven years after he was trained as a police constable in the 1950s. Bruce, however preferred to work as a fishing guide, and resigned. Since that time, the Ontario Provincial Police from the mainland have provided the policing on Wolfe Island.

The Act of Union passed in 1840 combined Upper and Lower Canada into the United Province of Canada. When the official announcement was made, Kingston became the capital city of Canada West.[29] With the strength of the Family Compact now diminished, the constitutional majority held the balance of power in the new responsible government.[30] The following year, on February 10, the administration of local affairs was transferred from the Court of Quarter Sessions to the town and district council, members of which were elected by popular vote. As a result of the new procedure, Wolfe Island constituents would elect their own representatives to sit on the Midland District Council at Kingston, but minor officials were approved by and subject to the district council.

The principals in the new administration were councillors, the township clerk, the tax collector, assessors, enumerators, and the township superintendent. Wolfe Island Township had two representatives on the district council, one of whom was the frequently elected Angus Cameron, owner of Garden Island. His fellow councillor depended on which other candidate was the more popular on the day of election. John Horne, a justice of the peace, lived in the village and held the office of township clerk for eight consecutive years. The township superintendent may have supervised or worked in conjunction with the tax collector, now called the treasurer.

To address the non-payment of taxes, council passed a bylaw in June 1848 stating that a list of names of all persons in tax arrears would be posted on the second Tuesday in November. Delinquents were given notice of eight days by signs posted in different sections of the township. If payment was not made, goods and chattels would be put for sale and proceeds retained equal to the amount owed, plus costs. William Randall was the bailiff. Research has unearthed a tax break, offered in 1844. An act had been passed in 1793 in an attempt to reduce and control wolves that were ravaging settlers' homes for food. The bounty per head was four dollars. By 1844, with the new legislation, bounty certificates (in lieu of scalps) could be presented by anyone living in the Midland District to the township collector for payment of taxes.

In 1850 a long-awaited change in the government of Wolfe Island Township occurred — a turning point in her history. The township could now elect its own officials and govern its own affairs. Henceforth, decisions affecting Wolfe Island would be made by a resident, experienced council knowledgeable of the conditions and needs of this isolated community. The first local municipal election took place in early January 1850. The following councillors were elected: Angus Cameron, John Grant, John Hawkins, Ronald McDonell, and James McRae. Angus Cameron was selected as township reeve and John Horne as township clerk. The first council meeting was held on January 21, 1850, in the newly erected common school #4 at the east end of the village.[31] Shortly thereafter a room in the Hitchcock House became the council chamber for monthly meetings until the present town hall was completed in 1859. R.M. Spankie (son of Dr. William Spankie of Wolfe Island) noted, "this old stone building (Hitchcock House) can claim recognition as a municipal parliament house along with its reputation as an inn."[32]

The Wolfe Island municipality seal was struck in 1850.

The council's first bylaw in 1850 established a common seal for the Wolfe Island municipality, emblazoned with the maxim *Par terre et par mer* along with symbols of islanders' livelihoods. Farm implements and a voyageur canoe, the first ferry of the late 1700s, portray the land and sea aspects of their daily lives.[33] This seal, along with sealing wax, were used to authenticate documents for many years until the style was upgraded to one that embossed official papers.[34]

Progress was made in the opening of new roads, the building of bridges (three over Reeds Creek) and improved ferry service to the mainland. Schools were established and older ones were upgraded. After so many years of apathy and indifference, Wolfe Island was finally able to move forward. The incorporation of the Township of Wolfe Island in 1854 gave birth to an autonomy that survived through hungry years and tight finances.

Edward Horsey, a noted Kingston architect, designed the Wolfe Island town hall in 1859. The edifice, a fine example of Italianate architecture, was constructed from stone quarried on the island. It cost twelve hundred dollars. Except for the concrete steps that replaced the original wooden ones along with renovations and interior upgrading, the town hall still stands as it did in earlier days, surviving as a symbol of

Wolfe Island's town hall was constructed on Main Street at Division in 1859, facing Kingston. Photo 1972.

the development of self-government in rural Ontario. The Historic Sites and Monuments Board of Canada declared this building to be an unusually sophisticated example of its type and commemorated its presence with a historic plaque in 1992.

By 1955 it became necessary to appoint a township clerk. C.S. Coffey was the first clerk, 1955–62, followed by Garfield Bennett, 1963–75, Mae Bennett, 1976–87, and Terry O'Shea from 1998 to the present.[35] Margaret Woodman, who in 1973 became the first woman to sit on council, served a number of terms. The second woman elected was Mildred Hawkins-Walton, who served from 1975–87.

The government of Ontario imposed the amalgamation of Wolfe, Garden, Simcoe, and Howe islands in 1998 to form the Township of Frontenac Islands. Effective that date, the title of *mayor* replaced the title *reeve* and a new seal was struck with the words *Corporation of Frontenac Islands*. In November 1997, municipal officers were elected for the newly formed township. Wolfe Island's Jan Hassellaar became mayor, along with six councillors, three of whom were from Wolfe Island: Albert Woodman (deputy), Wayne Grant, and James Vanden Hoek. Howe's representatives were Patrick Norris, Michael Garrah, and Paul Beseau. Terry O'Shea continued as clerk-treasurer. The new Mayor Hasselaar presided at the historic final meeting of the old council on December 22, 1997.[36] Initially set up with six members, council was subsequently reduced to four.

CHAPTER 16
Achieving Literacy: Libraries and Schools

A large proportion of pioneers who settled on Wolfe Island possessed average or better-than-average education, but not so their children, who had little or no formal schooling. Although there were numerous grammar schools in Kingston by 1820, illiteracy was commonplace among Wolfe Island's younger generation. In 1835, less than five percent could read. Alarming as the statistic may seem, illiteracy did not prevent them from making their way in life. New beginnings in a new land meant facing many challenges. The setting up of schools would come.

Alvah Bennett, born in the United States in 1792, was the son of a typical pioneer family who settled on Wolfe Island in 1807. His inability to read did not impede his leasing the ferry operation in 1808 from Samuel Hitchcock for three years. Bennett served in the War of 1812 and subsequently established and operated a hand-powered gristmill on Mill Point, an area still known by that name. Illiteracy did, however, preclude awareness of his entitlement to one hundred acres of land in return for his military service, in addition to his army pay at war's end.[1] Alvah retired on a half acre of land on St. Lawrence Street, immediately south of the Davis property more recently occupied by Enes Goslin.

Bennett was not the only pioneer achiever to lack a formal education. Thomas Davis followed Samuel Hitchcock as lessee of the ferry that ran to Kingston from the village, and Archibald Hitchcock, Samuel's son, succeeded Davis. Both were successful in the ferry business, but neither could read or write, and signed their petitions with an *X*.

Sheriffs Dawson and Duncan McRae were the top guns during the late 1800s in more than one way. They both read for the illiterate — a rather honest method of gaining awareness of everyone's business. But even the literate were generally not proficient with spelling, as manifested in the census lists as well as public and private documents. They frequently spelled what they heard phonetically — a practice that tends to hinder today's genealogical research. Some of my father's observations are noted here: Prisbiterian (Presbyterian), ingenear (engineer), prentis (apprentice), Fossett (Fawcett), Samull (Samuel).

Although improvised spelling cannot be attributed solely to the lack of reading material, newspapers and books were not accessible to the islanders. Neither the *Kingston Gazette* (later the *Standard*), published daily from its inception in 1810, nor the *British Whig*, published twice weekly beginning in 1834, was shipped to the island, as the *Whig-Standard* is today. Even had they been available by ferry, there was no distribution system across the island, and lending libraries had not yet been established. It was not until about 1840 that the Mechanics' Institute was founded in Kingston, allowing access to reading material for self-improvement and providing space for public lectures and displays. Wolfe Island had neither institute nor lending library for many years, except for what was available at the schools.

Some self-help or self-improvement publications were available, one of which my father noticed in a Wolfe Island home in 1930. The book, entitled *The Polite Letter Writer*, was published in the 1800s. In addition to pointing out the advantages of letter writing, it gave detailed instructions and some simple rules of composition, with examples of letters to businesses, relatives, and friends.

The need for a local library was a recurring theme and several attempts were made to establish one on the island during the 1900s. As recently as 1981, a provisional committee afforded taxpayers with a yes/no ballot to determine support; twelve of the fifteen townships in Frontenac County already had libraries. The referendum pointed out to Wolfe Island residents that they could enjoy the same benefits for an estimated ongoing increase of three dollars to four dollars per tax bill. A steering committee was struck and in a short time had secured suitable premises and raised the necessary thirty-five hundred dollars for the Frontenac County Library System membership fee. Previously,

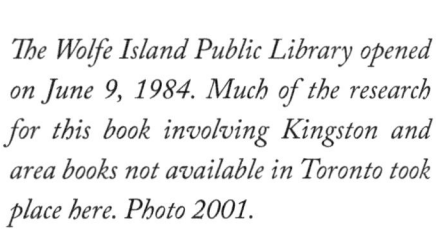

The Wolfe Island Public Library opened on June 9, 1984. Much of the research for this book involving Kingston and area books not available in Toronto took place here. Photo 2001.

Courtesy of Mable McRae.

one thousand dollars had been pledged for this project and responses to appeals for support and fundraising events raised over seven thousand dollars. The library opened on the target date of June 9, 1984.

Initially, the smoking room at the back of the Catholic Mutual Benefit Association (CMBA) hall on Division Street was used as a reading room until the new library, at the junction of highways 95 and 96, was opened for use by both community and summertime residents. Sharon (O'Shea) Hogan, a local resident, has been the librarian from the beginning and, in recent years, the number of users has hovered around 12,500 per annum.

The public school system in Ontario began in 1816, and by the 1840s basic schooling was available to everyone on the island, yet there were serious financial problems. Teachers considered their work simply as temporary employment and the school trustees were paying their salaries on an irregular basis. Lieutenant Colonel Ronald McDonell of Wolfe Island presented a petition, dated November 13, 1844, to the council regarding the salary of a schoolteacher in his township. This petition was one of many from the entire Midland District soliciting the action of council to assist teachers. On August 16, 1845, council gave the final reading to bylaw 38, authorizing taxing for school purposes. This was the beginning of the school-tax system, an assessment made at the municipal level totally separate from the government school fund of the time. The government grant was based on the total number of days of schooling received by all the pupils in the Midland District and then apportioned accordingly to each school. In 1843, the apportionment was the equivalent of one cent per pupil per day. Based on the method of apportioning funds it was crucial for the school trustees to discourage absenteeism. Should parents permit truancy, the government grant would be reduced, as would teachers' morale and their remuneration.

John Strachan, the ambitious superintendent of education for the Midland District during these difficult times, tackled the problems with vigour. In his brief to council dated November 7, 1845, he stated, "It is gratifying to report the general improvement especially that of intellectual instruction now more or less pursued by the teachers in almost every school … the diversity of textbooks no longer exists … and public examinations have been introduced with parents in attendance."[2] To top off his report, Strachan advocated that a model school be established in Kingston. Three years later the warden, in an address to the Midland District Municipal Council, noted another significant change in the education system when he said:

> No person at present can sufficiently testify to the value of this national system of education.… Therefore the councillors in their respective townships should be diligent in having adequate school rooms for the accommodation of the children and also be careful in forming the school sections of a sufficient size enabling the trustees to employ and reward competent teachers for their labour.[3]

From that time onward, education and teaching techniques improved throughout the whole Midland District as applied to the common or public school system — the separate school system was not yet in place on the island. At that time all pupils on the island, irrespective of religious affiliation, attended the common school nearest their homes. When Father Stafford was appointed priest in charge of Sacred Heart Church, Wolfe Island, his tireless efforts introduced the separate school system to the island in 1861.[4]

My father's research uncovered facts concerning fifteen schools, whose histories are recorded here. The first school on the north side of Wolfe Island is purported to have opened in 1833 in a log house in the Old Survey, on Front Road, one-half mile west of the village at the foot of Lambert's Hill, where the earliest settlers had established roots. A number was never assigned to this school. Rough-hewn wooden benches, without backs, sat on a dirt floor, but students were fortunate enough to have spellers, readers, slates, and some writing materials. Later, the school body was moved to another log house in the village at the north end of Leander Street,[5] built by Archibald Hitchcock Sr.

In the historical accounts written by R.M. Spankie and Edwin Horsey there is ambiguity as to whether the log schoolhouse at Lambert's Hill was physically moved piece by piece and reconstructed on Leander Street or whether the school buildings described were two separate log houses. According to Carmel Cosgrove, a Wolfe Island historian (recently deceased in her mid-nineties), the original house built by Archibald Hitchcock on Leander had many lives, even housing at one time the first Baker store, which later became Flynn's Saloon.

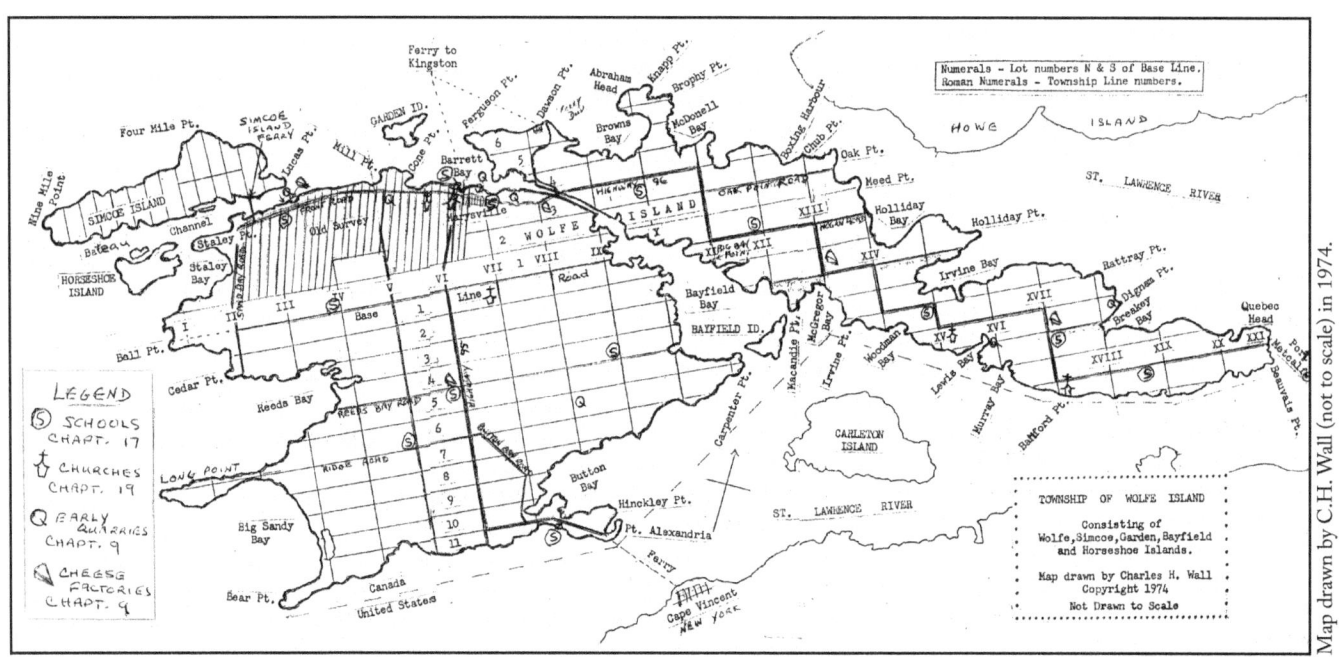

Map 11: Map of the Township of Wolfe Island circa 1860, marking the sites of early quarries, cheese factories, schools, and churches.

Johnny O'Shea noted that whisky could be purchased in bulk from a barrel in the front room of the building and, as its location was close to the ferry, the back room was used by the ladies to warm up with hot toddies after a cold ferry crossing.[6] During the late 1800s, Mrs. David Adair occupied this house for many years.

R.M. Spankie recalled "the first regular teacher on Wolfe Island was Miss Eunice Hinckley. She was hired in the old way and reimbursed by her patrons who took turns boarding her."[7] Boarding ultimately included paying the teacher twenty-five cents per child per month. From such rudimentary beginnings, education spread throughout the island, represented by at least thirteen one-room rural schools of log or frame construction and heated by a wood-burning box stove. Whether children travelled on foot, in horse-drawn cart, or by sleigh in winter, the sorry state of the roads made for arduous journeys.

SCHOOLHOUSES AT THE HEAD

The new "Hinckley" school (SS#5), a log cabin erected in 1823, was named after Samuel Hinckley, who provided the property. (See map 11 for locations of schools.) His daughter, Olivia, was the first teacher. A new frame school was built across the road opposite the present Point Alexandria Cemetery after the log structure burned. Some other teachers were Nettie Grant, Laura Murells, and John Smeaton. At one time all the students as well as the teacher, Olivia Horne, had the same great-grandmother, Olivia Hinckley. Mrs. Elizabeth Horne, well-known to islanders, taught there at a later date. It appears that men of the Horne family often married teachers as they brought new blood to the island.[9]

The Ridge School (SS#3) was built on land that abutted the Abbott family property at the Fourth Concession. This school was noted for fine teachers, two of whom became clergymen in their respective religious affiliations. Ruth Ann Pearce of Tilbury, Ontario, found a photocopy of a school certificate awarded to a Wolfe Island ancestor of hers (William Ellerbeck) dated Wolfe Island, September 21, 1841. It stated, "Honour all men, fear God, honour the king, love thy brothers. This is to certify that William Ellerbeck was a scholar in Ridge School and was diligent in his studies." It was signed by George Milligan,[10] who taught there in 1841 and was later appointed public school inspector for the County of Frontenac. After studying and obtaining his doctorate at Queen's University, he became a Presbyterian minister. John Farthing, who taught at the Ridge School in 1875–76, became an Anglican priest and eventually was elected bishop of Montreal. Pupils at this school came mostly from the Abbott, Cooke, Horne, and Spinning families in the early years. The only trustee that could be identified was Henderson Horne, who served circa 1875.

"Moran's School" (SS#1), adjoining Patrick Moran's property in the Reeds Bay area, was established as a common or public school prior to 1847. The 1861 census described the frame, one-room schoolhouse as being large enough to accommodate forty pupils, two per desk. Children of the Grant, Moran, Mosier, McGlynn, Bennett, Briceland, and O'Shea families were pupils here. Isabel O'Shea recalled the frame structure having curtains. The school covered grades one through ten and included gardening and agriculture, among the other subjects. In bad weather Isabel and her siblings were taken to school by their father in a horse and buggy, or by sleigh in winter with a covering of hay to keep them warm. In 1944, at the age of eighteen, Isabel taught at this school, then moved on to SSS#4 on the hill in the village in 1945.[11] Winston M. "Mike" Cosgrove (a native Wolfe Islander) taught there from 1948 to 1950 before moving to Lindsay, Ontario, during the 1980s to become vice-principal of an elementary school.

The George Friend School (SS#9), located near the corner of Base Line and Fourth, was built in 1904 to serve parts of the Third, Fourth, and Fifth concessions. George Friend was a long-serving trustee. During the early 1900s, Lena Davis, who lived in the village, taught there for many years. She walked the four miles to and from school daily and earned nine hundred dollars annually — the most highly paid teacher on the island. When the school was no longer needed, it was sold to Mrs. M. Doyle, who had the building moved to a lot on St. Lawrence Street opposite the Davis homestead, and converted it to a residence.

Due north of SS#9 is the original location of the Staley School (SS#2), not far from the north shore of the island where the Front Road meets the Third Line. It was built on property initially owned by Thomas Davis (lot 24,

Shown is the Township of Wolfe Island S.S. # 1 Simcoe Island class of 1928. Back row from (l–r): Thelma Eves, Donald Belyea, Ralph Eves, Carl Sudds, and Cecil Orr. Middle row (l–r): Anna Belyea, Vera Smith, George Eves, and Harrison Eves. Front row (l–r): are Freda Eves, Reta Eves, Vera Belyea, Sidney Eves, Kenneth Eves, and Rodney Orr.

Old Survey) and presently owned by Matt Flynn. Records indicate that this school section received an apportionment from the Common School fund, indicating that its history precedes 1840. In 1847, Staley School had the largest enrolment in the township, as it also included the children of Simcoe Island. The 1871 census shows two schoolmistresses, Catherine and Jane Dunlop (daughters of John Dunlop, the Simcoe Island lighthouse keeper).

According to an indenture dated February 20, 1883, an elementary school had been built on Simcoe Island, numbered SS#1.[12] Mabel, daughter of William H. Woodman of Wolfe Island, was the teacher. It was built for the elementary-school children of Simcoe Island, as the Staley School had come under the jurisdiction of the new Separate School Union in the 1860s (SSS#2). Simcoe Island residents were largely Protestant, so they preferred to have their own school facility. There was also an SS#1 on Garden Island that Wolfe Island children were allowed to attend until the island became incorporated as a village in 1866.

By 1890 the Staley School structure had been lengthened by ten feet, a raised platform installed for the teacher's desk, and the exterior clad with clapboard. A manual-training workbench was installed and equipped with a set of tools in 1938. For several years trustees Archie Staley, Samuel Taggart, and William Hawkins guided the school. Duff Cosgrove began his teaching career there in 1902, covering all subjects in all grades. His son, Thomas, also taught there in 1935–36.[13]

The Village School at the east end of Marysville on highway 96, initially named SS#4 and later PSS#4, was originally to provide schooling for children of Scottish descent. The first structure was built on the site of Richard Bolton's farm in 1850. A staffing difficulty must have arisen as a notice in Kingston's *Daily British American*, dated January 19, 1864, read, "Wanted immediately in school section #4 a female teacher having first or second class certificate." The advertisement was endorsed by John Hitchcock of Wolfe Island. The island's population was at its peak and perhaps classrooms were overcrowded. An ell addition, slightly smaller than the first section, was erected in 1897. Beginning in 1912, one room was used as a continuation school to provide the first two years of secondary school. In those days a Normal School certificate qualified a teacher to teach grades one through ten.

During the 1900s this school provided the basic education for nine students who went on to become physicians and lawyers. The doctors were Arthur Spankie, who practised at the Children's Hospital in New York City, brother William Spankie Jr., who practised in Calgary, and Sidney J.W. Horne, who became superintendent of the mental hospital in Orillia, Ontario. A courtyard between Earl Hall and the Anatomy Building at Queen's University in Kingston displays a brass plaque that reads: "Medical Quadrangle Plaques made possible through the Friend Trust." Three sons of Thomas Friend (the owner-operator of the general store at the foot of Leander on Wolfe Island for thirty-seven years) graduated in medicine: William (1929), Austin (1924), and Amos (1922). They practised medicine in the United States.[14] The village school's graduates who went on to law school were Lloyd Watts and the sons of the island's resident doctor William Spankie: Herbert Spankie of Calgary, and Ralph Spankie of Ottawa, who was at one time clerk of the Court of the Exchequer. Fanny Horne became a university librarian and the three Davis sisters, Elsie, Millie, and Annie, chose nursing careers. Elsie

The village school P.S.S. # 4 was located from its inception in 1850 at the east end of Marysville, just beyond the Seventh Line. After 1912, grades nine and ten were added to create a continuation school. Pictured here are twenty-two of the forty students in the 1915 class: Back row (l–r): Vera McDermott, Ethel Ranous, Mildred Davis, Kathleen Kenney, Oliver Davis, Mary Horne, Lena McDermott, and Bessie Adair. Middle row (l–r): Rita McDermott, Lillian McDermott, Emily Davis, Bertha Rattray, Louise Davis, and Lillian Kenney. Kneeling in front (l–r): Arthur Friend, Morris Walker, David Walker, George Kenney, Clarence Adair, Connie Horne, and Beverley Spence. (Last two names may be incorrect.) The small child behind Clarence Adair is Elsie McDermott, and the teacher is Jean Wood. Identification of the children was made by Ruth Hawkins. Both Captain Davis and Eileen Williamson, and the author of this book are descendants of pupils pictured here.

Davis, the Wolfe Island Public School health nurse in the 1920s, was also a fine musician and taught music in many of the island's schools.

PSS#4 was not the only school serving village children. Students were transferred to another location following the closure of the log cabin at the foot of Leander Street until the new village school opened in 1850.[15] Several interviews confirmed that the mid-1800s building sitting slightly askew on the west side of Centre Street was originally a

Another school, today a residence on Centre Street, shown on Walling Map of 1860, appears to jut on an angle into the roadway. A paved footpath leads to the building's side door. That this pathway is not in line with the road and leads to a side door suggests this was a very early school and meeting place, probably built before the road and at a time when there were few other structures in the village, photo 1973.

schoolhouse.[16] Its architecture betrays its former use. As the village was not surveyed showing streets and lots until 1857, it is assumed that this building was in an interim location, since a school is indicated on Centre Street on Walling's Survey Map of 1860. It was not assigned a number.

The first separate school (SSS#4), opened in 1861, was set on the hill in the village at the northwest corner of the Front Road and the Sixth Concession. Its solid brick construction allowed it to survive, and it still stands today, now converted to a residence. Billy Bolton recalled that halfway between his home and the school was George O'Brien's blacksmith shop at the north end of Victoria Street. The General Wolfe Hotel marina presently sits on the site. During wintertime, children on their way to school would stop at George's shop to warm up from the bitter cold.[17]

In January 1953, a new two-roomed schoolhouse, Sacred Heart Union Separate School, was built to the south of church, the first visible move towards a separate school system on the island. Prior to the formation of the Union Separate School Board on January 1, 1946, the four separate schools, #1, #2, #4, and #7, functioned as individual entities connected only in the sense that they taught the same Christian doctrine as part of their curriculum. With the Union they became one school system represented by three trustees. In 1970–71, four more classrooms were added and the students from other smaller rural locations were bussed to Sacred Heart School. The enlarged school was equipped with modern conveniences and teaching aids, a principal's office, and a fine gymnasium. The original SSS#4 on the hill also graduated many students in the early 1900s who sought professional careers or religious vocations,

The Sacred Heart Separate School Union System was inaugurated in January 1953. A new education facility was built just south of the church, which can be seen in the background, photo 1972.

Courtesy of C.H. Wall Collection.

including Howard Staley, chiropractor; Enroy Coyle, physician; and Charles Baker, R.J. Coyle, and James Ryan, all of whom were ordained to the priesthood.

James Dufferin Cosgrove of Sydenham arrived on the island in 1902 to take a teaching position at SSS#2. Appointed principal of the village separate school in 1904, he held the position for twenty-three years and taught all grades with one assistant teacher. His initial salary of four hundred dollars per year had escalated to one thousand dollars at the time of his retirement. Duff played soccer in his high school days at Sydenham and shared his knowledge of sports by coaching Wolfe Island baseball and hockey teams for over fifty years. Although somewhat abrupt in his elder years, he was intelligent, articulate, and much respected for his many abilities and utmost concern for the welfare of children committed to his charge.

In 1914, Duff Cosgrove was appointed clerk-treasurer of the township and held the position forty years. Other positions he held included secretary of the Wolfe Island Cheese Factory from 1924 and postmaster of Wolfe Island from December 1929 until his retirement in October 1956. His wife, the former Mary Louise Spoor, daughter of Richard J. Spoor, was an accomplished artist.

Mrs. Rodney McKenna (Kathleen Dillon), a long-time teacher in the separate school system, arrived on the island in 1926 and taught at SS#1 for five years. By 1952 she was at SSS#4, then moved to the Union Separate School on the Sixth Concession before transferring to the Sacred Heart School, where she continued to teach until 1971. In recognition of her years of service, Kathleen McKenna was given the honour of laying the cornerstone of the Sacred Heart School in 1953.

S.S. #6, the "Keyes' School," was named for the farm property on which it sat. Around 1870 the original log hut was replaced by the only limestone school building on the island. Photo 2003.

West of the canal and south on the Ninth Line is a school that still stands on the west side near Reeds Bay Road. This beautiful limestone structure with a frame entranceway is the Keyes' School (SS#6), so named as it sits on land adjoining the long-established Keyes farm. This school accommodated children of the west shore of Bayfield Bay, including those of the Keyes, Ryan, Hennessey, Wenborne, Bolton, and Charles families. The present building (the only school built of limestone on the island and truly a heritage building) replaced the original log structure in 1870; Bidwell Davis was the first teacher. The school is reputed to have provided elementary education for at least two nurses, five physicians, and one priest. Lorne McDonald, who later became a physician, attended this school up to grade seven, then transferred to PSS#4 to complete grades eight to ten. In 1939, students Arthur and Ken Keyes were chosen to attend the Royal visit to Kingston of King George VI and Queen Elizabeth.

To commemorate the coronation of George VI in May 1937, selected schools in Ontario received two acorns (male and female) from the British Royal Oak Trees of Windsor Forest. The trees are unique in that they remain green in wintertime, and spring growth pushes the old leaves off. Once they are forty years old they bear acorns. The Keyes' School received a package of these acorns, all of which were ceremoniously planted. One of these oaks remains by the school, a candidate for a commemorative plaque.[18] Boarded up, the Keyes' School awaits philanthropic support. Restoration could create a highlight for a tour of Wolfe Island's limestone buildings.

SCHOOLHOUSES AT THE FOOT

The first Fawcett School (SS#15), built of logs in 1862, was located on the south side of the main road at the Tenth Concession. Circa 1875, it was deemed to be too close to the road and was replaced by a frame building on a half-acre lot donated by Patrick Dawson. The earliest students were from the Knapp, Ryan, O'Brien, and O'Neill families who lived on what is now known as Brophy Point. Other children came from the Fawcett, Dawson, and McDonell families. As the student enrolment declined over time, the school was closed and sold to Oscar McReady, who relocated it in 1939.

SS#7, referred to as "MacLaren's School" in the early 1900s, was located on the northwest corner of the Twelfth and Base lines. The first schoolhouse, originally a public school, was built circa 1840 on property that had belonged to John J. Harris, father of Luther Harris. In 1908, a separate school (SSS#7) was erected on lot #1 in Concession Twelve, with Michael O'Neill as trustee. The two schools operated simultaneously for seven years. Although at one time forty-seven children attended SS#7, enrolment declined over time and its charter was annulled, and the building closed and put up for auction. Students who lived west of the Twelfth Concession were directed to SS#15 and those living east of the Twelfth went to SS#14.[19]

During its long history, "Smith's School" (SS#14), the first school to be established at the foot of the island, had at least four locations, all of which were at Irvine's Corners at the Fourteenth Concession, on or near John Smith's property. The first log building was erected in 1843 or possibly earlier. The fee arrangement for teachers included room and board (alternating from family to family) and twenty-five cents per pupil per month. Three children from the same family were taught for the cost of two.

By 1860 another schoolhouse was built at the northeast corner of the Fifteenth Concession and, fifteen years later, was relocated to George Woodman's property across the road, remaining there until about 1905. Having fallen into disuse, the school was sold to Jim O'Brien to be used as a blacksmith's shop.[20] The children of pioneer families Holliday, Montgomery, and Woodman, along with other children, attended each of the last two locations. A new frame building was erected at Irvine's Corners at approximately the same location of the first log structure that stood sixty-five years earlier. Miss Pannell was the first teacher in the new building, followed in 1909 by Dot (Campbell) Woodman. This school had five pupils when it opened: Madeline and Bessie Holliday, Willie Cramer, Laura Babcock, and Willie Harrison.

The penultimate school on the list is the O'Brien School (SS#8), also known as the Breakey's Bay School. A log structure located about one-quarter mile below Breakey's Bay Road on the west side of the Seventeenth Concession, it was built on property belonging to William Hennessey in 1859. When this first school was replaced around 1875, the location was shifted to the east side on property leased by John Dee from the Torres Estate. The interior was large enough for six to eight seats in each of two rows. Local people supplied wood, and perhaps started the fire in the wood stove as well. The first teacher was Miss Mary Mitchell, and some of the earliest pupils came from the Joy, Bartlett, and Patchin families. The children's parents were expected to buy the books and other class supplies.[21] Though early teachers were from the mainland, Flora Devlin recalls islander Margaret Holliday as being her teacher.

Several years later the building was upgraded to frame structure, and today is a summer home.

The last on the list of identifiable Wolfe Island schools was called the St. Lawrence School (SS#13), named for the local post office district. The children at the most easterly section of the island attended this log school, located initially on a plot of land adjoining John Heron's property on the north side of the main road near the Twentieth Concession. Built circa 1860, it was later replaced by a frame schoolhouse on the same site (apparently on a patch of poison ivy!). In 1897 this structure was moved across the road to property provided by George Gillespie, a location surrounded on three sides by the St. Lawrence River. The school was so far from mainland Canada via the village (approximately fourteen miles) that some of its earliest teachers were hired from the United States. Children of the Breakey, Armstrong, McFadden, and Rattray families were the earliest pupils, followed in later years by those from the Gillespie, Michea, and Woodman families. During its earliest days the school was also used as a meeting place for the Free Methodists. Mrs. Robert Bullis (Della Gillespie) told my father that the frame building was finally sold to W.P. Joslin to be used as a machine shop.

Within the first fifty or sixty years of their existence, many schoolhouses were relocated two or even three times, due mainly to being upgraded from log to frame construction, the shifting of pupil population, or the return of the land to farmers whose leases had expired. The Walling map of 1860 shows three schools that do not appear on any other map. Two of them were in the area of the George Friend School (SS#9), both on the Base Line, one at the Third Concession, and one at the Fifth. As the Friend school was not built until 1904 where the Base Line meets the Fourth, it is reasonable to assume that this school was replacing the two older structures. It was assigned number 9, the same number as one of the pre-existing schools. The abandoned school may have carried the number 10. In its early days it likely accommodated children from the Kemp, Yott, Michea, Grimshaw, and O'Reilly pioneer families.

The other school, marked only on the Walling map, was located about one-quarter of a mile south of Cold Springs on the east side of the Eighth Concession on the corner of property leased by James Abbott from the Allen Estate. Many years ago my father, while in Toronto, was engaged in conversation with an elderly gentleman and discovered that the stranger had been born on Wolfe Island. He told my father that when he was a boy on the island one public school was closed because the attendance had dropped to four pupils. The building was sold to a group who held lodge meetings in it for some time. My father had not been able to discover either the location of this school or the name of the lodge that may have used it. The Meacham map of 1878 shows an Orange Hall at the Sixth Concession and the Base Line, perhaps the building the gentleman remembered.

Reflections on the early history of education on Wolfe Island shed light on the reasons for a generation of illiteracy. Children certainly could not attend school when their families were fleeing difficult circumstances. Once these pioneers began to settle the land, young people were needed to work on the farming and other family duties. Lack of time, as well as funds, were early deterrents to schooling, but in due course the desire for education prevailed. All teachers were qualified in accord with mainland standards and Wolfe Island students were able to attend the secondary school in Kingston. Many went to the village continuation school for grades nine and ten before entering schools on the mainland. Island children grew up with a heightened sense of community and of self, fostered by the church and attendance at all-age schools. Facing larger unfamiliar groups in a strange school was never an issue.[22] By and large, the education received on Wolfe Island gave many the ability and assurance to succeed at the university level.

CHAPTER 17
Essential Services for an Isolated Community

During the early days of the 1800s, communications between the island and the mainland were messages or letters sent by bateau or steamship when ice and snow were not an issue. Travellers used a stagecoach, or a sleigh in winter, and the express stagecoach was available to transport mail and parcels. The opening of the Grand Trunk Railway from Toronto to Montreal in 1856 provided an alternative to horses.

POSTAL SERVICE

Early postal services in Canada were controlled from Britain. The closest post office in Kingston provided mail service to and from the island once weekly. Running regular ferry trips to Kingston, Archibald Hinckley assumed responsibility for mail transfer, and thus became Wolfe Island's first mail carrier. His wife Mary was the unofficial postmistress. It has been said that "Mary kept the letters in a large milk pan and change in an old fashioned teacup for her mail customers."[1] The government authorized her position officially on April 6, 1845, when a post office was established on the island. She continued to operate the business from her home until she retired in December 1857.[2]

On April 23, 1851, the postal service administration was transferred to Canada and the first Canadian stamps were issued: three-penny (domestic mail) and twelve-penny (to England) — stamps that are quite valuable today.[3] Canada officially changed its currency from British sterling to Canadian dollars on January 1, 1858, and postage stamps were issued the following year in denominations of 1, 5, 10, 12.5, and 17 cents.

After Mary Hitchcock retired, several successors assumed the role of postmaster until 1912 when the post office was moved to the premises of John Friend and Son, general merchants at the northeast corner of Main and Leander streets. Thom, John's son, was postmaster from April 1, 1912, until the fall of 1927 when the family moved from the island. The next two postmasters, James Dufferin "Duff" Cosgrove (appointed December 27, 1927) and his son Harold "Skee," are still remembered by the older generation. Skee was unwell for some time, and resigned on December 29, 1970, shortly before he died. A new post office building opened on September 30, 1970, with Giselle La Rocque as postmistress — a position she held for fourteen years. Her husband, William, had come to the island to manage the Kraft Cheese factory. After her retirement, Kingston supplied the postmasters.

In earlier days, three peripheral post offices functioned on the island to serve residents at the Foot. Located between the Seventeenth and Twelfth concessions, the St. Lawrence, the Allen, and the Central were opened in 1876, 1890, and 1906 respectively. Samuel Woodman was the initial mail carrier contracted to carry the post for these three offices. His son, Charlie, transferred all of the mail from the Foot to and from the village twice weekly. Most settlers travelled by boat, or in winter by sleigh, to pick up their mail as all three offices were located near the river. With the inauguration of rural mail delivery on December 31, 1914, these offices were closed.

The first mailman was William "Will" Ranous, a villager. He was responsible for weekly deliveries on Mondays, Wednesdays, and Fridays. Daily deliveries were initiated when John Cleary from Ferguson's Point took over the route in 1920. During the winter period, when the ferry was laid up, the municipal council set up a winter mail-carrying contract, permitting the transfer of mail to and from Kingston. A municipally owned ice punt was used when ice conditions were too unstable for the other modes of travel.

TELEGRAPH AND TELEPHONE

In 1848, the Great Northwest Telegraph Company ran cable from the mainland to Knapp Point, Wolfe Island, thence to the village and on to Cape Vincent to connect Ontario to New York State. Marysville was on this route and the first telegraph office was established in the building presently housing Fargo's store.[4] A whole new world of communication was opened to the islanders, which included most main points along the St. Lawrence River and Lake Ontario and mainland United States.

Forty-one years later (1889) the North American Telegraph Company installed the first telephones on the island. The company's cable followed much the same route as the telegraph, and the telephone switchboard was also installed in the same building as the telegraph office, by this time owned by Charlie Cummins.[5] He invited Mrs. Eva Prinyer of Bath, Ontario, to come and work as the telephone operator. Colonel Donald McDonald, U.E.L., who served under Sir John Johnson for seven years, had settled in the Quinte area and his only daughter married a native of France, whose surname was Prinyea. Eva may have been a descendant of this family.[6]

In 1906 ownership of the island telephone installations was transferred to the Bell Telephone Company. The telephone office was moved a few doors west of

Cummins' to the Coyle property and Eva became manager in 1914. Several years later the office was moved to a house at Main and St. Lawrence streets. Prinyer retired in 1941 and was succeeded by Lena Davis. At some point in the 1920s, Eva's daughter Rae, Kathleen Kenney, and Ella McRae joined the operation. In the early 1900s, Thursday was the unofficial telephone account collection day. Most islanders carried their produce to market on the 9:00 a.m. ferry, so the telephone office manager boarded the same boat to discuss delinquent accounts with those subscribers living a distance from the telephone office. While this may have been an unorthodox approach, the personal dunning apparently brought positive results.

Mable (Greenwood) McRae was seventeen in 1943 when she was hired as an operator. Lena Davis advanced to manager and remained in that role until 1958 when she was succeeded by Mable. She continued with a staff of six until the Wolfe Island system became automated. In November 1947 the island telephone installations were changed from the magneto system that required subscribers to turn a crank to signal the operator. The new system was a battery-operated switchboard on which a red signal lamp lit when a subscriber lifted the receiver.[7] The party-line aspect of the new installation certainly contravened the user's privacy.

Further progress was made in May 1960 when 14,300 feet of submarine cable was laid by way of a tug-guided, cable-laying barge from Kingston. The cable, weighing one hundred tons and containing 203 pairs of telephone lines, was the preliminary step toward dial service. It was then connected to an overland rural line from Mill Point to Horne's Point. The island's system became fully automated with a dial-operated system.

THE WOLFE ISLAND FIRE DEPARTMENT

The fire of 1977 that destroyed Fawcett's Red and White store, the attached apartment, and Ross Bustard's home and car, drove five people wearing only their night attire into sub-zero weather. The blaze was discovered about four o'clock in the morning and, before long, was out of control due to high winds and the fact that the island firefighters' pump had frozen. A pumper sent from the Kingston Fire Department helped to bring the fire under control after firemen bored through twenty-seven inches of river ice to create a conduit for pumping the water. Snow blowers were used to throw snow on the flames and between buildings to help prevent the fire from spreading.[8]

Fire has always been a major concern. Farmers' homes and barns, usually wooden structures, were vulnerable because of inadequate firefighting equipment and the lack of water-pumping facilities The village homes located in close proximity to each other were equally at risk. An example was the destructive village fire, of unknown origin, discovered in full blaze at four o'clock on the morning of March 14, 1946. When the flames were finally extinguished, Cummins' Lunch Counter on Main Street and the homes and barns of Dan La Rush and Leon McDermott were in ashes. The islanders' bucket brigade had proved no match for nature's blustery air currents. Had the wind turned slightly to the east, five or six more buildings could have been lost.

The following year, also in May, the village suffered another serious fire. This time it was a Marysville garage owned by Arnold "Cricket" Hawkins. The garage, situated on the north side of Main Street near the Sixth Concession, was completely gutted. The flames, fanned by a strong wind, threatened the whole village. All available islanders were summoned to help contain the fire and a mayday call was sent to Kingston. Fortunately, a Kingston pumper was able to contain the fire after laying 250 feet of fire hose to the river.

These events heightened awareness of the need for adequate fire protection for the islanders. However, apart from some discussion inside and outside of council, no action was taken, probably because the council was consumed with financial headaches regarding the *Wolfe Islander* (2) at the time. In the interim, Elwyn "Buck" Mullin, living on the north side of Main Street next to Fargo's store, decided to take the initiative. He purchased a small pumper in Alexandria Bay, New York. The pumper, mounted on a trailer, could be towed by car, and, where water was available, it was capable of throwing four streams of water simultaneously.

Increasing unrest around the lack of fire protection compelled council to take action. On November 1, 1952, they asked the Ontario Municipal Board for permission to issue debentures up to the amount of eleven thousand dollars over a period of five years to purchase standard fire equipment. Authorization was given for the purchase of a pumper, capable of pumping 250 gallons of water per minute, from the La France Company in Toronto. On June 5, 1953, a new bylaw established a volunteer fire brigade. A nineteen-member team was organized in 1955 and William McKenna was appointed fire chief. He held the post until June 1978, when he retired and Jake Heikamp assumed responsibility.[9]

A 2,500-gallon tank truck, formerly used to carry milk, was purchased in 1978 to transport additional water. In a move to further update their fire protection, the need for a new fire hall, spare tank truck, protective clothing, and radio equipment for all trucks was formally recognized. To finance those projects, it was suggested that a special mill rate be levied,[10] and the equipment was acquired over the next few years. Currently, a twenty-four member volunteer fire department, with James White as chief and Tim Hawkins as deputy-chief, provides fire protection for the island.

MEDICAL SERVICES

In times past, births on Wolfe Island were tended by midwives. The earliest recorded was Mary "Polly" Hitchcock, who had the distinction of caring for the baron's daughter, Charlotte. Dedicated islanders such as Noble Staley (1918–89) were always ready to transport the nurse or doctor to the afflicted. Staley's generous acts often involved crossing the ice to fetch a doctor from Kingston.[11] Physicians were summoned from the American side to care for the people at the Foot.

When the island's population peaked during the mid-1800s, there were as many as four physicians available. Although there is no verification of where or when they lived on the island, names of early resident practitioners included Dr. McCarthy, Dr. Cliff, Dr. McManus, Dr. Sauriel, Dr. Blenkinsopp, and Dr. Hunt.[12] From 1885 to 1930, Dr. William Spankie maintained an active practice. Although gruff in manner, rotund in appearance, and remembered for his large moustache, he was loved and respected by the community. He was successful in introducing a sense of public health and disease prevention to islanders and inspired a number of young women to enter the nursing profession. Leath Davis, a former Wolfe Islander, told me that three of his aunts — Mildred, Elsie, and Anne — encouraged by Dr. Spankie, took their nurses' training at Kingston General Hospital. Anne joined the army as a nursing sister during the Second World War. The military nursing included a post on the H.M.S. *Letitia*, the second Canadian hospital ship. Postwar she worked as supervisor of the Watkins Wing of Kingston General Hospital and retired from there in 1965.[13]

Islander Carmel Cosgrove, RN — candid, respected, and cherished by all — maintained her fiery Irish temperament to the end (August 2, 1912–February 1, 2007). She pursued her ambition to tend the sick and did so with great courage. The daughter of educator and postmaster Duff Cosgrove, Carmel was a pioneer in Kingston's industrial nursing field when she was employed at the shipyard from 1944 until her retirement. Her calm, take-charge demeanour was exactly what seriously injured shipyard workers needed in their times of crises.

Carmel's initial training at Kingston's Rockwood Psychiatric Hospital led to postgraduate studies at St. Joseph's Hospital in Toronto. During a subsequent position of operating-room supervisor at Kingston General Hospital, one of her patients, a baby with badly burned hands (caused by a mother's negligence) captured her heart. The Children's Aid Society allowed Carmel to raise the child and Bloorview Hospital, a facility for physically disabled children in Toronto, looked after the girl while Carmel worked at the shipyard. Presently, the child, now an adult, lives in Belleville, Ontario, her life enriched as a result of Carmel's compassion and intervention.[14]

Louise (Hawkins) Kenney Flynn's contributions to her Wolfe Island community cannot be overlooked. Encouraged by her mother and bolstered by moral values enforced during her rigid Irish Catholic upbringing, Louise — my aunt — applied and was accepted for nurses' training by the Sisters of St. Joseph at Hôtel Dieu Hospital in Kingston. In 1937, Louise and George Edward Kenney, a Great Lakes mariner, were wed. Seamen were away from March to November, so during these months Louise worked in the obstetrical department at Hôtel Dieu.[15] When their son Edward was born, George and Louise were living in Marysville, which allowed her to tend the needs of her immediate family as well as caring for local people. Their second child, Anne, was born in April of 1946, just seven months before her father died of heart failure.

One late summer day in 1946, when my mother and I were visiting Aunt Louise, she received a message. She hurried us (Mom, Edward, and myself) into the car and raced across the island to Horne's Point where Bill Horne awaited us with his pilot boat. In the channel, moving at a snail's pace, was the cargo ship *Cedarton*, skippered by Captain Mahoney. With him was my Uncle George, who had his captain's papers, but had assumed the role of mate as his health had deteriorated over time due to a heart problem. Horne drove up to the ship and cut the engine so that we were both moving at the same speed. Vern Yott, my uncle's close friend since childhood, threw a rope ladder over the side into our boat. Down came my uncle's valise, fastened by a rope, followed by my uncle securely locked into a safety harness. I was a youngster at the time, lacking the wisdom to realize how sick my uncle was. Instead, I was overwhelmed by the awesome experience of being out in the channel hugging that enormous ship while we brought my uncle to safety, and home for the last time. Louise soon found herself a widow with an infant, a small child, and an aging mother requiring her care.

Still unable to afford a telephone in the late 1940s, Louise depended on her sister Litta and brother-in-law Tupper Mosier, who lived nearby, to transfer phone messages whenever Louise was needed. She would pack her medical bag and Litta would stay with the family while her sister went to tend the sick or injured. Islander Elaine Berry commented that Louise Kenney was "as good as any doctor."[16] Working without trained assistants or the support of an ambulance was stressful. Her midwifery skills were required most often, but some cases really called for the assistance of a physician. When ice separated Kingston from Wolfe Island, physicians often refused to come, creating untenable situations for her when there were cases of uncontrollable bleeding. She felt helplessly abandoned.[17] As the years progressed and the ferry service improved, Louise responded less frequently to emergency calls but remained more active than ever as a bedside nurse to all who needed her.

After being widowed for nine years, Louise married fellow islander Edward Flynn. However, the seventies were difficult for her with the loss of several family members, including a five-year-old grandson.[18] At the age of sixty-six the tables turned; Louise suffered a heart attack and found it difficult to let others care for her. In 1967 she was awarded Canada's Centennial Medal. Reeve Tim O'Shea remarked that Louise had been both nurse and doctor to the islanders for over thirty years and demonstrated the essence of a true humanitarian.[19]

WOLFE ISLAND HEALTH CLINIC

The Wolfe Island Health Clinic, a converted mobile home, was opened in 1973 on property owned by Dr. George Merry, one of the founders. His wife Catherine,

Louise (Hawkins) Kenney Flynn is holding Canada's 1967 Centennial Medal presented to her in recognition of her outstanding humanitarian service to her community.

The Wolfe Island Health Clinic was opened in 1973 and operated for the first eight years by island residents, Dr. George Merry and his nurse wife, Catherine. Photo 1973.

a nurse, assisted him for the first eight years.[20] It was subsequently moved to a parcel of land donated by Mildred Hawkins-Walton, a driving force behind its founding and ongoing viability. Its new home is on the Sixth Line near the new location of the enlarged fire hall.

Dr. Alan McBride of Kingston held clinics two evenings each week during the 1980s and made house calls. Islanders soon had access to home-care service. Specially trained island residents Alice McKenna and Doris Eves looked after light housekeeping such as laundry, baths, light cooking, and the changing of sickroom bedding.[21] The next step was the service of the Victorian Order of Nurses (VON) in the person of Mrs. Adrienne Rose, another Wolfe Islander.

As physicians retired and younger doctors were reluctant to take the post, the clinic was closed for a few years until 2003, when Dr. Hans Westenberg of Kingston volunteered to hold a clinic weekly for a half day. Then, on May 5, 2008, the unthinkable occurred. Fire destroyed the clinic, valuable records, and equipment, but, thankfully, no lives were endangered as the clinic was not open. There is no doubt that a new, larger, and better-equipped clinic will take its place in the near future, thanks to the generous pledges received.[22]

AMBULANCE SERVICE

Dr. George Merry was the force behind Wolfe Island obtaining its first ambulance service and Dr. William Ghent of Hôtel Dieu Hospital acquired a previously used ambulance. The ambulance service upgraded the vehicle, trained a volunteer crew, and launched them for service. Some years later the Ministry of Health provided a fully equipped ambulance and ongoing skills upgrading for the dedicated round-the-clock crew. Emergency helicopter service for the critically ill was set up for the Frontenac Islands, particularly for winter months when the river crossings might impede a timely arrival at a Kingston hospital. By May 1992, funds raised through generous donations from Wolfe Island organizations and fundraising activities were used to purchase a "jaws of life." This equipment is often necessary to free the victim of an accident and allow the ambulance crew to get at the patient. With the government's amalgamation process instituted in 1998, the Wolfe Island Volunteer Ambulance Service became part of the Frontenac County Paramedic Services, requiring the level of training and upgrading for paramedics across the county to be standardized. Specialized training geared to farm hazards and accidents is also a regular part of volunteer preparation. It took many years for the medical care and emergency services to approach the quality carried out on the mainland.

From the services of one lone midwife dependent on others to transport her, to the sick or injured, to modern-day skilled volunteers able to provide emergency services, Wolfe Island has undergone a lengthy but rewarding metamorphosis in medical care.

CHAPTER 18
History of Wolfe Island Churches and Secular Societies

Until about 1825 most islanders travelled to Kingston for religious rites. Later, itinerant and visiting clergymen made occasional visits that increased in frequency as the population expanded. Services and ceremonies were conducted in the homes of adherents.

Funerals were community events with everyone helping to support the bereaved. Usually a local carpenter would construct a plain, custom-sized coffin painted with lamp black and with its interior lined with black fabric. Alex Fraser, an Anglican, was the last known coffin-builder on the island. Four men carried the coffin on their shoulders, alternating as necessary with four other bearers.[1] The service at home and cemetery usually consisted of a few prayers spoken extempore by one of the men. As burial is an act of mercy, the presence of clergy was not required.

In time, larger congregations planned the financing of their respective houses of worship and organized construction bees. The 1861 census recorded the denominations and enumerated 3,601 adherents by their faith: Roman Catholic, 1,563; United Church of England and Ireland, 1,116; Established Church of Scotland, 409; Methodist Episcopal, 277; Free Church of Scotland, 51; Wesleyan Methodists, 48; United Presbyterians, 44; Baptists, 40; Protestants (not designated), 21; no religion, 18; other Methodists, 11; New Connexion Methodists, 2; Unitarian, 1.[2] Aside from the four denominations that built churches, it was only possible to find information on the Baptists from the forgoing list.

My father was told that an unnamed Baptist minister from the United States used to cross the St. Lawrence River in the vicinity of Wolfe Island's Seventeenth Concession. He conducted services and preached on the shore of either the Niles or Bamford properties. As a result of this ministry, many islanders were baptized by immersion in the river.[3]

THE UNITED CHURCH OF ENGLAND AND IRELAND (TRINITY CHURCH)

During the relentlessly hot summer of 1845, a lot was surveyed by E.H. Kertland, a provincial land surveyor, and work began on Trinity Church. On October 6, 1845, George O. Stuart, rector of St. George's and Archdeacon of Kingston, conducted the cornerstone-laying ceremony. He was assisted by the Reverend Robert V. Rogers, rector of St. James, Kingston, and the Reverend Joseph A. Allen, the presumed first incumbent of the parish at Wolfe Island.[4]

The baroness de Longueuil (Caroline Coffin Grant) defrayed the expense of constructing the church, completed in 1846. Located in the village at lot 3 of the Old Survey on elevated land that permitted a fine view of Kingston and the bay, it has the distinction of being Wolfe Island's oldest church. Allowing that the interior of the church has undergone renovations and updating from time to time, the old Gothic-style limestone building still stands and serves as it has for over 160 years. The wooden carriage shed to the west has since been removed, as has the stable for the clergyman's horse and carriage, which was, at one time, located on the other side of the church.

By 1851 regular morning services were being held at Trinity Church, while afternoon services took place in Smith's log schoolhouse at Irvine's Corners. The school's namesake, John Smith, died in 1895 at the age of eighty and was buried in Christ Church Cemetery at the Foot. The first recorded marriage on the island was performed at Trinity by the Reverend T. Bousfield on March 7, 1852. The contracting parties were William Percival of Goderich, Ontario, and Sarah Going, sister of Captain Shirley Going of Wolfe Island. Baby Eliza Gass of Garden Island was registered on February 23, 1851, as the first baptism in Trinity Church. The first baptism on Wolfe Island to be registered was Eliza Ann Hackett on March 9, 1851, and the baptism of Lucy Ellen Garrett from Simcoe Island was registered on March 11, 1852.[5]

Reverend Bousfield, the parish incumbent, was a tireless worker. Along with regular Sunday morning services, he conducted three others on Sunday, travelling across the island on horseback to either schoolhouses or parishioners' homes. In spite of this fine record, a report indicated that the mission was in serious financial difficulties, and his salary was reduced.[6] The congregation consisted largely of impoverished tenant farmers unable to sustain the cost of church and incumbent. The Church Society removed Reverend Bousfield from his position, and for the next four years the mission was without an ordained priest.

The parishioners eventually realized the lack of accommodation for the incumbent was part of the problem. Reverend Allen had lived at Longueuil Castle and Reverend Patterson had lived in Kingston. A parsonage fund was established in 1855, and a church report for 1864 lists a stone parsonage as part of the ten-acre glebe. This building on the original seigneury lot was occupied until it was sold by the Anglican Diocese of Ontario on July 2, 1909, to George Friend, son of English immigrant John Friend and his wife Ann Wenbourne.[7] After a frame parsonage was built next to the church, Friend sold the property to Dr. William and Florence Areson of New Jersey on June 18, 1927. Reverend Henry Sharpe was appointed in 1858, and the island mission supported an incumbent for the next eighty-four years. But the lack of almsgiving continued. Among the Strachan Papers was a letter from the bishop to Reverend Sharpe referring to the "backwardness of the people" in contributing toward his support, as they had not been accustomed to so doing.[8]

CHRIST CHURCH

The congregation that met in Smith's schoolhouse was known as Christ Church. The Lord Bishop of Ontario, John Travers-Lewis, had purchased the northwest corner of Concession Sixteen, lot 6 south of the Base Line, from member John Montgomery for the nominal fee of five shillings. The church was built on this lot in 1862. A rough wooden shed that accommodated ten horses and buggies was to the north of the church, leaving the balance of the land available for a cemetery. In 1893 Christ Church added a thirty-six-square-foot vestry in the northwest corner of the building. The original altar from Trinity Church was transferred to Christ Church in 1896 after Anthony Malone of Garden Island presented a new altar to Trinity. The first pews, gifted by St. George's Cathedral, Kingston, and installed by Henry and Richard Holliday, were transported by the SS *Pierrepont*. Christ Church was consecrated on Ash Wednesday, February 20, 1901.[9]

Medical students were known at that time to invade Wolfe Island cemeteries to remove the newly interred bodies for anatomical studies. When Eliza Holliday was buried in 1892, her brothers took up watch with shotguns at her gravesite for a long period so her body would not be desecrated.[10]

Christ Church Anglican sits amidst its cemetery on the Fifteenth Concession at the foot of the island. Since 1930, many more grave markers have been erected, and the property has been enclosed with an iron fence. Photo 1930.

TRINITY CHURCH

An indenture of importance to Trinity Church, signed on June 9, 1865, assured the perpetuity of this church. The signatures were those of the five Wolfe Island trustees: Charles Armstrong, Joseph Bullis, Henry Percival, and Samuel Watts, all farmers, and Shirley Going, a gristmill owner. The sixth was that of the baroness de Longueuil. The document was a deed by which she granted to the above trustees all the lands and real property occupied by the Trinity United Church of England and Ireland on Wolfe Island:

> to be held by them and their successors in trust for a church where services could be held according to the established Church of England and Ireland …

> [B]ut the said party of the first part [the baroness] reserves to herself her heirs and assigns forever, and without being subject to any rent or charge of any kind whatever, the two pews next to the communion rails and in the centre aisle of the aforementioned church edifice.[11]

From that date on, the church held title to both the buildings and land, making it a candidate for heritage designation.

The fifth incumbent, Reverend Frank W. Kirkpatrick (son of Thomas, first mayor of Kingston, and brother of the Honourable Sir George Kirkpatrick, a member of Parliament), arrived on the island in 1864. During his ministry, church records showed that contributions were still sparse. When businessmen Reeve

Bishop Seagar of Kingston is pictured with Church Army Captain Stanley Jackson's Confirmation class on September 1, 1929, at Trinity Church. Although not identified, the children were from Simcoe and Wolfe islands. Captain Charles Wall would have prepared confirmées during his post in 1930–31.

Courtesy of C.H. Wall Collection.

Morey Spoor, Postmaster George Malone, and John F. Charles, superintendent of stores for Calvin and Breck, were the lay delegates for the fiscal year 1867–68, donations began to increase.

Trinity Church, French Gothic in design and built of island-quarried limestone, has a much more charming interior than the average country church. Three fleur-de-lis finials crown the carved-oak reredos. This French heraldic emblem, also symbolic of the Virgin Mary, caps the hymn-notice plaque, and is intricately carved into the prayer desks and the brass pedestal of the lectern. The pulpit was donated in memory of the seventh incumbent, Reverend James Godfrey, who served from 1873 to 1885. He and his wife Sarah, who predeceased him, were both laid to rest in the church's cemetery.

Trinity Church was the recipient of a new altar, donated in 1896 by Anthony Malone, postmaster of Garden Island. A new communion rail was dedicated at Easter 1908, given by Margaret and Thomas Lappin. Dr. Lappin may have been the island dentist during this era. Lay reader Garfield Bennett crafted the present baptismal font donated by him and his wife, Laura Mae, in memory of their son, Austin. The one stained-glass memorial window was donated in honour of A. Garfield Bennett, a native of Fogo Island, Newfoundland, by Grace and Garfield Kelly. The bell installed in the church tower bears an inscription placed there by the baroness, but the words have not been disclosed. Pew rental was introduced in 1891, and in 1893 new church pews were bought at a cost of $350. The pews, made of birch and elm with a mahogany finish, were furnished by Pennington, Baker, and Company of Hamilton and Dundas, Ontario.

ST. MARGARET'S HALL

When Reverend James Dawe suggested a parish hall during his incumbency (1932–38), members of both churches, in accord with the bishop, set up a building-fund committee. Margaret Ann Spankie of Kingston, sister of Dr. William Spankie, initiated the fundraising campaign with a donation of one thousand dollars and a further commitment of six hundred dollars. At her request a memorial to Dr. Spankie was incorporated into the hall — a handsome fieldstone fireplace.

St. Margaret's Hall was built in 1935 on church-owned property on the river side of Front Road opposite the church. Through the efforts of Reverend Dawe, the hall was debt free by 1937 when he and Mrs. Dawe carried out a mortgage-burning ceremony with festivities for the parishioners.[12] When my father was the Church Army incumbent at Trinity, he played an influential role in the Young Peoples' Association and met his future wife there. St. Margaret's continues as a major centre for the island community.

CEMETERIES

While Christ Church sits amidst its cemetery, the Trinity Church lot lies adjacent to its burial ground. Numerous early settlers are interred in this historic place, perhaps the most notable being the baron and baroness de Longueuil. Some of the larger family plots contain up to seven or eight generations, yet one wonders how many early pioneers were buried in small family plots on their own properties. Some children of

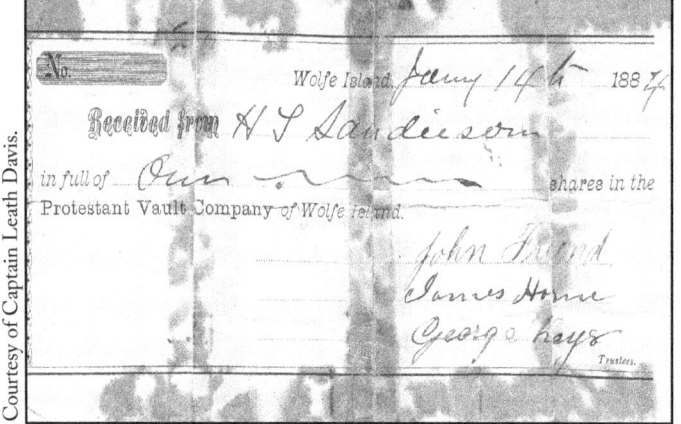
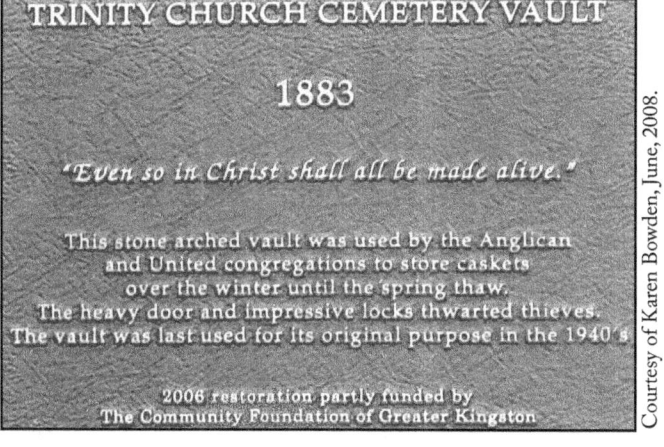

TOP: Trinity Anglican Cemetery's stone arched vault was erected in 1883 with funds raised on a shareholder basis between the Anglican and Methodist congregations. Caskets with the deceased were stored there in winter to await the spring thaw. In the 1940s, the vault was closed but was restored in 2006, an initiative taken by Canon Carr. This photo also shows side and rear views of Trinity Church to the left. Photo 2009. BOTTOM LEFT: This is an actual shareholder's receipt for the Protestant Vault Company, Wolfe Island, 1884. BOTTOM RIGHT: The plaque mounted on the limestone vault commemorates the vault's purpose and the need for restoration, June 2006.

the Alexander Kiell family were laid to rest their farm on Bear Point.[13]

One attractive piece of architecture within the Trinity Cemetery is the stone vault. For decades its was difficult to see from the road as it was overgrown with ivy and other plants. The vault was constructed in 1883 to accommodate caskets awaiting the spring thaw. The current incumbent of Trinity Church, Reverend Canon Carr, loath to see the historical structure crumble, sought restoration funding. Local stonemason Kevin Frost (a Simcoe Island ferry captain) was contracted to restore the vault in 2007. As space in the cemetery is basically sold out, plans for developing the vault as a columbarium for cremated remains will increase capacity.[14]

There have been a number of Anglican incumbents since the church's inception and each has had a special place in the hearts of their parishioners. Reverend Carr, affectionately known as Chris, has won the hearts of islanders regardless of their religious persuasion.

THE CATHOLIC CHURCH

Initially, the Catholic congregation of Wolfe, Garden, Simcoe, and Mud islands attended St. Mary's Cathedral in Kingston. As the population grew, priests crossed the river to hold services or attend the sick. Early stations or divine office were celebrated at John B. McDonell's home four miles east of the village. Later, Hiram O. Hitchcock, a Protestant, offered his home in the village. On his deathbed, Hitchcock was given the last rites of the Catholic Church.[15]

The Catholic Mission of Wolfe Island was formed in 1852 under the auspices of Father Farrell in Kingston, and established as such in 1854 by Bishop Phelan, coadjutor and administrator of the archdiocese of Kingston. The first island church, dedicated as the Church of the Sacred Heart of the Blessed Virgin Mary, was a limestone building erected on four acres of donated land valued at approximately two thousand dollars.[16]

There are two versions regarding the origin of the four-acre lot and the donor. Firstly, Dr. John McRae from Inverness and his wife Anne held part ownership of lot 1, Concession Six (NBL) by the mid-1830s. After Anne was widowed in 1838, she purchased the ninety-acre lot 5 (Old Survey), from which four acres were severed in 1841 and donated by her for the first church and cemetery. Secondly, Mary McRae, James Hector's wife of Glengarry, has been credited with donating the land, but they arrived on the island later and, although they never lived on lot 5, it is apparent that they obtained the patent for John and Anne's original property on the Sixth Line in 1848. It seems possible that James may have been Dr. John McRae's son by a previous marriage.[17]

The substantial stone structure also contained living quarters for its first resident pastor, Reverend John Foley. His pastorate lasted from November 1854 to October 1861, during which time the diocese purchased a house on four acres of land adjoining the church from Mr. Porter Fuller of Cape Vincent. Father Foley lived there until his death in 1861, and is remembered for encouraging people to join the temperance society.[18] Later, Father Michael Stafford was appointed to the Mission. He lived in the house for two years until it burned in 1863. He purchased another four-acre lot with a stone

The second Catholic Church of the Sacred Heart of the Blessed Virgin Mary was erected in 1869. Note the horses and buggies in the foreground. Photo 1910.

house owned by the baroness. This may have been the one depicted on the 1860 Walling map as Elmlodge. It was used as a parsonage until Stafford was transferred to the mission at Lindsay, Ontario. He remains revered for his influence on the education of Catholic youth, and is credited with establishing and furnishing the first separate schools on the island.[19] The small stone parsonage was used as such until 1901 when the present imposing brick mansion was built.

Reverend M.J. Graham replaced him as pastor in May 1868 for a period of fifteen months, followed by the Reverend Edward H. Murray. Recognizing the need for a larger church, he set out to realize this goal. People gave so generously they were also able to purchase an eight-acre grove from Hiram Hitchcock for one thousand dollars. The cornerstone was laid by Bishop Horan on June 20, 1872, and the church was completed towards the end of that year.[20] During his five years in office, Father Murray "worked with great energy and zeal for the welfare of the people committed to his care."[21] The second church, also constructed of limestone, was set on the newer property close to and facing the turnpike. Sometime later the first church was sold to Harry Card for salvage of the stone and lumber.

Reverend Thomas Spratt succeeded Father Murray in 1874, and, by 1887, the bishop of Kingston was encouraging the congregation to raise funds to improve and enlarge the church.[22] This mission was accomplished with the laying of the cornerstone in 1915 by the Most Reverend M.J. Spratt, brother of Reverend Thomas and Archbishop of the Kingston Diocese. In the cornerstone were placed the names of Archbishop Spratt and the new incumbent Father Fleming, the date of the ceremony, samples of coins of the realm, and copies of

The third and present Church of the Sacred Heart was dedicated in 1918. Stone from the second church constitutes the foundation of the front stairway. Photo 1995.

the *Daily British Whig*, the Toronto *Globe*, the *Catholic Record,* and the *Canadian Freeman*. Unfortunately, in 1915, after forty-one years as pastor, Father Thomas died before he could see the new church completed.

This third and present church was dedicated on June 11, 1918, by Archbishop Spratt. Built of limestone quarried from behind the brick parsonage, the imposing edifice of Gothic revival architecture mimics the Norman style of the middle ages. J. Fowler and Son of Kingston were the architects and R. Sheehy of Peterborough, Ontario, was the contractor. The contract price was $56,600, but its final cost was closer to ninety thousand dollars. Outside measurements were 165 feet by ninety-five feet wide.[23]

Reverend J.P. Fleming was the pastor on the day of dedication, followed in succession by Reverend P.J. McKiernan in 1923, Reverend R.A. Carey in 1928, Reverend J.F. Feeney in 1935, Reverend Joseph Shannon in 1942, and the memorable Reverend James S. Ryan, a native Wolfe Islander, in 1948. When Ryan celebrated his golden jubilee in the priesthood at his parish church on June 10, 1972, the title of *monsignor* was conferred upon him. This was the same service at which Wolfe Islander and Franciscan friar Tod Laverty, OFM, was ordained to the priesthood.

Mable McRae's grandfather, William Hawkins, was a caretaker of Sacred Heart Church during the late 1800s. On one occasion, while he was on a ladder cleaning the top of the reredos, he accidentally knocked one of the angels to the floor. Hawkins lived on the Old Survey and his neighbour was Dr. Ed Adams Deming, a young man studying to be a plastic surgeon. Using his artistic ability, Deming created a new angel to match the broken one's former beauty. The following summer the doctor returned with it from his home in Connecticut.[24]

The Old Cemetery, located behind the present parsonage beside the site of the first Catholic church, is historic, its markers indicating the gravesites of numerous pioneers born in the 1700s. Although tombstones reveal French, English, and Scottish heritage, almost two thirds of them represent counties of Ireland. The newer cemetery is on the east side of the Sixth Line, across the road from the present church.

Another day of significance for the parish was on October 19, 1901, when Wilfred Kingsley was ordained to the priesthood. The son of William and Mary Kingsley, who had settled on a portion of lot 3 on the east side of the Eighth Line, he obtained his elementary education on the island and completed his academic and seminary studies in Kingston and Toronto. After ordination, Father Kingsley's further studies took him to Rome for a doctorate in Canon Law. This opened the door for him to become secretary to Archbishop Gauthier in Kingston on his return to Canada. Reverend Dr. Kingsley's last assignment before his retirement was as pastor of the Church of the Good Thief at Portsmouth, and chaplain of the Kingston Penitentiary during the time of the incarceration of the notorious gangster Norman "Red" Ryan.[25] It seems that Dr. Kingsley would, from time to time, arrange fresh-air leave for Red Ryan by inviting him to cut the grass at the church.

SACRED HEART PARISH HOUSE

The brick parsonage that Father Spratt had constructed by 1901 was used as both a summer retreat and retirement home for priests within the archdiocese for eighty years. In 1985 this beautiful mansion underwent a metamorphosis. It acquired a widow's walk, magnificent new

Sacred Heart Parish House was owned and used by the diocese from its completion in 1901 to 1985 when it was sold. It sits on land that juxtaposes the Anglican and Catholic church properties. The initial Catholic cemetery is situated behind the parish house. Photo 1988.

Courtesy of Mable McRae.

gardens, and a completely transformed interior when the property was sold and converted into a bed and breakfast named Wolfe Manor. The main floor parlour remains much the same as the original, with the tall, handsome oak mantel and fireplace creating a dominating presence in the room.

Perhaps the only children on Wolfe Island to grow up in this parsonage were Father James Ryan's niece, Margaret, and two nephews, James and Paul Johnson. Their mother, Edna, was his sister. After the tragic loss of Edna's husband in a farming accident, Ryan took them under his roof. Edna became the rectory housekeeper and each of the children had their chores. When groups of visiting priests were gathered, the children were servers at table. All of this became the way of life for them. Father Ryan loved American-made cigarettes and Mogan David wine, and when his nephew, James, worked on Horne's ferry to Cape Vincent he would procure the cigarettes.

Father Ryan frequently worked surreptitiously to help those in need. He often picked up nurse Louise Kenney when summoned to an accident or someone's sickbed. After she was widowed with two children, her son Edward told Father Ryan that someone had been leaving a goose at their back door each Christmas. One year Edward was fast enough to look out when he heard a car door slam, and sure enough it was Father Ryan.

Many benevolent gestures are recorded about this gentle but no-nonsense man. He could often be found in coveralls painting the church, chinking the masonry, or cutting grass, as he maintained both the church and the schoolyard. His niece, Margaret, remained at the rectory until she was married (her uncle James officiating), and, as Margaret tells the story, she had a perfectly normal, happy upbringing.[26] The first Dutch family to immigrate to Wolfe Island after the Second World

The Vollerings were the first Dutch family to arrive on Wolfe Island after the Canadian liberation of the Netherlands during the Second World War. They were sponsored by Father Ryan.

War, the Vollerings, will never forget Father Ryan, as he sponsored them when they came to Canada.

Monsignor Ryan became ill in 1974 and died five years later. Reverend Michael E. Farrell administered the parish until 1981 when Reverend R.C. Vickers assumed the post, which he held until 1986. The next incumbent, Reverend J. Appelman of the Mission Hill Missionaries, was in charge of Sacred Heart Church for twelve years until 1998. He holds a special place in the hearts of immigrants of post-Second World War Holland, his homeland. A brief incumbency in 1998 held by Reverend Karl Clemens was followed by Reverend Eugene O'Reilly, who returned to the place of his birth to take charge of his home parish — a role cut short by his death in September 2003. As he fulfilled his personal mandate of inspiring ecumenism on Wolfe Island, he is revered among the island's parishioners. Vern Yott recalled O'Reilly fondly, as their ancestors had come to Wolfe Island at the same time and, as boys, Vern and Eugene had attended school together.[27] By the summer of 2004, Father René LaBelle had succeeded Father O'Reilly, and the ubiquitous Reverend Raymond De Sousa has currently been the apostolate.

Another local property owned by the Catholic archdiocese was Horseshoe Island off the western tip of the Old Survey. The island had been used as a boys' camp for many years, and, when the archdiocese made the decision to sell it in 1948, Dr. Vincent Corrigan, formerly of Kingston, purchased the island. Buildings that existed on Horseshoe at the time were carted by scow to Simcoe Island and Reeds Bay to serve as additions to existing houses. After the Corrigans built their cottage and their family expanded, their summer compound grew from one to eight cottages.[28]

THE METHODIST CHURCH

Early Methodists on Wolfe Island were served by the Methodist Episcopal Church until about 1900. As their headquarters were in the United States, congregations were called American Methodists. A Loyalist, William Losee, was their first appointed itinerant minister along the St. Lawrence River. He arrived in 1791 and concentrated his efforts on the settlers of the Quinte area, his itinerant preaching tours taking him as far as Kingston. From all accounts, William Losee just disappeared early in his ministry. Seemingly, he had fallen in love with a young lady, but while he was away on a preaching tour, another itinerant minister won her. This so upset him that Losee is said to have become mentally unbalanced and left the area.

It is not known exactly who formed the nucleus of the Methodist congregation on Wolfe Island, but during the 1850s services were being held in houses, most often that of George Keyes. The first Methodist church on Wolfe Island was established around 1857–58 on the Ninth Concession, mainly through Keyes's efforts. Reverend J.N.D. West was the first minister of the congregation that met in an old converted house located on property owned by William Keyes. Another nearby building became the first parsonage.

On Sunday, March 15, 1874, the St. Lawrence Methodist Church was opened on the Seventeenth Line Road and dedicated to serve the people at the foot of the island. Wells Bamford, a United Empire Loyalist, donated the land for the church and cemetery. Three parishioners, George and Samuel Woodman and William Rattray, defrayed fifty percent of the cost of construction. The generosity of George W. Woodman led

The St. Lawrence Methodist Church was built on the Seventeenth Concession on land donated in 1874 by Wells Bamford, U.E.L. The church was destroyed by lightning-precipitated fire on August 7, 1957. Photo 1930.

St. Lawrence Cemetery, located beside this church, had been used for the burials of many Methodist Loyalists long before the church was built. No burial records had been kept for these early settlers and few grave markers exist. The burial vault, which had decayed over time, was later rebuilt on a shareholder basis in Trinity Church Cemetery.

THE PRESBYTERIAN CHURCH

The official name of the Presbyterian Church in the 1850s was the Established Church of Scotland. Presbyterians on Wolfe Island applied this name to their congregation and their first place of worship. Erected in 1856, the church was named St. Andrew's, in keeping with the Scottish tradition. The property, at the corner of Seventh and the South Base Line, was purchased from Thomas Tarrant, who, with his wife, Ann, had emigrated from England and settled in the area. The church was built by contractor Azel Cook and his committee: William Grant, J. McDonald, George Michea, and George Stokes.

to the steeple being erected in 1895. However, lightning struck the church on August 7, 1957, causing the whole structure to burn to the ground.[29] The loss of the steeple was also a loss to mariners for, when in that area of the river, they would line up the steeple visually with a particular pine tree as a navigational marker. After the church burned and the old pine fell, a lighthouse had to be erected at Bamford Point. The only thing saved from the church was the communion set, likely because it had been taken to a parishioner's home to be polished.[30] The

Reverend David Cameron was the first pastor, assisted by Donald Ross, the first student minister. The initial elders were Azel Cook, George Michea, and War of 1812 veteran John Unwin. After the church was demolished in a windstorm, the presbytery approved its relocation in the village on the east side of Division Street, just south of Eliza. Shirley Going deeded the land to church trustees Nelson Dean, David Donnelly, and James Horne.[31] The church relied on student ministers from Queen's University during the early years, followed by pastors Reverend K.C. McLeod, Reverend J. Sinclair, Reverend H.V. Workman, Reverend D.T. Lancaster, and Reverend A.M. Russell.

In 1925 the Methodist and Presbyterian congregations joined to form one church named Wolfe Island United Church, operating under the Kingston Presbytery of the Bay of Quinte Conference, Canada. The Presbyterian church building was moved in 1951 and physically incorporated with the former Methodist Church building to become St. Andrew's Hall. Its former site became part of the new public elementary school, SS#4. Point Alexandria Cemetery, formerly under the aegis of the Presbyterian Church, transferred to the United Church.[32]

The plain stained-glass windows were redesigned in an ecclesiastical sense in recent years. Eight windows in the nave of the church now depict some Wolfe Island history, occupations of their donors, and those held dearly in memory.[33] The church commissioned resident artist Linda Sutherland for this task, and her interpretation was so well-received that, after Father O'Reilly's death in September 2003, the church trustees engaged her to redesign the front entrance transom in his memory. The dedication service took place on October 9, 2005, with Terry Wood, lay pastor, presiding.

In May 1974 the United Church congregation celebrated its fiftieth anniversary with fifty-five subscribing families participating. Reverend R. Sweeney officiated. Elders at the time were G.W. Keyes (honorary), J.A. Keyes, G. Joslin, Grant Pyke, and T. Vanden Hoek.[34]

Wolfe Island United Church incorporated the Presbyterian and Methodist congregations with church union in 1925. This photo was taken after the installation of new stained glass windows in 2005.

The Horne and Point Alexandria cemeteries (United Church), with Button Bay in the background.

HORNE CEMETERY AND POINT ALEXANDRIA UNITED CHURCH CEMETERY

One of the earliest settlers of Point Alexandria, Demetrius Spinning (1803–61), reserved land for a cemetery in what came to be lot 10 in Concessions Seven and Eight. He permitted the construction of a school across the road for Presbyterians to use for church services and Sunday school until they could build closer to Marysville. This land, later acquired by the Horne family, is known as the old part of the Point Alexandria United Church Cemetery. In more recent years Bruce Horne donated land as the old portion of the cemetery had no further burial space.[35]

CATHOLIC MUTUAL BENEFIT ASSOCIATION HALL

Although the Catholic congregation was without a parish hall for social functions, the Catholic Mutual Benefit Association (CMBA) Hall was always available to them. The association built the hall under the direction of Father Spratt in the late 1800s when benevolent societies were in vogue. This capacious, two-storey frame building became the busiest place in town. In earlier times the upper level was used for business meetings while the lower level served as a dance hall, theatre, banquet room, or space for political meetings. A constant round of "balls" was held there, organized by the various religious and social groups of the community. Music was provided by local family bands, and the climax of the evening was always a midnight dinner provided by the women of the sponsoring group. Old-timers still refer to these events as "the good old days." The CMBA Hall still stands at its original location south of, and connected to, the back of the town hall. The Anglicans, Methodists, and Presbyterians were each permitted to use the hall gratis once annually during the early 1900s. In later years, the building functioned as a parish hall until 1952, when the parochial social activities were held in the new separate-school building on the Sixth Line. In 1976, the CMBA hall and property were sold to the township.

The late 1800s was a period when the majority of people subscribed to the church or denomination of their choice. Many also opted for membership in a secular organization, some wanting material benefits without church commitment. And so it was that established lodges and new societies offering fraternal, benevolent, and social fellowship, such as the Masonic, Workmen's, and Orange lodges, were spawned.

MASONIC LODGE

Circa 1876, members of a Masonic lodge were holding meetings in a brick building on the hill beside the Hitchcock House. The lodge was known as the Hiram Lodge No. 342, and meetings were convened monthly on the Fridays on or before the full moon. Hiram O. Hitchcock was the lodge's chief supporter, but the group had a short lifespan due to lack of financial support and interest. Around 1891 — shortly after Hitchcock's death in 1889 — the lodge surrendered its charter and the building was used by other groups for meetings, card parties, dances, and for overflow accommodations from the Hitchcock House Hotel.

WORKMEN'S LODGE

The Ancient Order of United Workmen was a benevolent insurance association made up of wage earners. The official title for this local lodge was Wolfe Island Lodge No. 260 AOUW. They held monthly meetings with collection of membership dues of $1.44 per month. The order paid death benefits to deceased members' families and endeavoured to improve the moral, intellectual, and social conditions of its members.[36] Daniel Cattanach, a carpenter living at the southeast corner of Main and Leander, was treasurer for several years. The Workmen's Lodge ceased operations in 1917.

CHOSEN FRIENDS

Another group, registered as Lodge No. 7, met in the large hall over Tom Friend's general store. Members of this Chosen Friends Society wore an attractive membership pin bearing the initials *F.A.P.* This island lodge seems to have focused on social activities, one of them being their annual oyster supper.[37] The Canadian Order of Chosen Friends made its debut circa 1898, but the lifespan of this lodge for both men and women on Wolfe Island is not known. The society had a life insurance policy on each member, operating in a similar manner to the AOUW. When this lodge closed, members surrendered their charter to the Hamilton, Ontario, headquarters. In 1943, the Reliable Life Insurance Co. emerged from the ashes of this society.[38]

THE ORANGE ORDER

The Orange Order was initially organized in 1795 in Northern Ireland as a secret political society to foster and protect Protestantism. A substantial number of Irish immigrants had settled in the vicinity of Kingston in the early 1800s and Orange lodges proliferated throughout the area, including Wolfe Island. The island's chapter was named the Prince of Wales Loyal Orange and Temperance Lodge No. 495. They met in their own building at the southeast corner of the Sixth and Base lines, adjoining the property of Absalom Briggs. He was listed in the 1857–58 edition of the Kingston directory as a deputy district master. This would indicate that the lodge was well-established during the 1850s, as it required at least eight years to acquire the position held by Briggs.

One might wonder how important a role the island Orangemen played in the demonstration that occurred at the Kingston harbourfront on Tuesday, September 4, 1860. About thirty thousand people had gathered to welcome Albert Edward, the nineteen-year-old Prince of Wales, who was on a visit to Canada. Among the throng of well-wishers was a group of three thousand Orangemen in full regalia, representing forty-six area Orange lodges.[39]

The whole community had put considerable expense into plans to receive the prince with a public reception. A ball at the Crystal Palace in the Kingston Fairgrounds had been arranged in his honour. The Orange Society had expected the prince to pass through the Orange arch decorated with flying banners and their insignia. Had he done so, he would have appeared to be in defiance of the Catholic Church. However, Catholic dignitaries sent out a sincere welcome and beckoned him to land where he would be escorted safely to City Hall.[40]

The Duke of Newcastle, advisor to the prince, noted the religious and political implications and sent a message ashore that the prince would not disembark until the Orangemen divested themselves of all regalia, arches, and banners. This request was not honoured. City officials boarded the prince's ship, the *Kingston*,[41] a steamer that had been refitted and decorated for carrying the prince and his party. They presented their addresses, but the overall situation caused further discontent between Catholics and Protestants in Kingston.[42] The *Kingston* slipped away towards Picton and Belleville. The royal party encountered similar occurrences at scheduled stops, but the events in Kingston did not interfere with Wolfe Island's recognition of the royal visit. The township council had resolved to provide illumination for the occasion and authorized the expenditure of twenty-four dollars for the creation of four bonfires on sites easily observed from Kingston.[43]

An amusing story amid the events of September 1860 is a tale of comeuppance. Two Catholic gentlemen shared a few drinks at a Wolfe Island village inn one Thursday evening when the Orange Lodge was in session. They rode horseback along the Sixth Line by the lodge on their way home. As a prank, they backed up against the wooden door, tickled their horses' groins, and made a hasty retreat after the horses had kicked in the doors.[44]

THE WOMEN'S INSTITUTE

"For Home and Country," the motto of inspiration and motivation for country and farm women throughout the nineteenth century, was conceived through the combined efforts of a farm woman named Adelaide Hunter Hoodless of St. George, Ontario, and her fervent advocate Erland Lee, a farmer's grange leader. After having lost a child due to the consumption of unpasteurized milk, Adelaide crusaded for the remainder of her life to have household sciences incorporated into the school curriculum. She was ultimately the impetus behind the funding for the Macdonald Institute (Guelph) for the study of home economics, opened in 1902. Her vision inspired Lee to help her draw up a constitution for the first Women's Institute at his farmhouse near Stoney Creek, Ontario, in 1897.[45]

Wolfe Island's Dr. William Spankie urged the women of the community to become members and form their own chapters. The institute empowered its members to influence and shape policies in their communities and provinces both nationally and internationally. Chapters sprung up quickly across Canada, two of them being established on Wolfe Island in 1927, one in the village and one formed at the foot of the island.[46] This organization afforded rural women the opportunity to discuss their problems and to work together to improve their standard of homemaking and citizenship.

The St. Lawrence Chapter at the foot of the island elected Alvira (Woodman) Gillespie as their first president, and Mary (Gordon) McFadden as first secretary. The impressive number of twenty-seven charter members attended the inaugural meeting in Annie Niles's home.[47] On April 16, 1927, a meeting to found the

The first St. Lawrence Women's Institute meeting was held at the home of John and Annie Niles on May 11, 1927. Seated (l–r) are: Mary McFadden, secretary-treasurer; Shelley Henderson; Tilley Niles; Annie Niles; and John Niles. Standing beside John is Inez Woodman. Lying on the ground and sitting in the foreground are Wallace Niles and John Niles Jr. Photo 1930.

Wolfe Island chapter was held in the township hall, and all the forty women present became charter members, with Mrs. McAllister president, Mrs. John Weir secretary-treasurer, and Mrs. R. McCready the first district director. Before the end of the first year their membership had mushroomed to seventy-nine, and five years later, in 1931–32, to 101 under the leadership of president Mrs. Oscar Fawcett and Mrs. William Mosier, the secretary-treasurer.

Women shared their talents such as quilt-making, knitting, embroidery, tatting, and sewing work clothes. In time these ladies of various cultural backgrounds excelled at needlework, leatherwork, sewing, and rug-making. They sold their wares to raise funds for worthy causes, thus demonstrating their commitment to good works, and were heavily involved in the formation and sponsorship of many 4-H homemaking clubs over the years. During wartime the Women's Institute was globally called upon to meet the needs of refugees and orphans from war-torn countries. Minute notes attest to the measures of gratitude expressed by worldwide relief organizations.[48]

When the Women's Institute chose Lady Tweedsmuir, wife of the governor general, as their patron, they undertook the maintenance of a chronological history of their association and notable events occurring in their villages or communities. The resultant "Tweedsmuir Village Histories" have become of such value to historians that many libraries now house these reference materials.

Former MP Flora MacDonald marked the St. Lawrence Chapter's Golden Jubilee in 1977 as their guest speaker. As both chapters were founded in the same year, they celebrated their Diamond Jubilee on May 1, 1987.

Mrs. Keyes was honoured posthumously. Joan O'Shea noted that the quest for better nutrition and home sanitation was a factor that contributed to the founding of the Women's Institute in 1897.[49] Annie Niles, almost 104 years of age at the time, attended, her lifespan covering that of the Institute. The Honourable Ken Keyes, a native Wolfe Islander, was the guest speaker.

Collectively, Wolfe Island members and similar organizations around the world total over nine million. They are known as "The Associated Country Women of the World," and are recognized at the United Nations as a non-governmental organization.

APPENDIX I
Gravesites: Early Settlers from England

Sacred Heart Cemetery
Rebecca Fry, born 1831, Sommersetshire, died July 7, 1863 (wife of David Healey)

Trinity Cemetery
Frederick Whitmarsh, born 1818, Dinder, Sommersetshire, died February 25, 1871
Clarence Coxall, born circa 1823, Bedfordshire, drowned circa 1859
Theophilis Vale, born 1794, St. Martins, London, died September 22, 1875
Thomas Fox, born 1774, Devonshire, died May 11, 1850
Thomas Wills, born 1803, Devonshire, died June 30, 1880
    Wife: Sophia Wills, Devonshire, born 1812, died August 14, 1880
John Craine, born 1800, Isle of Man, died October 20, 1881

Samuel Watts, born 1801, County Kent, died May 20, 1878
    Wife: Phoebe Darling, born in the United States
John Wright, born 1857, London, died 1902
William Bullis, born 1794, Staffordshire, died September, 1871
    Wife: Elizabeth Blake, born 1792, Leicestershire, died 1870
Mary Parks, born 1759, Yorkshire, died 1833 (former wife of Reverend William Smythe)
Thomas Sluman, born 1789, died 1857
John Tarrant, born 1805, Hampshire, died 1885
    Wife: Clemence Tarrant, born 1811, Hampshire, died 1881

APPENDIX II
Gravesites: Early Settlers from Ireland

Sacred Heart Cemetery

Thomas Briceland, born 1818, County Donegal, died October 27, 1906
    Wife: Mary McGill, born 1825, County Armagh, died October 22, 1906

Dennis Hagerty, born 1863, County Kerry, died September 19, 1905

John Dee, born 1815, County Kerry, died (date unknown)
    Wife: Hannah Healey, born 1825, County Cork, died (date unknown)

Michael Flynn, born 1814, County Cork, died 1898
    Wife: Ellen Collins, born 1827, County Cork, died 1902

Mary McCallum, born 1798, County Antrim, died September 24, 1873
    Husband: John Dawson, born 1797, County Kilkenny, died July 8, 1882

Rose Cunningham, born 1790, County Down, died September 6, 1866

William Murphy, born 1800, Queen's County, died May 1, 1883
    Brother: Patrick Murphy, born 1805, Queen's County, died August 13, 1880
    Brother: John Murphy, born 1796, Queen's County, died August 1, 1874

Patrick Duffy, born 1794, County Monaghan, died November 20, 1870

James Coyle, born 1830, County Armagh, died February 23, 1868
    Wife: Catharine Kelly, born 1816, County Fermanagh, died March 10, 1881

Thomas Hogan, born 1791, County Clare, died April 10, 1870
    Wife: Ann O'Grady, born 1811, County Clare, died Decembet 10, 1885

Patrick O'Reilly, born 1804, County Cavan, died April 23, 1857
    Wife: Rose Garvey, born 1813, County Cavan,

died June 27, 1881
Patrick Lyons, born 1793, County Roscommon, died Dececember 25, 1871
> Wife: Sabina Monaghan, born County Roscommon, died November 21, 1866

Patrick Scanlon, born 1830, Parish of Cloyn, County Cork, died December 1, 1880

Ann Dwyer, born 1790, Parish of Lochmore, County Tipperary, died March 10, 1871

Bernard Quinn, born 1818, County Roscommon, died January 22, 1862
> Wife: Ellen McNight, born 1815, County Limerick, died September 22, 1883

Michael Cushion, born 1838, County Wexford, died August 17, 1862

John Davis, born 1808, County Wicklow, died September 24, 1877

John Buggy, born 1819, Parish of Ableix, County Queen's, died April 2, 1857

Oliver Fanning, born 1804, County Kilkenny, died January 9, 1867

Ann Boleyn, born 1819, County Queen's, died February 26, 1883
> Husband: John Johnson, born County Queen's, died March 4, 1875

John Hawkins, born 1798, County Down, died November 2, 1874

Edward Nugent, born 1827, County Armagh, died July 26, 1857

John McDonald, born 1829, County Queen's, died April 2, 1857

John Kinsella, born 1826, County Wexford, died October 9, 1858
> Wife: Catherine Kinsella, born 1814, County Wexford, died January 14, 1864

John Dignem, no information listed in cemetery records
> Wife: Elizabeth Dignem, born 1808, County Cavan, died February 5, 1881

Rosana Conley, born County Monaghan (wife of Terence Conley)

Patrick McCafferty, born 1808, County (unknown), died August 27, 1856
> Wife: Ann McCafferty, born 1800, County (unknown), died January 9, 1882

William Doolan, born 1797, County Queen's, died July 23, 1891
> Wife: Mary Terrell, born 1824, County Queen's, died March 30, 1890

Daniel Whelan, born 1800, County Queen's, died February 15, 1867

Thomas Phair, born 1845 County Fermanagh, died March 22, 1879
> Father: Thomas Phair, born 1809, County Fermanagh, died August 25, 1853

Trinity Anglican Cemetery

Henry Percival Pittadro, born September 21, 1826, County Queen's, died December 11, 1893

George Malone, born May 16, 1812, Kinsale, Ireland, died April 27, 1886

John Marshall, born 1794, County Armagh, died December 22, 1860

Ann Gillespie, born 1826, County Armagh, died December 11, 1868

Christ Church Anglican Cemetery

Robert Keys, born 1818, County Leitrim, died February 17, 1896

APPENDIX III
Gravesites: Early Settlers from Scotland

Protestant

Peter Grant, born 1812, Invernesshire, died July 24, 1857
    Wife: Isabella Kennedy, buried Sacred Heart Cemetery

David Cramand, born 1825, Dundee, died March 27, 1889
    Sister: Barbara, born 1829–?

Mary Brown, born 1807, Aberdeenshire, died November 16, 1869

Mary McKay, born 1794, Sutherlandshire, died July 27, 1876
    Husband: John S. McDonald, born 1800, Sutherlandshire, died February 28, 1870

Duncan McRae, born 1799
    Wife: Margaret McRae, born 1809

James Rattray born 1762, (probably Perth), died 1859

Elizabeth Rattray, born 1796, (probably Perth), died 1874

Lewis Kiell Sr. (widower), Inverness, brought four children in 1831, dates of birth and death unknown
    Daughter: Margaret (Kiell) Marlow, born 1813, Inverness, died 1896
    Son: Alexander, born 1819, died 1892
    Wife: Lovina Cool, born 1836, died 1883, Wolfe Island
    Son: Lewis Jr., born 1817 died October 5, 1913
    Wife: Ann Dawson, born 1827, died 1901, Wolfe Island
    Son: Peter, born 1815, date of death unknown
    Wife: Mary Abbott, born 1829, died Wolfe Island

Henry Sandieson, born 1830, died 1892
    Wife: Elizabeth (Betsy), born 1825, died 1896

James Berry, born 1802, died 1862

John Horne, born 1798, died 1887

William Henderson, born 1821, died 1899

Alexander Irvine, born 1821, died 1852

Roman Catholic

Isabella Kennedy, born 1819, Invernesshire, died 1875 (wife of Peter Grant)

Jessie McRae, born 1825, Invernesshire, died January 22, 1898

Thomas Nicholson, born 1842, Scotland, died July 15, 1868

Anne McRae (widow of Dr. John McRae), born 1793, Scotland, via Glengarry, Ontario, died 1866
- Daughter: Hannah McRae Cuff, born 1819, died 1887
- Daughter: Jesse McRae Baker, born 1822, date of death unknown

James Hector McRae, born 1818, died 1900, and wife Mary McRae, born 1831, died 1885, probably both from Kintail, Scotland

Margaret McDonald, born 1833, Scotland, died 1863 (wife of Donald McDonell)

APPENDIX IV
The Cone Surname

The name Cone has been spelled as Coan, Corn, Coon, and Coun on maps and records in Kingston's Land Transfer Office. The 1822 Chewett map shows Samuel Coan as the lessee for Old Survey #9, which includes the eastern third of Mill Point, then named Cone Point. Simultaneously, waterfront lots on Button Bay were leased in the names of S. Coun and G. Coun. A Darius Augustus Coon is noted in the Pyke family lineage (married Nellie Pyke in 1891), but it is difficult to align this family with the Cones, as this man would have been born one hundred years later. Although the illiteracy of the time may have been the primary reason for spelling inaccuracies, the full family lineage of the noted Cones could be traced from their initial arrival in America from Scotland at Connecticut. These records may be found in Jefferson County, New York, records.

Wolfe Island's Samuel Cone (1769–1854) and his brother Darius (1763–?) may have fled to Wolfe Island as Loyalists within a few years of the deaths of their parents Nathanial Cone Jr. (1790) and Mary Graves (1792). Samuel and Darius Cone were two of fourteen siblings. They left Wolfe Island as mysteriously as they arrived, evidently without wives or issue. It was not possible to trace any of the other spellings of the name *Cone* in Jefferson County, New York.

APPENDIX V
Wolfe Islanders and Simcoe Islanders Who Fought for Their Country

Those who perished during the First World War:
Frederick Davis, Richard Edwin Davis, Irwin Kelly, James Ernest Matier, Andrew McRae, John Rogers, Edwin Jobe Walker

Those who served in and survived the First World War:
Howard Abbott, Ambrose Alarie, Wilfred Banting, John Belyea, "Peg Leg" Blake, John Daly, Leonard Darragh, Norman Eves, Herbert Sudds, Henry Fargo, Leo Hogan, James Kenney, John Keyes, Lincoln Kiell, Stanley Kiell, David Henry Matier, George McAllister, Ed McKenna, George O'Brien, Dr. James O'Reilly, Charles V. Patterson, Bert Smith, George Bruno Spoor, Melville Staley

Those who perished during the Second World War:
Millard Horne, Earl Joslin, Francis Payne

Those who served in and survived the Second World War:
George Alarie, Gerald Alarie, Clarence Adair, Donald Belyea, Jack Briceland, Hubert Leslie Bullis, Cameron Burke, Bill Bustard, Arthur Campbell, Dr. G. Carson, Charles Coffey, Cecil Conley, Preston Conley, Robert Corcoran, Charlie Cosgrove, Robert Crothers, William Crothers, Howard Cummings, Anne Davis, Chuck Davis, Hank Davis, Paul Davoud, James Dawe, Leon Docteur, Eddie Edwards, Harrison Eves, Ralph Eves, Sanford Eves, R.F. Fawcett, Bill Flynn, Slim Flynn, Bill Hawkins, Ralph Henderson, Roland Henderson, Eddie Hogan, Eugene Hogan, Harry Hogan, Jack Hogan, Jerry Hogan, Ralph Hogan, Dee Horne, Lawrence Horne, Gene Hulton, Percy Jermany, Don Keeley, Harold Keeley, George Kenney, Stan Keogh, Vinton Keogh, Louis Kiell, Tom King, Howard MacDonald, Art MacDonald, Gordon MacDonald, Allan MacAddo, Geraldine MacAdoo, Bernie McColley, Charlie McColley, Leon McDermott, John H. McDonald, Alice McCready, Emmett McDonnell, Bill McFadden, Glenn Mosier, Buck Mullin, Neill O'Brien, Rodney Orr, Jack O'Shea,

Walter Patterson, Hilda Russell, Delbert Sudds, Lesley Sudds, Garnet Tarrant, Robert Tarrant, Maurice Twynham, Ray Wade, Bill Watts, Bill Whitmarsh, Stanley Woodman, Austin Yott, Vern Yott.

Those who served in peacekeeping and military operations other than war:
Simon Berry, Jason Baird, Ronald Barber, Chris Batley, Jim Calvin, Steve Cumpsty, Elise Huffman, Margaret Knott, Walter Knott, Jamie Sanford, Joseph Sanford, Patricia Sanford, Terry Sanford, Leonard Skinner, Natalie Stoyko, Patrick Stoyko, George Turnbull, Keith Walton, Ruby White.

Ongoing Canadian participation in peacekeeping missions to war-torn nations has often included the skills of dedicated Wolfe Islanders. Lieutenant Colonel David Patterson, a Canadian Armed Forces instructor at the Kingston base, has called Wolfe Island home for the past several years. Gradually inspired by the history of this area, he has engaged in the pursuit of the circumstances surrounding Wolfe Islanders lost in battle. Patterson's resolve has succeeded in finding the burial places of some of those who perished. Their names have been added to the rolls and recalled at the annual Remembrance Day observance at the town hall. Of late, this event has heightened the awareness of all present to the legacy of service given by these many young people.

NOTES

Introduction: The People of Wolfe Island
1. Charles Wall, my father, wrote this introduction in 1978 when the islands that he mentioned were all that comprised Wolfe Island Township. During the amalgamation process imposed by the provincial Conservative government in 1998, Howe Island was added to the list and the township name was changed to the Township of Frontenac Islands.
2. Wolfe Island Public Library was opened in 1984.

Chapter 1 — In The Beginning
1. Mark Badham, curator, Miller Museum of Geology, Queen's University, Kingston, Ontario. Personal interview in June 2006, followed by email communication August/September 2006.
2. *Ibid.*
3. *Ibid.*
4. Glacial history information taken from graphs created by Mark Badham, mounted in Miller Museum of Geology, Queen's University, Kingston.
5. Robert Gilbert, "Landscape of Southeastern Ontario and Kingston Region," in *Bulletin 453*, published by the Geological Survey of Canada (1994).
6. O. Salad Hersi and G.R. Dix, "Black Riverian Lithostratigraphy: Ottawa Embayment Eastern Ontario," *Canadian Journal of Earth Science* 36 (1999), 2047.
7. "Limestones of Ontario," no. 5, part 2, in *Geological Surveys of Canada*, Ottawa Bureau of Mines (1903), 43–45.
8. B.A. Liberty, "Paleozoic Geology of Wolfe Island, Bath, Sydenham and Gananoque Areas," *Geological Surveys of Canada* no. 70 (1971), 35.
9. Information from Robert Barnett, a technician with the Department of Invertebrate Paleontology, Royal Ontario Museum, Toronto, 1976, at the time of Charles Wall's consultation with him.
10. Liberty, "Paleozoic Geology of Wolfe Island," 5, 6.
11. Information from Mark Badham, curator, Miller Museum of Geology.
12. Liberty, "Paleozoic Geology of Wolfe Island," 6.
13. *Ibid.*
14. Liberty, "Paleozoic Geology of Wolfe Island," 35.
15. Information from Mark Badham.
16. *Ibid.*
17. Interview, Charles Wall with Leonard Mosier, Wolfe Island, 1930.
18. Interview, Charles Wall with Theresa (La Fleur) McGarvey, Wolfe Island, 1930.

Chapter 2 — Long Island Standing Up
1. R. Bruce Morrison and C. Roderick Wilson, *Native Peoples: The*

2. Jon Nelson, *Quetico: Near to Nature's Heart* (Toronto: Dundurn Press, 2009), 68.
3. The material found at this site is currently with the Archaeological Survey of Canada under the heading of Brophy Site (National Museums Canada).
4. Major James F. Pendergast was awarded an honorary doctorate of science degree by McGill University in June 1976. He was considered to be one of the best amateur archaeologists in Canada. *Kingston Whig-Standard*, June 8, 1976.
5. W.J. Wintemberg, *Artifacts from Ancient Graves and Mounds in Ontario*, series 3, vol. 22 (Ottawa: Royal Society of Canada, 1928), 177, 195.
6. Michael W. Spence, "A Middle Woodland Burial Complex in the St. Lawrence Valley," *Anthropology Papers #14*, National Museum of Canada (1967), 11.
7. William Stone, as quoted in Spence, 11.
8. T.R. Glover and D. D. Calvin, *A Corner of The Empire, The Old Ontario Strand* (Toronto: Macmillan, 1937), 45.
9. Ronald Wright, *Stolen Continents* (Toronto: Penguin, 1991), 115.
10. *Ibid.*, 12.

Chapter 3 — Enter the French
1. From *http://library.thinkquest.org/c006522/explorationcartier.php*, accessed on January 3, 2009.
2. From *http://www.civilization.ca/vmnf/theseigneurs*, accessed on August 24, 2003, re-accessed January 3, 2009.
3. From *http://www.greatcanadianlakes.com/ontario*, accessed February 10, 2009.
4. William Canniff, *The Settlement of Upper Canada* (Toronto: Dudley & Burns, 1869. Fifth printing, Belleville, ON: Mika Publishing, 1983), 9.
5. Mary Druke, *Native Peoples: The Canadian Experience* (Toronto: McClelland & Stewart, 1986), 304.
6. Ronald Wright, *Stolen Continents* (Toronto: Penguin Books, 1992), 125.
7. R. Vachon Rogers, "An Old Conveyance," *Queen's Quarterly*, vol. 1, no. 2 (July 1893–April 1894), 13.
8. J. Castell Hopkins, *French Canada and the St. Lawrence* (Philadelphia, PA: John Winston Co., 1913), 164.
9. R.M. Spankie, "Wolfe Island, Past and Present," in *Proceedings of the 15th Annual Meeting of the New York State Historical Association* (New York: New York Historical Association, 1914), 212.
10. *Ibid.*, 212. Author's Note: The linear and monetary equivalents at the time are as follows: one league = three miles or 84 arpents; one toise = 6.4 feet; square toise = 41 square feet; One arpent = 192 feet; square arpent = 5/6 acre; one livre = one dollar Canadian (fixed equivalent in 1958); 8.1 arpents = one league = three miles.
11. Rogers, "An Old Conveyance," 16, 17.
12. Spankie, "Wolfe Island, Past and Present," 213.
13. R. Cole Harris, *The Seigneurial System in Early Canada* (Montreal: McGill-Queen's University Press, 1984), 42.
14. *Ibid.*, 26.
15. Rogers, "An Old Conveyance," 20.
16. The *Dictionnaire national des canadiens français 1608–1760* reveals many spellings of the name Curotte, the main one being "Curaux" under which Martin's lineage is recorded. (Montreal: Institute Geneologique Drouin, 1965), 329.
17. Richard Preston, ed., *Kingston: Before the War of 1812* (Toronto: Champlain Society University of Toronto Press, 1915), xxxviii.
18. Hubert C. Burleigh, *Forgotten Leaves of Canadian History* (Kingston: Brown and Martin, 1973), 5.
19. Library and Archives Canada, RG 4, B-28, Internal Correspondence, Traders' Licences.
20. Library and Archives Canada, C-11A7, 303–305.
21. Library and Archives Canada, MG-11, Q313 part I: 300, 301.
22. Reformed Church of Quebec, *http://www.erq.gc.ca/english/ourhistory.html*, accessed on January 3, 2009.
23. Brian Rollason, ed., *County of a Thousand Lakes* (Lindsay, ON: Frontenac City Council, John Deyell Co., 1982), 483.
24. Author interview with Isabel O'Shea, Kingston, Ontario, in June 2005.
25. R. Cole Harris, *The Seigneurial System in Early Canada* (Montreal: McGill-Queen's University, 1984), 72.

Chapter 4 — Lineage of the Barony of Longueuil
1. Bruce Trigger, *The Children of Aataentsic: A History of the Huron People to 1660* (Kingston: McGill-Queen's University Press, 1976), 668.
2. *Donnés* were devout laymen attached to the Jesuit missions in the mid-1600s. They took vows and wore the religious habit.

3. Wallace G. Breck, "The Le Moynes, Longueuil, Kingston and Wolfe Island," *Historic Kingston* 37 (Kingston: Historical Society, 1989), 2. This paper, written by Professor Wallace Breck formerly of Queen's University, contained contributions from some Wolfe Islanders, including Peg and Ken White, who currently own the property where Ardath was located.
4. Ibid., 3. Charles Le Moyne would go on to receive numerous honours.
5. *Toronto Telegram*, November 26, 1970.
6. Wallace G. Breck, "The Le Moynes, Longueuil, Kingston and Wolfe Island," 3
7. *Ibid.*, 10.
8. *Ibid.*, 13.
9. David Roberts, *Dictionary of Canadian Biography*, vol. 5 (1801–1820) (Toronto: University of Toronto Press, 2000), 369.
10. *Ibid.*, 374.
11. "Marie-Charles Joseph Le Moyne," *Dictionary of Canadian Biography*, 1836–1850, http://www.biographi.ca, accessed August 5, 2008, and March 6, 2009.
12. Roy Fleming, "Recollections of a Visit to Ardath Castle, Wolfe Island in 1902," *Kingston Whig-Standard*, June 1942.
13. Daniel François, *Histoire des grandes familles français du Canada* (Montreal: Eusebe Senecal, 1867).
14. *Dictionary of Canadian Biography*, vol. 5, 501.
15. Sir John Johnson (1742–1830), son of Sir William Johnson, was a Loyalist leader in the American Revolution. He ultimately moved to Canada, and became superintendent of Indian Affairs in 1782.
16. Roy Fleming, "Recollections of a Visit to Ardath Castle, Wolfe Island in 1902."
17. Hubert C. Burleigh, *Forgotten Leaves of Canadian History, Kingston* (Kingston: Brown and Martin, 1973), 54.
18. R.M. Spankie, "Wolfe Island, Past and Present," 232.
19. Loyalist Collection at the University of New Brunswick, New Brunswick Museum Archives, Loyalist documents 1755–1880, MIC-Loyalist FC LSC. N4 M8 A7L6, Reel 2.
20. Gerald Craig, *Upper Canada: The Formative Years 1784–1841*, 2nd ed. (Toronto: McClelland & Stewart Ltd., 1963, 1991), 13, 14.
21. Roy Fleming, "Recollections of a Visit to Ardath Castle, Wolfe Island, 1902."
22. Katherine Hale, "Canadian Houses of Romance, 1926," from Hubert C. Burleigh, *Kingston! Oh Kingston* (Kingston: Arthur Britten Smith 1987), 596. The name "Katherine Hale" was the nom-de-plume of Amelia Beers (Warnock) Garvin (1878–1956) of Toronto.
23. B. Osborne and D. Swainson, *Kingston: Building on The Past* (Westport, ON: Butternut Press, 1988), 264.
24. "Old Survey," Wolfe Island, Ontario, Land Transfer Office, Kingston, Ontario.
25. Brian Rollason, ed., *County of a Thousand Lakes: History of County of Frontenac 1673–1973* (Lindsay, ON: John Deyell Co., 1982), 498.
26. Fern Small and Ken Collins, *Trinity Anglican Church Cemetery Records Wolfe Island* (booklet) (Ontario Genealogical Society, Ottawa Branch, 1973).
27. Strachan Papers, Anglican Diocesan Archives, York (Toronto mid-1800s), 10.
28. *Ibid.*, 10.
29. Dr. D.M. Schurman, "Bishop Strachan and the Archdeaconry of Kingston, 1830–1840," in *Historic Kingston*, vol. 8 (1971), 28.
30. Archives of the Anglican Diocese of Ontario, Kingston, Ref. 3W1, 3, Trinity Anglican Church, Wolfe Island.
31. *Ibid.*, 3W1, 17 and 3W1, 29.
32. *Ibid.*, 2K9, 102.
33. "Old Survey," Wolfe Island, Ontario, Land Transfer Office, Kingston, Ontario.
34. *Kingston Whig Standard*, June 1946.
35. Winston M. Cosgrove, *Wolfe Island, Past and Present* (Lindsay, ON: J. Deyell and Co. 1966), 5, 6.
36. Archives of the Anglican Diocese of Ontario, Kingston, Ref. 3W13, 210, Trinity Anglican Church, Wolfe Island.
37. *Ibid.*, 5K2, 153.
38. *Ibid.*, 4K7, 467.
39. Blairfindie (Grant Allen's middle name) was taken from the name of the seigneury in France belonging to one of his seventeenth century ancestors.
40. Interview with Joan O'Shea, Wolfe Island, June 2004.
41. See *http://www.chriswillis.freeserve.co.uk/grantallen.htm*, accessed on August 28, 2006.
42. Donald Forsdyke, "Grant Allen, George Romans, Stephen J. Gould and the Evolution of Their Time … And Who Was the Kingston Lady," in *Historic Kingston*, vol. 52 (2004), 95–103.

Chapter 5 — What's in a Title?
1. A "church glebe" refers to land owned by a parish church, including the rectory and cemetery.
2. National Archives of Canada, Ref. RG1, L3, vol. 286, 299, 300.
3. Gerald M. Craig, *Upper Canada: The Formative Years* (Toronto: McClelland & Stewart, 1963), 171.
4. *Ibid.*, 172.
5. William Canniff, *The Settlement of Upper Canada* (Toronto: Dudley & Burns, 1869. Fifth printing, Bellville, ON: Mika Publishing, 1983), 339.
6. Craig, *Upper Canada: The Formative Years*, 185.
7. National Archives of Canada, Ref. RG1, vol. 87 (1805), 46.
8. *Ibid.*, Upper Canada Land Petitions Ref. RGI, L3, vol. 87, 76.
9. *Ibid.*
10. *Ibid.*, Ref. MG 11, Q313, Part 1, 299.
11. *Ibid.*, Ref. RG1 L3, vol. 286, 63K.
12. *Ibid.*, "Upper Canada Land Petitions," RG1, L3, vol. 5 "A" Bundle, 10.
13. *Ibid.*
14. *Ibid.*
15. National Archives of Canada, Ref. RGI, L3, vol. 286, L10, 63N.
16. For information on Gourlay's questionnaire, see F. Murray Greenwood and Barry Wright, eds., *Law, Politics and Security Measures, 1608–1837, Canadian State Trials*, vol. 1 (Toronto: Osgoode Society, 1996), 697–702.
17. Joe Fiorito, *Toronto Star* (Canadian Press News Service), August 30, 2004.
18. R. Vachon Rogers, "An Old Conveyance," *Queen's Quarterly*, vol. 1 (July 1893–April 1894), 12.
19. National Archives of Canada (Colonial Office, London, England), Q328, Pt. 2, 238–46.
20. Rogers, "An Old Conveyance", 11.

Chapter 6 — Whence Did They Come
1. William Canniff, *The Settlement of Upper Canada* (Toronto: Dudley & Burns, 1869. Fifth printing, Belleville, ON: Mika Publishing, 1983), 636.
2. See Brian Osborne and Donald Swainson, *Kingston: Building on the Past* (Westport, ON: Butternut Press, 1988), 23, 26, 28.
3. Information provided to the author from Ruth Ann (Ellerbeck) Pearce of Tilbury, Ontario, regarding her ancestral history, a letter to author dated September 18, 2005, based on a record of the life story of Emmanuel Ellerbeck and that of his issue as compiled by Emmanuel's grandson (Ruth Ann Ellerbeck Pearce's uncle, Robert Ellerbeck).
4. Hubert C. Burleigh, *Forgotten Leaves of Canadian History, Kingston* (Kingston: Brown and Martin, 1973), 83.
5. *Ibid.*, 81.
6. *Ibid.*, 92.
7. Information from Ruth Ann (Ellerbeck) Pearce.
8. Archives of the Anglican Diocese of Ontario, ref. 3W3, 222. Trinity Anglican Church, Wolfe Island.
9. Canniff, *The Settlement of Upper Canada*, 185, 188.
10. Russell Waller, U.E., Wolfe Island 1851 Census, 33.
11. T.R. Glover and D.D. Calvin, *A Corner of the Empire: The Old Ontario Strand* (Toronto: Macmillan, 1937), 83.
12. Canniff, *The Settlement of Upper Canada*, 574.
13. Kenneth Bagnell, *The Little Immigrants* (Toronto: Macmillan, 1980): Inside cover flap.
14. Interview with Eugene Hulton, Wolfe Island, September 20, 2006.
15. Interview with Flora Devlin, Wolfe Island, September 14, 2005.
16. Canniff, *The Settlement of Upper Canada*, 137.
17. Thomas G. Anderson, *Reminiscences: Loyalist Narratives from Upper Canada* (Toronto: J.J. Talman, 1946), 123.
18. Brian Rollason, ed., *County of a Thousand Lakes: History of Frontenac County 1673–1973* (Lindsay ON: John Deyell Company, 1982), 483.
19. Canniff, *The Settlement of Upper Canada*, 403.
20. Research by Charles Wall in 1930–31 identified the name as Boxing Harbour. Current signage spells the name as Boxen.
21. Helen Litton, *The Irish Famine* (Dublin, Ireland: Wolfhound Press, 1994), 100. See also, Donald MacKay, *Fight from Famine: The Coming of the Irish to Toronto* (Toronto: McClelland & Stewart, 1990. Third edition, Toronto: Dundurn Press, 2009).
22. Susan MacDonald-Dill, B.A., M.B.A., U.E. (born on Wolfe Island). Researched and compiled McDonell/MacDonald ancestral history, unpublished manuscript obtained June 12, 2004.
23. Burleigh, *Forgotten Leaves of Canadian History, Kingston*, 44.
24. *Ibid.*, 46.
25. Bishop Alexander Macdonell (1762–1840) was born Alexander McDonell in Scotland. At some point in his life, the spelling of his name was changed. Over the years there have

been many variations on the initial spelling of this surname. The two earliest were McDonald and McDonnell. Other variations on Wolfe Island include McDonell, MacDonell, Macdonell, and MacDonald.

26. Canniff, *The Settlement of Upper Canada*, 304.
27. Lt. Col. Louis J. Flynn, *Built On A Rock: The Story of the R.C. Church in Kingston 1826–1976* (Kingston: Catholic Archdiocese, 1976), 12.
28. Canniff, *The Settlement of Upper Canada*, 306.
29. Alexander McDonell, Roman Catholic priest, bishop, and politician, b.1762 Glen Garry Scotland, d. 1840 Dumfries, Scotland. Entered by J.E. Rea, *Dictionary of Canadian Biography* vol. 7, 1836–1850 (Toronto: University of Toronto/University of Laval, 2000).
30. J.K. Johnson, *Historical Essays on Upper Canada* (Toronto: McClelland & Stewart, 1975), 257.
31. Canniff, *The Settlement of Upper Canada*, 306.
32. Time and space do not permit us to record more of this clan's lineage and their contributions to the island community. Theresa Broeders and her brother Brian McDonald have shared information from their McDonell-McDonald family genealogy for this study. The lieutenant colonel was their great-great-grandfather. His tombstone is one of the oldest in the first Sacred Heart of the Blessed Virgin Mary Catholic Cemetery, which lies just west of the present church.
33. Interview with Isabel O'Shea, September 22, 2005, Kingston, Ontario.
34. *Columbia Encyclopedia* (New York: Columbia University Press, 1967), 521.
35. Interview with Flora Devlin, September 20, 2005, Wolfe Island, Ontario.
36. Fern Small and Ken Collins, *Sacred Heart of the Blessed Virgin Mary Roman Catholic Church Cemetery Records*, Wolfe Island, no. 76-15 (Ottawa: Ontario Genealogical Society, Ottawa Branch, 1976), 1.
37. Interview with Johnny O'Shea, June 9, 2006. Information shared in 1993 with O'Shea by descendants of the McRae family, and provided by Brian MacDonald, genealogy chair, Wolfe Island Historical Society, September 20, 2007.
38. Email communication with Gordon McRae, "Wolfe Island Family Connections," December 2007. He is a descendant of these early McRaes.
39. Flynn, *Built on a Rock*, 161.
40. Nelie H. Casler, *Cape Vincent and Its History* (Watertown, NY: Hungerford-Holbrook Co., 1906), 146.
41. *Ibid.*, 150.
42. Interview with Johnny O'Shea on Wolfe Island, June 9, 2006.
43. Casler, *Cape Vincent and Its History*, 141.
44. *Ibid.*, 152.
45. Taken from Coleman Hinckley's contribution to *The History of Jefferson County: New York* (Philadelphia, PA.: L.H. Everts and Co., 1878), 321.
46. Casler, *Cape Vincent and Its History*, 151.
47. Donald Creighton, *The Empire of the St. Lawrence* (Toronto: Macmillan, 1970).
48. Casler, *Cape Vincent and Its History*, 152.
49. Information from a framed document hanging on a wall of the Cape Vincent Historical Museum, New York.
50. Casler, *Cape Vincent and Its History*, 202.
51. *Ibid.*
52. Hart Massey (the family originally emigrated from Vermont) built an industrial empire based on farm equipment. A devout Methodist, he was noted for his philanthropic work, leaving such legacies as Toronto's Massey Hall, Hart House at the University of Toronto, and the Fred Victor Mission.
53. Casler, *Cape Vincent and Its History*, 174.
54. Eloise Brière, comp. "The French History of Northern New York State," in *Franco-American-Quebec Heritage Series* (Albany: State University of New York, 1986), 14–17.
55. Casler, *Cape Vincent and Its History*, 211.
56. *Ibid.*, 143.
57. Information from an interview with Mary (Hinckley) (Hamilton) of Cape Vincent, New York, June 21, 2006.
58. Edwin E. Horsey, *Notes on Wolfe Island*, from Charles Wall's personal collection, believed to have been published for the Kingston Historical Society in 1941. 19.
59. *Ibid.*, 9.
60. Meeting with Mary (Hinckley) Hamilton of Cape Vincent, village historian, in company with Johnny O'Shea, Wolfe Island historian, to discuss Cape Vincent history, June 21, 2006.
61. Interview with Captain Leath Davis of Kingston, June 28, 2007.
62. Casler, *Cape Vincent and Its History*, 143.

63. From Mary (Hinckley) Hamilton, June 21, 2006.
64. *Ibid.*
65. *Ibid.*
66. *Ibid.*
67. Coleman Hinckley's chapter in *The History of Jefferson County*.
68. Information from Susan MacDonald-Dill, June 12, 2004.
69. Burleigh, *Forgotten Leaves of Canadian History, Kingston*, 123.
70. Letter from Rachel (Jamieson) Horne regarding family history, dated July 3, 2006.
71. *Watertown Daily News*, January 7, 1936, provided by Bruce Horne of the Horne Ferry Company.
72. Letter from Rachel (Jamieson) Horne, July 3, 2006.

Chapter 7 — A Teapot in a Tempest
1. J. Castell Hopkins, *French Canada and the St. Lawrence* (Philadelphia, PA: John Winston Co., 1913), 136.
2. *Ibid.*, 40.
3. *Ibid.*, 290.
4. From www.thecanadianencyclopaedia.com, accessed April 23, 2005. The Canadian Encyclopedia, Quebec Act and American Revolution, 2005, Historica Foundation of Canada.
5. *Toronto Star* (Canadian Press), June 30, 2003. See also Osborne and Swainson's *Kingston: Building on the Past*, 27.
6. Edwin Horsey, *Notes On Wolfe Island* (Kingston: Kingston Historical Society, 1941), 3.
7. Richard A. Preston, *Kingston: Before The War of 1812* (Toronto: University of Toronto Press, 1959), 264.
8. Hubert C. Burleigh, "The Romance of Fort Frontenac," in *Kingston! Oh Kingston*, ed. Arthur Brittion Smith (Kingston: Brown and Martin, 1987), 113.
9. Bruce Elliot, *Irish Migrants in the Canadas* (Montreal: McGill-Queen's University Press, 1988), 132.
10. Nelie Casler, *Cape Vincent and Its History* (Watertown, NY: Hungerford-Holbrook Co., 1906), 132.
11. "The American Naval Attack on Kingston, Nov. 10, 1812," reported in *Kingston Gazette*, from *Historic Kingston* vol. 6 (Belleville, ON: Mika Publishing, 1974), 50.
12. R.M. Spankie, "Wolfe Island, Past and Present," in *Proceedings of the 15th Annual Meeting of the New York State Historical Association*, vol. 13 (1914), 219.
13. The Holland Land Company, organized by Dutch bankers in 1796, was active in the settlement of much of New York State.
14. William Canniff, *The Settlement of Upper Canada* (Toronto: Dudley & Burns, 1869. Fifth printing, Belleville, ON: Mika Publishing, 1983), 171.
15. William Lyon Mackenzie (1795 Aberdeen, Scotland–1861 Toronto). An ardent Reformer, he shared his views through his newspaper, the *Colonial Advocate*.
16. Hubert C. Burleigh, *Forgotten Leaves of Canadian History, Kingston* (Kingston: Brown and Martin, 1973), 113.
17. John Montgomery, "An Account of an Escape from Fort Henry," in Hubert C. Burleigh, *Kingston! Oh Kingston* (Kingston, ON: Brown and Martin, 1987), 319.
18. Burleigh, *Forgotten Leaves of Canadian History, Kingston*, 114.
19. G.F. Stanley, "William Johnston: Pirate or Patriot?" in *Historic Kingston*, vol. 6 (Belleville, ON: Mika Publishing, 1974), 15.
20. E.A. Theller, *Canada in 1837–38* (Philadelphia, PA: Henry Anners, 1841): 308.
21. Stanley, "William Johnston: Pirate or Patriot?" 27.
22. Casler, *Cape Vincent and Its History*, 20.
23. *Ibid.*, 27.
24. *Ibid.*, 34.
25. Stanley, "William Johnston: Pirate or Patriot?" 13.
26. B.S. Osborne and D. Swainson, *Kingston: Building on the Past* (Westport, ON: Butternut Press, 1988), 29, 30.
27. *The Thousand Islander and Rideau Voyageur*, Gananoque, Ontario, July 15, 1972.
28. Mary Druke, *Native Peoples: The Canadian Experience* (Toronto: McClelland & Stewart, 1986), 316, 317.
29. From http://www.navy.forces.gc.ca, accessed on September 2, 2005.
30. "R.M.C. Toronto: Canadian Magazine, 1895," in Hubert C. Burleigh, *Kingston! Oh Kingston* (Kingston: Brown and Martin, 1973), 560.
31. Interview with Johnny O'Shea, June 9, 2006.
32. A compilation by Russell Waller, U.E., based on the Wolfe Island 1851 census. 1, 4, 9, 14, 15, 18.
33. The term "skedaddler" was coined by Americans during the American Civil War, according to Webster's dictionary online, http://www.merriam-webster.com, accessed on March 16, 2009.
34. *Kingston Whig-Standard*, June 19, 1974.
35. Interview with Johnny O'Shea, June 9, 2006.
36. Interview with J. Dufferin Cosgrove of Wolfe Island by Charles Wall during 1967.

37. Interview with Johnny O'Shea, June 9, 2006.
38. Alvin Armstrong, "Fenian Scare," in *Kingston Whig-Standard*, 1973, part of the "Historic Kingston" series.
39. Brian Rollason, ed. *County of a Thousand Lakes: History of County of Frontenac, 1673–1973* (Lindsay, ON: John Deyell Company, 1982), 104.
40. Theresa (La Fleur) McGarvey, "Wolfe Island's Early Days," in *I Remember When* (Kingston, ON: Kingston Jaycettes, 1973), 1–6. (A compilation of essays written by Kingstonians who were former Wolfe Islanders.)
41. Edwin Guillet, *Early Life in Upper Canada* (Toronto: Ontario Publishing Co. Ltd., 1933), 329, 719.
42. Ontario Archives, not indexed. Charles Wall acquired a photocopy in September 1981.
43. Alvin Armstrong, "Prohibition Days," in the *Kingston Whig-Standard*, "Historic Kingston" series, October 26, 1973.
44. Ibid.
45. C.W. Hunt, *Booze, Boats and Billions* (Toronto: McClelland & Stewart, 1988), 37.
46. Ibid., 29.
47. Ibid., 40.
48. Ibid., 23.
49. Ibid., 285.
50. *Kingston Whig-Standard*, no date given, a newspaper clipping from a scrapbook in the author's possession, only identified as written in 1943.
51. Shawn Thompson, *River's Edge*, (Burnstown, ON: General Store Publishing, 1991), 54.
52. Ibid., 57.
53. Ibid.
54. Ibid., 58.

Chapter 8 — Establishing Roots

1. William Canniff, *The Settlement of Upper Canada* (Toronto: Dudley & Burns, 1869. Fifth printing, Belleville, ON: Mika Publishing, 1983), 636.
2. Agnes M. Machar, *The Story of Old Kingston* (Toronto: Musson Book Co. Ltd., 1908), 59.
3. Information about the cruse lamp and Berry family history from author's interview with Elaine Berry, Wolfe Island, June 14, 2005.
4. Information on the Hitchcock lamp from notes given to Charles Wall in 1970, from Flora King of Wolfe Island.
5. A. Skinner, *Watertown, New York: A History* (Watertown NY: Manufacturers' Aid Association, 1876), 106. Additional information provided by researchers Greg Hall and Tim Baty of the New York Air Brake Company of Watertown.
6. Machar, *The Story of Old Kingston*, 59.
7. Ibid., 64.
8. From Charles Wall's interview with Mabel (Woodman) Eves, 1931.
9. R.M. Spankie, "Wolfe Island, Past and Present," in *Proceedings of the 15th Annual Meeting of the New York State Historical Association*, vol. 13 (1914), 220.
10. Canniff, *The Settlement of Upper Canada*, 201.
11. Ibid., 213.
12. Theresa (La Fleur) McGarvey, "Wolfe Island's Early Days," in *I Remember When* (Kingston: Kingston Jaycettes, 1973), 5.
13. Information obtained by Charles Wall from Garfield Bennett, the township clerk, Wolfe Island, in the mid-1960s when Tim O'Shea was reeve.
14. R.M. Spankie, "Wolfe Island, Past and Present," in dialogue with Richard Davis, 220.

Chapter 9 — Early Industries and Livelihoods

1. Donald Creighton, *The Empire of the St. Lawrence* (Toronto: Macmillan, 1956), 149.
2. Edward Wilkes Rathbun (1842–1903) took over the sawmill established by his father at Mill Point (Desoronto) in 1848, and by 1872 the mill was producing up to fifty million board feet of lumber annually. An astute businessman, he broadened his lumbering enterprise into manufacturing and navigation. For more information on lumbering in Canada, see Donald MacKay, *The Lumberjacks* (Toronto: Natural Heritage Books/Dundurn Press, 2007).
3. William Buckingham and George Ross, "The Hon. Alexander Mackenzie," excerpt from Hubert C. Burleigh's *Kingston! Oh Kingston* (Kingston: Brown and Martin, 1987), 343.
4. Nick and Helma Mika, *Kingston, Historic City* (Belleville, ON: Mika Publishing, 1987), 146.
5. Creighton, *The Empire of the St. Lawrence*, 346.
6. Buckingham and Ross, "The Hon. Alexander Mackenzie," 347.
7. Interview with Donalda Parkes of Toronto, a descendant of the William Stevenson family, May 5, 2004.

8. Library and Archives Canada, Upper Canada Land Petitions RGI, L3, vol. 535, W20/21.
9. Wolfe Island Cheese Factory, Cheese Board accreditation reg. #866.
10. Interview with Johnny O'Shea, Wolfe Island, June 10, 2004.
11. Silver Springs Cheese Factory, Cheese Board accreditation reg. #672.
12. Ontario Cheese Factory, Cheese Board accreditation reg. #421.
13. New St. Lawrence Cheese Factory, Cheese Board accreditation reg. #88.
14. Tweedsmuir History, Wolfe Island, courtesy of the St. Lawrence Women's Institute.
15. *Ibid.*
16. Gilt Edge Cheese Factory, Cheese Board accreditation reg. #864.
17. Interview with Edmund Taggart, a former employer at Kraft, Wolfe Island, on June 16, 2004.
18. *Ibid.*
19. *Ibid.*

Chapter 10 — Down to the Sea
1. William Ratigan, *Great Lakes Shipwrecks and Survivals* (Grand Rapids, MI: Wm. B. Eerdman, 1960), 102.
2. Interview with retired Captain Leath Davis of Kingston, June 29, 2007.
3. *Ibid.*
4. Interview with Johnny O'Shea, June 20, 2005.
5. Ratigan, *Great Lakes Shipwrecks and Survivals*, 268.
6. Documented discussions between Captain Lewis Orr and Charles Wall during the 1960s.
7. *Daily British Whig*, Kingston, May 23, 1890.
8. *Ibid.*, June 16, 1890.
9. *Ibid.*, June 17, 1890.
10. Willis Metcalfe, *Canvas and Steam on Quinte Waters* (Picton, ON: Prince Edward County Historical Society, 1968), 120.
11. Ratigan, *Great Lakes Shipwrecks and Survivals*, 71, 73.
12. *Ibid.*, 181.
13. *Ibid.*, 260.
14. Metcalfe, *Canvas and Steam on Quinte Waters*, 49.
15. Environment Canada, Meteorological Services of Canada, Great Lakes Division, courtesy Chris Marshall, 2004.
16. Interview with Edward Kenney, Wolfe Island, June 20, 2004.
17. James Foster Robinson, *Kingston Whig Magazine*, 1970s (specific date of publication not known). The Main Duck Islands lie almost due south of Amherst Island, southwest of Wolfe Island's Bear Point in line with Charity Shoal.
19. French-Canadian sea shanty of 1885. See Ratigan, *Great Lakes Shipwrecks and Survival*s, 247.
20. Sanford Eves, *Simcoe Island: An Eves Perspective* (Cobourg, ON: Haynes Printing Co., 1994), 6. Excerpt from "Ballad of Nine-Mile Point.

> The Jessie Breck with timber on deck
> Capsized in a summer squall
> The Captain and all the crew were lost
> The waters claimed them all
> It was eighteen ninety in the month of May
> When normally peaceful waters play
>
> Many a ship has made the trip
> To the bottom of the lake
> Within the ray of the beacon bright
> When the storms they could not take
> And there's many a grisly tale to tell
> Of sailors who have gone through hell.

Chapter 11 — Garden Island: One Man's Empire.
1. Author unknown, "Journal of a Voyage to North America," London 1761, from Hubert C. Burleigh's *Kingston! Oh Kingston*, ed. Arthur Britton Smith (Kingston: Brown and Martin, 1987), 2.
2. Marion Calvin Boyd, *The Story of Garden Island* (Kingston: Hanson & Edgar Ltd., 1973), 1.
3. Donald Swainson, "Dileno Dexter Calvin" Dictionary of Canadian Biography Online, *http://www.biographi.ca*, accessed March 16, 2009.
4. Donald Swainson, *Garden Island: A Shipping Empire* (Kingston: Marine Museum of the Great Lakes, 1986).
5. *Ibid.*, Swainson.
6. Swainson, "D.D.Calvin," Dictionary of Canadian Biography Online.
7. Brian Rollason, ed. *County of a Thousand Lakes: History of County of Frontenac. 1673–1973* (Lindsay, ON: John Deyell Company, 1982), 484.

8. *Ibid.*, 141.
9. D.D. Calvin, *A Saga of the St. Lawrence* (Toronto: Ryerson Press, 1945), 147.
10. Interview with retired Queen's University Professor Duncan McDougall, June 15, 2005.
11. Swainson, Dictionary of Canadian Biography Online.
12. *Ibid.*
13. The year 1858 marked the inception of the currently used Canadian dollar.
14. Swainson, *Garden Island: A Shipping Empire.*
15. Kingston Marine Museum of the Great Lakes 2004 exhibition "The Mighty Calvins." See website: *http://www.marmuseum.ca*, accessed July 21, 2004.
16. *Ibid.*
17. The International Seamen's Union founded in Chicago, Illinois, was an American maritime trade union that operated from 1892 until 1937. Opposed to organized labour, Calvin broke the union formed among his sailors by importing seamen from Scotland. The union was formed by maritime labour representatives from the United States' Pacific, Great Lakes, and Gulf Coast regions.
18. Swainson, Dictionary of Canadian Biography Online.
19. *Ibid.*
20. *Ibid.*
21. J.H. Meacham, *Historic Illustrated Atlas of Frontenac County* (Belleville, ON: Mika Publishing, 1878), 90.
22. B.S. Osborne and D. Swainson, *Kingston: Building on the Past* (Westport, ON: Butternut Press, 1988), 190.
23. Rollason, *County of a Thousand Lakes*, 236.
24. *Encyclopedia Britannica* vol. 2 (Chicago: University of Chicago, 1984), 575, 576.
25. Boyd, *The Story of Garden Island*, 28.
26. Swainson, *Garden Island: A Shipping Empire.*
27. Interview with Queen's University Professor Duncan McDougall, June 15, 2005.
28. *Limelight* (Kingston Historical Society newsletter, January 2005), 4.

Chapter 12 — The Lifeline: Wolfe Island Ferries

1. R.M Spankie, "Wolfe Island, Past and Present," in *Proceedings of the 15th Annual Meeting of the New York State Historical Association* (1914), 217.
2. *Ibid.*, see Appendix B, 237.
3. *Ibid.*
4. Edwin E. Horsey, *Notes on Wolfe Island* (Kingston Historical Society, March 1941), 10.
5. National Archives of Canada, Upper Canada State Papers, RG1, E3, vol. 25, 149–151.
6. Richard A. Preston, *Kingston: Before the War of 1812* (Toronto: University of Toronto Press, 1959), 264.
7. National Archives of Canada, RG1, E3, vol. 28, 43.
8. *Ibid.*
9. Horsey, *Notes on Wolfe Island*, 10.
10. National Archives of Canada, RG1, E3, vol. 29.
11. *Ibid.*, RG1, E 3, vol. 35.
12. Spankie, "Wolfe Island, Past and Present," 225.
13. Horsey, *Notes on Wolfe Island*, 11.
14. *Ibid.*
15. *Ibid.*
16. Anna G. Young, *Great Lakes Saga* (Owen Sound, ON: Richardson, Bond, and Wright, Ltd., 1965), 60.
17. Interview with Mary (Hinckley) Hamilton, Cape Vincent, New York, June 2006.
18. *Daily British Whig* (Kingston), May 26, 1858.
19. Spankie, "Wolfe Island, Past and Present," 244; reprinted in the Kingston *Daily British Whig*, February 8, 1912.
20. *Watertown Daily News*, January 6, 1873.
21. Horsey, *Notes on Wolfe Island*, 13.
22. *Daily British Whig*, July 17, 1902.
23. *Ibid.*, June 22, 1904.
24. *Ibid.*, March 30, 1905.
25. *The Globe and Mail*, July 13, 1946.
26. Remark made by Captain Carnegie to a news reporter, overheard by a young mariner later to become Great Lakes and *Wolfe Islander* ferry captain, Captain R.F. Fawcett, and shared with Charles Wall.
27. Because the first *Wolfe Islander* had been retired from service prior to the registration of this vessel, it was not requisite to name her *Wolfe Islander II* and so she is referred to by the numeral 2.
28. *Kingston Whig-Standard*, August 28, 1946.
29. *Kingston Whig-Standard*, "Island Ferries Sink," May 11, 1964.
30. Interview with Billy Bolton, Wolfe Island, September 3, 2005.
31. *Kingston Whig-Standard*, February 3, 1974.

32. "The Bubble System," Ontario Ministry of Transportation and Communication fact sheet, March 1974.
33. *Ministry of Transportation and Communication News*, August 1975.
34. Interview with Edward Kenney, former supervisor of Marine and Structural Services, Kingston District, Ministry of Transportation, 2005.
35. *Kingston Whig-Standard*, September 23, 1985, in conjunction with interview with Edward Kenney.
36. *Kingston Whig-Standard*, January 14, 1950, conversations between Captain Sisty and R.F. Fawcett, long-time friends and sailing companions, in January 1950 shortly after the episode occurred.
37. Interview with retired Captain Elwood Woodman, Wolfe Island, September 2004.
38. *Ibid.*
39. *Ibid.*
40. Municipal Council Minutes as included in Spankie, "Wolfe Island, Past and Present," 231.
41. George Copway (1818–69) spent the first part of his life as a Methodist missionary and much of the second part as a writer and travelling speaker. He was an accomplished orator. This quote comes from one of his speeches given in 1850.

Chapter 13 — Coping With the Hazards of Isolation
1. Walter S. Herrington, "Pioneer Life Among the Loyalists in Upper Canada," in H.C. Burleigh, *Kingston! Oh Kingston*, ed. Arthur Britton Smith (Kingston: Brown and Martin, 1987), 162.
2. *The Kingston Argus*, May 26, 1846.
3. Joe Fossey, *The Scoot: Its History and Development* (Barrie, ON: Georgian Copy and Printers, April 2004), 7.
4. *Ibid.*, 5.
5. *The Kingston Argus*, March 26, 1862, and Edwin E. Horsey, *Notes on Wolfe Island* (1941), 12.
6. *Ibid.*
7. R.M. Spankie, "Wolfe Island, Past and Present," 246.
8. *Kingston Whig-Standard*, March 1943.
9. *Ibid.*, March 1946.
10. *British Whig*, January 13, 1886.
11. *Kingston Whig-Standard*, March 19, 1946.
12. Interview with Beulah (Watts) Flynn, summer 1956.
13. Account provided for this history by near victims Darrell and Fern Small, Ottawa, Ontario, June 2004.
14. *Toronto Telegram*, December 27, 1955.
15. Prospectus of Pyke Salvage and Navigation Co. Ltd., Kingston.
16. Interview with Grant Pyke Jr. and retired Captain R.F. Fawcett, September 2004.
17. *Ibid.*
18. Correspondence with Flora Devlin, October 15, 2005.
19. Annette Phillips, "The Islands," *Kingston Whig-Standard*, January 10, 1998.
20. Margaret Knott, "What's New on Wolfe Island," *The Heritage*, January 13, 1998.
21. Jack Chiang, "Kingston: A City Under Siege," *Kingston Whig-Standard*, January 17, 1998.
22. Correspondence with Lois and Sidney Eves, May 2006.
23. Murray Hogben, "Wolfe Islanders Reflect," *Kingston Whig-Standard*, January 1998.
24. Julia White, "Kingston This Week," *Kingston Whig-Standard*, January 21, 1998.
25. Correspondence with Flora Devlin, October 15, 2005.

Chapter 14 — Establishing Transportation Links
1. William Canniff, *The Settlement of Upper Canada* (Toronto: Dudley & Burns, 1869. Fifth printing, Belleville, ON: Mika Publishing, 1983), 408.
2. Ann Lukits, *Kingston Whig-Standard*, July 21, 1976.
3. Consultation with township clerk, Terry O'Shea, Wolfe Island, June 9, 2005.
4. National Archives of Canada, Upper Canada State Papers RG1, E3, vol. 34 D.
5. *Ibid.*
6. *Ibid.*
7. *Ibid.*
8. Interview with Johnny O'Shea, Wolfe Island, June 21, 2006.
9. Archives Ontario, "Midland and Prince Edward Districts Exhibiting Manner in which They Have Been Divided into Townships, Consessions and Lots," Code A-16, container N-2530C. Publius V. Elmore's map, 1836.
10. Archives Ontario, "Located Districts, Province of Upper Canada, Describing New Settlements and Townships etc. Adjacent Frontiers," compiled and corrected from latest surveyors

in the surveyor general's office, Miscellaneous Map Collection, Ref.# C 279-0-0-0-76, Container N-2307. Map, 1836, by James Wylde, surveyor.
11. Township of Frontenac Islands (Wolfe Island Office), communication with the treasurer by phone, September 26, 2006.
12. Interview with Mable McRae, June 19, 2008.
13. Petition and map courtesy of Queen's Archives, Ref.#2999, surveyor's report 1841. Archivist Jeremy Heil.
14. Communication with Brian McDonald, chair, Genealogy, Wolfe Island Historical Society, June 2008.
15. Edwin C. Guillet, *Early Life in Upper Canada* (Toronto: Ontario Publishing Co. Ltd., 1933), 536.
16. Bylaw 150 of the Township of Wolfe Island, May 5, 1879.
17. *Kingston Gazette*, January 22, 1819.
18. Bylaw 150, Wolfe Island.
19. Guillet, *Early Life in Upper Canada*, 536.
20. B. Osborne and D. Swainson, *Kingston: Building on the Past* (Westport, ON.: Butternut Press, 1988), 158.
21. William Dewey, *Suggestions Urging the Construction of a Railroad from Rome to Watertown and Cape Vincent* (Watertown, NY: J. Green, 1844).
22. Canadian currency equivalents compared to British sterling in use at the time.
23. Dewey, *Suggestions for Urging the Construction of a Railroad*.
24. Minutes of Municipal Council of Wolfe Island, December 2, 1857.
25. Prospectus and engineer's report published by the *Kingston Daily News*, Kingston, Ontario. A copy is held in the Toronto Reference Library.
26. R.M. Spankie, "Wolfe Island, Past and Present," 225.
27. *Kingston Daily News*, October 14, 1851.
28. Osborne and Swainson, *Kingston: Building on the Past*, 158.
29. Edwin E. Horsey, *Notes on Wolfe Island*, 15.

Chapter 15 — Marysville Comes Alive

1. R.M. Spankie, "Wolfe Island, Past and Present," in *Proceedings of the 15th Annual Meeting of the New York State Historical Association*, vol. 13 (New York: New York Historical Association, 1914), 221.
2. J.H. Meacham, *Illustrated Historical Atlas, Frontenac, Lennox & Addington Counties* (Belleville, ON: Mika Publishing, 1878), 38.
3. Interviews conducted by Charles Wall and research at Land Transfer Office, Kingston in the 1970s.
4. Discussions between Charles Wall and Marie and Arthur Baker, Wolfe Island, 1970.
5. *Ibid.*
6. Interviews between Charles Wall and Msgr. Charles Baker during the 1980s.
7. *Encyclopedia Britannica* vol. 5, (Chicago: University of Chicago, 1884), 2.
8. Interview with Theresa Fargo, Wolfe Island, June 9, 2005.
9. Interview with Johnny and Joan O'Shea, Wolfe Island, June 9, 2006.
10. Interview with siblings Margaret (Johnson) Commercial, Rochester, New York, and James Johnson, Kingston, June 14, 2007.
11. History of Mrs. Wenbourne's enterprises, related by her to Charles Wall during the 1930s.
12. Interview with Johnny O'Shea, June 23, 2006.
13. Researched by Charles Wall during the 1970s.
14. Researched by Theresa Broeders, Wolfe Island, 2007.
15. Interviews of Wolfe Islanders conducted by Charles Wall over the 1960s and 1970s.
16. Observation and interviews conducted and recorded by Charles Wall from 1930 to 1931.
17. Charles Wall's research, 1970s.
18. Theresa Broeder's research, 2007.
19 Interviews, Margaret Commercial and James Johnson, June 2007.
20. Edwin, C. Guillet, *Early Life in Upper Canada* (Toronto: Ontario Publishing Co. Ltd., 1933), 617.
21. Edwin E. Horsey, *Notes on Wolfe Island*, 16.
22. *Ibid.*, 16.
23. *Ibid.*
24. Many years later, in 1916, the Penny Bridge was replaced by the La Salle Causeway, which greatly facilitated the journey across the bridge.
25. William Canniff, *The Settlement of Upper Canada* (Toronto: Dudley & Burns, 1869. Fifth printing, Belleville, ON: Mika Publishing, 1983), 542.
26. Archives Ontario, Grand Jury Report, April 1844, of the Court of Quarter Sessions for the Midland District.
27. *Ibid.*

28. 1850s bylaws, Township of Wolfe Island.
29. B. Osborne and D. Swainson, *Kingston: Building on the Past* (Westport, ON: Butternut Press, 1988), 81, 356.
30. Agnes Machar, *The Story of Old Kingston* (Toronto: Musson Book Co. Ltd., 1908), 201.
31. Spankie, "Wolfe Island, Past and Present," 226.
32. *Ibid.*, 227.
33. Wolfe Island Seal, researched and documented by Mildred Hawkins-Walton, Wolfe Island councillor, from 1975 to 1987.
34. Consultation with Terry O'Shea, township clerk, September 16, 2007.
35. Minutes of Wolfe Island Township Council Meeting, November 1997.
36. Charles Wall's research, 1970s.

Chapter 16 — Achieving Literacy: Libraries and Schools

1. R.M Spankie, "Wolfe Island, Past and Present," in *Proceedings of the 15th Annual Meeting of the New York Historical Association*, vol. 13, (New York: New York Historical Association, 1914), 219.
2. Strachan Papers.
3. Ontario Archives, Common School Act (Provincial), January 1, 1847, Warden of Midland District Municipal Council.
4. Edwin E. Horsey, *Notes on Wolfe Island* (Kingston: Kingston Historical Society, 1941), 20. Initially, the differing systems were identified as: SS school section (common), SSS, separate school section (Catholic), PSS, public school section.
5. Spankie, "Wolfe Island, Past and Present," 221.
6. Interviews with Wolfe Island historians Carmel Cosgrove and Johnny O'Shea during June 2004.
7. Spankie, "Wolfe Island, Past and Present," 221.
8. This 1823 date is in conflict with the opening date of the school at Lambert's Hill, both purported to be the first school on the island. My research has been unable to resolve the discrepancy.
9. Interview with Carmel Cosgrove at Rideaucrest, Kingston, June 13, 2004.
10. Information from Ruth Ann Pearce, Tilbury, Ontario, January 2005–February, 2006, re: ancestor, William Ellerbeck.
11. Interview, Isabel O'Shea, Kingston, September 17, 2005.
12. "Tweedsmuir Histories," Wolfe Island Library.
13. Interview, Charles Wall with Winston (Mike) Cosgrove during the late 1960s.
14. Correspondence with Harry Friend of Kingston (great nephew of Thomas Friend of Wolfe Island), April 12, 2005.
15. "Tweedsmuir Histories."
16. Interview with Anita (O'Connell) Janzer, Wolfe Island, June 16, 2005.
17. Interview with Billy Bolton, Wolfe Island, September 26, 2005.
18. Interview with Geneva and Arthur Keyes, Wolfe Island June 8, 2004.
19. "Tweedsmuir Histories."
20. Interview, Charles Wall with Bessie (Holliday) Kenney during the 1970s.
21. Interview with Flora Devlin, Wolfe Island, September 20, 2005.
22. R.J. Harris, *Toronto Star*, May 4, 1979. Harris was a former principal and teacher at Marysville Public School, Wolfe Island. Title of the article is not known.

Chapter 17 — Essential Services for an Isolated Community

1. R.M. Spankie, "Wolfe Island, Past and Present," *Proceedings of the 15*th *Annual Meeting of the New York Historical Association*, vol. 13 (New York: New York Historical Association, 1914), 221.
2. Canada Post Office, Public Relations, Marketing, File 11-11-2, December 6, 1971.
3. Bill Coates, "Coates and Coates," Philatelic Company, Toronto, 2004.
4. Alvin Armstrong, *Kingston Whig-Standard*, "History Series," Part 151.
5. Captain Brian Johnson, *Kingston Whig-Standard*, March 8, 2008.
6. William Canniff, *The Settlement of Upper Canada* (Toronto: Dudley & Burns, 1869. Fifth printing, Belleville, ON: Mika Publishing, 1983), 113.
7. Interview with Mable McRae, Wolfe Island, June 12, 2008.
8. Sylvia Graham, *Kingston Whig-Standard*, January 31, 1977.
9. Correspondence between Charles Wall and Weir McRae, March 19, 1978.
10. *Kingston Whig-Standard*, October 23, 1978.

11. Dan Hogan, *Kingston Whig-Standard*, 1989.
12. "Tweedsmuir Histories," Wolfe Island Library.
13. *Kingston Whig-Standard*, Obituary, September 10, 1979.
14. Interview with Carmel Cosgrove at Rideaucrest, Kingston, June 23, 2004.
15. Nicholas Taggart, Wolfe Island, unpublished paper, "Nursing Alone," written in 1994 about the life of his grandmother, Louise (Hawkins) Kenney Flynn.
16. Interview with Elaine Berry, Wolfe Island, June 27, 2005.
17. Taggart, "Nursing Alone."
18. *Ibid.*
19. *Kingston Whig-Standard*, 1967. No author or article title given.
20. A. Lukits, *Kingston Whig-Standard*, May 5, 2008.
21. "Tweedsmuir Histories," Wolfe Island Library.
22. A. Lukits, *Kingston Whig-Standard*, May 6, 2008.

Chapter 18 — History of Wolfe Island Churches and Secular Societies

1. R.M. Spankie, "Wolfe Island, Past and Present," in *Proceedings of the 15th Annual Meeting of the New York State Historical Association* vol. 13 (New York: New York Historical Association, 1914): 223.
2. 1861 Wolfe Island Census.
3. Information given to Charles Wall by Bessie (Holliday) Kenney during 1971.
4. *Kingston Herald*, October 7, 1845.
5. Fern Small and Ken Collins, "Trinity Anglican Church Cemetery Records Wolfe Island," #75-10, published by the Ontario Genealogical Society, Ottawa Branch, 1975.
6. Anglican Church of Canada General Synod Archives, Kingston. Colonial Church Society Report, 1854.
7. Land Transfer Office, Kingston, Ontario, June 2004.
8. Strachan Papers, Anglican Diocesan Archives (York), 10.
9. Christ Church, Wolfe Island cemetery records.
10. *Ibid.*
11. Strachan Papers, recorded in registrar's office for County of Frontenac, lib. 4, folio #2, memorial #58, Township of Wolfe Island.
12. St. Margaret's Hall, researched by Canon Christopher Carr, Trinity Anglican Parish.
13. Kiell family history, Keith Keill, Joyceville, Ontario, researched by Leonard Marlow, descendant of early Kiells on Wolfe Island.
14. Justification for restoration funding, researched by Canon Christopher Carr, 2006.
15. Records of the Catholic Mission of Wolfe Island, as recorded by Father Thomas Spratt, pastor, 1886.
16. Lieutenant Colonel Louis J. Flynn, *Built on a Rock: The Story of the Roman Catholic Church in Kingston (1826–1976)* (Kingston: Catholic Archdiocese, 1976), 286.
17. Researched by Brian McDonald, chair, Genealogy, Wolfe Island Historical Society.
18. Records of the Catholic Mission of Wolfe Island.
19. *Ibid.*
20. *Ibid.*
21. *Ibid.*
22. *Ibid.*
23. *Ibid.*
24. Interview with Mabel McRae, June 24, 2008.
25. Flynn, *Built on a Rock*, 323.
26. Interview with Margaret Commercial, Rochester, New York, and James Johnson, Kingston, June 14, 2007.
27. Interview with Vern Yott, Wolfe Island, June 27, 2007.
28. Information shared by Douglas and Michael Corrigan, Wolfe Island, June 2006.
29. Taken from an account of the Methodist Church History, Wolfe Island, written for the "Tweedsmuir History."
30. Interview with Connie and Elwood Woodman, June 21, 2008.
31. Methodist Church History.
32. Synopsis of church history, cemetery records (Horne's Point, Point Alexandria, and St. Lawrence), Ontario Genealogical Society, Kingston Branch, November 2006.
33. Methodist Church History.
34. Interview with Connie and Elwood Woodman, June 21, 2008.
35. Ontario Genealogical Society, Kingston branch.
36. Brian Rollason, ed., *County of a Thousand Lakes, History of County of Frontenac, 1673–1973* (Lindsay, ON: John Deyell Company, 1982), 235.
37. Communication with Harry Friend of Kingston, October 2005.
38. From http://www.reliablelifeinsurance.com, accessed on March 23, 2009. The company is based in Hamilton, Ontario.
39. *The Weekly British Whig*, September 7, 1860.
40. Edwin E. Horsey, *Kingston: A Century Ago* (Kingston Historical Society, 1938), 488.

41. *Ibid.* For more on the *Kingston* and the regal visit, see Walter Lewis and Rick Nelson, *River Palace: The Many Lives of the Kingston* (Toronto: Dundurn Press, 2008).
42. Horsey, *Kingston: A Century Ago*, 488.
43. Minutes of Wolfe Island Township Council, 1860.
44. Interview with Johnny O'Shea, Wolfe Island, 2005.
45. "Tweedsmuir Histories," Wolfe Island Library. At the time a legal document required a man's signature. Erland Lee signed the constitution for the Women's Institute on behalf of Adelaide Hunter Hoodless and her supporters.
46. *Ibid.*
47. Excerpt from a letter written by Lulu Keyes (date unknown), "Tweedsmuir History," Wolfe Island Library.
48. Excerpts from Women's Institute Minutes, Wolfe Island, compiled by Linda Val Hal, 1993.
49. Reg Whitty, *Kingston Whig-Standard*, June 3, 1987.

Appendix IV: The Cone Surname
1. See *http://www.geocities.com/heartland/fields/9304*, accessed on October 10, 2008.

SELECTED BIBLIOGRAPHY

Anderson, Thomas G. *"Reminiscences": Loyalist Narratives from Upper Canada.* Edited by J.J. Talman. Toronto: Champlain Society of Upper Canada, 1946.

Bagnell, Kenneth. *The Little Immigrants.* Toronto: Macmillan of Canada, 1980.

Boyd, Marion Calvin. *The Story of Garden Island.* Kingston: Hanson & Edgar, 1973.

Brière, Eloise. *The French History of Northern New York State.* Franco-American Quebec Heritage Series. Albany: University of New York Press, 1986.

Buckingham, William and George Ross. "The Honourable Alexander Mackenzie." In *Kingston! Oh Kingston.* Edited by H.C. Burleigh. Kingston: Brown and Martin, 1987.

Burleigh, Hubert, C. *Forgotten Leaves of Local History.* Kingston, ON: Brown and Martin, 1973.

Calvin, D. D. *A Saga of the St. Lawrence.* Toronto: Ryerson Press, 1945.

Canniff, William. *Settlement of Upper Canada.* Toronto: Dudley & Burns, 1869. Fifth printing, Belleville, ON: Mika Publishing, 1983.

Casler, Nelie. *Cape Vincent and its History.* Watertown, NY: Hungerford-Holbrook Company, 1906.

Cosgrove, Winston. *Wolfe Island, Past and Present.* Lindsay, ON: J. Deyell and Company, 1966.

Brian Rollason, ed. *County of a Thousand Lakes*: *History of Frontenac County 1673–1973.* Lindsay, ON: John Deyell Company, 1982.

Craig, Gerald M. *Upper Canada, the Formative Years 1784–1841.* Toronto: McClelland & Stewart, 1963.

Creighton, Donald. *The Empire of the St. Lawrence.* Toronto: Macmillan, 1956.

Daniel, François. *Histoire des grandes familles français du Canada.* Montreal: Eusebe, Senecal, 1867.

Druke, Mary. *Native Peoples: The Canadian Experience.* Toronto: McClelland & Stewart, 1986.

Elliot, Bruce. *Irish Migrants in the Canadas.* Montreal: McGill-Queen's University Press, 1988.

Evert, L.H. *History of Jefferson County, New York, 1797–1878.* Philadelphia: L. H. Evert and Co., 1878.

Eves, Sanford Sydney. *Simcoe Island: An Eves Perspective.* Cobourg, ON: Hayne's Printing Co. Ltd., 1994.

Flynn, Lieut. Col. Louis J. *Built on a Rock: The Story of the Roman Catholic Church in Kingston (1826–1876).* Kingston: Brown and Martin for the Archdiocese of Kingston, 1976.

Forsdyke, Donald. "Grant Allen, George Romans, Stephen J. Gould and The Evolution of Their Time … and who was The Kingston Lady?" In *Historic Kingston*, vol. 52. Kingston: Kingston Historical Society, 2004.

Fossey, Joe. *The Scoot: Its History and Development.* Barrie, ON: Georgian Copy and Printers, 2004.

Glover, I.R. and T.D. Calvin. *A Corner of The Empire.* Kingston: Brown and Martin, 1973.

Guillet, Edwin C. *Early Life in Upper Canada.* Toronto: Ontario Publishing Company Ltd., 1933.

Hale, Katherine. "Canadian Houses of Romance, 1926." In *Kingston! Oh Kingston.* Edited by H.C. Burleigh. Kingston: Brown and Martin, 1987.

Harris, R. Cole. *The Seigneurial System in Early Canada.* Montreal: McGill-Queen's University Press, 1984.

Herrington, Walter S. "Pioneer Life Among the Loyalists in Upper Canada." In *Kingston! Oh Kingston.* Edited by H.C. Burleigh. Kingston: Brown and Martin, 1987.

Hopkins, J. Castell. *French Canada and The St. Lawrence.* Philadelphia: John Winston Co., 1913.

Horsey, E.E. *Kingston a Century Ago.* Kingston: Kingston Historical Society, 1938.

Hunt, C.W. *Booze, Boats and Billions.* Toronto: McClelland & Stewart, 1988.

Johnson, J.K. *Historical Essays on Upper Canada.* Toronto: McClelland & Stewart, 1975.

Litton, Helen. *The Irish Famines.* Dublin, Ireland: Wolfhound Press, 1994.

Machar, Agnes. *The Story of Old Kingston.* Toronto: Musson Book Co. Ltd., 1908.

Metcalfe, Willis. *Canvas and Steam on Quinte Water.* Picton, ON: Prince Edward Historical Society, 1968.

Mika, Nick and Helma. *Kingston: Historic City.* Belleville, ON: Mika Publishing, 1987.

Montgomery, John. "An Account of An Escape From Fort Henry." In *Kingston! Oh Kingston.* Edited by H.C. Burleigh. Kingston: Brown and Martin, 1987.

Morrison, R. and C. Roderick Wilson. *Native Peoples: The Canadian Experience* Toronto: McClelland & Stewart, 1986.

Osborne, B. and D. Swainson. *Kingston: Building on the Past.* Westport, ON: Butternut Press, 1988.

Preston, Arthur, and Leopold LaMontagne. *Royal Fort Frontenac.* Toronto: University of Toronto Press for the Champlain Society of Upper Canada, 1958.

Preston, Richard A. *Kingston Before the War of 1812.* Toronto: University of Toronto Press, 1959.

Ratigan, William. *Great Lakes Shipwrecks and Survivals.* Grand Rapids, MI: Wm. B, Eerdman's Pub. Co., 1960.

Schurman, Dr. D.M. "Bishop Strachan and the Archdeacon of Kingston 1830–1840." In *Historic Kingston* vol. 8. Kingston: Kingston Historical Society, 1971.

Skinner, A. *Watertown, New York: A History.* Watertown, NY: Manufacturer's Aid Association, 1876.

Spankie, R.M. "Wolfe Island, Past and Present." In *Proceedings of the 15*th *Annual Meeting of the New York State Historical Association,* vol. 13. New York: New York Historical Association, 1914.

Stanley, G.F. "William Johnson: Pirate or Patriot." In *Historic Kingston* vol. 6. Kingston: Kingston Historical Society, 1974.

Stewart, J.D. and I.E. Wilson. *Heritage Kingston.* Kingston: Queen's University Press, 1973.

Swainson, Donald. *Garden Island: A Shipping Empire.* Kingston: Marine Museum of the Great Lakes, 1986.

Theller, E.A. *Canada in 1837–38.* Philadelphia: Henry Anners, 1841.

Thompson, Shawn. *River's Edge.* Burnstown, ON: General Store Publishing, 1991.

Trigger, Bruce. *The Children of Aataentsic.* Kingston: McGill-Queen's University Press, 1976.

Wright, Ronald. *Stolen Continents: The Iroquois.* Toronto: Penguin, 1992.

Young, Anna G. *Great Lakes Saga.* Owen Sound, ON: Richardson Bond and Wright Printers Ltd., 1965.

INDEX

1869 Burleigh Fortification Survey, 51, 114
79th Highlanders (Cameron Highlanders), 149
84th Royal Highland Regiment, 49, 105

Abbott, Howard, 273
Abbott, James, 77, 235
Abbott, Mary, 269
Abbott family, 227
Abraham's Head, 30
Act of Union, 101, 213
Adair, __ (Mrs. David), 214, 227
Adair, Bessie, 230
Adair, Clarence, 181, 230, 273
Adams, __ (Mr.), 77
Ainos Cheese Co., 132
Alarie, George, 181, 273
Alarie, Gerald, 181, 273
Alarie, Vincent, 127
Albany, New York, 103, 178
Albert Edward, Prince of Wales, 261
Alexandria Bay, New York, 103, 240
Algonquin First Nation, 34, 38

Allen:
  Caroline, 60, *see also* Caroline Machar, 58
  Charles Grant Blairfindie, 54, 60, 61, 278
  Charlotte (Grant), 54, 56–58, 60, 61, 240
  Dora Maude Carleton, *see* Dora Maule Machar
  Eliza Josephine (Mrs. Henry F.), 60
  Frederica Blanche Emily, 57
  Henry F., 60
  Reverend Joseph Antisell, 54, 56–61, 107, 211, 246
Allen, C.R. (surveyor), 206
Allen, Captain James, 74
Allen, William, 212
Allen Estate, 59, 62, 130, 235
Allen family, 53, 57–60
Allen Post Office, 238
Allen Street (Marysfield), 60
Alwington House (Kingston), 52, 53, 54, 57–61
America (steamer), 90, 202

American Civil War (1861–1865), 90, 107, 283
American Methodists, 256
American War of Independence, American Revolution, 49, 50, 2, 63, 71, 79, 81, 85, 86, 96, 105, 278
Amherst, Governor Jeffrey, 95, 217
Amherst Island, 40, 63, 97, 103, 142, 174, 203, 217, 285
Ancient Order of United Workmen (AOUW), 141, 142, 260
Anderson, Captain Thomas G., 76
Anglican Diocese of Ontario, 57, 246
Ansley, Amos, 67, 68
Appelman, Reverend J. (Mill Hill Missionaries), 83, 256
Apps, Molly, 173
Apps, Syl (MPP), 173
Ardath Castle (formerly Longueil Castle), 21, 51–53, 59, 60, 61, 107, 125, 154, 277
Areson, Florence, 55
Areson, Dr. William, 45, 55, 56, 246
Areson family, 55, 56, 246

Areson House, 54, 55, 125
Armstrong, Charles, 248
Armstrong family, 235
Auburn, New York, 103
Augustus (steamer), 137
Ault Bros. Milk Co., 130–32

Bagot, Sir Charles, 54
Baker:
    Arthur, 208, 210
    Charles E. (Monsignor), 210, 211, 232
    Edward, 209, 219
    Eliza "Banny" (Spoor), 209–11
    Joseph Stafford, 209, 210
    Margaret (Payne), 210
    Marie, 207, 208, 210
    Michael, 209, 211
    Sadie, 210
Baker, Catherine, 78
Baker, John, 78
Baker, Michael, 78
Baker's (Bakers') General Store, 134, 206, 209, 210, 212, 215, 217, 226
Baldwin, Sarah Ann, 119
"Ballad of Nine-Mile Point," 147, 285
Bamford, Volty, 112, 216,
Bamford, Wells, 77, 245, 256, 257
Bamford Point, 77, 257
Baptist(s), Baptist Church, 125, 154, 156, 245
Barnett, Robert, 245
Baron V de Longueuil, *see* Charles William Grant
Barrett, __ (fisherman), 128
Barrett, Isaac T., 77
Barrett, James, 75
Barrett, J.J., 193
Barrett, S.T., 211
Barrett Bay, 114, 189, 200, 201
Barrett Street, 211
Barriefield, Ontario, 51, 89
Barriefield Escarpment, 105

Barriefield Military Base, 182
Bartlett family, 234
Bass Rock, 26, 27
Bassitt, John, 78
Bateau Canal, 166, 200, 201
Bateau Channel, 45, 140, 141, 147, 169, 186
Bates, Captain George, 171, 175, 180, 183, 184
Bates, Margaret (Hawkins), 180
Bathurst, Henry (3rd Earl) (colonial secretary), 69
Battle of Chouagen, 95
Battle of Windmill Point (1838), 101, 103
Bavaria (schooner), 143
Bay of Quinte Conference, 258
Bayfield Bay (Big Bay), 74, 84, 85, 113, 189, 200, 233
Bayfield Island (Mud Island), 19, 189, 218
Bayfield, Admiral Henry Wolsey, 189
Bayview Cottage, 51, 53
Bear Point, 24, 38, 95, 251, 285
Beaver, Joseph, 216
Beekeeping, 133–34
Bell Telephone Co., 238
Belyea:
    Anna, 228
    Bert, 129
    Donald, 228, 273
    Fred, 129
    John, 129, 273
    Vera, 228
Bennett, Alvah, 60, 78, 98, 99, 160, 223
Bennett, Austin, 249
Bennett, A. Garfield, 249
Bennett, Garfield, 222, 249, 284
Bennett, James S., 215
Bennett, John, 215
Bennett, Laura Mae, 222, 249
Bennett, Truman S., 130
Bennett family, 227
Berry, Elaine, 115, 242
Berry, James, 114, 115, 269

Berry, Marianne, 119
Berry, Robert, 169
Berry, Simon, 274
Berry family, 82
Bertram Engine Works (Toronto), 169
Beseau, Paul, 222
Bienville, *see* Jean-Baptist Le Moyne
Big Sandy Bay, 113, 140, 202
Black Pond, 99, 118
Blair Hotel, 193
Blanchard, Sarah (Mrs.), 61
Blenkinsopp, Dr. __, 240
Bloorview Hospital (Toronto), 241
Bobcaygeon limestone, 25
Bolton, Nellie, 147
Bolton, Richard, 229
Bolton, W.H., 216, 217
Bolton, Wilfred "Billy," 172, 231
Bolton family, 233
Bolton and Bolton, Wheelwrights, 217
Boleyn, Ann, 268
Bonaparte, Joseph (King of Spain), 87
Bonapartist(s), 86, 87
Bonnie Prince Charlie, 79, 81
Booth Fisheries, 109, 129
Boulton, Henry, 70
Bousfield, Reverend T., 58, 246
Boxing Harbour Hotel, 77
Boyd, Alberta Victoria, 211
Boyd, Marion (Calvin), 149
Bradshaw, Isabella, 89, *see also* Isabella Hinckley
Bradstreet, Colonel John, 95, 104
Brant, Joseph, 105, 189
Brant, Molly, 105
Breakey's Bay, 125, 169
Breakey's Bay School, 234
Breck and Booth Co. (Garden Island), 142
Breck and Booth Co. (Kingston), 206
Breck, Dr. Wallace, 61, 277
Breck, Ira Allen, 142, 151
Briceland, __ (Mrs.), 215

Briceland, Frank, 213
Briceland, Jack, 273
Briceland, Thomas, 267
Briceland family, 227
Briceland farm, 75
Briggs, Absalom, 165, 178, 261
Briggs, David, 88
Briggs, "Dode," 106, 192
Briggs, George, 178
Briggs Daily Express, 178–79
Briggs family, 88
British Act of Emancipation (1834), 74
British Empire Show (Central Ontario District), 131
British Royal Oak Trees (Windsor Forest), 233
Brock, General Isaac, 9
Brockville (steamer), 101
Broeder family, 83
Broeders, Theresa, 280
Bromley, Guy, 30
Brooks, __ (Professor), 163
Brophy, Mary, *see* Mary Darling
Brophy Point, 30, 31, 33–35, 68, 174, 178, 181, 233
Brophy Point Site, 30, 31, 276
Brown, Mary, 80
Brown, Mary, 269
Brown, Daniel, 162
Brown, Wilf, 186
Brown family, 82
Browne, Jemima, 91, *see also* Jemima Horne
Browne family, 90
Brulé, Etienne, 38
Bruyière, Margaret, 216
Bruyière, Oliver, 216
Btuyière family, 43
Buade, Count Louis Henri de Frontenac, 29, 39
Bubble system, 172, 173
Buck (Deer) Island, 104
Buckley, Susan, 119

Bullis, Elizabeth (Blake), 265
Bullis, Della (Gillespie) (Mrs. Robert), 235
Bullis, Hubert Leslie, 273
Bullis, John, 216
Bullis, Joseph, 248
Bullis, William, 78, 265
Burial mounds, 30, 31, 33
Burke, Cameron, 273
Burleigh, H.C., 42
Busch, Arabella (Hinckley), 73
Busch, __ (Mr.), 141
Busch, J., 78
Busch, John A., 127
Busch, John H., 73
Busch, Sara Ann (Ellerbeck), 73
Busch family, 77, 178
Bustard, Bill, 273
Bustard, Ross, 207, 239
Bustard family, 78
Button Bay (Granis Bay), 33, 88, 105, 170, 191, 197, 259, 271
Button Bay Road, 191
Button Bay Site, 31, 33
Bylaw # 150 (statute labour), 194, 195

Cadotte, George, 140
Cadotte, Leo, 181
Cadotte family, 43
Calvin:
    __ (Mrs. Hiram A.), 157
    Catherine (Wilkinson) (Mrs. D.D.), 157
    Dileno Dexter "D.D.," 21, 149, 150–57, 199, 286
    Hiram A. 151, 157
    Marion, *see* Marion Boyd
    Meg, *see* Meg d'Esterre
Calvin, Jim, 274
Calvin and Breck Co., 151, 249
Calvin, Breck and Rees Co., 139, 152
Calvin and Breck Shipbuilding and Lumber Merchant Co., 142

Calvin and Son Co., 152
Calvin Company (Garden Island), 34, 53, 123, 124, 126, 135, 137–41, 143, 151, 155, 158, 166, 170, 197, 216
Calvin Company Ltd., 152, 153, 156
Calvin Company Scrip, 155
Cambro-Silerian limestone, 24
Camel, 72
Cameron, Captain Angus, 149, 150, 154, 158, 165, 199, 220
Cameron, Reverend David, 257
Cameron, John, 193
Campbell, Alexander, 90, 193
Canada, William, 140
Canada Steamship Lines, 168
Canadian Centennial Medal (1967), 242
Canadian Clergy Reserves Corp., 64, 97
Canadian Currency, 237, 289
Canadian Freeman, 253
Canadian National Exhibition, 134
Canadian Order of Chosen Friends, 260
Canadian Postal Service, 237–38
Cape Vincent, New York, 21, 74, 84–93, 97, 99, 101, 104, 107, 109, 111, 120, 127, 129, 130, 135, 155, 166–68, 177–79, 190, 191, 193, 195, 197, 199, 200–02, 214, 217, 238, 251, 255
Cape Vincent Historical Museum, 86, 281
Card, Harry, 210, 217, 252
Card, Lloyd, 169
Card, Richard, 217
Card, William "Billie," 217
Carey, Reverend R.A., 253
Carleton, Sir Guy (Lord Dorchester), 48, 72, 96, 105
Carleton Island, 49, 77, 84, 86, 96–98, 100, 104, 105, 189
Carnegie, Andrew, 155
Carnegie Endowment, 155
Carnegie, Captain Ross, 170, 287
Carnegie, John, 168
Carnegie, Robert H., 168

Carpenter Point, 24, 189
Carr, Christopher (Canon), 14, 55, 250, 251
Carr, Connie, 55
Carruthers Point, 202
Carson, Dr. G., 273
Cartier, Jacques, 37–39
Cartwright, Richard (Hon.), 67, 96, 161
Casey family, 78
Cassidy, H., 128
Castle Grant (Scotland), 49
Cataraqui (later Kingston), 34, 37–39, 42, 71, 72, 96, 97, 104, 105, 189
Cataraqui, Seigneury of, 39
Cataraqui, Township of, 72–74
Catatarqui River, 34, 39, 218
Catholic Archdiocese of Kingston, 256
Catholic Mission of Wolfe Island, 251
Catholic Mutual Benefit Association (CMBA), 225, 259
Catholic Record, 253
Cattanach (Cattanagh), David, 216
Cattanach (Cattanagh), Donald, 216
Cattanagh, Daniel, 260
Cauchois (Curaux):
    Jacques, 41–44
        Elizabeth (Prudhomme), 41
        Madeleine, 42, *see also* Madeleine Curaux
Cayuga First Nation, 34, 105
Cedar Island, 40, 97, 142, 178
Cedarton (cargo ship), 138, 241
Central Post Office, 238
Champlain, Samuel de, 34
Charles, John F., 249
Charles family, 233
Charlèvoix, Reverend Pierre François Xavier de, 149
Chateau Ardath, *see* Ardath Castle
Chaumont Bay, 97
Chaumont, Jacques, *see* Jacques Le Ray de Chaumont
Chauncey, Commodore Isaac, 97

Chewett, J., 65
Chewett Map of 1822, 65, 77, 271
Children's Aid Society, 241
Chosen Friends Society, Lodge # 7, 260
Chrétien, Jean (Hon.), 187
Christ Church Anglican, 247, 268
Christian Reformed Church of Quebec (Huguenots), 43
Chub Point, 27, 77
Church Army of Canada, 13, 111, 112, 248, 249
Church of England Incorporated Synod, Diocese of Ontario, 55, 58
Church of England Mission, 56
Church of Scotland, 64,
    established, 245, 257
    free, 245
Church of the Good Thief (Portsmouth), 254
Church of the Sacred Heart of the Blessed Virgin Mary, 51, 81, 125, 143, 226, 251–53, 256, 265, 267, 269, 280
City of Kingston (steamer), 152
Cleary, John, 238
Cleary family, 196
Clemens, Reverend Karl, 256
Clench and Crawford (wheelwrights), 217
Clergy Reserves, 51, 57, 65, 66, 69, 100, 125, 149
Cliff, Dr. __, 240
Clovis Culture, 29, 30
Club (OPP Constable), 112
Cochrane, Hugh F., 143
Coffey, C.S., 222
Coffey, Charles "Charlie," 213, 273
Coffin, Caroline, 50, *see also* Baroness Caroline Grant
Coffin, General John, 50
Coffin family, 54
Cold Springs, 26, 130–32, 235
Cold Springs Cheese Factory, 131
Cole, Claude "King," 109

Comet Foundation, 174
Commercial, Margaret (Johnson), 289, 292
Commercial Hotel, 192
Cone:
    Darius Augustus, 88, 271
    Mary (Greaves), 271
    Nathanial, 271
    Samuel, 66, 77, 84, 88, 89, 191, 271
Cone family, 76, 85, 271
Cone Point, 45, 51, 159, 160, 176, 271
Conley, Cecil, 273
Conley, Norman, 110, 111, 140
Conley, Preston, 273
Conley, Rosana, 268
Conley, Terence, 268
Conley family, 78, 110
Constitutional Act of 1791, 64, 66, 96, 217
Cook, Azel, 257
Cook, Charles, 88
Cook, Daniel, 123
Cook, Hiram, 150, 151, 155
Cook, Robert, 88
Cooke, Francis, 90
Cooke family, 227
Coon, Darius Augustus, 271
Coon, Nellie (Ryan), 271
Cooper, C.W., 139
Copway, George, 139
Cornwall, Ontario, 33, 79, 100, 132, 211
Corrigan, Douglas, 292
Corrigan, Michael, 292
Corrigan, Doctor Vincent, 256
Cosgrove, Carmel, 226, 241
Cosgrove, Charlie, 273
Cosgrove, James Dufferin "Duff," 106, 130, 131, 229, 232, 238
Cosgrove, Harold, 174
Cosgrove, Winston M. "Mike," 228
Counter, John, 150, 197, 200
Court of Quarter Sessions, 88, 159, 163, 190, 218, 219

Coxall:
    Amelia (Darby), 212
    Clarence, 265
    Johnnie, 212
Coxe, Grace, 85, *see also* Grace Le Ray de Chaumont
Coyle, Dr. Enroy, 232
Coyle, R.J., 232
Coyle Property, 238
Craig-Russell farms, 127
Craine, John, 134, 211, 265
Craine, Joseph, 134
Crawford, Captain James, 169
Crawford, Fred, 215
Crawford, John, 143
Crawford, Susannah, 143
Cross Street, 132, 211
Crown Land, 51, 63, 65–70, 97, 106
Crumby, Davey, 75
Crumpet, Tommy, 183
Cruse lamp, 114, 284
Crysler farm, 99
Crystal Palace (Kingston), 261
Cummins, Charles "Charlie," 176, 213, 238
Cummins, Howard, 181
Cummins General Store, 212
Cummins' Lunch Counter, 238, 239
Cummins' Wharf, 176
Cumpsty, Steve, 274
Curaux (Curotte):
    Amable, 42, 43, 63
    Martin, 42
    Jacques François, 42
    Madeleine (Cauchois), 42
    Michel, 42, 43, 63
Curaux (Currotte) brothers, 41, 42, 44, 50, 63, 64, 66, 68, 95
Cushion, Michael, 268

D.D. Calvin (steam timber drougher), 153
D'Esterre, John Kinnear, 158
D'Esterre, Meg (Calvin), 158

Darling, Mary (Brophy), 35
Darroch, Lois, 69
Daryeau, J.C., 181
Daryeau family, 43
Davis, Albert, 181, 216
Davis, Allan, 129
Davis, Anne "Annie" (Registered Nurse), 229, 241, 273
Davis, Bidwell, 233
Davis, Clarence, 129, 216
Davis, Charles S., 193
Davis, Edwin, 273
Davis, Elsie (Registered Nurse), 229, 241
Davis, Emily, 230
Davis, Frederick, 273
Davis, Gillison "Gill," 215, 216
Davis, Hank, 273
Davis, Harriet, *see* Harriet Winbourne
Davis, Captain Henry Leath, 137, 138
Davis, James, 77
Davis, James, 88
Davis, James, 137
Davis, Jim, 129
Davis, John, 268
Davis, John H., 129
Davis, Joseph, 216
Davis, Leander, 211
Davis, Captain Leath, 88, 138, 230, 241
Davis, Lena, 228, 239
Davis, Louise, 230
Davis, Mary Hinckley (Mrs. Thomas), 88, 161, 205, *see also* Mary Hitchcock
Davis, Mildred (Registered Nurse), 229, 230, 241
Davis, Olive, *see* Olive Spoor
Davis, Oliver, 213, 230
Davis, Captain Oliver "Chuck," 137, 273
Davis, Peter C., 193
Davis, Richard, 88
Davis, Richard Edwin, 273
Davis, Thomas, 77, 88, 98, 160, 161, 195, 205, 214, 223,

Davis, Thomas Jr. "Tom," 165, 166, 205, 228
Davis, William, 77, 192
Davis, Captain William, 137
Davis family, 76, 88, 89, 90, 128
Davis Hotel, 192
Davis Quarry, 125, 193
Dawe, Reverend James, 249, 273
Dawson, __ (Mrs.), 211
Dawson, Ann, *see* Ann Kiell
Dawson, Captain George, 152
Dawson, James, 273
Dawson, John, 78, 165
Dawson, John Sr., 108
Dawson, Mary (McCallum), 78, 267
Dawson, P. (Reeve), 195
Dawson, Patrik, 233
Dawson, Captain Thomas, 152
Dawson, Sheriff Thomas, 108, 223
Dawson family, 106, 176, 233
Dawson Wharf (dock), 165, 173, 176
Dawson's Point, 172, 174, 176
Davoud, Paul, 273
Deforge, Anthony, 140
de Longueuil, Barony, 47–62
de Longueuil, Lieutenant Raoul, 61
De Reuter family, 27, 83
De Sousa, Reverend Raymond, 256
Dean, Nelson, 257
Dee, John, 234, 267
Deming, Doctor E. Adams, 353
Denyke, Captain Andrew, 96, 161
Devlin, Flora (McDonald), 81, 185, 187, 234
Devereau family, 43
Devlin, John, 75
Devlin, Mike, 75
Devlin family, 78
Dewey, William, 197
Diamond Jubilee (Women's Institute), 263
Dickens, Charles, 54
Dickson, Dr. __, 33

Dignem:
    Elizabeth, 268
    John, 268
    William, 125, 126, 131
Diocese of Ontario, Anglican, 55, 57, 58, 246
Dionne, Emile, 56
Dix, Captain James, 143
Dixon, John, 139
Dobbs, Reverend __, 58
Docteur, Alexander, 87
Docteur, Martin, 87
Dominion Marine School (Toronto), 138, 175
Donnelly, David, 257
Dorey, Matthew, 137
Doucett, George (Hon.), 171
Dout family, 43
Doyle, __ (Mrs. M.), 228
Doyle, Sir Arthur Conan, 61
Ducey family, 43
Duffy, Patrick, 267
Dunlop:
    Catherine, 229
    Jane, 229
    John, 229
Durham, Governor General Lord, 101, 103
Dutch immigration, 71, 76, 83, 255

Ecclemont, Olivia, 77
Eccles, James, 128, 129
Edinborough, Arnold, 158
Edwards, Eddie, 273
Edwards, Pauline, 175
Edwards, Rowen, 93
Ellerbeck:
    Lieutenant Emmanuel, 71–73
    Harriet Louise, 74
    Richard, 72
    Richard Abbott, 73, 74
    Sarah (Mrs. E.), 72
    Sarah (Howard) (Mrs. R.A.), 73, 74
    Sarah Ann, 73, *see also* Sarah Ann Busch
    William W., 73
Ellis, Delila, 81, *see also* Delila McRae
Elmlodge, 50, 51
Erie Canal, 197
Ernie's Lunch, 208, 214
Esselton, R.M. 85
Evert's History of Jefferson County, New York, 90
Eves:
    Doris, 243
    Freda, 228
    George, 228
    Harrison, 228, 273
    Kenneth, 228
    Lois, 186
    Mabel, 116, *see also* Mabel Woodman
    Norman, 273
    Reta, 228, *see also* Reta Hulton
    Sanford, 147, 273
    Sidney, 186
    Thelma, 228, *see also* Thelma Butler
Exchange Bank of Clayton (New York), 103

Family Compact, 64, 66–69, 100, 101, 218, 219
Fanning, Frederick, 78, 195
Fargo:
    Clifton, 213
    Henry, 273
    Merritt, 213
    Stephen "Steve," 186, 213
    Theresa, 213
Fargo's (general store), 131, 176, 210, 238, 240
Farrell, Reverend M.E., 251, 256
Farthing, Bishop John, 227
Fawcett, __ (Mrs. Oscar), 263
Fawcett, Fern, *see* Fern Small
Fawcett, Frank, 196
Fawcett, Marette, 61
Fawcett, Captain Richard F., 61, 126, 138, 173, 175, 184, 185, 273, 287
Fawcett, Sidney, 207
Fawcett family, 233
Fawcett's Red and White store, 207, 208, 239
Feeney, Reverend J.F., 253
Fence viewer, 190, 218
Fenians, 107, 155
Ferguson, Captain __, 175
Ferguson, Father John, 175
Ferguson, John, 75
Ferguson's Point, 74, 108, 114, 139, 151 196, 238
Fern's Point Lock, 12
Ferry Inn, 108, 165
Fertian, __ (Mrs.), 140
Fleming, Father J.P., 134, 252, 253
Fleming, Roy, 52
Fleury d'Eschambault, Marie-Anne Catherine, 48
Flower, Governor Roswell P., 115
Flynn:
    Edward, 242
    Ellen, 119
    Ellen (Collins) (Mrs. M.), 267
    James, 216
    John, 137
    Louise (Hawkins) Kenney, 241, 242
    Matthew "Matt," 137, 229
    Michael, 119, 267
    Slim, 273
    Thomas, 137
    William, 273
Flynn family, 78
Flynn's Saloon, 226
Fogo Island, Newfoundland, 249
Foley, Reverend John, 251
Folger, Benjamin, 167
Folger, Fred, 167
Folger, Henry, 167

Folger Brothers, 90 166–68, 169, 201, 202
Fort Frontenac, 39, 40, 42, 47, 50, 72, 95, 97, 104, 189
Fort Haldimand, 104, 105
Fort Henry, 100, 106, 125, 145
Fort Niagara, 79
Fort Presentation, 95
Fort Wallace, 102, 103
Fowler, Ida, 87
Fowler, J. and Son (Kingston), 253
Fox, Marion (Mrs.), 182
Fox, Thomas, 265
Fraser, Alex, 245
Freisland, Province of (Holland), 83
French Creek (Clayton, New York), 102, 103
French Foreign Legion, 61
French Revolution, 41, 86
French Squadron, 105
Friend:
    Dr. Amos, 229
    Ann (Wenbourne) (Mrs. J.), 246
    Arthur, 230
    Dr. Austin, 230
    George, 55, 228, 246
    Harold, 207
    John, 78, 207, 208, 237, 246
    Thomas "Tom," 207, 208, 260
    Dr. William, 229
Frontenac Axis, 24
Frontenac County Library System, 224
Frontenac County Paramedic Services, 244
Frontenac Islands, Township of, 149, 190, 222, 275
Frost, Kevin, 251
Fuller, Porter, 251

Gaelic, 79–81
Ganounkouesnot (Wolfe Island), 12, 40
Garden Island, 19, 21, 34, 120, 123, 124, 135, 137–44, 146, 149–58, 166, 167, 169, 175, 180, 182, 184, 199, 216, 220, 229, 246, 247, 249
Garden Island naval brigade, 107
Garrah, Michael, 222
Garrett, Lucy Ellen, 246
Garrison House, 97, 98
Gass, Ann Eliza, 246
Gauthier, Archbishop Joseph C.H., 254
Gazelle (steamer), 167
General Wolfe Hotel, 163, 165, 213, 231
George Friend School (S.S. #9), 228, 235
George Thurston (schooner), 142
George, Frank, 141
George, John, 114
George, John, 214
Ghent, Dr. W.R., 203, 243
Gibson, John, 201
Gildersleeve:
    Charles, 166
    Henry, 200, 201
    James P., 201
    Lucretia, 201
    W., 128
Gillespie, Alvira (Woodman), 262
Gillespie, Charlie, 112, 131
Gillespie, Della, *see* Della Bullis
Gillespie, George, 234
Gillespie, Mary (Mrs. R. Sr.), 119
Gillespie, Robert Sr., 119
Gillespie family, 235
Gillow family, 142
Gilt Edge Cheese Factory, 130, 131
Glacial striations, 26, 27, 124
Glen Garry, Scotland, 79
Glengarry County, of, 77, 79–81, 91, 93, 251
Glengarry Fencibles Regiment, 79
Glengarry Regiment, 80
Godfrey, Reverend James, 249
Godfrey, Sarah, 249
Going, Captain Shirley, 20, 59, 107, 175, 176, 211, 246, 248, 257
Going, Sarah, 246
Gooderham and Worts Distillery (Toronto), 152

Gordon, Mary, *see* Mary McFadden
Gore, Lieutenant-Governor Francis, 67, 68
Gorget, 31, 32
Goslin, Enes, 223
Gourlay, Robert Fleming, 68, 69, 279
Graham, Reverend M.J., 252
Grand Trunk Railway, 125, 179, 237
Grande Île (Wolfe Island), 12, 29, 40, 42, 50, 51, 84, 96, 100
Granite Hill Factory (Pittsburgh Township), 131
Grant:
    Charles Colmore (Baron VII), 62
    Charles James Irving (Baron VI), 50, 52, 54, 61
    Charles William "Baron Grant" (Baron V), 47, 50–54, 57, 58, 68–70, 75, 76, 80, 200
    Charlotte, 50, 54, 56, 57, *see also* Charlotte Allen
    David, 44
    Captain David Alexander, 49–51, 63–66, 68–70, 74, 75, 105, 149
    Marie-Anne Catherine (Fleury D'Eschambault) (Le Moyne) (Baroness), 48–50
    Dr. Michael David, 61, 62
    Raoul, *see* Raoul de Longueuil
    Raymond David, 61
    Ronald Charles (Baron X), 61
    William, 49
    William (Hon.), 48–50
Grant, John, 220
Grant, Nettie, 227
Grant, Wayne, 220
Grass, Captain Michael, 71, 72
Gravelly Point, New York, 84, 85, 97
Gray, John, 137
Great Depression, 60, 82, 110
Great Lakes shipwrecks, 140–47
Great Northwest Telegraph Co., 238
Great Western Railroad, New York, 197

Greaves, Mary, *see* Mary Cone
Greenwood, Charles, 136
Greenwood, George, 75
Greenwood, Mable, *see* Mable McRae
Greenwood, Maxime Sr. "Max," 217
Greenwood, Norah, 214
Greenwood, Vincent, 59, 124, 215
Greenwood Quarry, 126
Grenadier Island, 98, 167
Griffin, Ed, 216
Griffin, Isadore, 216
Griffin's Blacksmith Shop, 216
Grimshaw Estate, 73
Grimshaw family, 142, 235
Grindle, Edward, 167
Grindle family, 43
Guérin, Aimé, 157
Gulf and Lake Navigation Co., 138
Gull River limestone, 25
Gurnsey, C.F., 181
Gurnsey, Claytus, 130, 131
Gurnsey, Harold, 131

H.M.S. *Letitia* (Canadian hospital ship), 138
H.M. Stanley, 14
Hackett, Eliza Ann, 246
Hagerman, C.A. (Judge), 54
Haldimand, Governor Frederick, 49, 63, 96, 104, 105
Halfway House, 84, 85
Hall family, 196
Hall Shipping Co. (Montreal), 138
Hallas, Squire __, 78
Halpenny, Reverend William, 196
Harper, Francis A., 72
Harris, Luther, 77
Harrison, President William, 103
Harrisville, New York, 87
Hasselaar, Jan, 163, 222
Hasselaar, Mae, 163
Hasselaar family, 83

Hassler, F.R., 86
Hatfield, T.A., 207, 208
Hawkins:
    Arnold "Cricket," 170, 217, 239
    Bill, 273
    Joe, 215
    John, 220, 268
    Louise, 170, *see also* Louise Kenney Flynn
    Margaret, 180, *see also* Margaret Bates
    Oliver, 60, 217
    Patrick, 60
    Ruth, 230
    Tim, 240
    William, 140, 229, 253
Hawkins family, 78
Hawkins-Walton, Mildred, 222, 243
Head, Sir Francis Bond, 127
Heikamp, Jake, 240
Helwig, David, 160
Henderson, Arthur, 131
Henderson, Captain N. George, 142
Henderson, Ralph, 273,
Henderson, Roland, 273
Henderson, Shelley, 262
Henderson, William, 82
Hennessey, William, 234
Hennessey family, 233
Hercules (steamer), 43
Heron, John, 234
Hickory Island, 102
Highlander (tug), 143
Hillcrest Street, 53, 61, 211
Hillier, Major George, 162
Hinckley:
    Arabella, 73, *see also* Arabella Busch
    Coleman Joseph Jr., 21, 90, 130, 167, 178
    Captain Coleman Sr., 89, 166, 167, 178
    Dexter, 178, 179
    Eunice, 227

Henry, 35, 178, 179
    Mary "Polly," 88, 115, 205, 214, 216, *see also* Mary Davis/Mary Hitchcock
    Mary (Mrs. S.), 88
    Minerva, 88, 89, *see also* Minerva Mosher
    Ola, 170, *see also* Ola Mullins
    Olivia, 89, *see also* Olivia Spinning
    Rodney, 88
    Samuel "Sam," 66, 67, 88, 89, 91, 99, 101, 190, 191, 195, 227
Hinkley Express, 178
Hinckley family, 76, 85, 90, 91
Hinckley Inn, 89
Hinckley School (SS #5), 227
Hinckley's Point, Wolfe Island, 85, 88, 90
Hitchcock:
    Archibald Jr., 89, 115, 128, 161–64, 193, 205, 218, 223
    Archibald Sr., 160, 193, 226
    Hiram O., 195, 251, 252, 260
    John, 205, 229
    Mary "Polly" (Hinckley) (Davis), 89, 115, 161, 162, 165, 237, 240
    Oliver, 205, 216
    Robert, 115
    Samuel, 21, 77, 159, 160, 223
Hitchcock House, 81, 115, 125, 162, 163, 165, 202, 220, 260
Hitchcock Lamp, 20, 115
Hitchcock Lamp Co., 115
Hobson, Alex, 78
Hoek, T. Vanden, 258
Hogan, Ann (O'Grady), 267
Hogan, Eddie, 273
Hogan, Eugene, 273
Hogan, Gertrude, 183–84
Hogan, Harry, 273
Hogan, Howard, 173
Hogan, Ralph, 273
Hogan, Sharon (O'Shea), 225
Hogan, Thomas, 267
Hogan, W.J., 181

Holland Land Co., New York, 100, 282
Holliday:
    Bessie, 234, *see also* Bessie Kenney
    Eliza, 247
    Henry, 216, 247
    John, 114
    Madeline, 234
    Margaret, 234
    Richard, 247
Holliday Bay, 27, 43
Holliday family, 78, 234
Holliday Point, 35, 118
Hoodless, Adelaide Hunter, 262
Horan, Bishop Edward J., 252
Horne:
Angeline (Mrs. Thomas Jr.), 89
    Bill, 92, 241
    Bruce, 92, 259
    Connie, 230
    Elizabeth (Mrs.), 227
    Fanny, 229
    George, 92
    George Darrell "Dee," 91–93, 273
    Henderson, 227
    Hugh, 130, 213
    James, 257
    John, 82, 90, 91, 193, 220, 269
    Lawrence, 273
    Louise, 85, *see also* Louise Smith
    Olivia, 227
    Rachel (Jamieson), 93
    Robert, 131
    Robert Andrew, 142
    Robert Sr., 91
    Dr. Sidney J.W., 229
    Thomas Darrell Jr., 89, 91, 193
    William, 91
    William "Bill" Sr., 91, 179
    William Esmond, 92, 170
Horne family, 78, 90, 91, 93, 128, 227, 259
Horne's Ferry, 83, 89, 91, 92, *see also* W.E.
    Ferry Co., 170, 253

Horne's Point, 74, 93, 179, 214, 239, 241
Horseshoe Island, 19, 25, 40, 128, 141, 169, 218, 256
Horsey, Edward, 21
Horsey, Edwin E., 226
Horton, Orin, 212
Hôtel Dieu Hospital (Kingston), 241, 243
Howard, Sarah, 73, *see also* Sarah Ellerbeck
Howe, C.D. (Hon.), 171
Howe Island, 40, 41, 57, 60, 169, 186, 203, 213, 217, 222, 275
Hudson's Bay Co., 123
Huffman, Elsie, 274
Hulton, Eugene "Gene," 138, 273
Hulton, Henry, 75
Hulton, James, 75
Humphries, David, 202
Hunt, Dr. __, 240
Hunters' Lodges, 100, 101, 107
Huot family, 43, 77
Huron First Nation, 34, 38
Huron Mission of Sainte-Marie, 47
Huron-Petun culture, 33
Hutchinson, Tom, 130

Iberville, *see* Pierre Le Moyne
Ice harvesting, 135
Ice storm, January 1998, 184–87
Île aux Cochons, 149
Île Cauchois, 41
Île Ste Hélèna, 50, 86
Illiteracy, 99, 223, 235, 271
Ingersoll Cheese Factory, 130
Inn on the Island (Hitchcock House), 162
Irish Rebellion, 1798, 79
Iroquois Confederacy, 34, 39, 48, 105
Irvine, Alexander, 269
Irvine, Richard C., 77
Irvine family, 88
Irvine's Corners, 234, 246
Island Grill Restaurant, 207
Island Wanderer (steam vessel), 202

Islander (steamer), 177
Ives, Abner, 161, 162, 164
Ives, George, 165
Ives, John, 165
Ives, Captain H., 177

Jacobite Highlanders, 79, 81
Jacques Cartier (ferry), 91, 92
Jessie H. Breck (schooner), 141, 142, 146, 147, 285
Jesuit(s), 40, 47, 48, 95, 277
John Counter (freight-car ferry), 200
John Friend and Son Co., 207
Johnson:
    Archibald Kennedy, 70
    John (Sir), 49, 63, 70, 79, 88, 105, 238, 278
    Maria (Langan), 70
    William (Sir), 79, 105
Johnson, Edna, 255
Johnson, James and Paul, 255
Johnson, John, 268
Johnston:
    John, 103
    Kate, 102, 103
    William "Bill," 102, 103, 107, 161
Jolliffe, Anthony, 152
Jollife family, 43
Jones, __ (Mr.), 74
Jones, George, 131
Jones family, 74
Joslin, Al, 77
Joslin, Ebenezer, 77
Joslin, G., 258
Joslin, W.P., 235
Joy family, 234

Kelly, Garfield, 249
Kelly, Grace, 249
Kelly, Irwin, 273
Kelly, R.J., 216
Kelly, William, 137

Kelsey, Eber, 85
Kemp, John, 181
Kemp, Sarah, *see* Sarah Michea
Kemp, William "Willy," 141
Kemp family, 142, 235
Kenney:
    Captain Clarence, 138
    Edward, 125, 145, 241
    Gail, 125
    Captain George Edward, 230, 241
    Captain James, 138, 273
    Kathleen, 13, 230, 239, *see also*
        Kathleen Wall
    Lillian, 230
    Louise (Hawkins) (Mrs. G. E.), 241,
        242, 255, *see also* Louise Flynn
Keogh, James, 131
Keogh, Stan, 273
Keogh, Vinton, 273
Kertland, E.H., 246
Keyes:
    Arthur, 233
    Elsie (Allum), 121
    George, 256
    G.W., 158
    J.A., 258
    John, 131, 273
    Kenneth, 12, 124, 216, 233, 263
    Thomas, 213
    William, 256
Keyes' Schoolhouse, 125, 233
Keystone Shipping Line, 138
Kiell:
    Ann (Dawson), 269
    Alexander, 251, 269
    Lewis, 173
    Lewis Senior, 269
    Margaret, *see* Mararet Marlow
King's College (York), 66, 97
King's Own Yorkshire Light Infantry, 61
King's Royal Regiment (New York), 72
Kinghorn, Campbell and Hinckley, 90, 166, 167, 200, 201
Kinghorn, C.M., 90
Kingsley:
    John, 134
    Mary, 134, 254
    Reverend Doctor Wilfred, 134, 254
    William, 134, 254
Kingston (steamship), 261
Kingston and Cape Vincent Express Co., 178
Kingston Archaeological Society, 32
Kingston Cheese Board, 131
Kingston Daily News, 199
Kingston Flying Club, 181
Kingston Fire Department, 239, 240, 244
Kingston Gazette, 99, 224
Kingston General Hospital, 156, 183, 241
Kingston Harbour, 168, 169, 172, 202
Kingston Historical Society, 61, 158
Kingston market, 35, 117, 120, 128, 129, 214
Kingston Penitentiary, 23, 54, 61, 125, 219, 254
Kingston Presbytery, 258
Kingston Stave Forwarding Co., 150
Kingston Whig-Standard, 30, 256, 174
Kingston Yacht Club, 169
Kirkpatrick, Sir George (Hon.), 248
Kirkpatrick, Reverend Frank W., 248
Kirkpatrick, Thomas, 169, 248
Kirkpatrick, T.W., 164
Knapp Point, 238
Knapp family, 233
Knott, Margaret, 274
Knott, Walter, 185, 274
Kotté, Lewis, 45, 73, 189
Kraft Company, 131–33
Kyle, Joseph, 201
Kyle family, 78

La Fargeville, New York, 150
La Fleur, Peter, 43, 81
La Fleur, Theresa, *see* Theresa McGarvey
La France Co. (Toronto), 240
La Londe, Alfred, 215
La Londe, François, 214, 215
La Rocque de Roberval, Jean-François, 37
La Rocque, Giselle, 238
La Rocque, William "Bill," 132
La Rush:
    __ (Mrs.), 176
    Antoine, 207
    Dan, 239
    Dora, 207
    Gary, 182, 183
    Gordon, 134
    Harold, 207
    Richard "Dick," 134, 176
La Salle Causeway, 290
La Salle, Réné Robert Cavelier, 39–41, 43, 68, 149, 189
Lacey, Dan, 118
Lacey, John Sr., 181
LaForce, H., 45
Lambert family, 43, 77
Lambert Quarry, 126, 128
Lambert's Hill, 51, 126, 197, 211, 226, 290
Lancaster, Reverend D.T., 258
Landry, N.A., 163
Langan:
    Charlotte, 68, 70
    Julia, 68, 70, *see also* Julia Leslie
    Maria, 68, 70, *see also* Maria Johnson
    Patrick, 44, 49–51, 57, 63, 64, 66–70, 74, 75, 77, 88, 90, 105, 141
Lappin, Margaret, 249
Lappin, Dr. Thomas, 249
Larkin, John, 207, 213
Lathrop, Hiram, 106
Laura E. Calvin (schooner), 152
Laurentian Eastern Group, 30
Laverty, Frank, 75
Laverty, Friar Tod, 75, 253
Lawrence, Frank, 140

Le Blanc Henri, 140
Le Moyne :
    Charles (Charles the Elder), 39, 40, 41, 47
    Charles "the Younger" (Baron I), 48
    Charles (Baron II), 48
    Charles Jacques (Baron III), 48
    Charlotte Catherine (de Gray), 48
    Jean-Baptiste "Bienville," 40
    Marie-Catherine Josephe, 48
    Marie-Charles Josephe, 48, 49
    Pierre "Iberville," 40, 48
Le Ray de Chaumont:
    Grace (Coxe), 85
    Jacques, 85
    Vincent, 85–87
Leander Street, 160, 205, 207, 208, 211, 213, 215–17, 226, 229, 230, 238, 260
Ledford, Captain John, 60
Ledford Point, 60
Lee, Erland, 262
Leslie, James (Hon.), 70
Leslie, Julia (Langan), 68
Lewis, Dexter, 140
Leslie Estate, 74
Liberty, B.A., 24, 25, 27
Limekilns, 114
Livesey, Dr. R.J., 163
Livingstone, H.M., 33
Livingstone family, 196
Long Point (Wolfe Island), 110, 111, 128
Longueuil Seigneury, 41, 48–50
Longueuil Castle, 21, 48, 52, 53, 57, 59, 80, 125, 246
Longueuil, Benjamin, 216
Losee, William (Pastor), 256
Louis XIV, King, 38, 39, 41, 44, 69
Lowery, Bruce, 110

MacAdoo, Allan, 174
McAdoo, Geraldine, 273
Macaulay, W., 128

MacDonald, Captain Allan, 170
MacDonald, Flora, 81
MacDonald, Flora (MP), 263
MacDonald, John A. (Sir), 21, 72, 125, 156, 197, 200
MacDonald Institute (Guelph), 262
Macdonell, Bishop Alexander, 79
MacFarlane, J. (J.P.), 128
Machar, Agnes Maule, 60
Machar, Caroline (Allen) (Mrs. J. Maule), 60
Mackenzie, Alexander, 105, 125
Mackenzie, William Lyon, 100, 282
Madigan-Hyland Co. (New York), 202
Madison, President James, 96
Magnetic anomalies, 145–46
Mahoney, Captain __, 241
Main Duck Islands, 103, 109, 110
Maisonneuve, Governor, 47
Maitland, Samuel, 212
Maitland, Sir Peregrine, 69, 161, 162
Mallorytown, Ontario, 114
Malone, Abraham, 155
Malone, Anthony, 247, 249
Malone, George, 249, 268
Manaling, A. (J.P.), 128
Manion, Gene, 181
Markland, Thomas (J.P.), 128
Marlow, Margaret (Kiell), 269
Marlow, Shirley, 182
Marsh, George, 134, 193
Marsh, William, 78
Marshall, John, 268
Marshall, William, 155
Martello Towers (Kingston), 106, 125, 168
Martin, Albert, 133
Marysburgh Vortex, 143–45
Marysville, Ontario, 13, 21, 25, 26, 30, 35, 44, 52, 58, 60, 74, 84, 88, 89, 91, 124, 131, 149, 176, 177, 195, 205–22, 229, 230, 238, 239, 241, 259

Masonic Lodge:
    Cape Vincent, 86
    Hiram Lodge No. 342, 260
Massey, Hart, 86, 281
Matier, Ernest, 273
Matier, David Henry, 273
Matier, James, 215
Maud (steamer), 165–66
Maude (ferry), 90, 165, 166
Mayflower, 71, 85, 90
McAllister, __ (Mrs.), 263
McAllister, George, 273
McAvoy, Patrick, 215
McBride, Dr. Alan, 243
McCarthy, Dr. __, 240
McCaul, John, 78
McColley, Bernie, 273
McColley, Charlie, 273
McComb, John, 84
McCready, __ (Mrs. R.), 263
McCready, Elsie, 230
McCready, Keith, 181
McCready, Nancy, 81, *see also* Nancy McRae
McCready, Oscar, 170
McDermott:
    Elsie, 230
    Lena, 230
    Leon, 181, 239, 273
    Lillian, 230
    Orville "Tricky," 110, 181
    Patrick "Paddy," 126, 180
    Rita, 230
    Sadie, 230
    Vera, 230
McDonald, Brian, 193, 280
McDonald, Donald, 141, 142
McDonald, Colonel Donald, 238
McDonald, John, 268
McDonald, John H., 273
McDonald, John S., 269
McDonald, Lorne, 233
McDonald, Malcolm, 217

McDonald, Hugh, 193
McDonell, Alexander, 79
McDonell, Father Alexander, 79
McDonell, Allan, 79
McDonell, George, 126, 270
McDonell, John, 79
McDonell, John B., 251
McDonell, Lieutenant Colonel Ronald Ban, 80, 220, 225, 280
McDonell, Margaret (McDonald), 270
McDonell, Mary, 81, *see also* Mary La Fleur
McDonell, Mary (Brown), 80
McDonell family, 128, 233
McDougall, Duncan, 157, 158
McFadden, Bill, 273
McFadden, Mary (Gordon), 262
McFadden family, 235
McFarland Co. (Kingston), 126
McGarvey, Theresa (La Fleur), 27
McGlynn, John, 120
McGlynn, Patrick, 120
McGlynn family, 227
McGrath, Peter, 75
McKendry Quarries Ltd. (Kingston), 127
McKenna:
    Alice, 243
    Ed, 273
    James, 215
    Kathleen (Dillon) (Mrs. Rodney), 232
    William, 240
McKiernan, Reverend P.J., 253
McLaren, Allan, 163, 202
McLaren, Elizabeth, 81, *see also* Elizabeth McRae
McLaren, Emily, 163
McLaren, Mac, 163
McLeod, Angus, 205
McLeod, Reverend K.C., 258
McManus, Dr. __, 240
McRae:
    Andrew, 273
    Andrew J., 217
    Anne, 81, 251, 270
    Delila (Ellis) (First Mrs. W.), 81
    Duncan (Sheriff), 81, 223, 269
    Ella, 239
    Elizabeth (Mclaren), 81
    George, 81
    George Sr., 59
    Gordon, 32
    James Hector, 81, 191, 193, 213, 220, 270
    Jessie, 270
    Dr. John, 81, 251
    Nancy (McCready) (second Mrs. W.), 81
    Mable (Greenwood), 82, 180, 239, 253
    Margaret (Mrs. D.), 81, 269
    Mary (Mrs. J.H.), 81, 251, 270
    Weir, 81, 82
McRae Bros. General Store, 213
McRae family, 75, 82, 128
McRae Place, 81, 213
Mechanics' Institute, 155
Merry, Catherine, 242–43
Merry, Dr. George, 242–43
Metcalfe, Willis, 144
Methodists: 214, 257, 258, 260, 281, 287
    American Methodists, 256
    Free Methodists, 235
    Methodist Episcopal, 245
    Methodist Episcopal Church, 256
    New Connexion Methodists, 245
    Wesleyan Methodists, 245
Mexico Bay, New York, 143
Michea:
    James, 141, 142
    Joseph, 141
    Miriam, 141, 142
    Sarah (Kemp), 140
    Captain Thomas, 141, 142
Michea family, 141, 142, 235
Middle Woodland burial complex (St. Lawrence Valley), 33
Midland City (steamer), 166
Midland District, 64, 65, 67, 191, 193, 217, 220, 225
Midland District Municipal Council, 219, 225
Mill Hill Missionaries, 83
Mill Point, 46, 51, 60, 159, 160, 191, 197, 199, 223, 239, 271
Miller, George, 140
Milligan, George, 227
Milner, Joseph, 200
Mississauga First Nation, 34, 105, 116, 118
Mitchell, Mary (Miss), 234
Mohawk First Nation, 34, 105
Monroe, Jane, 87, *see also* Jane Docteur
Montcalm, Marquis Louis Joseph de, 95, 189
Montgomery, Edith, 117
Montgomery, John, 100, 101
Montgomery family, 234
Montmorency, Bishop de Laval, 39
Montreal (steamer), 140
Moore, Herman, 91
Moore, Rodney, 91
Mosher (Mosier, Moshier):
    Lewis, 77, 193
    Minerva (Hinckley), 89
    Nicholas, 77, 89, 117, 193
    Reuben, 77
Mosier:
    __ (Mrs. William), 263
    Danny, 186
    Glenn, 27
    Leonard "Tupper," 27, 247
    Lewis Jr., 193
    Litta (Hawkins) (Mrs. L.), 242
Mosier family, 43, 77, 90, 128, 186, 191, 209, 227
Mowat, Oliver (Hon.), 108
Muckian, Tom, 178, 179
Mullin:
    Elwyn "Buck," 142, 145, 170, 240, 273

John, 141, 142
Reba, 170
Rollie, 170
William, 141, 142
Mullin Family, 106
Murphy:
    John, 267
    James, 134
    Patrick, 267
    William, 267
Murphy family, 75, 78, 183
Murphy's Seafoods (Kingston), 116
Murray Bay, 27
Murray, Reverend Edward H. , 252
Murray, Lieutenant George, 107
Murray, Governor James, 96

Napoleon, 86, 87
Napoleonic War, 75, 81, 123
New York Central Railroad, 168
Nichol, Cecil, 129
Nicholls, James (J.P.), 163
Nicholson, Monsignor J.F., 211
Nicholson, Thomas, 270
Nicholson's Island, 143
Nickle, W.F. (K.C.), 70
Nickle, Folger and Hinckley Co., 90
Niles:
    Annie, 262, 263
    George, 131
    John, 77, 262
    John Jr., 262
    Tilley, 262
    Wallace, 262
Niles family, 245
Norris, Patrick, 222
North American Telegraph Co., 238
North West Co., 123
Norway (schooner), 137, 143

O'Brien:
    George, 231
    George, 273
    James "Jim," 215, 216, 234
    John "Jack," 216
    Neill, 273
O'Brien family, 78, 233
O'Brien School (SS#8), 234
O'Brien's Butcher Shop, 213
O'Conner, Edward, 78
O'Reilly:
    Reverend Eugene CSB, 256, 258
    James, 273
    Patrick, 268
    Rose (Garvey), 268
    Tom, 215
O'Reilly family, 78, 235, 256
O'Shea:
    Isabel, 44, 80, 227
    Joan (Ledford), 60, 213, 263
    John "Johnny," 81, 106, 130, 134, 214, 227
    Michael, 169
    Sharon (Hogan), 225
    Terry, 222
    Timothy (Reeve), 202, 242
O'Shea's Cheese Factory, 130, 131
O'Shea family, 80, 227
Ogdensburg, New York, 34, 95
Ogle, Clarence, 182
Old Cone Road, 191, 193, 195
Old French Survey, 42, 43–46, 50–52, 55, 59, 60, 64, 65, 70, 80, 84, 91, 119, 125, 131, 191, 192, 193, 205, 211, 216, 226, 229, 246, 251, 253, 256, 271
Ontario Archaeological and Historic Sites Board, 103
Ontario Cheese Factory, 131
Ontario Milk Marketing Board, 133
Ontario Northland Co., 138
Ontario Provincial Police (OPP), 110, 112
Ontario Temperance Act, 109
Orange Order (Loyal Orange Lodge), 143, 235, 260, 261
Ordovician Period, 23, 24
Orr:
    Cecil, 228
    Captain Lewis, 141, 146
    Nathaniel, 181
    Rodney, 228, 273
Orser, Jeremiah, 117
Orser family, 77
Oswego, New York, 72, 95, 104, 109, 110, 143

Palatine German(s), 71, 72, 76
Parkes, Donalda, 127
Passenger pigeon, 117
Patchin family, 234
Pathmasters, 194–95
Patron's Directory, Meacham's Historic Atlas of Frontenac County, 1878, 76–78
Patterson, Reverend __, 246
Patterson, Charles V., 273
Patterson, Lieutenant Colonel David, 274
Patterson, Walter, 274
Payne, Francis, 273
Payne, Margaret, 210, *see also* Margaret Baker
Payne, Robert, 273
Peachey, James, 73, 189
Pearce Ruth Ann (Ellerbeck), 227
Pendergast, Major James F. , 30, 31, 276
Pennington, Baker and Co. (Hamilton), 249
Penny Bridge, 89, 218, 290
Percival:
    Henry, 248
    Shirley (Going), 246
    William, 246
    William (P.L.S.), 205
Petrie's Tavern (Point Frederick), 218
Peugnet, Theophilus, 86
Phelan, Bishop Patrick, 251
Pickett's Ferry, 203
Picquet, Father François, 95
Pierrepont (steamer), 21, 74, 90, 167, 176, 202, 247

Pierrepont II (sidewheeler), 167, 168
Pigeon Island, 89, 128, 129, 161, 216
Plains of Abraham, 11, 12, 29, 42, 95
Point Alexandria Cemetery, 74, 142, 227, 258
Point Frederick, 100, 105, 161, 218
Point Peninsula Culture, 30, 31, 33
Point Petre, Ontario, 143
Port Metcalfe, 77, 127, 139, 195
Port Putnam, New York, 84, 85
Posthumus family, 83
Postal sevice, 237–38
Prescott, Ontario, 99, 101, 139, 151
Preston, Raymond, 140
Preston family, 273
Prevost, Sir George, 67, 68
Price, Charles, 131
Price, D., 106
Prince Edward (steamer), 166
Prince Edward, County of, 110, 143
Prince of Wales Loyal Order and Temperance Lodge #495, 261
Prinyer, Eva (Mrs.), 238, 239
Prinyer, Rae, 239
Prohibition, 110, 111, 140
Prohibition League of Ontario (1874), 109
Provincial Marine, 105
Prudhomme, Elizabeth, *see* Elizabeth Cauchois
Publius, V. Elmore, 191
Putnam, Abijah, 84
Pyke:
    Dexter, 31, 127
    George H., 127
    George Sr., 174, 180
    Grant Jr., 185, 258
    Captain Grant, 127, 179, 183, 184, 258
    Jake, 185
    Jason, 185
    Mary (Mae) (Mrs. Rodney), 119, 182
    Nellie, 271, *see also* Nellie Coon

Pyke family, 127
Pyke Farm Site, 31, 33
Pyke farms, 180, 184
Pyke Salvage and Towing Co., 179, 183, 189

Quebec Act (1774), 96
Quebec & Ontario Line, 138
Quebec Head (Wolfe island), 174
Queen Victoria (schooner), 150
Queen's University (Kingston), 25, 61, 138, 157, 158, 163, 227, 229, 257, 277
Queenston Heights, Battle of, 98
Quigley, Mary, 119, 120
Quigley, Patrick, 119
Quist, Alex, 132

Radford, Captain J.H., 53, 108, 109
Raftsman (paddlewheel steamer), 165
Rainny, John L., 152
Randall, William, 220
Ranous, Ethel, 230
Ranous, William "Will," 238
Rathbun, Edward Wilkes, 284
Rathbun and Co. (Desoronto), 124
Ratigan, William, 143
Rattray:
    Bertha, 230
    Elizabeth (Mrs. J.), 82, 269
    George, 131, 132, 210, 213
    James, 82, 269
    William, 256
Rattray family, 235
Rattray's Cheese Factory, 131
Réal, Pièrre François (Count), 86, 87
Rebola, 170
Reeds Bay, 77, 118, 139, 141, 167, 191, 215, 227, 256
Reeds Bay Road, 25–27, 215, 233
Reeds Creek, 27, 119, 123, 221
Reginald (steamer), 140
Rémy de Courcelles, Governor, 39

Renshaw:
    John, 77
    Mary, 77
    Matthew, 77
    Olivia (Ecclemont), 77
    Sarah, 77
Rhodes, Minister John, 203
Rhythmic Flow, 145
Richardson, Senator Henry Wartman, 54
Rideau Canal, 23, 125
Ridge Road, 26, 89
Ridge School (S.S.#3), 227
Rixton, Randy, 133
Robert Gaskin (schooner), 152
Robinson, Attorney General John Beverley, 69, 162
Robinson, James Foster, 146
Robinson, T.W., 197
Rock Island, 103
Rockport Navigation Co. Ltd., 168
Rockwood Psychiatric Hospital (Kingston), 241
Rogers, John, 273
Rogers, Reverend Robert V., 246
Roman Catholic, 20, 40, 41, 43, 48, 49, 50, 60, 71, 79, 81, 87, 96, 134, 214, 219, 241, 245, 256, 259, 261, 270
    Catholic Church, 75, 81, 83, 212, 251–54, 261
Rome, New York, 84, 89, 90, 103, 197, 199
Roney, Captain Henry, 107, 155, 170
Roney, Gordon, 53, 92, 170
Rose, Adrienne (Mrs.) (VON), 243
Rosière (France), 87
Rosière, New York, 87
Ross, Donald, 257
Ross, Major John, 72
Rousseau, Edward, 108, 109
Rousseau, Peter, 108
Rousseau family, 43
Royal Military College, 105, 125, 187
Russell, Craig, 170, 171, 216

Russell, Hilda, 274
Russell, Reverend A.M., 258
Ryan, Andrew, 216
Ryan, Reverend James S., 232, 253, 255, 256
Ryan, Norman "Red," 254

Sackets Harbor, New York, 34, 38, 96, 97, 102, 103, 110
Sacred Heart Church Cemetery, 143, 265, 267, 280
Sacred Heart Union Separate School (SSS#4), 231, 232
Sadie, 170
Salmon fishery, 118, 128, 129
Sammons:
    Isaac, 74
    Joseph, 74
    Matthew, 74
    Uriah, 74
Sandieson, Elizabeth, 269
Sandieson, Henry, 213, 269
Saucy Sally (iceboat), 171
Saunders, Captain __, 100
Sauriel, Dr. __, 240
Seaman's Union, 154
Schenectady, New York, 89
School of Navigation, Queen's University, 138
Scottish Settlement, 75, 80, 123, 134, 193
Second World War, 61, 82, 83, 92, 109, 138, 171, 241, 255, 256, 273
Seymour, Benjamin (MPP), 197
Shannon, Reverend Joseph, 253
Shanty Creek, 113
Sharpe, Reverend Henry, 253
Sharpie (ice punt), 181
Sheehy, R., 253
Sherman, Perthinea, 119
Sherwood, Sheriff Justus, 117
Seigneur de Blairfindie, 49
Silver Springs Cheese Factory, 130, 131
Simcoe, Lieutenant Governor John Graves, 29, 74, 96

Simla (steamer), 137
Sinclair, Reverend J., 258
Sir Robert Peel (steamer), 103
Sisters of St. Joseph, 241
Sisty, Captain Joseph, 174
Sjonger, Gepke, 83
Sjonger family, 83
Skedaddlers, 106, 107
Sluman, Gilbert, 213
Sluman, Thomas, 193, 265
Small, Brian, 30
Small, Fern (Fawcett), 182
Small, Holly, 182, 183
Small, Leslie, 182
Small, Lieutenant Darrell, 182
Smeaton, John, 227
Smith:
    Bert, 273
    David John, 128
    Henry, 129
    Henry Jr. (MPP), 197
    John, 234, 246
    Louise (Horne), 85
    Vera, 228
Smith's School (SS#14), 234, 246, 247
Smither family, 196
Snake Island, 97, 202
Snake Island lighthouse, 141
Snell:
    John, 143
    Thomas, 143
    William, 143
Sorel, Quebec, 72
Spankie:
    Dr. Arthur, 229
    Herbert, 229
    Margaret Ann, 249
    Ralph M., 99, 220, 226, 227, 229
    Dr. William, 130, 207, 229, 240, 241, 249, 262
    Dr. William Jr., 229
Spence, Michael W., 31, 33

Spinning:
    Damon, 89
    Daniel, 85
    Demetrius, 89, 119, 259
    Edwin, 89
    Humphrey, 85
    Jerusa (Standish), 85
    Olivia (Hinckley), 89
    Othniel, 86
Spinning family, 89, 90, 227
Spinning Hotel, 91, 106
Spook Hill, 118
Spoor:
    Eliza, 209, *see also* Eliza Baker
    George Bruno, 134, 273
    Harriet (Turcotte), 218, 219
    Mary Louise, 232, *see also* Mary Louise Cosgrove
    Morey, 77, 193, 218, 219, 24
    Olive (Davis), 219
    Richard J. 232
Spratt, Archbishop Michael J., 252, 253
Spratt, Father Thomas, 134, 252, 254, 259
Saint Andrew's Hall, 258
Saint Andrew's Presbyterian Church, 257
Saint George's Cathedral (Kingston), 58, 205, 246, 247
Saint James Anglican Church (Kingston), 57, 60, 246
Saint James Cathedral (Toronto), 69
Saint John's Anglican Church (Portsmouth), 57, 60
Saint John's Church (Cape Vincent), 87
Saint Joseph Hospital (Toronto), 241
Saint Joseph's Missionary Society, 83
Saint Lawrence Cemetery, 82, 257
Saint Lawrence Chapter (Women's Institute), 262, 263
Saint Lawrence Cheese Factory, 131, 132
Saint Lawrence College Navigation (Kingston), 138
Saint Lawrence Methodist Church, 256, 257

Saint Lawrence Post Office, 238
Saint Lawrence River Steamboat Co., 90, 166–68, 179, 201
Saint Lawrence School (S.S.#13), 88, 234
Saint Lawrence Seaway, 92, 126
Saint Margaret's Hall, 249
Saint Mark's Anglican Church (Barriefield), 57
Saint Mary's Cathedral (Kingston), 23, 125, 251
Saint Mary's of the Lake Hospital, 72
Saint Michael the Archangel (Belleville), 211
Saint Paul's Anglican Church (Kingston), 57
Stafford, Father Michael, 50, 226, 251, 252
Stahl (Staley), Martin, 78
Staley:
    Archibald "Archie," 229
    Captain Charles, 141–43
    Howard, 232
    Melville, 273
    Noble, 240
Staley family, 128
Staley Point, 44
Staley School (SS#2) (SSS#2, 1860), 228, 229
Staley Wharf, 193
Standish, Jerusa, 85, *see also* Jerusa Spinning
Standish, Myles, 85
Stevenson:
    Andrew Craig, 127
    Clifford Andrew, 127
    Eliza, 127
    Margaret, 127
    William, 127
Stewart, Dr. H.A. (MP), 171
Stokes, George, 257
Stone, William L. 33
Strachan, Bishop John, 57, 64, 66, 69, 79, 125, 225
Strawberry (sailing vessel), 165
Stuart, Venerable Archdeacon, 57

Sudds family, 77
Sudds:
    Anna, 192
    Carl, 228
    Delbert, 274
    Eva, 19
    Herbert, 273
    Lesley, 274
    Nora, 192
    Victor, 110
Sutherland, Linda, 258
Sweeney, Reverend R., 258
Sylph (schooner), 99

Taggart, Edmund "Eddy," 133
Taggart, Samuel, 229
Tarrant:
    Ann (Mrs. T.), 257
    Clemence (Mrs. J.), 265
    Garnet, 274
    Hattie, 207
    Howard, 112, 207, 208
    John, 78, 265
    Robert, 274
    Thomas, 257
Tarrant store, 207
Taylor:
    Ambrose, 216
    George, 216
    Peter, 216
    Wilson, 216
Terminal Woodland Period, 29, 33
Tetro, Robert, 168
The Associated Country Women of the World, 263
The Big Crack, 180, 181
The Garden Island (barque), 152, 153
The Passage, 191
The Ridge, 26
The Wolfe (steamboat), 164
Thiery-Primot, Catherine, 47, *see also* Catherine Le Moyne

Thomas Fawcett (ferry), 169
Thousand Island Ivy Lea Bridge, 168, 203
Thousand Islands Boat Co., 166
Thousand Islands Bridge Authority (New York), 202
Timber rafting, 85, 150–52
Tobin, Patrick, 60
Todd, John, 137
Travers-Lewis, Bishop John, 247
Treaty of Ghent (1814), 100
Treaty of Paris (1763), 44, 96
Trenton Air Base, 203
Trenton Group (limestone), 24, 26
Trinity Church, Trinity United Church of England and Ireland, Trinity Anglican Church, 48, 49, 51, 54, 57, 111, 125, 208, 214, 246–48
Trio, 153
Turcott, Michael, 134
Turnbull, George, 274
Tweedsmuir Village Histories, 263
Tynham, Maurice, 274

Underground Railway, 74
Union Separate School Board, 231
Unitarian Church, 245
United Church of Canada, 196, 258
United Empire Loyalists, Loyalists, 42–44 52, 63, 64, 66, 71–74, 76–78, 80–82, 88, 93, 96, 104, 115, 257, 271
United Presbyterians, 245
United Province of Canada, 219
United States (steamer), 101
Unwin, John, 257

Vale, Theophilis, 265
Valencia (schooner), 140
Van Strien family, 83
Vanden Hoek, James, 222
Vanden Hoeck, T., 258
Vérendryé, Pièrre Gaultier de Varennes, 44
Verulam Limestone, 25, 26

Vickers, Reverend R.C., 256
Victoria, Queen of England, 62, 101, 166, 211
Villa St. Lawrence, 74
Village Continuation School (SS#4) (PSS#4), 235
Village of Garden Island, 156
Vollering family, 83, 255
Von Schoultz, Nils, 101, 103

W. Davis Hotel, 192
W.E. Horne Ferry Co., 92, 170, 253
Wagner, Douglas, 181
Wall, Charles, 13, 14, 111, 208, 248, 275
Wall, John, 181
Wall, Kathleen (Kenney) (Mrs. Charles), 13, *see also* Kathleen Kenney
Walker, David, 230
Walker, Edwin Job, 273
Walker, Morris, 230
Walton, Keith, 213, 274
Walton, Mildred, 213
War Assets Corporation, 171
War of 1812, 77, 79, 86, 96–100, 143, 223, 257
Watertown, New York, 90, 100, 101, 103, 115, 127, 190
Watertown (steamer), 155, 167
Watertown and Rome Railroad, 179, 197
Watts:
    Bert, 179
    Bill, 274
    Lloyd, 229
    Samuel, 78, 248, 265
Waubic (steamer), 167, 168
Webster, John, 214
Weir, __ (Mrs. John), 263
Weir, John, 213
Welland Canal, 23, 125
Wells Island, 103
Wenbourne, Ann, 246, *see also* Ann Friend
Wenbourne, Harriet (Davis) "Hattie," 214

Wesleyan Methodists, 245
West, Reverend J.N.D., 256
Western Berg, Dr. Hans, 243
White:
    Dorothy (Mrs.), 216
    Ken, 45
    James, 240
    Peg (Mrs. Ken), 45
    Robert, 181
    Ruby, 274
White's Lane, 53
Whitmarsh:
    Bill, 274
    Ernie 213
    Frederick, 265
    Frederick "Fred," 59, 213, 214
    George "Butch," 59, 213
    Sarah (Mrs. Fred), 59
Whitmore, Laurinda, 119
Whitmore, Mina, 119
William Darrell (ferry), 92
Wills, Thomas, 212, 268
Wilson, G., 181
Wintemberg, W.J., 31
Wisconsin (steamer), 167
Wolfe Island, Township of, 19, 21, 63, 120, 138, 149, 150, 194, 198, 218–21, 226
Wolfe Island Bakery, 213
Wolfe Island Canal, 24, 85, 90, 166, 167, 178, 201
Wolfe Island Cheese Factory, 130, 232
Wolfe Island Fire Department, 260
Wolfe Island Health Clinic, 242, 243
Wolfe Island Lodge # 260 (AOUW), 260
Wolfe Island Railway and Canal Co., 199, 200
Wolfe Island Rowing Club, 219
Wolfe Island Town Hall, 222
Wolfe Island Township Council (1850), 80
Wolfe Island United Church, 258, 259
    United Church Cemetery, 259
Wolfe Island Volunteer Ambulance Service, 244

Wolfe Island, Kingston and Toronto Railway Co. Inc., 197–99
Wolfe Islander I, 137, 168–70, 192
Wolfe Islander (2), 170–72 174, 175, 183, 184, 240, 287
Wolfe Islander III, 19, 158, 173, 175, 176, 203
Wolfe, General James, 11, 96
Wood, Jean, 230
Wood, lay pastor Terry, 258
Woodman:
    Albert, 222
    Alvira, 262, *see also* Alvira Gillespie,
    Bruce, 219
    Charlie, 238
    Dot (Campbell), 234
    Captain Elwood, 174, 175
    Francis, 180
    George, 217, 234, 256
    Inez, 262
    Mabel, 192, 229
    Margaret, 222
    Mary (Mrs. W.G.), 133
    Samuel, 238, 256
    Stanley, 274
    William G., 133
    William H., 229
Woodman family, 234, 235
Woodman House Hotel, 215
Workman, Reverend H.V., 258

Yott:
    Austin, 274
    Rodney, 137
    Vern, 138, 241, 256, 274
Yott family, 235

ABOUT THE AUTHOR

Barbara Wall La Rocque's career was as a Toronto teaching-hospital operating-room supervisor and later a nursing consultant for insurance companies. Her avocation is as a classical vocalist trained at the Royal Conservatory of Music in Toronto and she has been a soloist in several Toronto church and concert choirs. After her father's death in 1993, her penchant for music continued, but she changed her focus to writing with the goal of finishing her father's manuscript on Wolfe Island's history.

Barbara's matrilineal roots, coupled with a keen interest in genealogy and history, inspired her to engage in creative non-fiction writing with the assistance of the Humber College School for Writers. She embarked upon a labour of love and respect for her father's dedication to Wolfe Island to ensure that his earlier work was not in vain.

A Torontonian all of her life, Barbara presently lives in Leaside with her husband, Lloyd. They have two adult daughters, Karen and Lesley, and more recently are enjoying their grandson Ryan, born at the outset of this venture. The family frequently travels to Wolfe Island.

OF RELATED INTEREST

BELLEVILLE
A Popular History
Gerry Boyce
978-1-55002-863-8 $32.99

Belleville traces its beginnings to the arrival of the United Empire Loyalists. For thirty years the centre of the present city was reserved for the Mississauga First Nation, until the land was "surrendered" to white settlers and a town plot was laid out in 1816. Early influences include the first railway in 1856, Ontario's first gold rush in 1866, and prominent citizens such as noted pioneer author Susanna Moodie and Sir Mackenzie Bowell, Canada's fifth prime minister.

QUETICO
Near to Nature's Heart
Jon Nelson
978-1-55488-396-7 $35.00

Quetico Park in northwestern Ontario, long-recognized as a gem among parks, celebrates its 100th anniversary in 2009. Combining thorough research with threads of his own extensive involvement with the park, the author presents an insightful look into both Quetico's natural and human history. The result is a splendid tribute to a very special place.

A KINGSTON ALBUM
Glimpses of the Way We Were
Marion Van de Wetering
978-0-88882-200-0 $19.99

This album follows the history of Kingston from the founding of Fort Frontenac and the accompanying French settlement of Cataraqui in 1673 to its present-day incarnation as a popular tourist and travel destination. In addition to its fine military tradition, Kingston has also been the centre of commerce, shipping, industry, education, and government in the region.

Available at your favourite bookseller.

DUNDURN
www.dundurn.com

Tell us your story! What did you think of this book? Join the conversation at
www.definingcanada.ca/tell-your-story
by telling us what you think.

www.ingramcontent.com/pod-product-compliance
Lightning Source LLC
Chambersburg PA
CBHW080543230426
43663CB00015B/2695